By MINGO ITO
In collaboration with
NIPPON COLUMBIA CO., LTD.

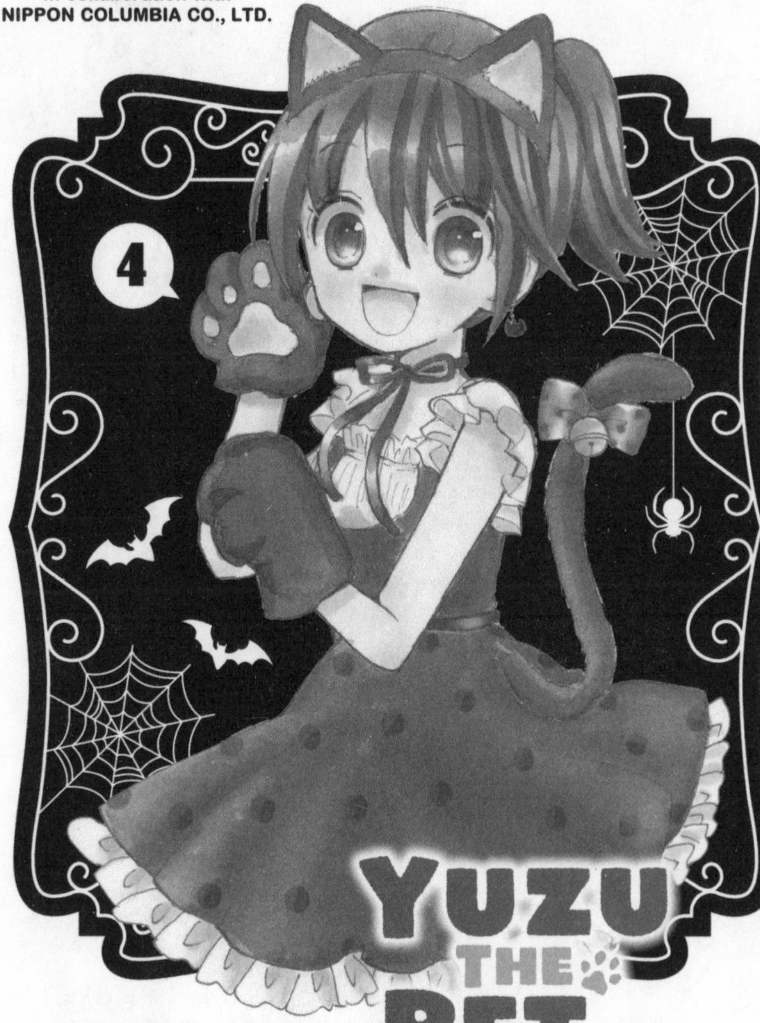
4

YUZU THE PET VET

MEDICINE

Story

YUZU MORINO IS IN THE FIFTH GRADE. SHE'S ALSO SCARED OF ANIMALS... ONE DAY, AFTER HER MOM IS HOSPITALIZED, YUZU MOVES IN WITH HER UNCLE AKIHITO. AND GUESS WHAT? HE'S THE VETERINARIAN AT BOW MEOW ANIMAL HOSPITAL! EVERY DAY IS BUSY, AND HE COULD ALWAYS USE AN EXTRA SET OF HANDS—GOOD THING YUZU'S HERE TO HELP! LATELY, SHE'S BEEN LEARNING ABOUT HOW SPECIAL A BOND WITH A PET CAN BE. WHO DO YOU THINK SHE'LL MEET TODAY?

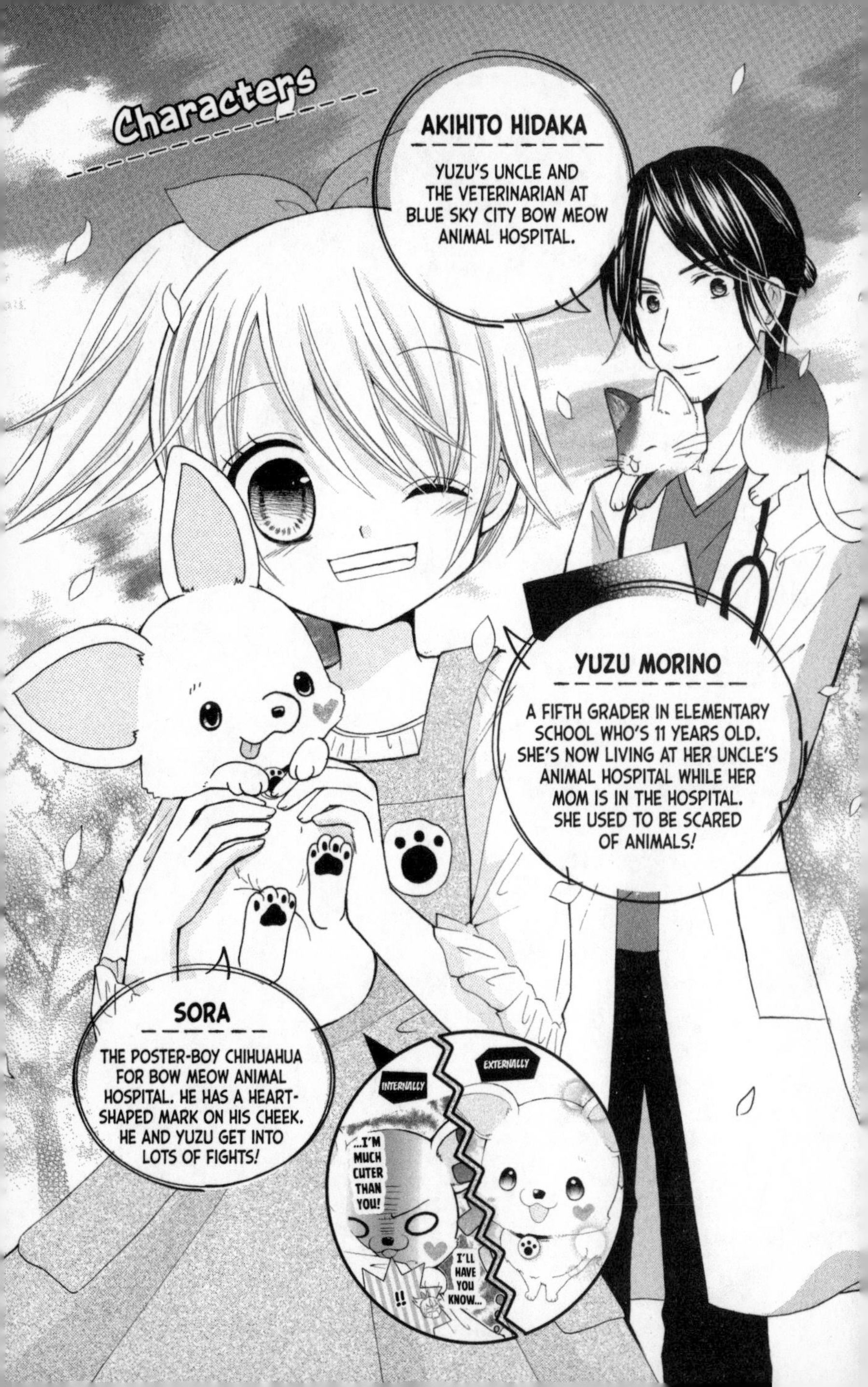
Characters
AKIHITO HIDAKA
YUZU'S UNCLE AND THE VETERINARIAN AT BLUE SKY CITY BOW MEOW ANIMAL HOSPITAL.
YUZU MORINO
A FIFTH GRADER IN ELEMENTARY SCHOOL WHO'S 11 YEARS OLD. SHE'S NOW LIVING AT HER UNCLE'S ANIMAL HOSPITAL WHILE HER MOM IS IN THE HOSPITAL. SHE USED TO BE SCARED OF ANIMALS!
SORA
THE POSTER-BOY CHIHUAHUA FOR BOW MEOW ANIMAL HOSPITAL. HE HAS A HEART-SHAPED MARK ON HIS CHEEK. HE AND YUZU GET INTO LOTS OF FIGHTS!
EXTERNALLY
INTERNALLY
I'LL HAVE YOU KNOW...
...I'M MUCH CUTER THAN YOU!
!!

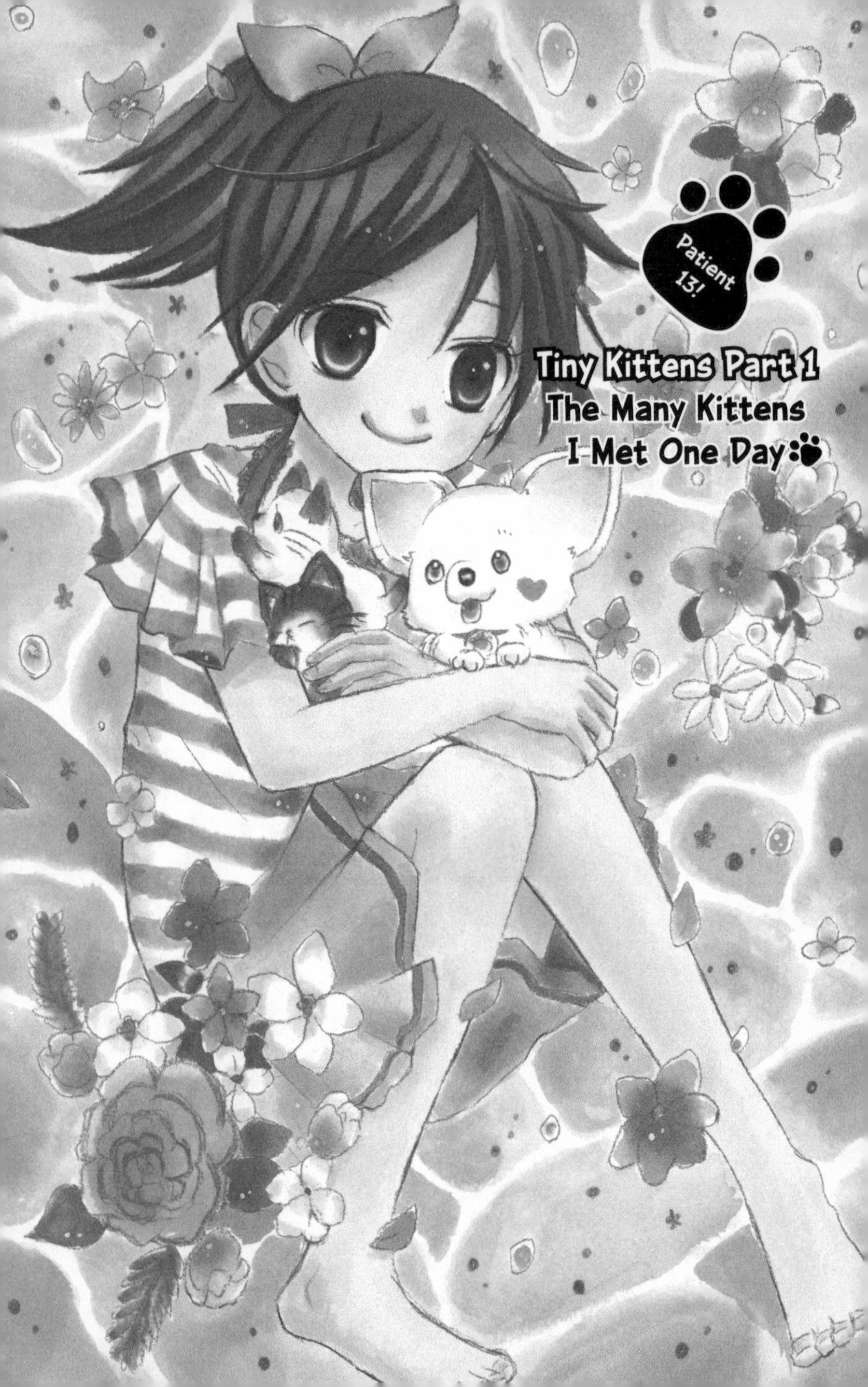
Patient 13!
Tiny Kittens Part 1
The Many Kittens I Met One Day

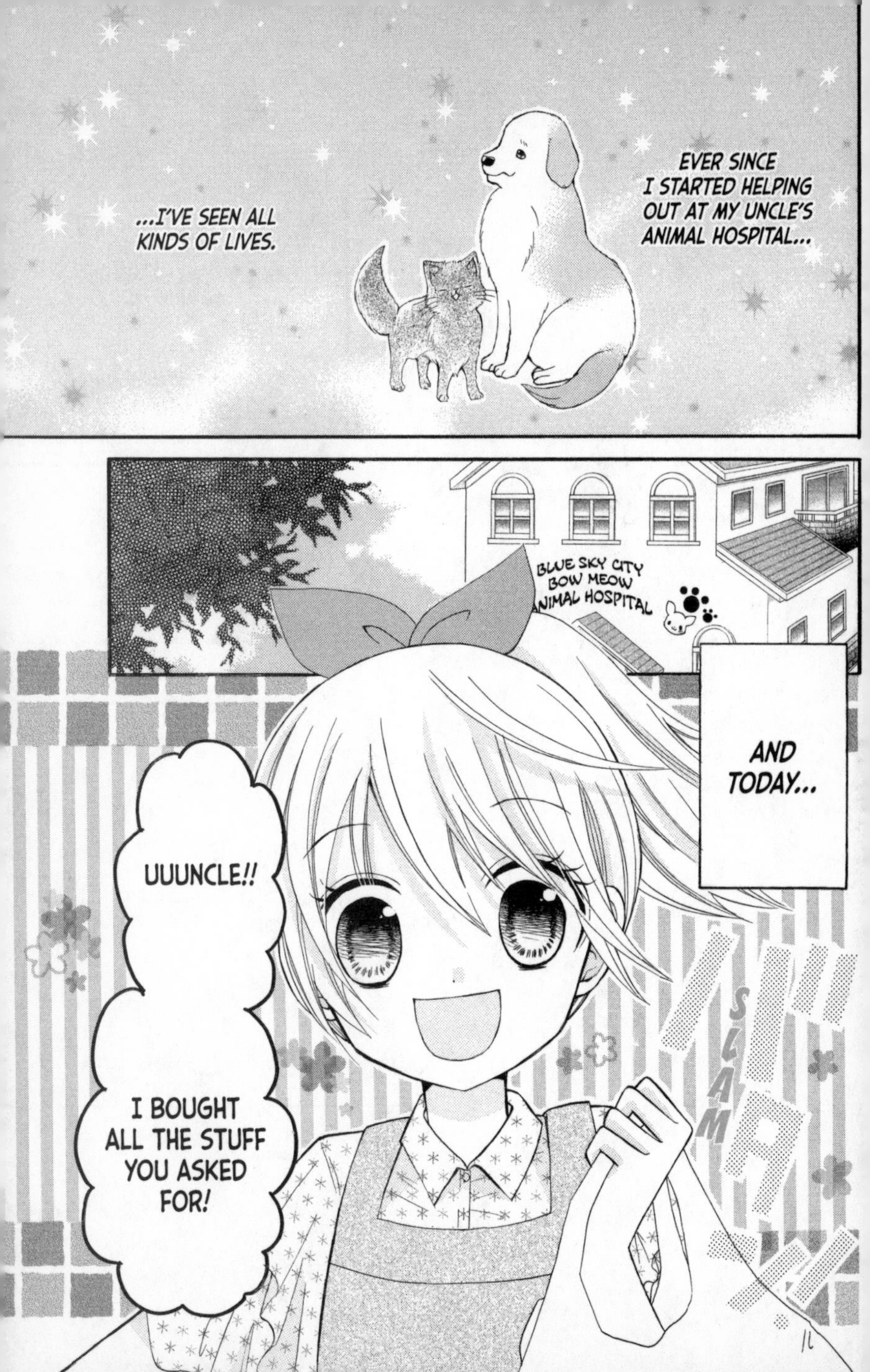
EVER SINCE I STARTED HELPING OUT AT MY UNCLE'S ANIMAL HOSPITAL...
...I'VE SEEN ALL KINDS OF LIVES.
BLUE SKY CITY BOW MEOW ANIMAL HOSPITAL
AND TODAY...
SLAM
UUUNCLE!!
I BOUGHT ALL THE STUFF YOU ASKED FOR!

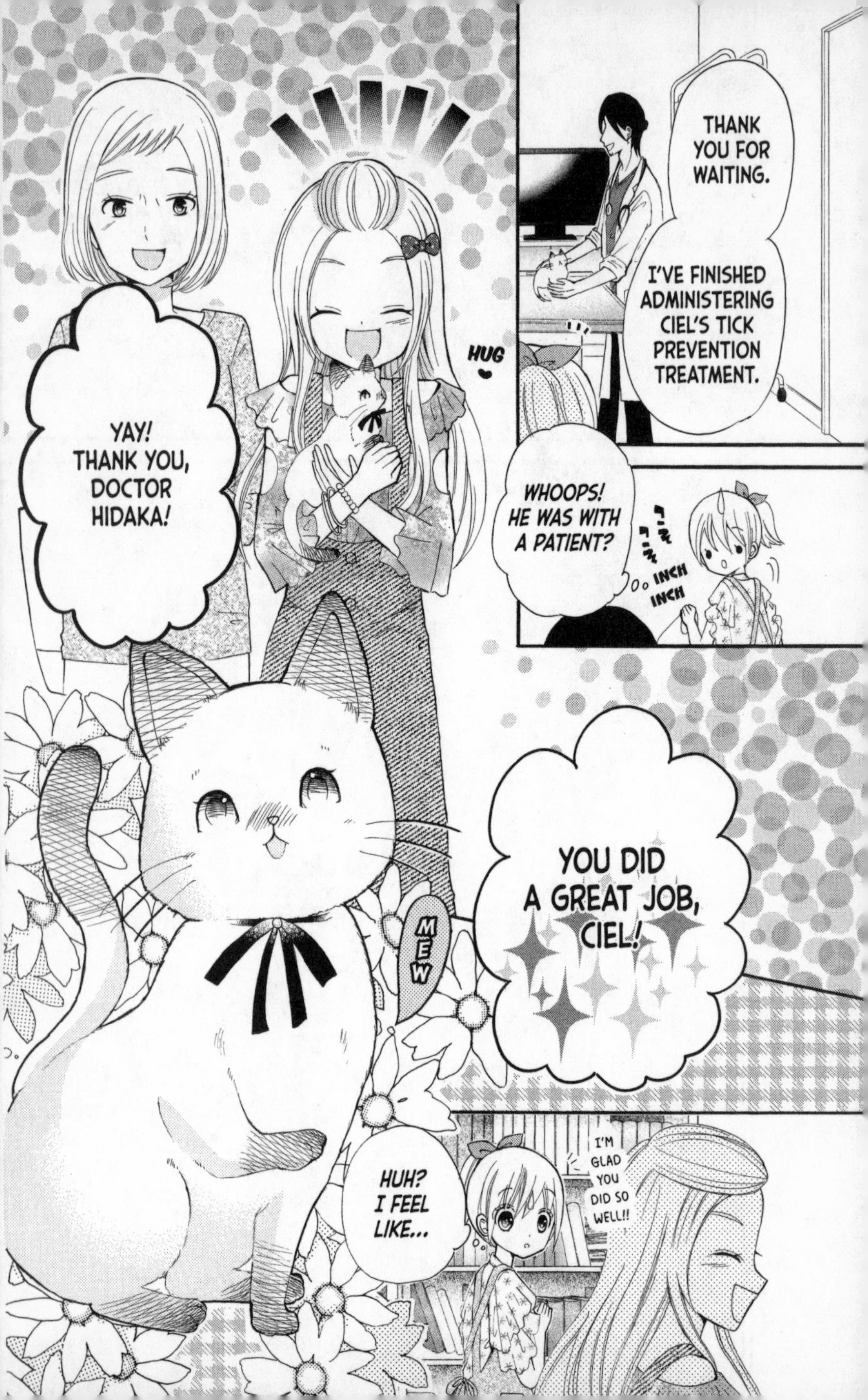
THANK YOU FOR WAITING.
I'VE FINISHED ADMINISTERING CIEL'S TICK PREVENTION TREATMENT.
WHOOPS! HE WAS WITH A PATIENT?
INCH INCH
HUG
YAY! THANK YOU, DOCTOR HIDAKA!
YOU DID A GREAT JOB, CIEL!
MEW
I'M GLAD YOU DID SO WELL!!
HUH? I FEEL LIKE...

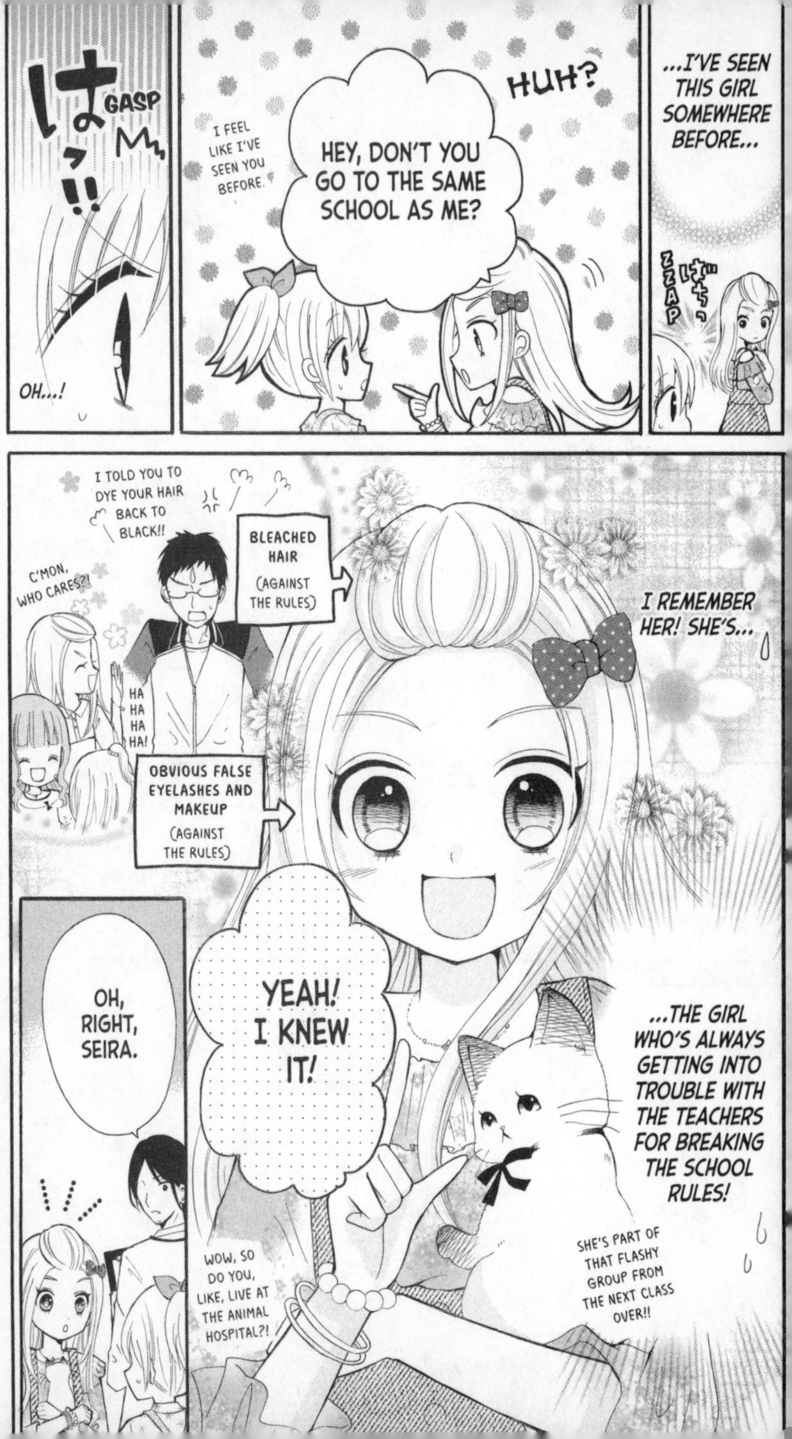
...I'VE SEEN THIS GIRL SOMEWHERE BEFORE...
ZZZAP
HUH?
HEY, DON'T YOU GO TO THE SAME SCHOOL AS ME?
I FEEL LIKE I'VE SEEN YOU BEFORE.
GASP
OH...!
I REMEMBER HER! SHE'S...
...THE GIRL WHO'S ALWAYS GETTING INTO TROUBLE WITH THE TEACHERS FOR BREAKING THE SCHOOL RULES!
SHE'S PART OF THAT FLASHY GROUP FROM THE NEXT CLASS OVER!!
I TOLD YOU TO DYE YOUR HAIR BACK TO BLACK!!
BLEACHED HAIR (AGAINST THE RULES)
C'MON, WHO CARES?!
HA HA HA HA!
OBVIOUS FALSE EYELASHES AND MAKEUP (AGAINST THE RULES)
YEAH! I KNEW IT!
WOW, SO DO YOU, LIKE, LIVE AT THE ANIMAL HOSPITAL?!
OH, RIGHT, SEIRA.
...!

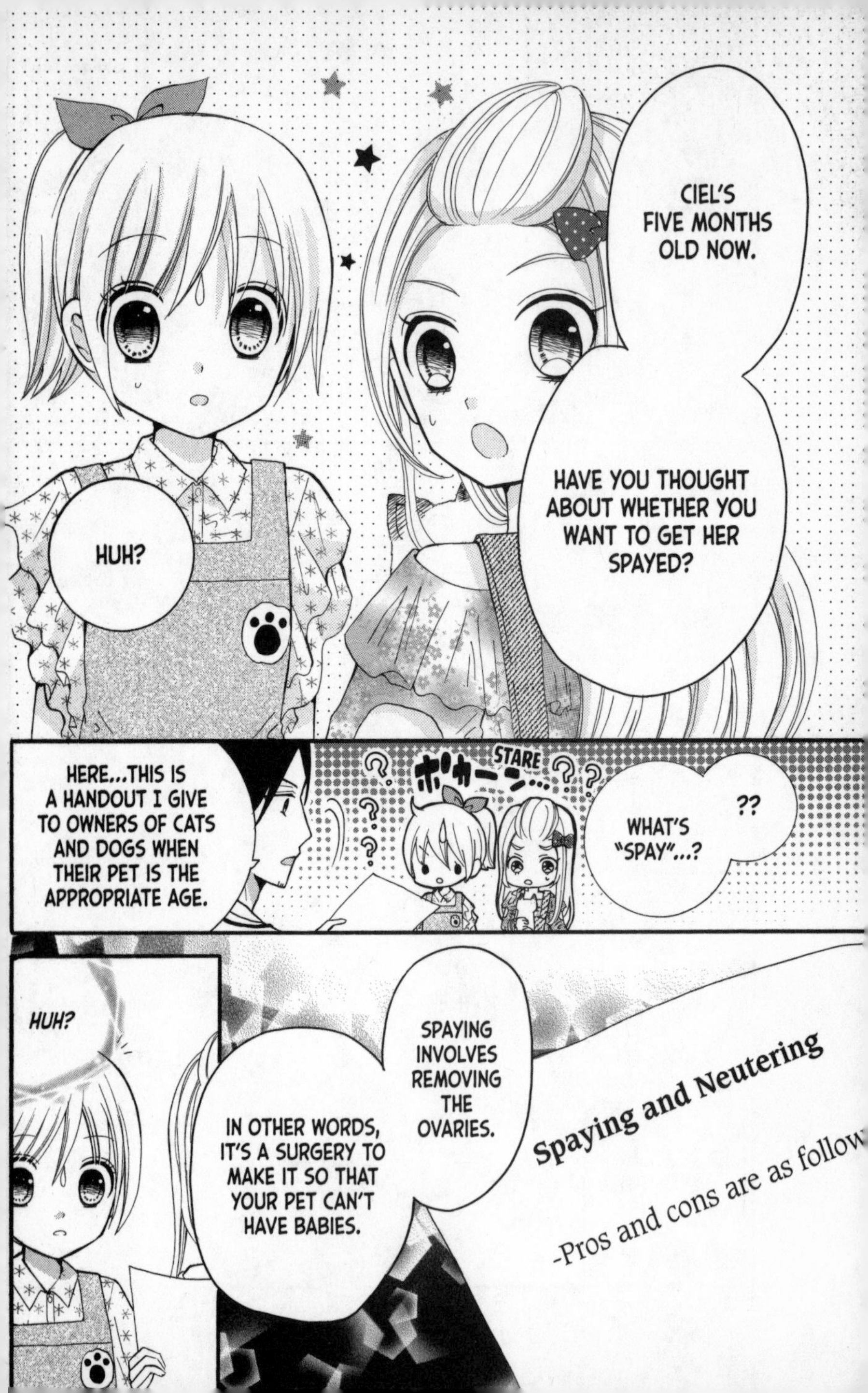
CIEL'S FIVE MONTHS OLD NOW.
HAVE YOU THOUGHT ABOUT WHETHER YOU WANT TO GET HER SPAYED?
HUH?
??
WHAT'S "SPAY"...?
STARE
ポカーン…
HERE...THIS IS A HANDOUT I GIVE TO OWNERS OF CATS AND DOGS WHEN THEIR PET IS THE APPROPRIATE AGE.
Spaying and Neutering
-Pros and cons are as follow
SPAYING INVOLVES REMOVING THE OVARIES.
IN OTHER WORDS, IT'S A SURGERY TO MAKE IT SO THAT YOUR PET CAN'T HAVE BABIES.
HUH?

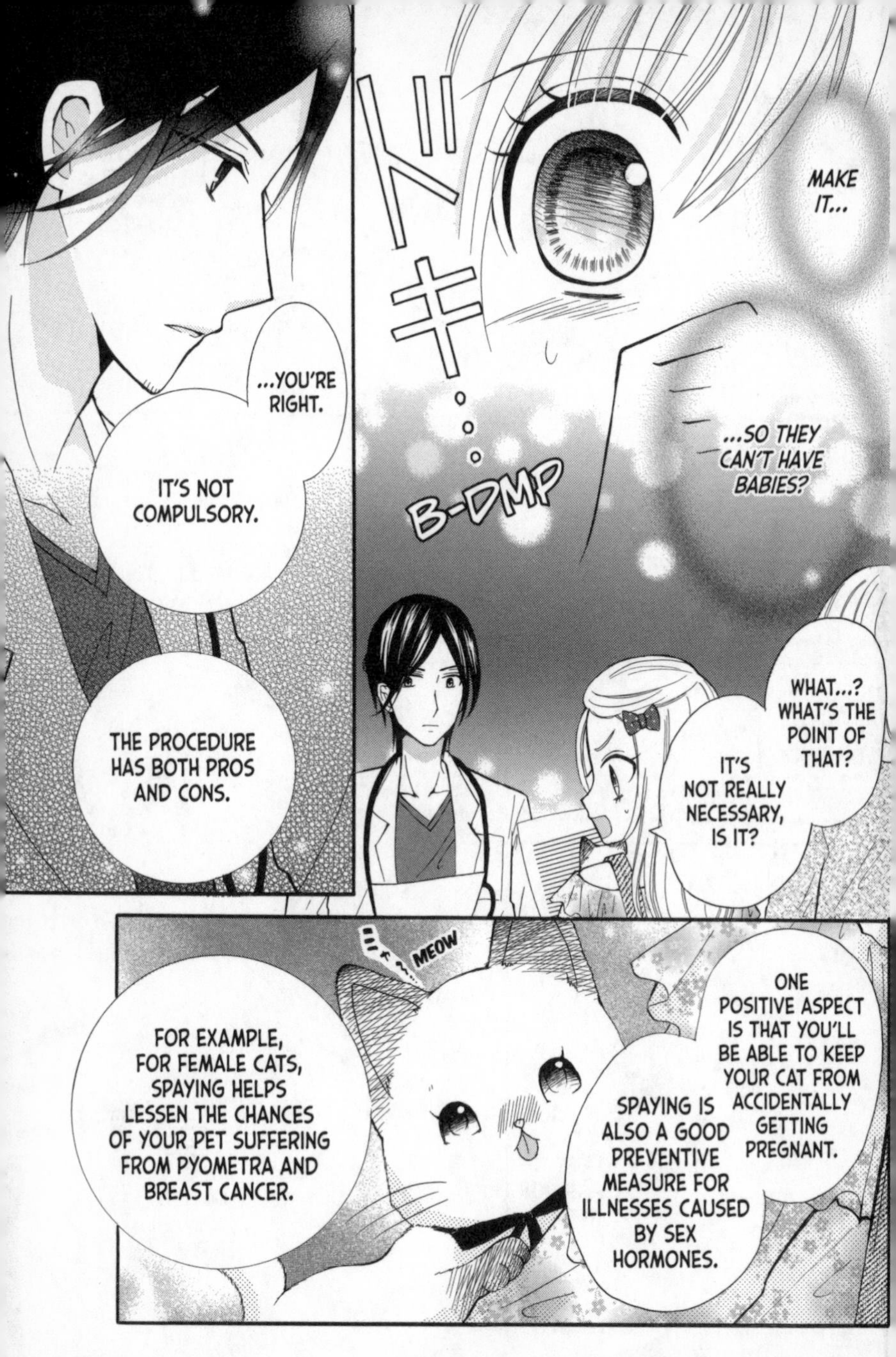
MAKE IT...
...SO THEY CAN'T HAVE BABIES?
ドキ
B-DMP
WHAT...? WHAT'S THE POINT OF THAT?
IT'S NOT REALLY NECESSARY, IS IT?
...YOU'RE RIGHT.
IT'S NOT COMPULSORY.
THE PROCEDURE HAS BOTH PROS AND CONS.
ONE POSITIVE ASPECT IS THAT YOU'LL BE ABLE TO KEEP YOUR CAT FROM ACCIDENTALLY GETTING PREGNANT.
SPAYING IS ALSO A GOOD PREVENTIVE MEASURE FOR ILLNESSES CAUSED BY SEX HORMONES.
MEOW
FOR EXAMPLE, FOR FEMALE CATS, SPAYING HELPS LESSEN THE CHANCES OF YOUR PET SUFFERING FROM PYOMETRA AND BREAST CANCER.

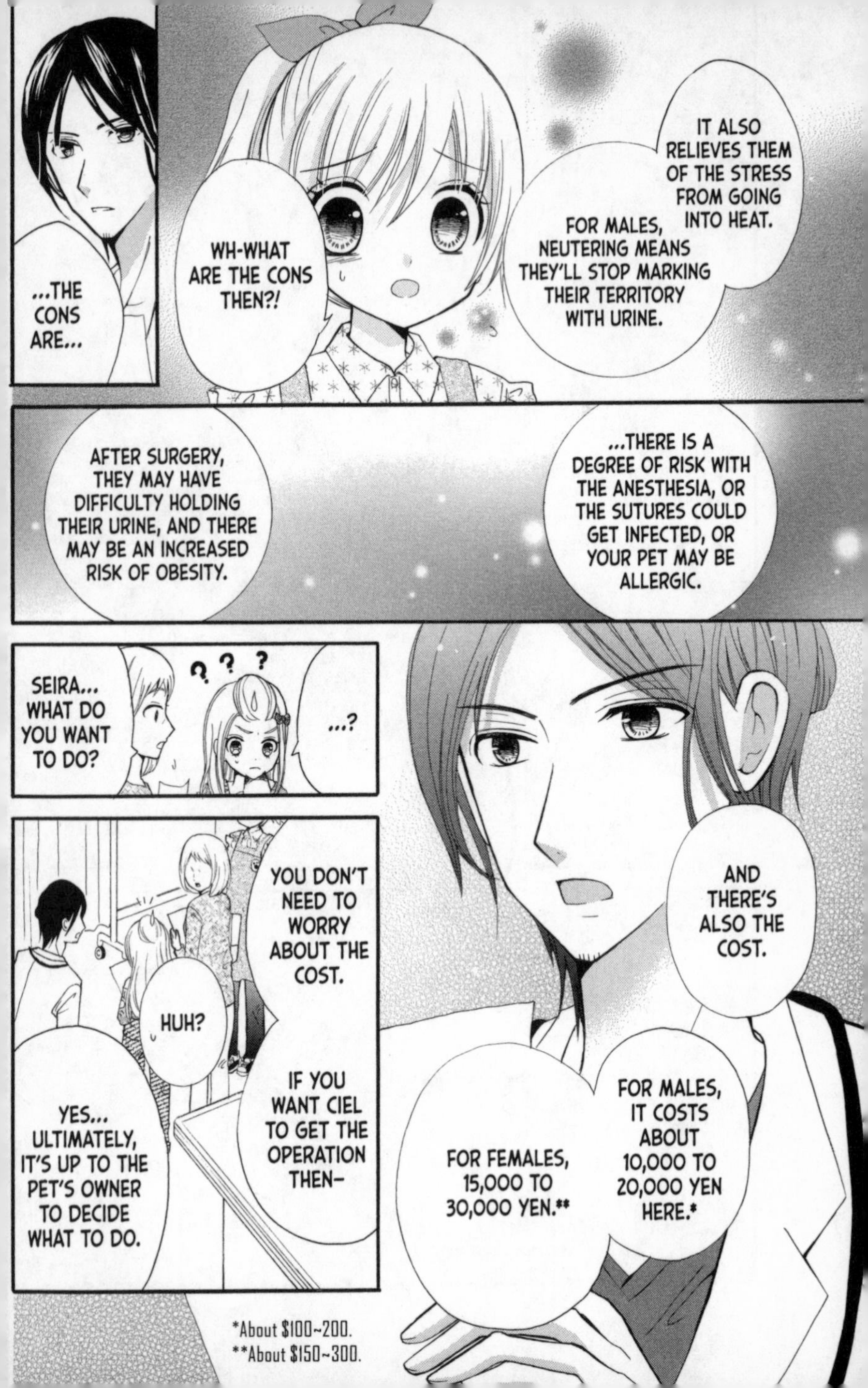
IT ALSO RELIEVES THEM OF THE STRESS FROM GOING INTO HEAT.
FOR MALES, NEUTERING MEANS THEY'LL STOP MARKING THEIR TERRITORY WITH URINE.
WH-WHAT ARE THE CONS THEN?!
...THE CONS ARE...
...THERE IS A DEGREE OF RISK WITH THE ANESTHESIA, OR THE SUTURES COULD GET INFECTED, OR YOUR PET MAY BE ALLERGIC.
AFTER SURGERY, THEY MAY HAVE DIFFICULTY HOLDING THEIR URINE, AND THERE MAY BE AN INCREASED RISK OF OBESITY.
AND THERE'S ALSO THE COST.
FOR MALES, IT COSTS ABOUT 10,000 TO 20,000 YEN HERE.*
FOR FEMALES, 15,000 TO 30,000 YEN.**
...?
? ? ?
SEIRA... WHAT DO YOU WANT TO DO?
YOU DON'T NEED TO WORRY ABOUT THE COST.
IF YOU WANT CIEL TO GET THE OPERATION THEN–
HUH?
YES... ULTIMATELY, IT'S UP TO THE PET'S OWNER TO DECIDE WHAT TO DO.

*About $100~200.
**About $150~300.

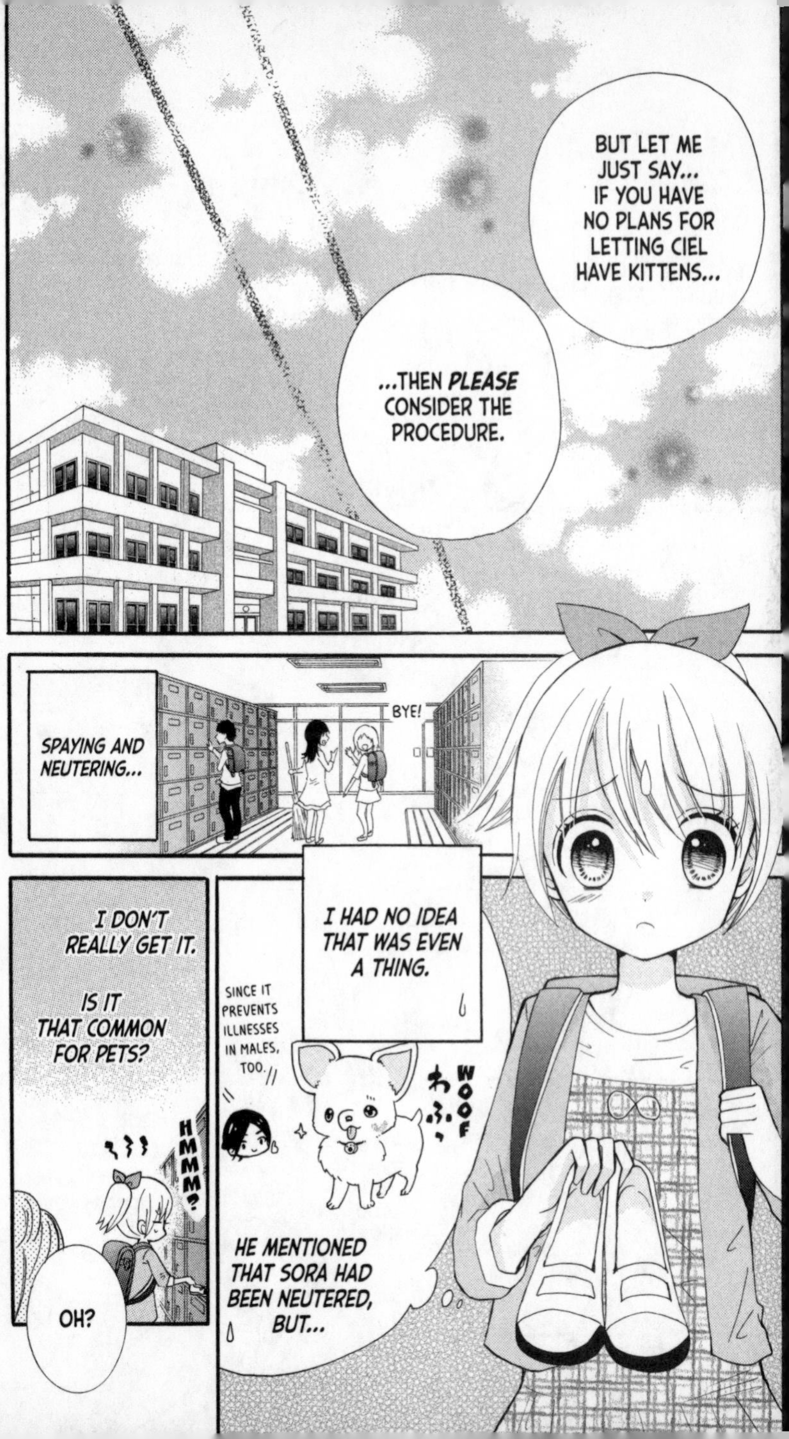
BUT LET ME JUST SAY... IF YOU HAVE NO PLANS FOR LETTING CIEL HAVE KITTENS...
...THEN *PLEASE* CONSIDER THE PROCEDURE.
BYE!
SPAYING AND NEUTERING...
I HAD NO IDEA THAT WAS EVEN A THING.
HE MENTIONED THAT SORA HAD BEEN NEUTERED, BUT...
SINCE IT PREVENTS ILLNESSES IN MALES, TOO.
わふ, WOOF
I DON'T REALLY GET IT.
IS IT THAT COMMON FOR PETS?
HMMM?
OH?

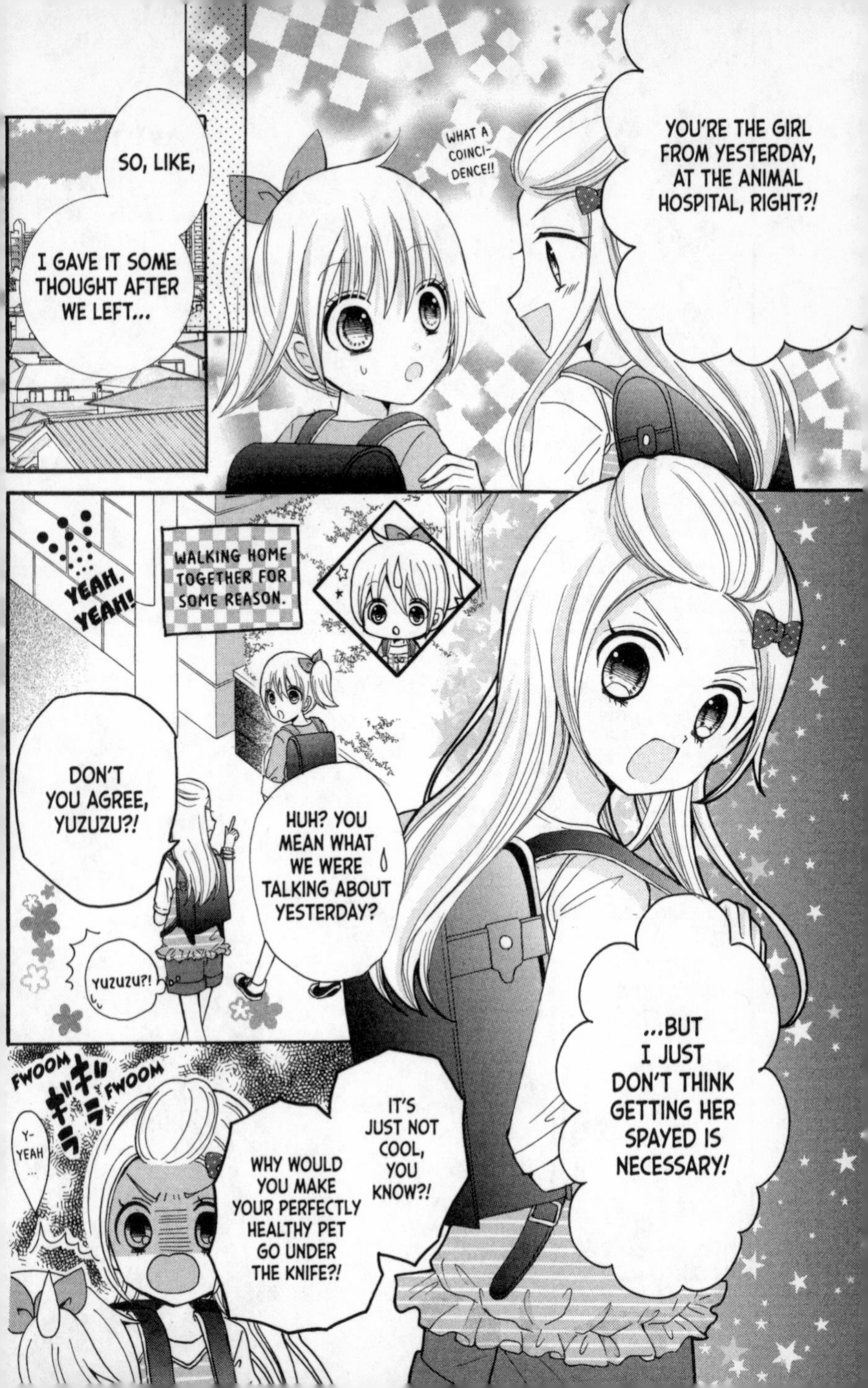
YOU'RE THE GIRL FROM YESTERDAY, AT THE ANIMAL HOSPITAL, RIGHT?!
WHAT A COINCIDENCE!!
SO, LIKE,
I GAVE IT SOME THOUGHT AFTER WE LEFT...
...BUT I JUST DON'T THINK GETTING HER SPAYED IS NECESSARY!
WALKING HOME TOGETHER FOR SOME REASON.
YEAH, YEAH!
DON'T YOU AGREE, YUZUZU?!
YUZUZU?!
HUH? YOU MEAN WHAT WE WERE TALKING ABOUT YESTERDAY?
FWOOM
ギラギラ
FWOOM
IT'S JUST NOT COOL, YOU KNOW?!
WHY WOULD YOU MAKE YOUR PERFECTLY HEALTHY PET GO UNDER THE KNIFE?!
Y-YEAH...

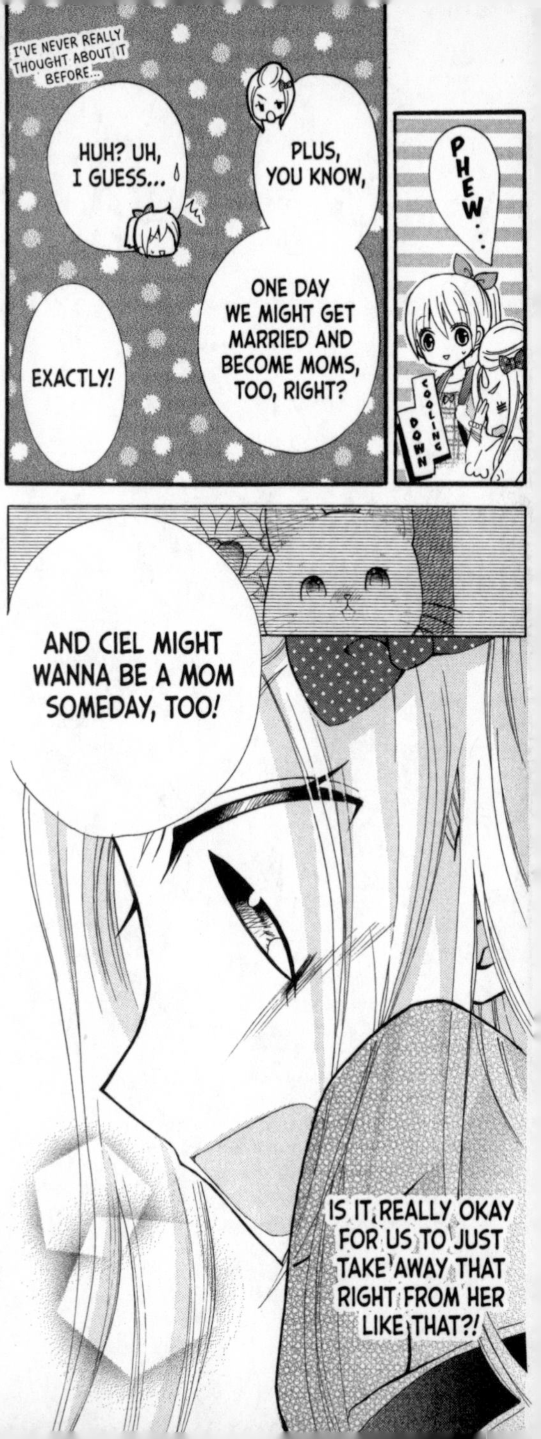
PHEW...
COOLING DOWN
PLUS, YOU KNOW,
ONE DAY WE MIGHT GET MARRIED AND BECOME MOMS, TOO, RIGHT?
HUH? UH, I GUESS...
I'VE NEVER REALLY THOUGHT ABOUT IT BEFORE...
EXACTLY!
AND CIEL MIGHT WANNA BE A MOM SOMEDAY, TOO!
IS IT REALLY OKAY FOR US TO JUST TAKE AWAY THAT RIGHT FROM HER LIKE THAT?!

GREETINGS.

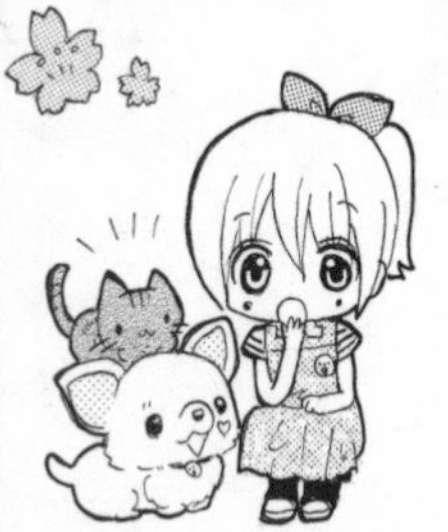

YUZU THE PET VET HAS REACHED VOLUME 4! THANK YOU SO MUCH FOR BUYING IT!!

I'M SURPRISED AT HOW FAST TIME FEELS TO BE PASSING RECENTLY. I WAS THINKING IT WAS ALMOST HALLOWEEN, BUT THEN CHRISTMAS WAS SUDDENLY RIGHT AROUND THE CORNER... OR THAT THE YEAR IS COMING TO A CLOSE, BUT THEN NEW YEAR'S DAY IS SUDDENLY LONG GONE. IN JAPAN, THIS VOLUME WENT ON SALE IN THE SPRING—A GOOD ✧ TIME TO ENJOY THE CHERRY BLOSSOMS LIKE YUZU AND THE ANIMALS ON THE COVER. ✿

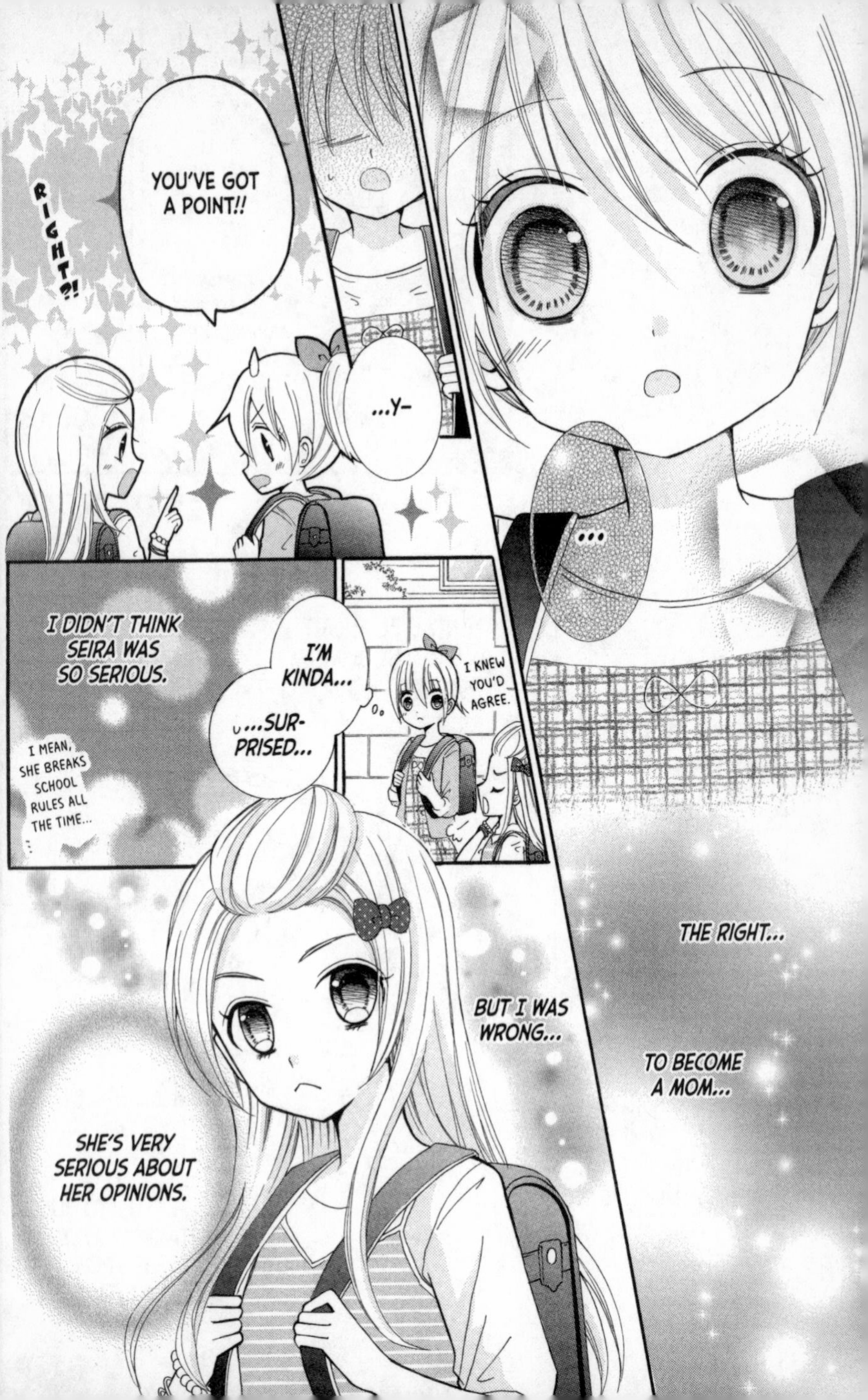
YOU'VE GOT A POINT!!
RIGHT?!
...Y–
...
I KNEW YOU'D AGREE.
I'M KINDA...
...SUR-PRISED...
I DIDN'T THINK SEIRA WAS SO SERIOUS.
I MEAN, SHE BREAKS SCHOOL RULES ALL THE TIME...
BUT I WAS WRONG...
SHE'S VERY SERIOUS ABOUT HER OPINIONS.
THE RIGHT...
TO BECOME A MOM...

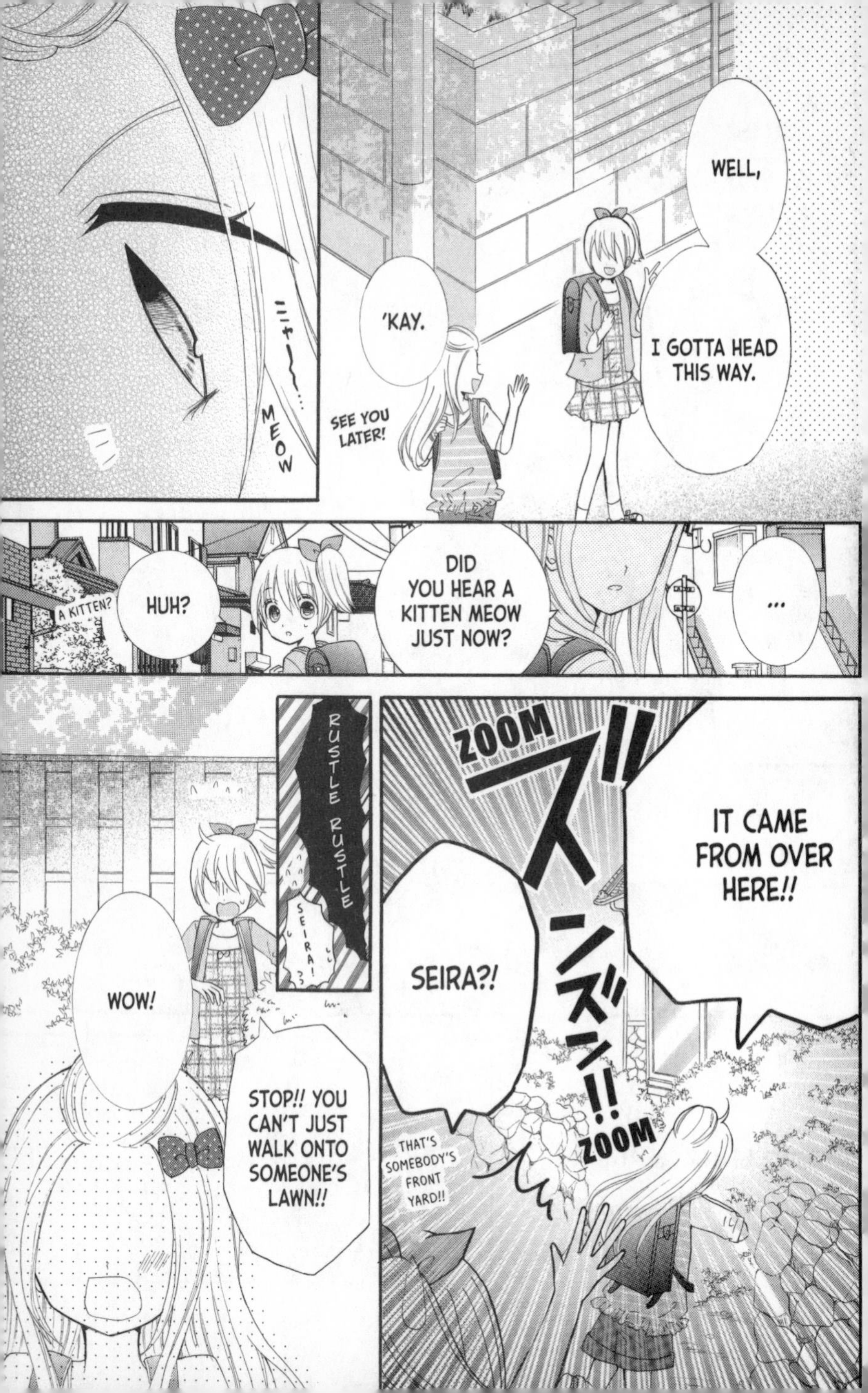
WELL,
I GOTTA HEAD THIS WAY.
'KAY.
SEE YOU LATER!
ニャー〜…
MEOW
…
DID YOU HEAR A KITTEN MEOW JUST NOW?
HUH?
A KITTEN?
ZOOM
IT CAME FROM OVER HERE!!
SEIRA?!
ZOOM
THAT'S SOMEBODY'S FRONT YARD!!
RUSTLE RUSTLE
SEIRA!
WOW!
STOP!! YOU CAN'T JUST WALK ONTO SOMEONE'S LAWN!!

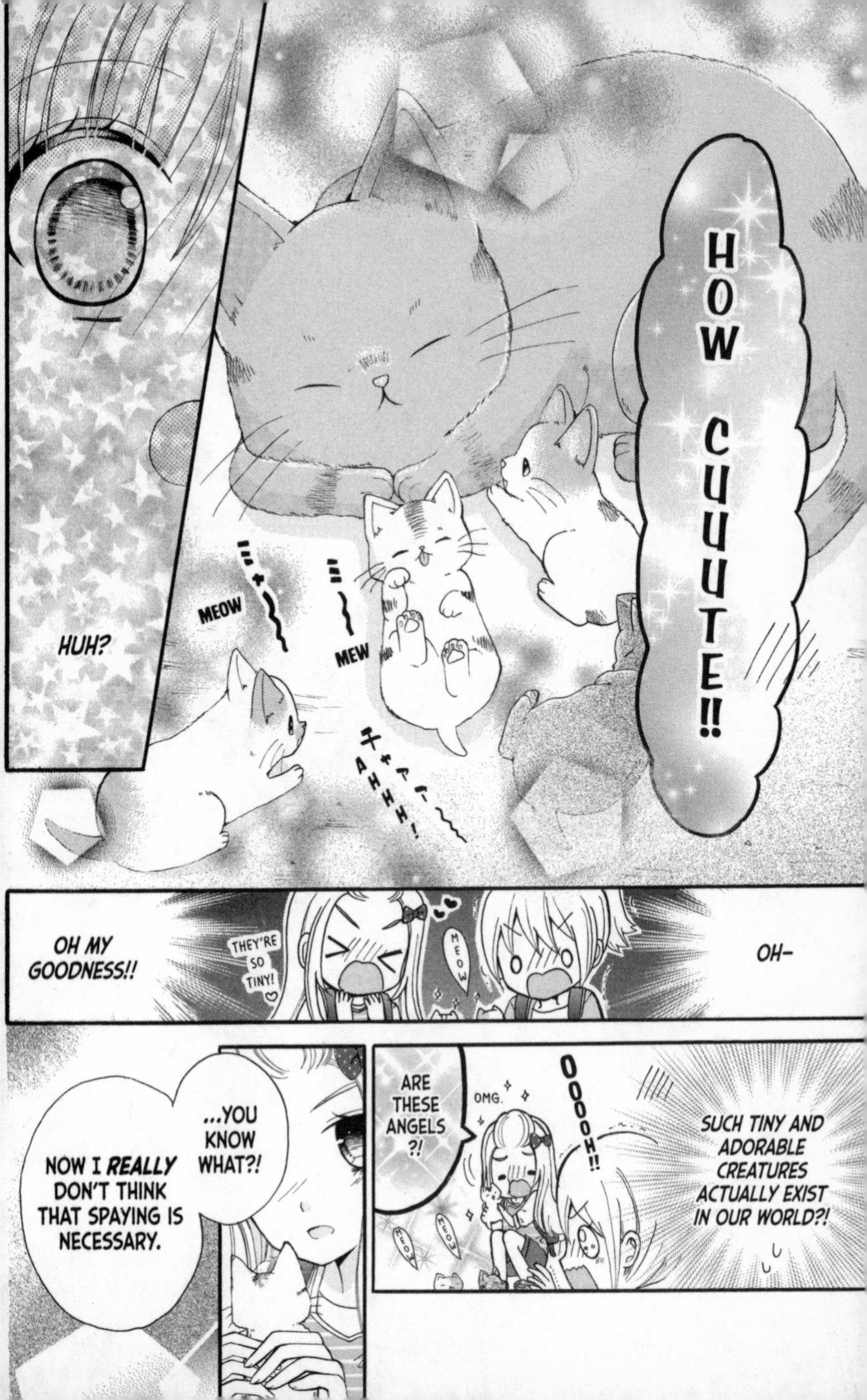
HOW CUUUTE!!
MEW
MEOW
AHHHH!
HUH?
OH–
MEOW
THEY'RE SO TINY!
OH MY GOODNESS!!
SUCH TINY AND ADORABLE CREATURES ACTUALLY EXIST IN OUR WORLD?!
OOOOOH!!
OMG.
ARE THESE ANGELS?!
MEOW
MEOW
...YOU KNOW WHAT?!
NOW I REALLY DON'T THINK THAT SPAYING IS NECESSARY.

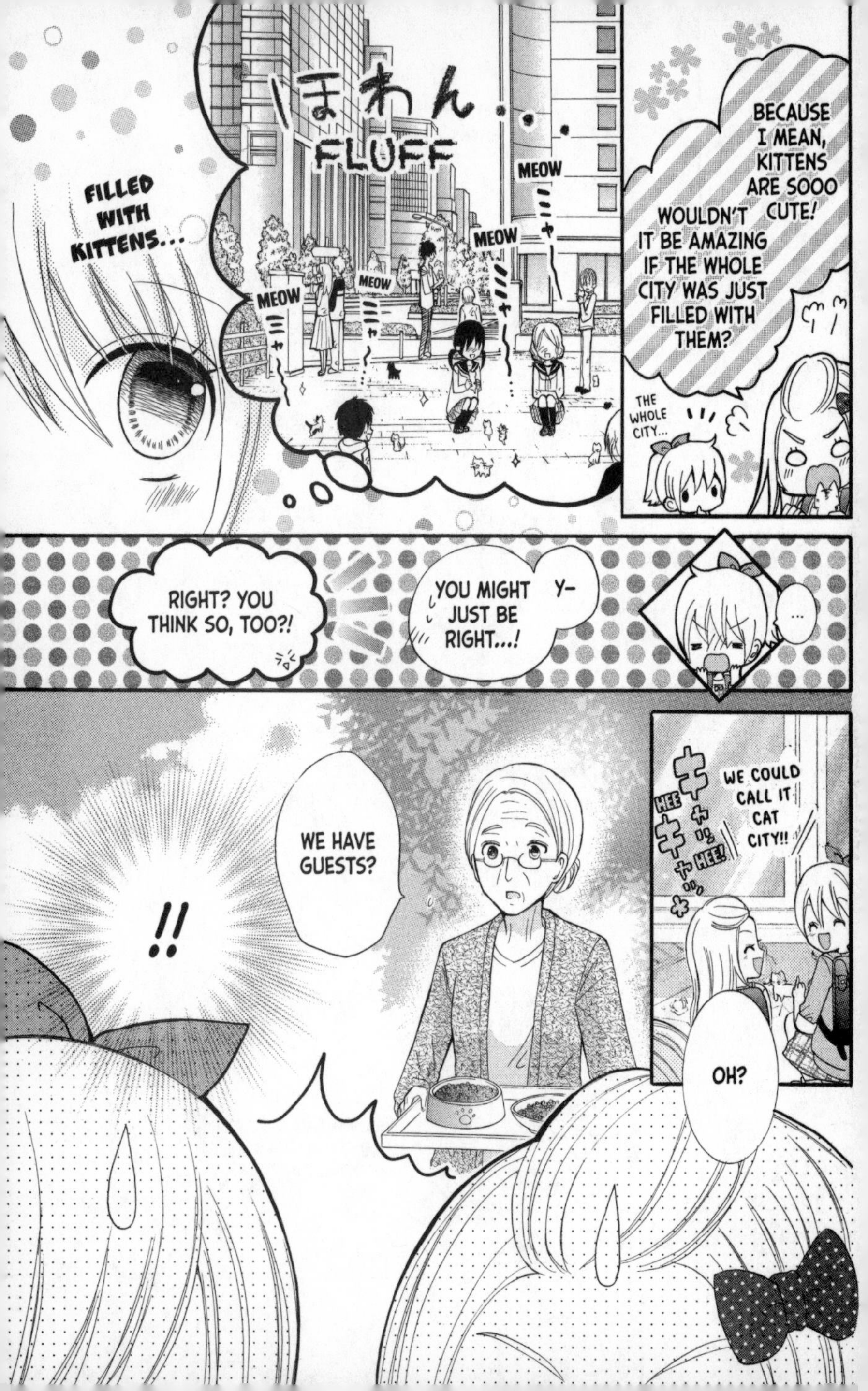
BECAUSE I MEAN, KITTENS ARE SOOO CUTE!
WOULDN'T IT BE AMAZING IF THE WHOLE CITY WAS JUST FILLED WITH THEM?
THE WHOLE CITY...
ほわん
FLUFF
MEOW
MEOW
MEOW
MEOW
FILLED WITH KITTENS...
...
Y–
YOU MIGHT JUST BE RIGHT...!
RIGHT? YOU THINK SO, TOO?!
WE COULD CALL IT CAT CITY!!
HEE HEE!
OH?
WE HAVE GUESTS?
!!

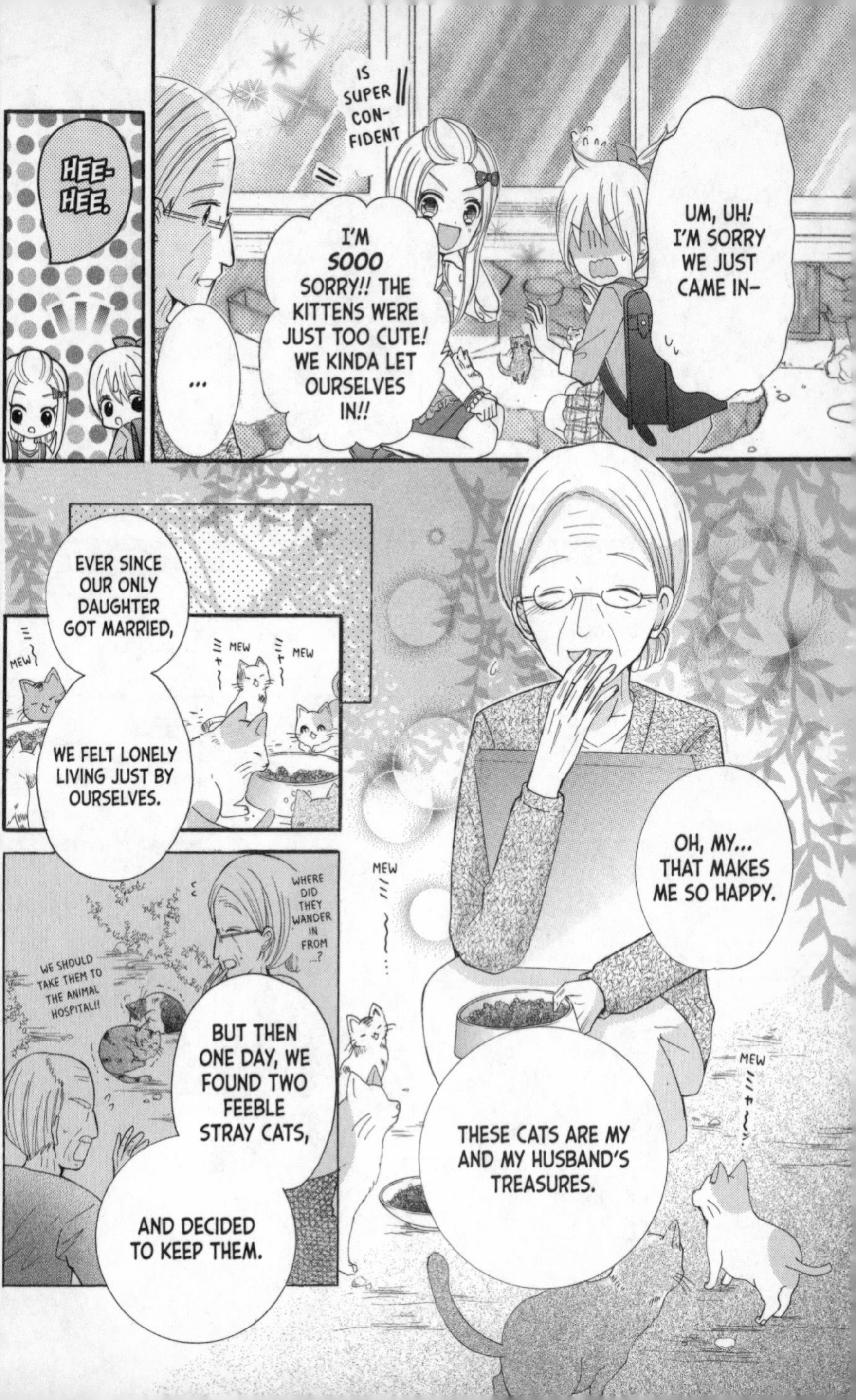
UM, UH! I'M SORRY WE JUST CAME IN-
IS SUPER CONFIDENT
I'M SOOO SORRY!! THE KITTENS WERE JUST TOO CUTE! WE KINDA LET OURSELVES IN!!
...
HEE-HEE.
OH, MY... THAT MAKES ME SO HAPPY.
MEW
MEW
THESE CATS ARE MY AND MY HUSBAND'S TREASURES.
EVER SINCE OUR ONLY DAUGHTER GOT MARRIED,
MEW
MEW
MEW
WE FELT LONELY LIVING JUST BY OURSELVES.
WHERE DID THEY WANDER IN FROM ...?
WE SHOULD TAKE THEM TO THE ANIMAL HOSPITAL!!
BUT THEN ONE DAY, WE FOUND TWO FEEBLE STRAY CATS,
AND DECIDED TO KEEP THEM.

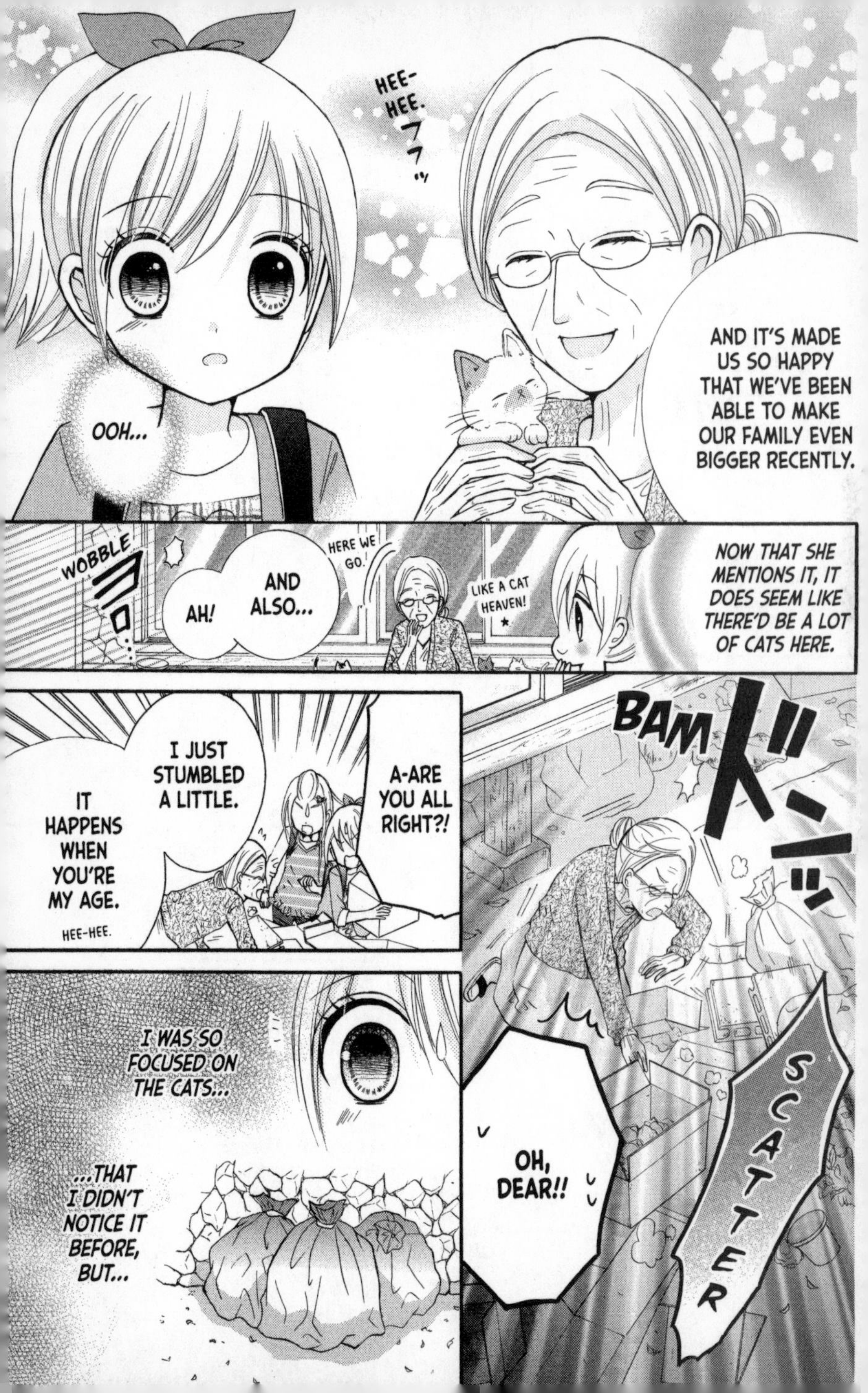
AND IT'S MADE US SO HAPPY THAT WE'VE BEEN ABLE TO MAKE OUR FAMILY EVEN BIGGER RECENTLY.
HEE-HEE.
OOH...
NOW THAT SHE MENTIONS IT, IT DOES SEEM LIKE THERE'D BE A LOT OF CATS HERE.
LIKE A CAT HEAVEN! ★
HERE WE GO.
AND ALSO...
AH!
WOBBLE
BAM
OH, DEAR!!
SCATTER
A-ARE YOU ALL RIGHT?!
I JUST STUMBLED A LITTLE.
IT HAPPENS WHEN YOU'RE MY AGE.
HEE-HEE.
I WAS SO FOCUSED ON THE CATS...
...THAT I DIDN'T NOTICE IT BEFORE, BUT...

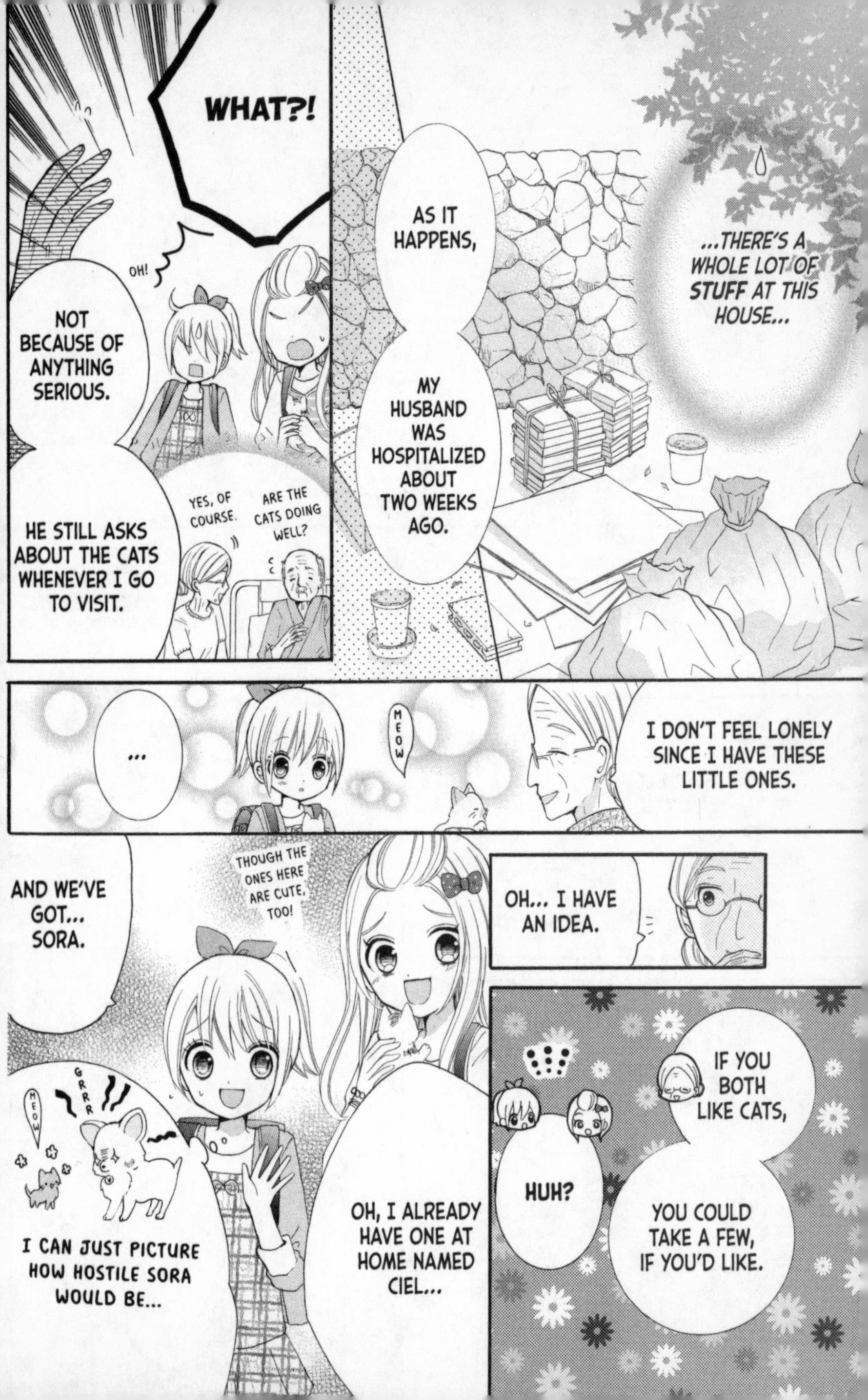
...THERE'S A WHOLE LOT OF STUFF AT THIS HOUSE...
AS IT HAPPENS,
MY HUSBAND WAS HOSPITALIZED ABOUT TWO WEEKS AGO.
WHAT?!
OH!
NOT BECAUSE OF ANYTHING SERIOUS.
ARE THE CATS DOING WELL?
YES, OF COURSE.
HE STILL ASKS ABOUT THE CATS WHENEVER I GO TO VISIT.
I DON'T FEEL LONELY SINCE I HAVE THESE LITTLE ONES.
MEOW
...
OH... I HAVE AN IDEA.
IF YOU BOTH LIKE CATS,
HUH?
YOU COULD TAKE A FEW, IF YOU'D LIKE.
OH, I ALREADY HAVE ONE AT HOME NAMED CIEL...
THOUGH THE ONES HERE ARE CUTE, TOO!
AND WE'VE GOT... SORA.
GRRR
MEOW
I CAN JUST PICTURE HOW HOSTILE SORA WOULD BE...

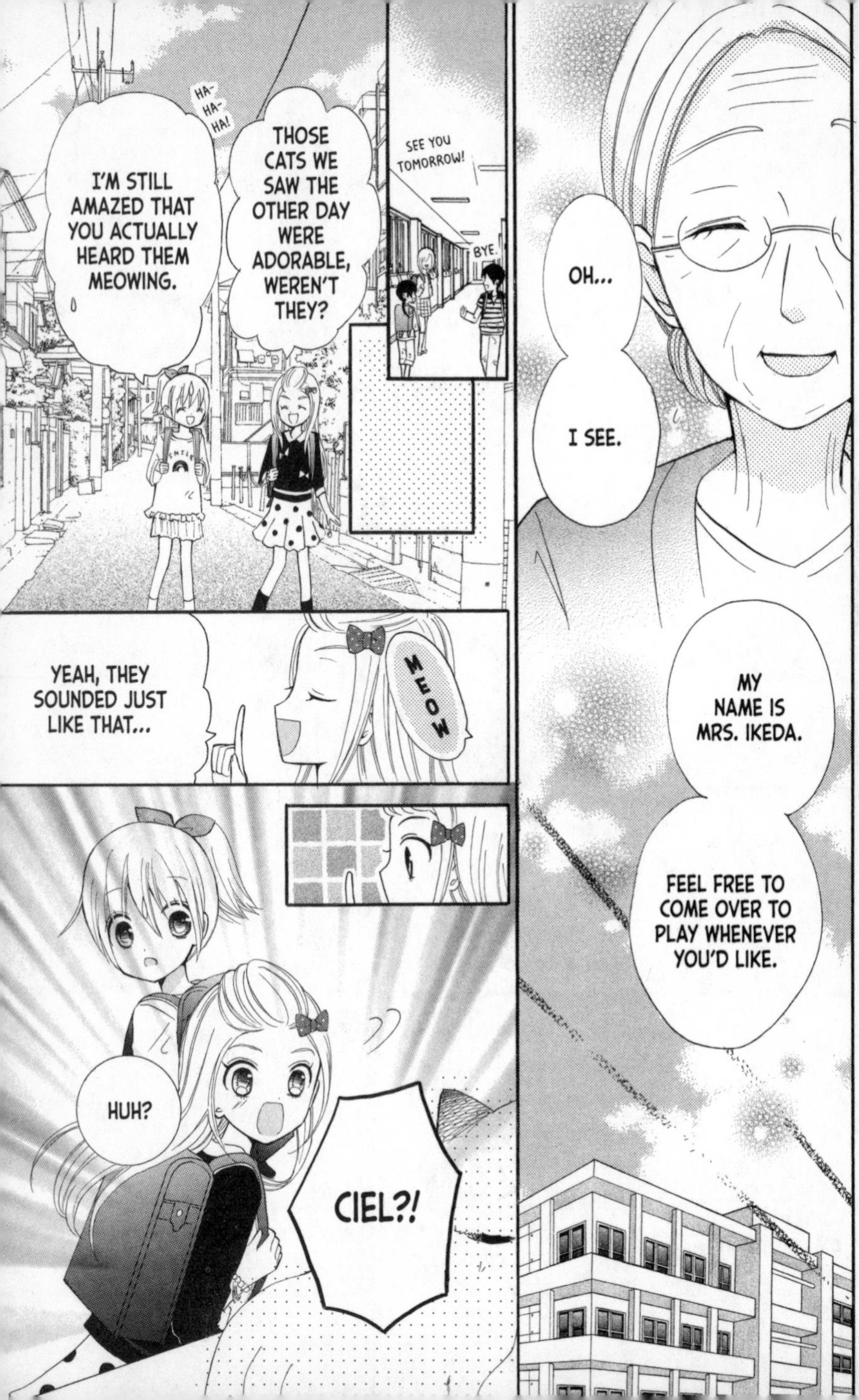
OH...
I SEE.
MY NAME IS MRS. IKEDA.
FEEL FREE TO COME OVER TO PLAY WHENEVER YOU'D LIKE.
SEE YOU TOMORROW!
BYE.
THOSE CATS WE SAW THE OTHER DAY WERE ADORABLE, WEREN'T THEY?
HA-HA-HA!
I'M STILL AMAZED THAT YOU ACTUALLY HEARD THEM MEOWING.
MEOW
YEAH, THEY SOUNDED JUST LIKE THAT...
CIEL?!
HUH?

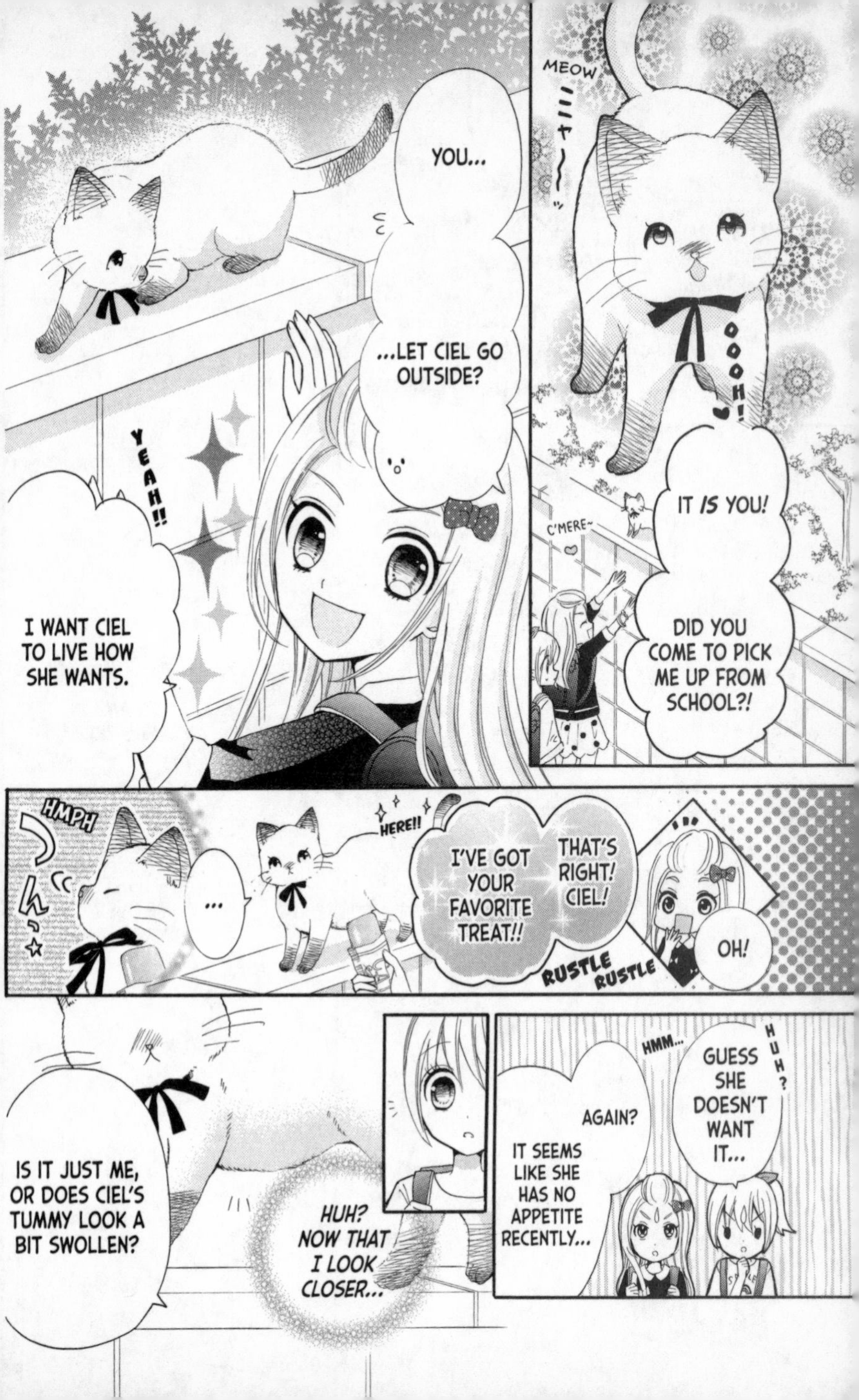
MEOW
ニャ〜ッ
OOOH!
IT *IS* YOU!
C'MERE~
DID YOU COME TO PICK ME UP FROM SCHOOL?!
YOU...
...LET CIEL GO OUTSIDE?
YEAH!!
I WANT CIEL TO LIVE HOW SHE WANTS.
OH!
RUSTLE RUSTLE
THAT'S RIGHT! CIEL!
I'VE GOT YOUR FAVORITE TREAT!!
HERE!!
...
HMPH
つん☆
GUESS SHE DOESN'T WANT IT...
HUH?
HMM...
AGAIN?
IT SEEMS LIKE SHE HAS NO APPETITE RECENTLY...
HUH? NOW THAT I LOOK CLOSER...
IS IT JUST ME, OR DOES CIEL'S TUMMY LOOK A BIT SWOLLEN?

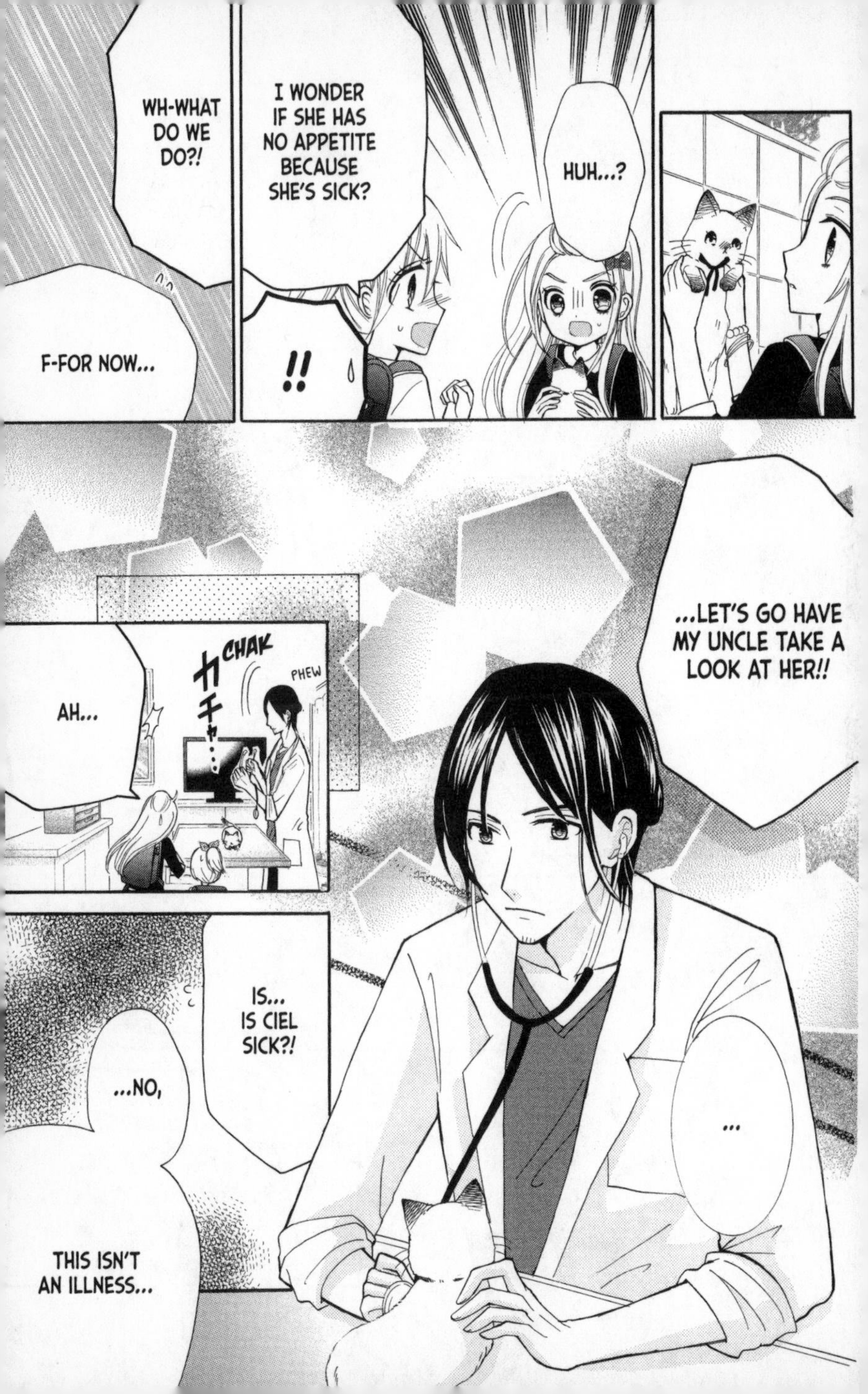

HUH...?
!!
I WONDER IF SHE HAS NO APPETITE BECAUSE SHE'S SICK?
WH-WHAT DO WE DO?!
F-FOR NOW...
...LET'S GO HAVE MY UNCLE TAKE A LOOK AT HER!!
PHEW
カチャ
CHAK
AH...
...
IS... IS CIEL SICK?!
...NO,
THIS ISN'T AN ILLNESS...

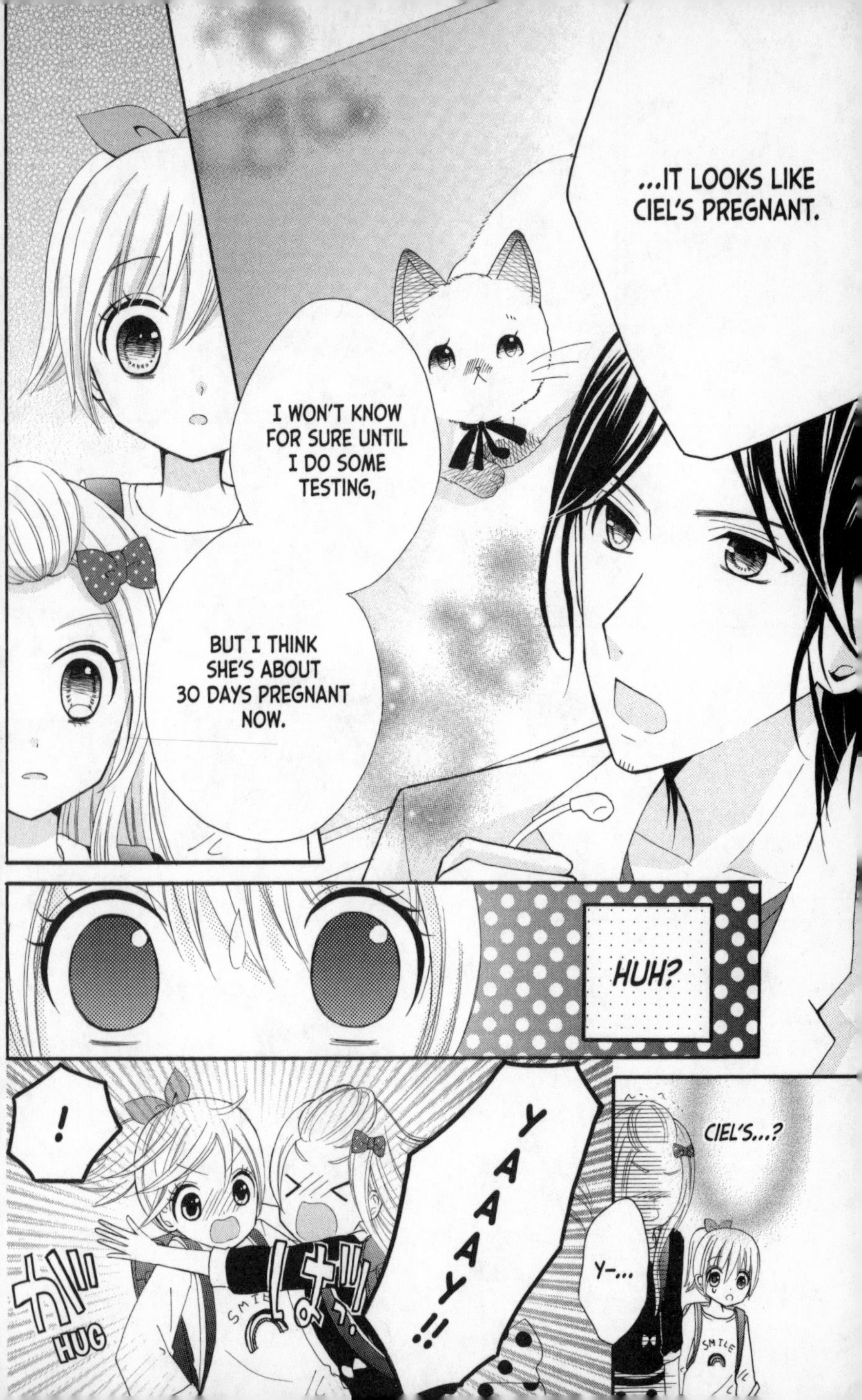
...IT LOOKS LIKE CIEL'S PREGNANT.
I WON'T KNOW FOR SURE UNTIL I DO SOME TESTING,
BUT I THINK SHE'S ABOUT 30 DAYS PREGNANT NOW.
HUH?
CIEL'S...?
Y-...
YAAAAY!!
!
HUG

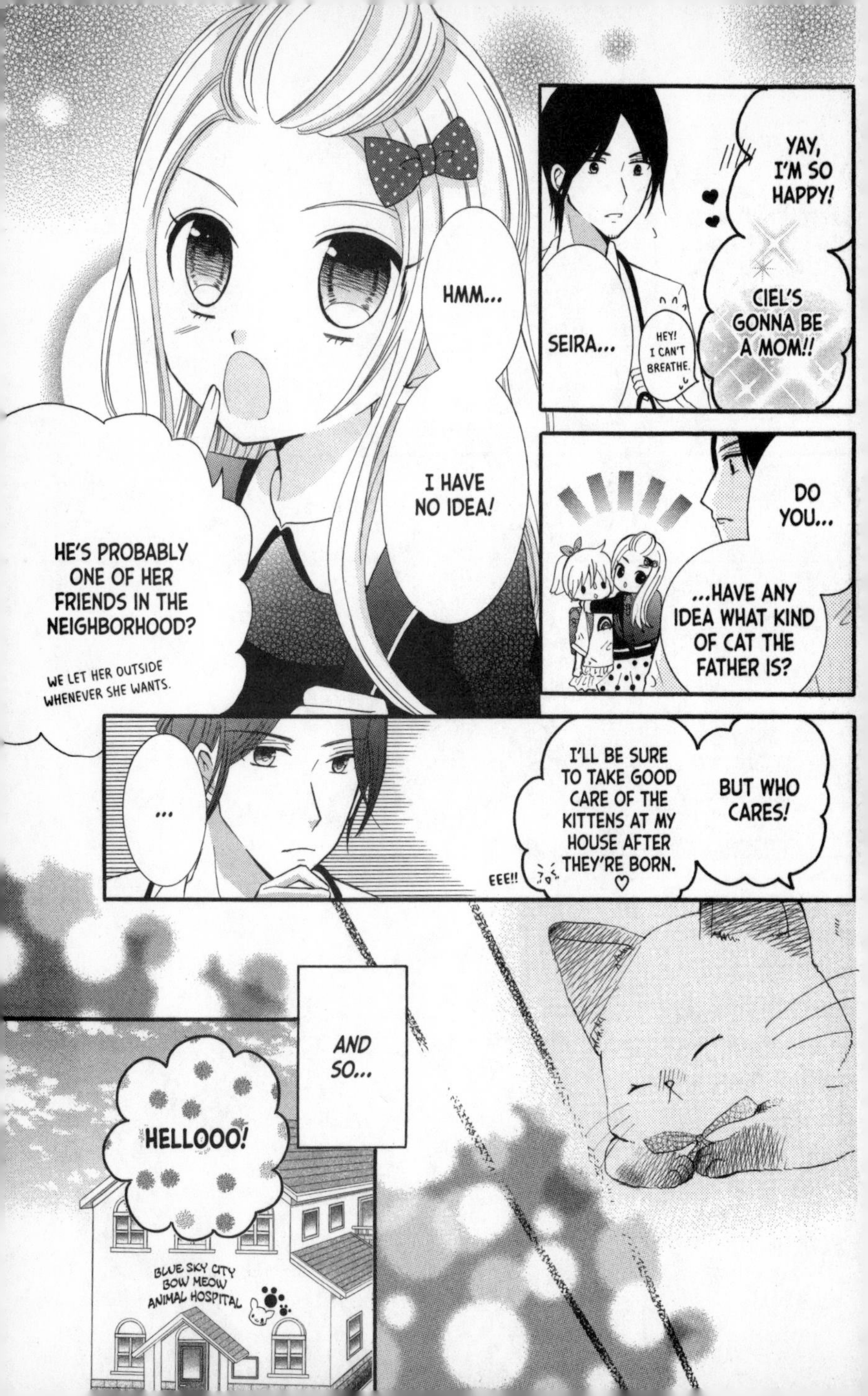
YAY, I'M SO HAPPY!
CIEL'S GONNA BE A MOM!!
HEY! I CAN'T BREATHE.
SEIRA...
DO YOU...
...HAVE ANY IDEA WHAT KIND OF CAT THE FATHER IS?
HMM...
I HAVE NO IDEA!
HE'S PROBABLY ONE OF HER FRIENDS IN THE NEIGHBORHOOD?
WE LET HER OUTSIDE WHENEVER SHE WANTS.
BUT WHO CARES!
I'LL BE SURE TO TAKE GOOD CARE OF THE KITTENS AT MY HOUSE AFTER THEY'RE BORN.
EEE!!
...
AND SO...
HELLOOO!
BLUE SKY CITY BOW MEOW ANIMAL HOSPITAL

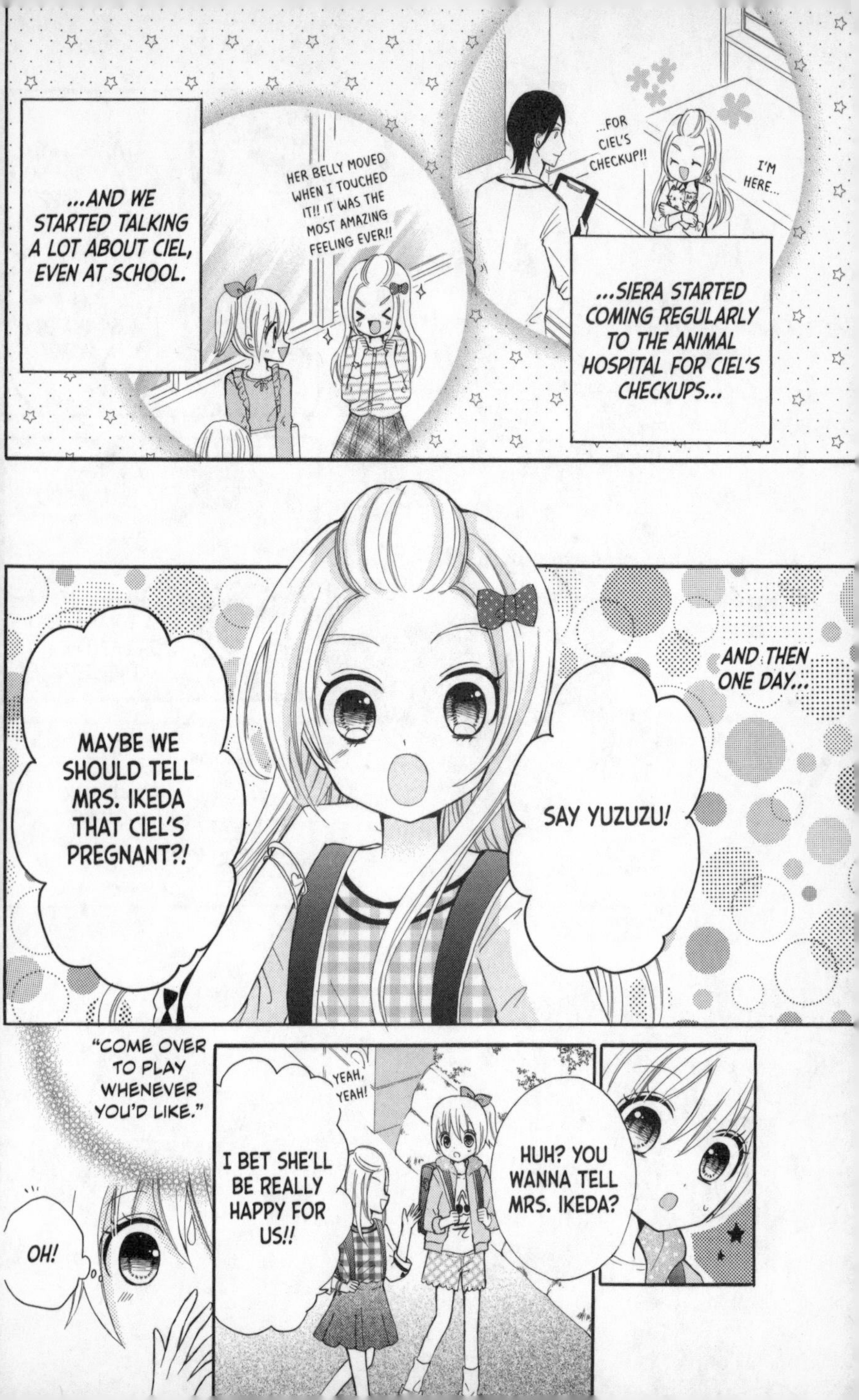

I'M HERE...
...FOR CIEL'S CHECKUP!!
...SIERA STARTED COMING REGULARLY TO THE ANIMAL HOSPITAL FOR CIEL'S CHECKUPS...
HER BELLY MOVED WHEN I TOUCHED IT!! IT WAS THE MOST AMAZING FEELING EVER!!
...AND WE STARTED TALKING A LOT ABOUT CIEL, EVEN AT SCHOOL.
AND THEN ONE DAY...
SAY YUZUZU!
MAYBE WE SHOULD TELL MRS. IKEDA THAT CIEL'S PREGNANT?!
HUH? YOU WANNA TELL MRS. IKEDA?
YEAH, YEAH!
I BET SHE'LL BE REALLY HAPPY FOR US!!
"COME OVER TO PLAY WHENEVER YOU'D LIKE."
OH!

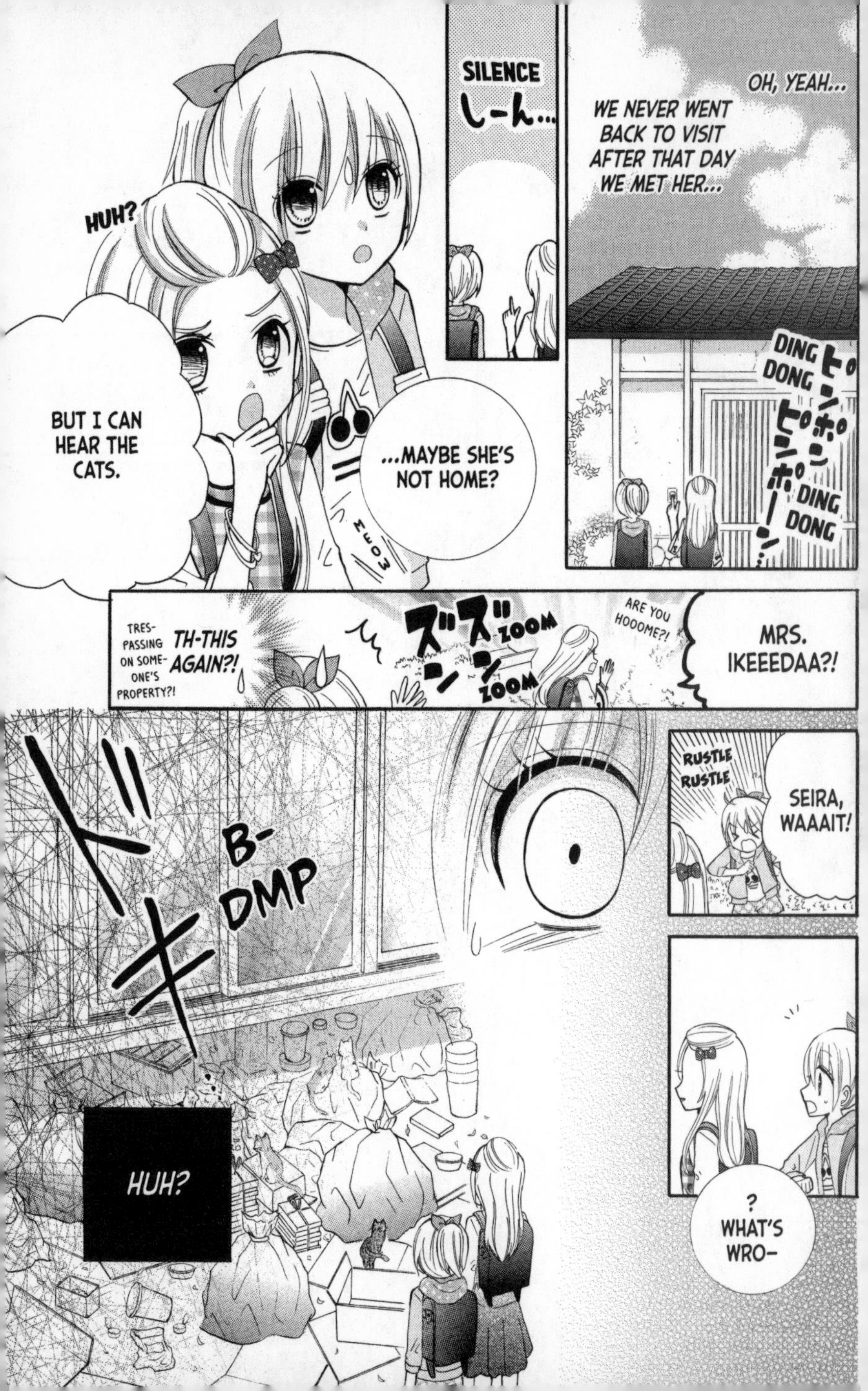
OH, YEAH...
WE NEVER WENT BACK TO VISIT AFTER THAT DAY WE MET HER...
ピンポン ピンポーン
DING DONG
DING DONG
SILENCE
しーん...
...MAYBE SHE'S NOT HOME?
HUH?
MEOW
BUT I CAN HEAR THE CATS.
MRS. IKEEEDAA?!
ARE YOU HOOOME?!
ズン ズン
ZOOM
ZOOM
TH-THIS AGAIN?!
TRES-PASSING ON SOME-ONE'S PROPERTY?!
SEIRA, WAAAIT!
RUSTLE RUSTLE
? WHAT'S WRO-
ドキ
B-DMP
HUH?

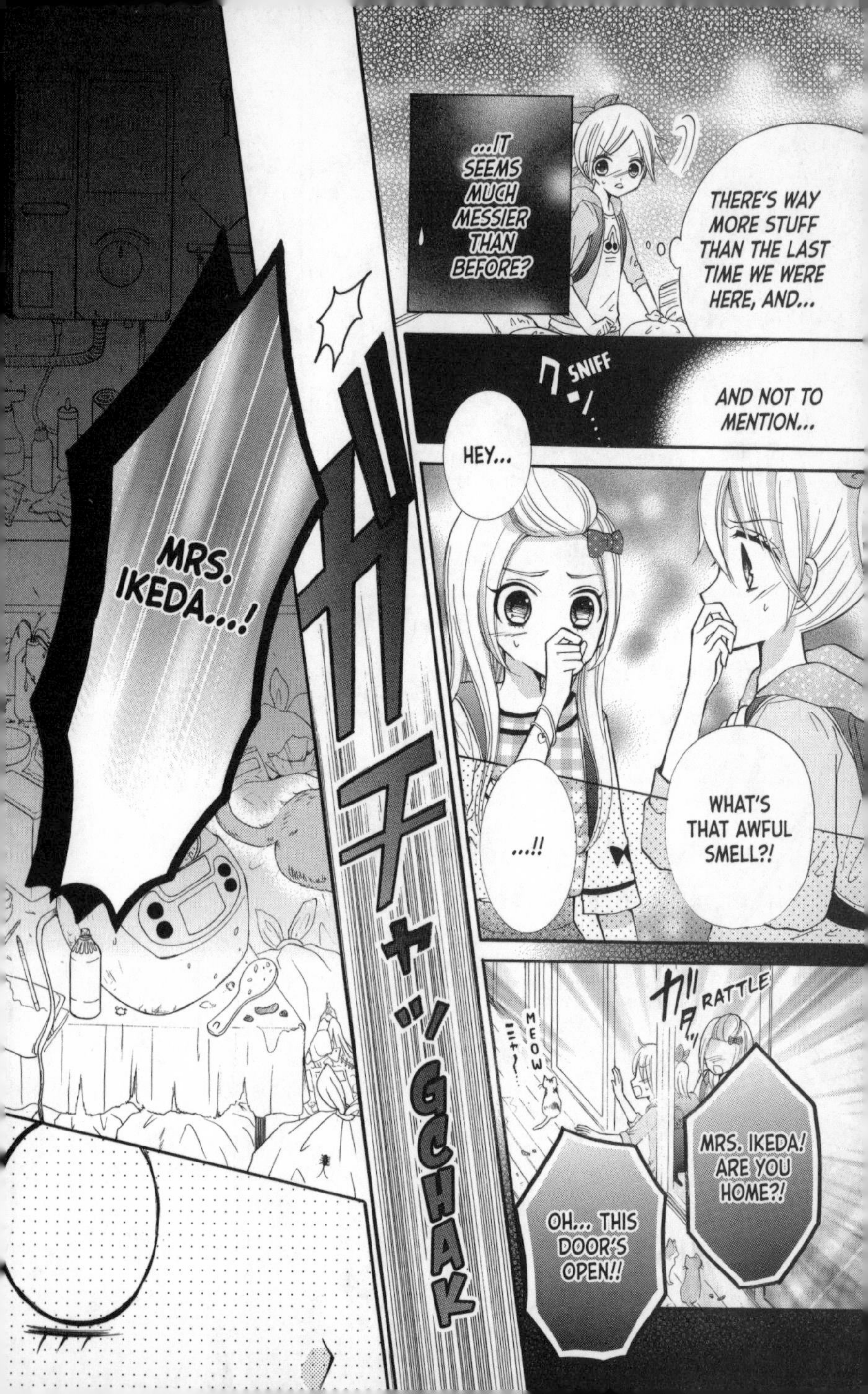
THERE'S WAY MORE STUFF THAN THE LAST TIME WE WERE HERE, AND...
...IT SEEMS MUCH MESSIER THAN BEFORE?
AND NOT TO MENTION...
SNIFF
HEY...
WHAT'S THAT AWFUL SMELL?!
...!!
RATTLE
MEOW
MRS. IKEDA! ARE YOU HOME?!
OH... THIS DOOR'S OPEN!!
GCHAK
MRS. IKEDA...!

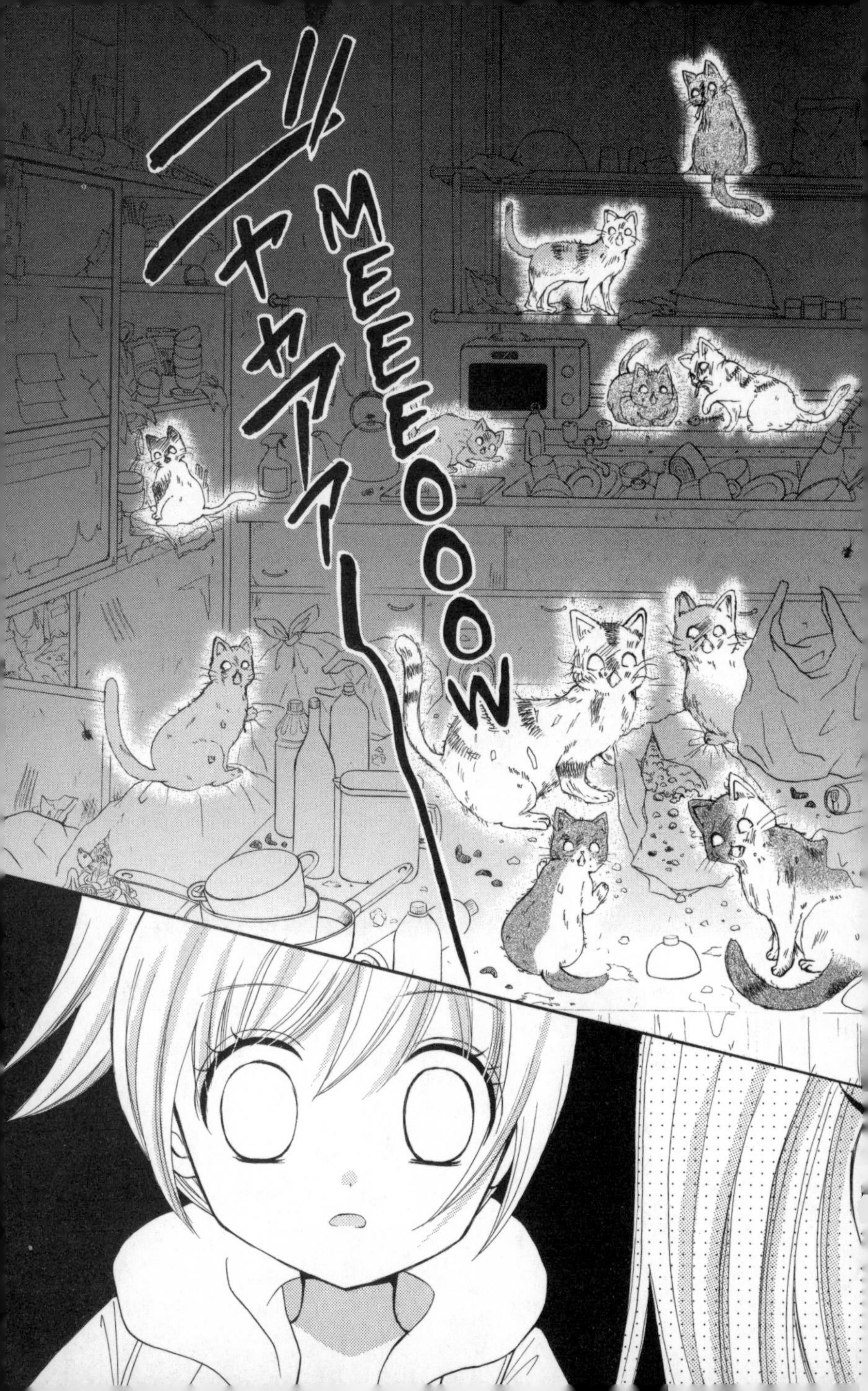
ニャァァァ
MEEEOOOW

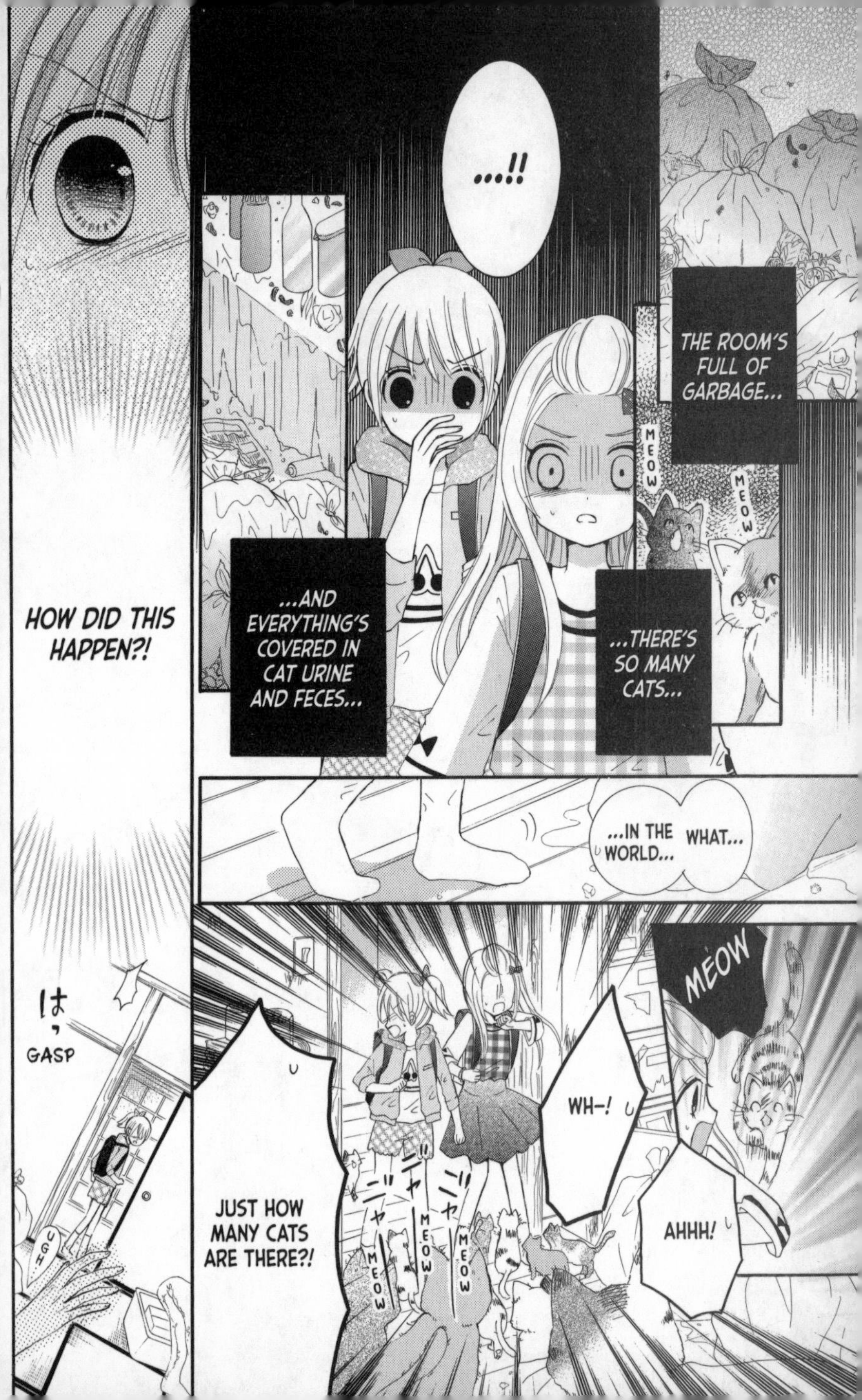
...!!
THE ROOM'S FULL OF GARBAGE...
MEOW
MEOW
...THERE'S SO MANY CATS...
...AND EVERYTHING'S COVERED IN CAT URINE AND FECES...
WHAT...
...IN THE WORLD...
MEOW
AHHH!
WH-!
ニ゛ャ
MEOW
ニ゛ャ
MEOW
ニ゛ャ
MEOW
JUST HOW MANY CATS ARE THERE?!
HOW DID THIS HAPPEN?!
は、
GASP
UGH

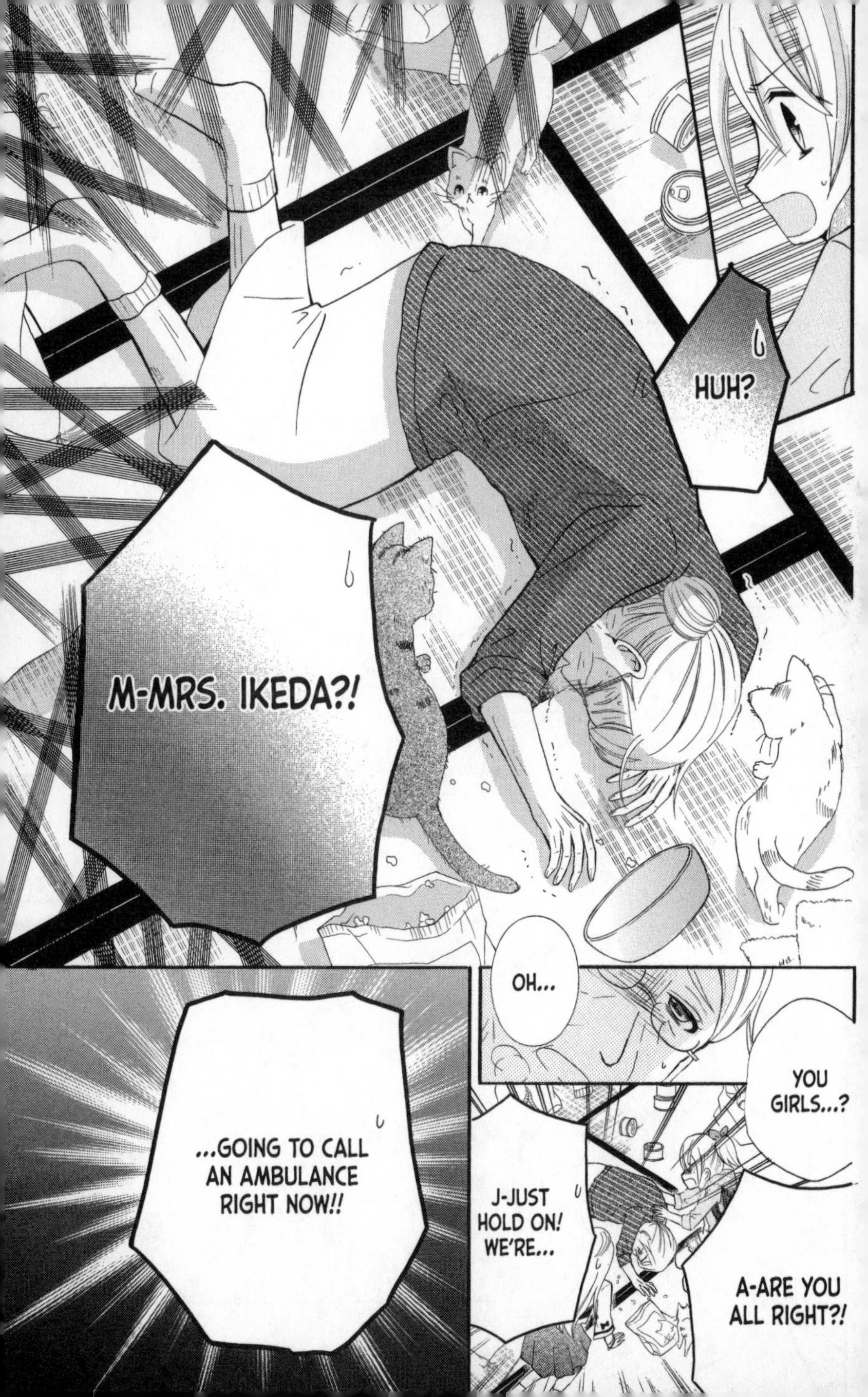
HUH?
M-MRS. IKEDA?!
OH...
YOU GIRLS...?
A-ARE YOU ALL RIGHT?!
J-JUST HOLD ON! WE'RE...
...GOING TO CALL AN AMBULANCE RIGHT NOW!!

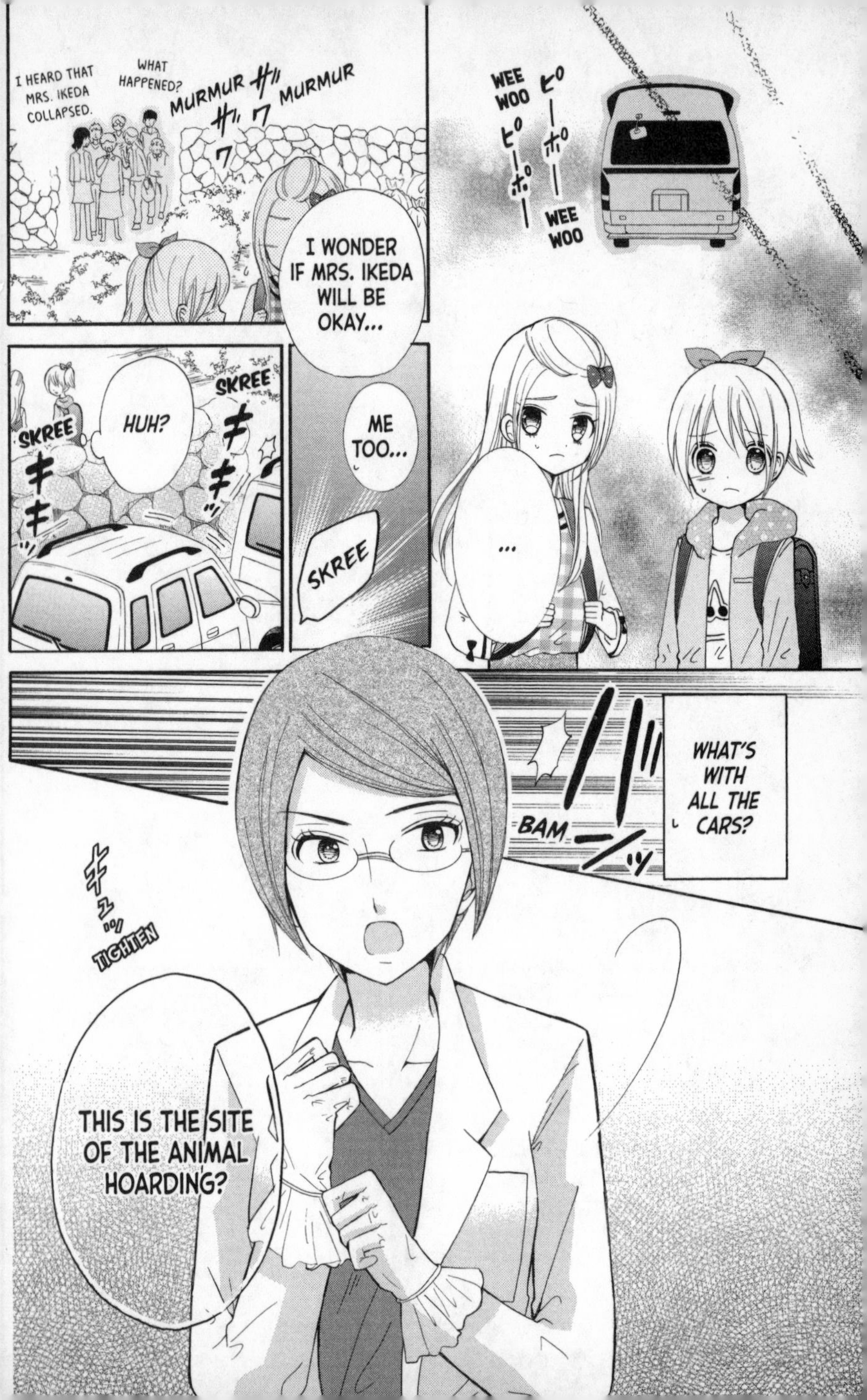
WEE WOO
WEE WOO
WHAT HAPPENED?
I HEARD THAT MRS. IKEDA COLLAPSED.
MURMUR MURMUR
I WONDER IF MRS. IKEDA WILL BE OKAY...
...
ME TOO...
SKREE
SKREE
SKREE
HUH?
WHAT'S WITH ALL THE CARS?
BAM
TIGHTEN
THIS IS THE SITE OF THE ANIMAL HOARDING?

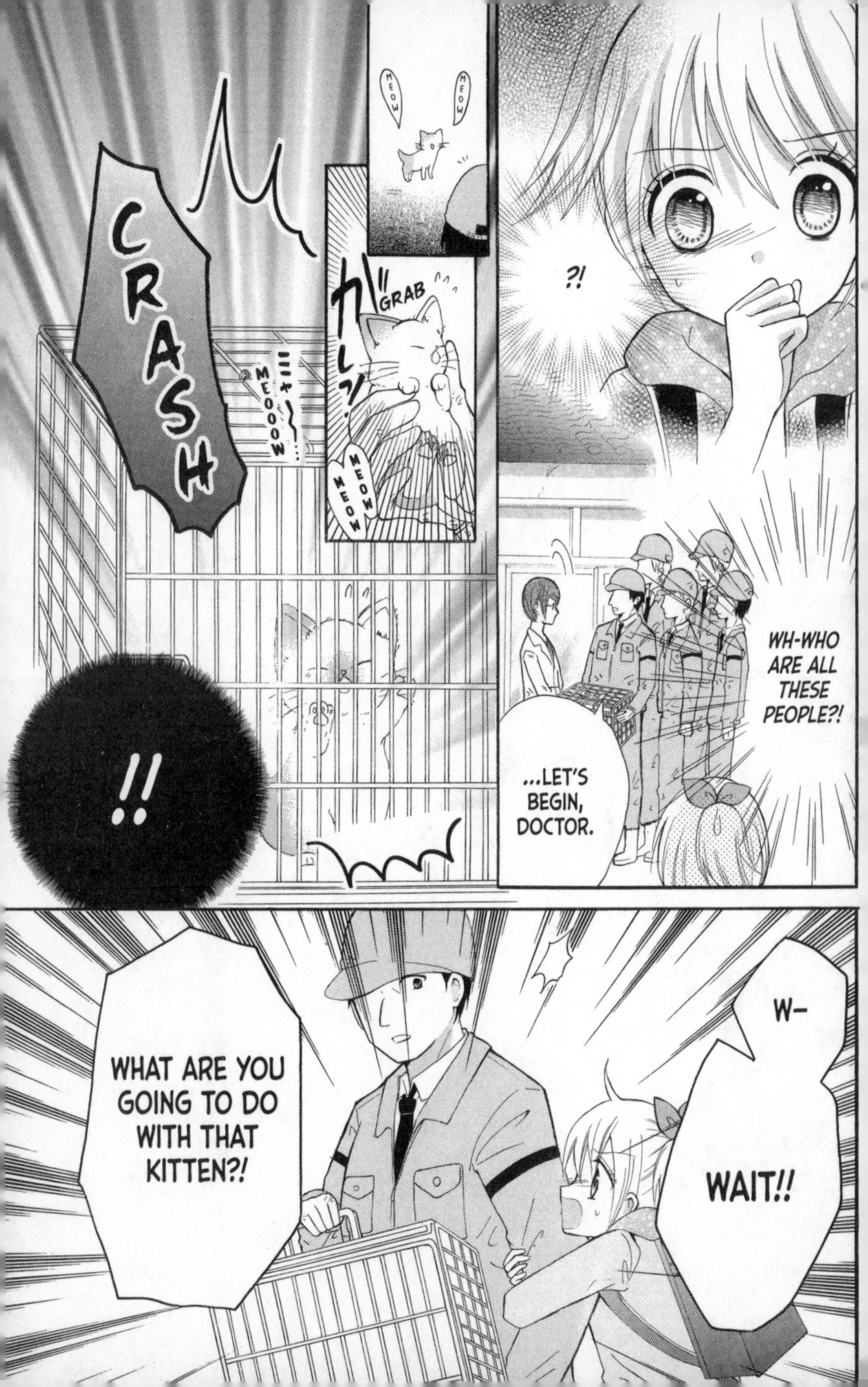
?!
WH-WHO ARE ALL THESE PEOPLE?!
...LET'S BEGIN, DOCTOR.
MEOW
MEOW
GRAB
MEOW MEOW
CRASH
MEOOOW
!!
W-
WAIT!!
WHAT ARE YOU GOING TO DO WITH THAT KITTEN?!

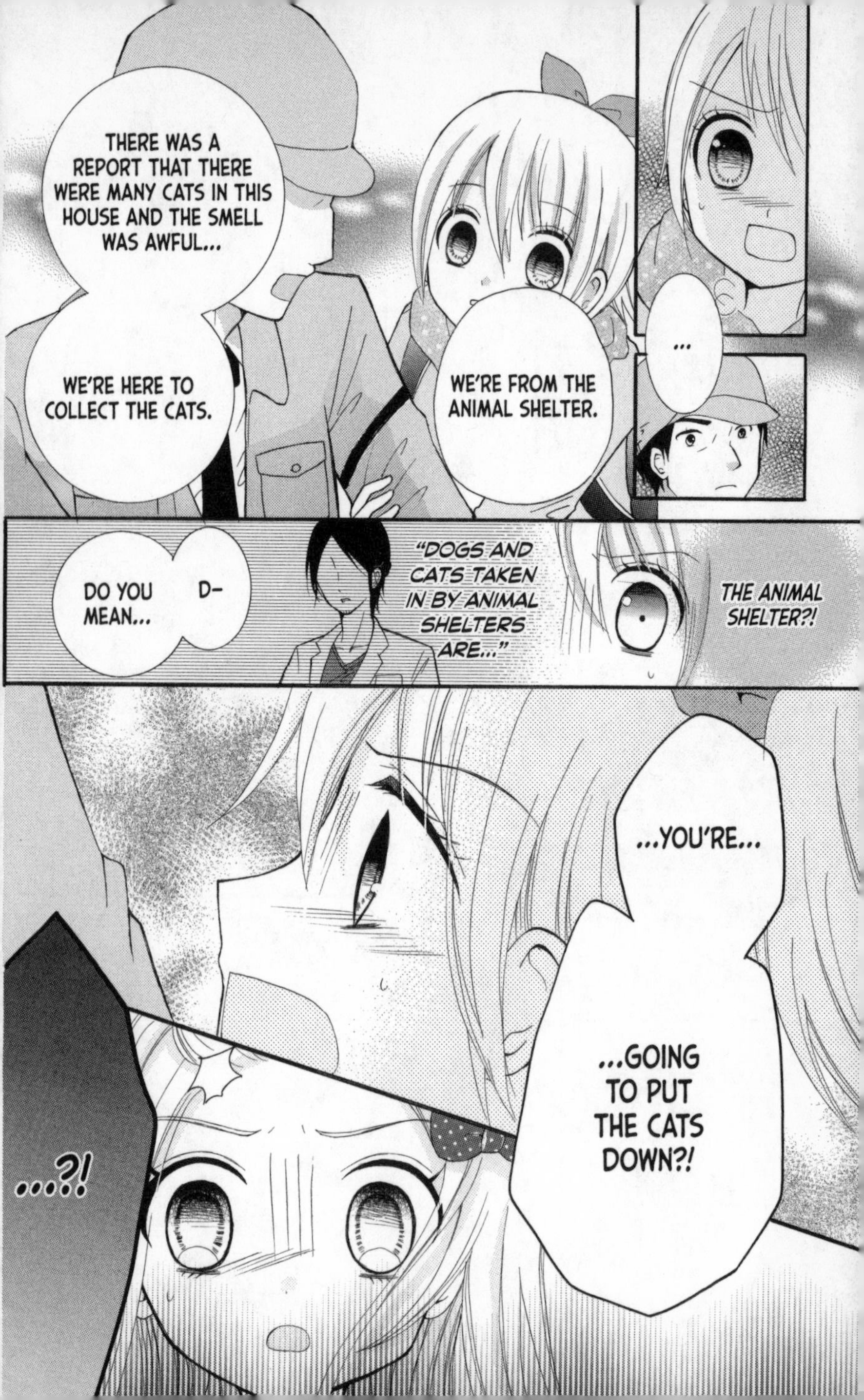
...
WE'RE FROM THE ANIMAL SHELTER.
THERE WAS A REPORT THAT THERE WERE MANY CATS IN THIS HOUSE AND THE SMELL WAS AWFUL...
WE'RE HERE TO COLLECT THE CATS.
THE ANIMAL SHELTER?!
"DOGS AND CATS TAKEN IN BY ANIMAL SHELTERS ARE..."
D-
DO YOU MEAN...
...YOU'RE...
...GOING TO PUT THE CATS DOWN?!
...?!

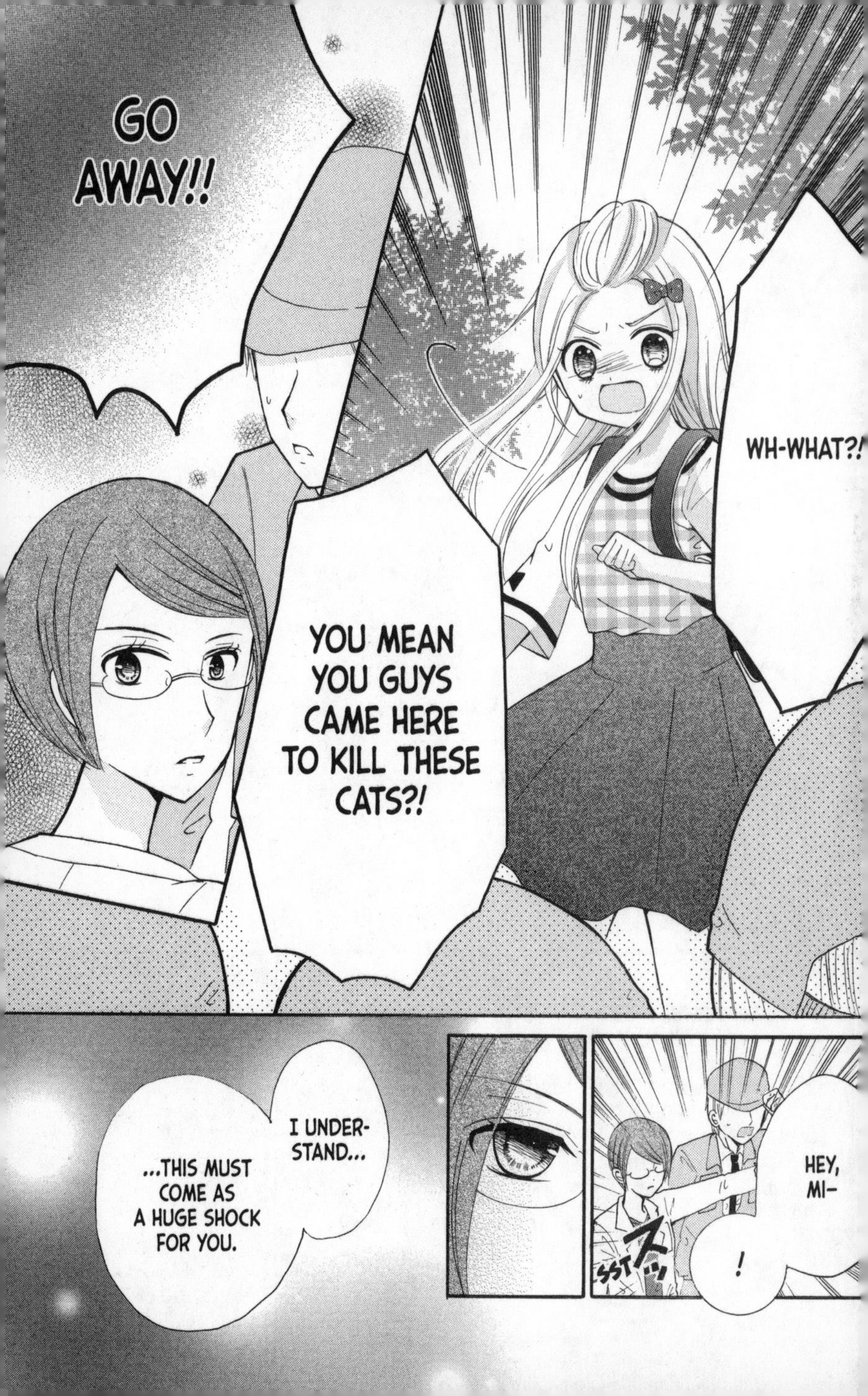
WH-WHAT?!
YOU MEAN YOU GUYS CAME HERE TO KILL THESE CATS?!
GO AWAY!!
HEY, MI-
!
SST
I UNDER-STAND...
...THIS MUST COME AS A HUGE SHOCK FOR YOU.

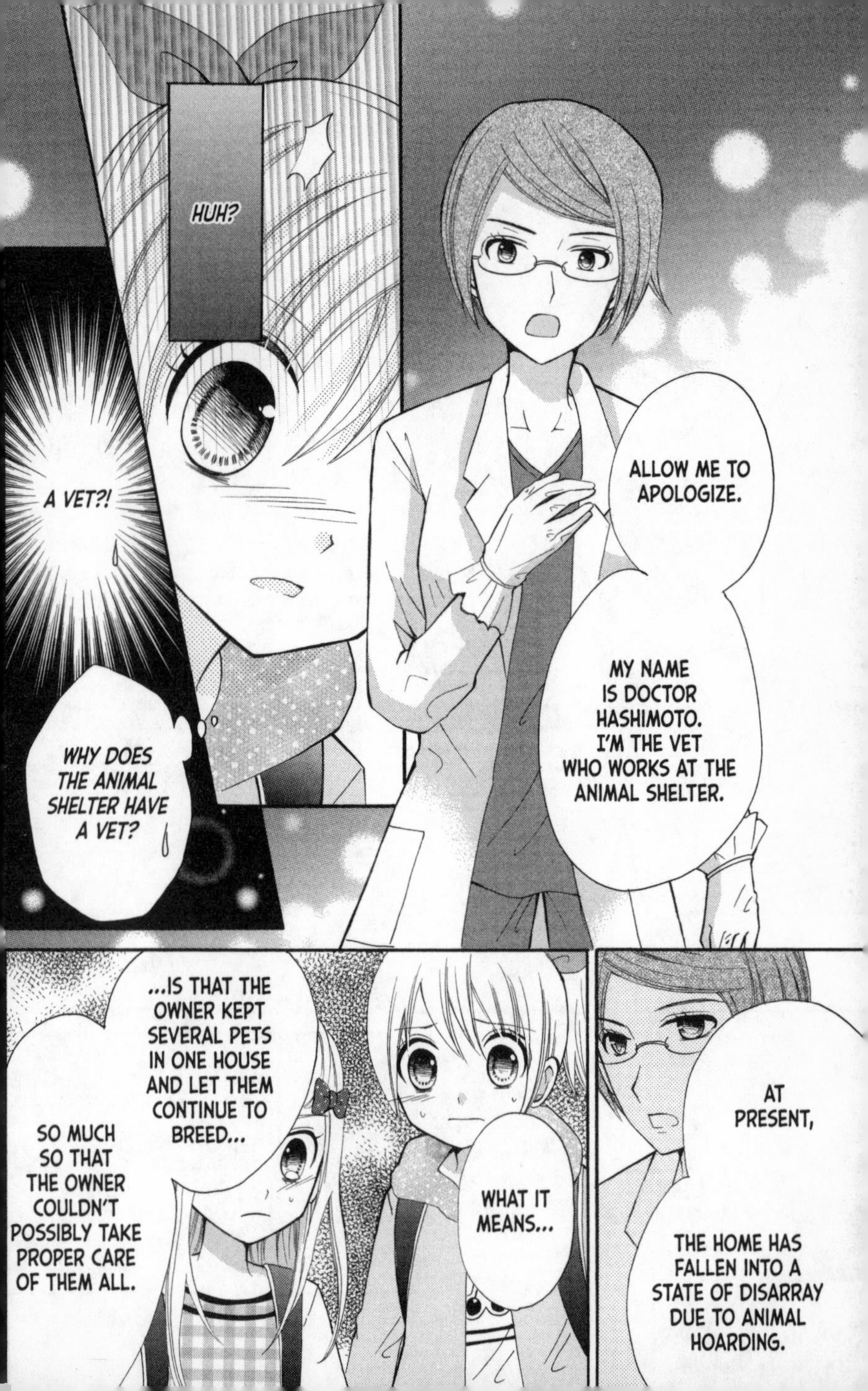
ALLOW ME TO APOLOGIZE.
MY NAME IS DOCTOR HASHIMOTO. I'M THE VET WHO WORKS AT THE ANIMAL SHELTER.
HUH?
A VET?!
WHY DOES THE ANIMAL SHELTER HAVE A VET?
AT PRESENT,
THE HOME HAS FALLEN INTO A STATE OF DISARRAY DUE TO ANIMAL HOARDING.
WHAT IT MEANS...
...IS THAT THE OWNER KEPT SEVERAL PETS IN ONE HOUSE AND LET THEM CONTINUE TO BREED...
SO MUCH SO THAT THE OWNER COULDN'T POSSIBLY TAKE PROPER CARE OF THEM ALL.

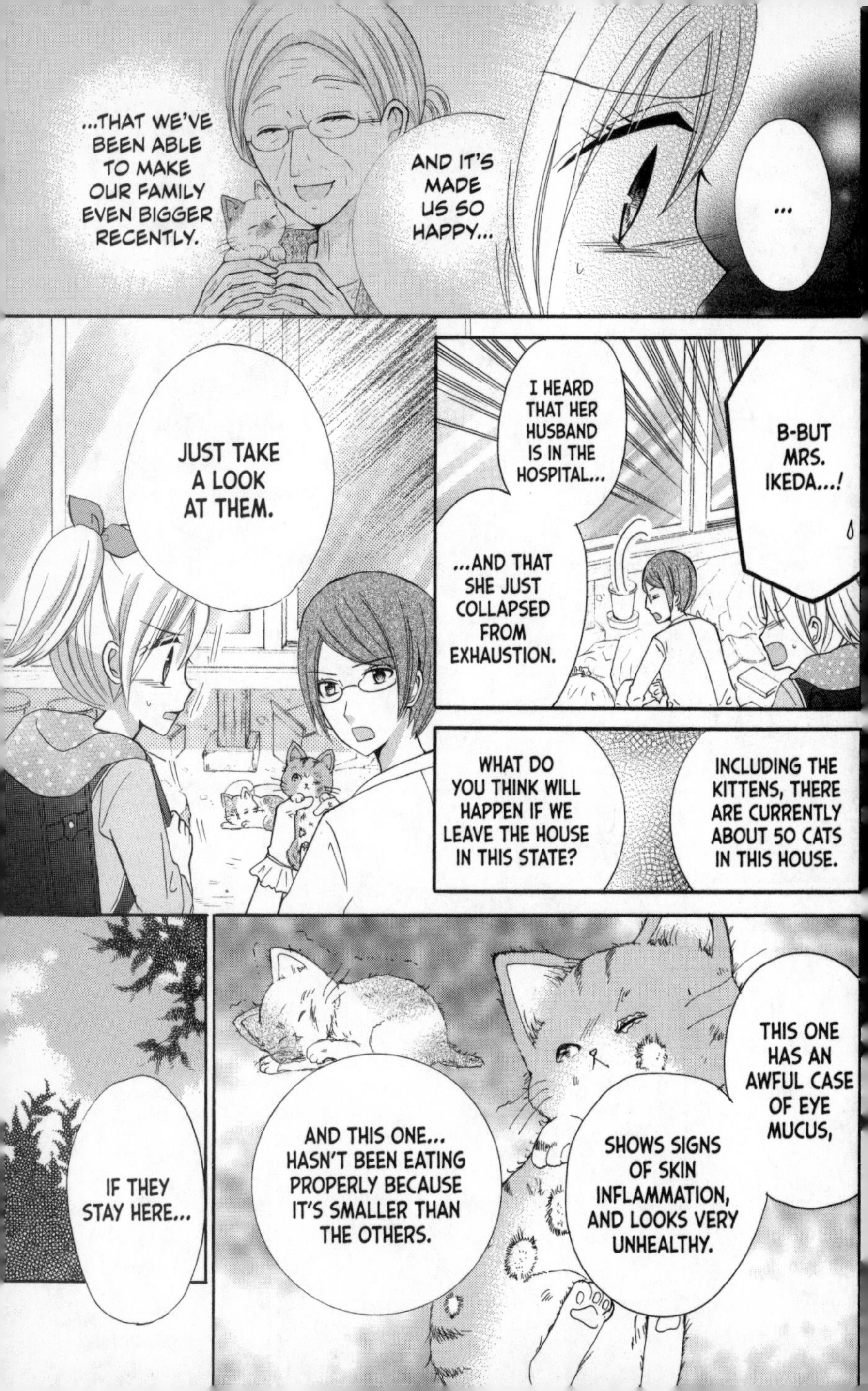
AND IT'S MADE US SO HAPPY...
...THAT WE'VE BEEN ABLE TO MAKE OUR FAMILY EVEN BIGGER RECENTLY.
...
B-BUT MRS. IKEDA...!
I HEARD THAT HER HUSBAND IS IN THE HOSPITAL...
...AND THAT SHE JUST COLLAPSED FROM EXHAUSTION.
INCLUDING THE KITTENS, THERE ARE CURRENTLY ABOUT 50 CATS IN THIS HOUSE.
WHAT DO YOU THINK WILL HAPPEN IF WE LEAVE THE HOUSE IN THIS STATE?
JUST TAKE A LOOK AT THEM.
THIS ONE HAS AN AWFUL CASE OF EYE MUCUS,
SHOWS SIGNS OF SKIN INFLAMMATION, AND LOOKS VERY UNHEALTHY.
AND THIS ONE... HASN'T BEEN EATING PROPERLY BECAUSE IT'S SMALLER THAN THE OTHERS.
IF THEY STAY HERE...

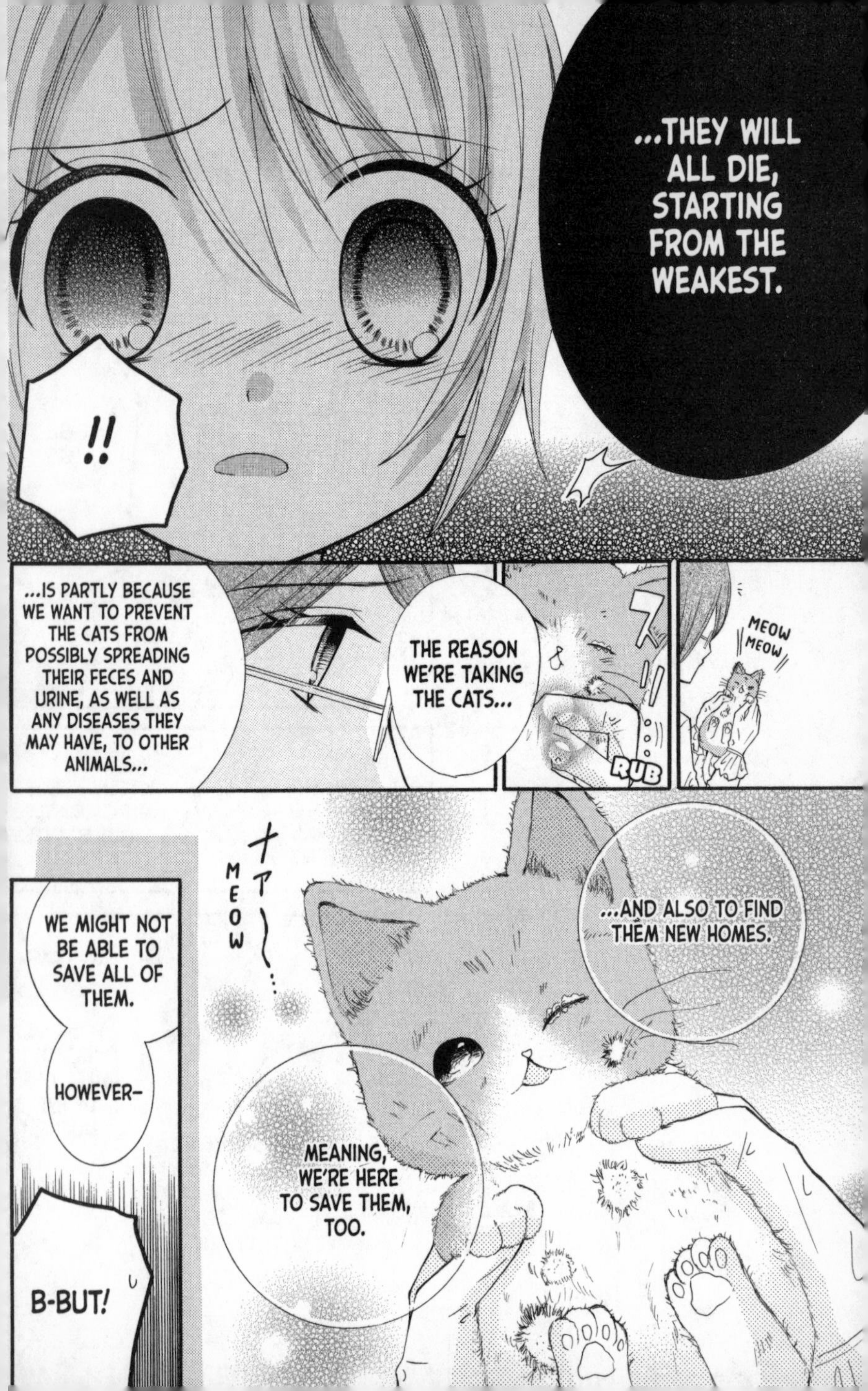
...THEY WILL ALL DIE, STARTING FROM THE WEAKEST.
!!
MEOW MEOW
RUB
THE REASON WE'RE TAKING THE CATS...
...IS PARTLY BECAUSE WE WANT TO PREVENT THE CATS FROM POSSIBLY SPREADING THEIR FECES AND URINE, AS WELL AS ANY DISEASES THEY MAY HAVE, TO OTHER ANIMALS...
...AND ALSO TO FIND THEM NEW HOMES.
MEOW
MEANING, WE'RE HERE TO SAVE THEM, TOO.
WE MIGHT NOT BE ABLE TO SAVE ALL OF THEM.
HOWEVER–
B-BUT!

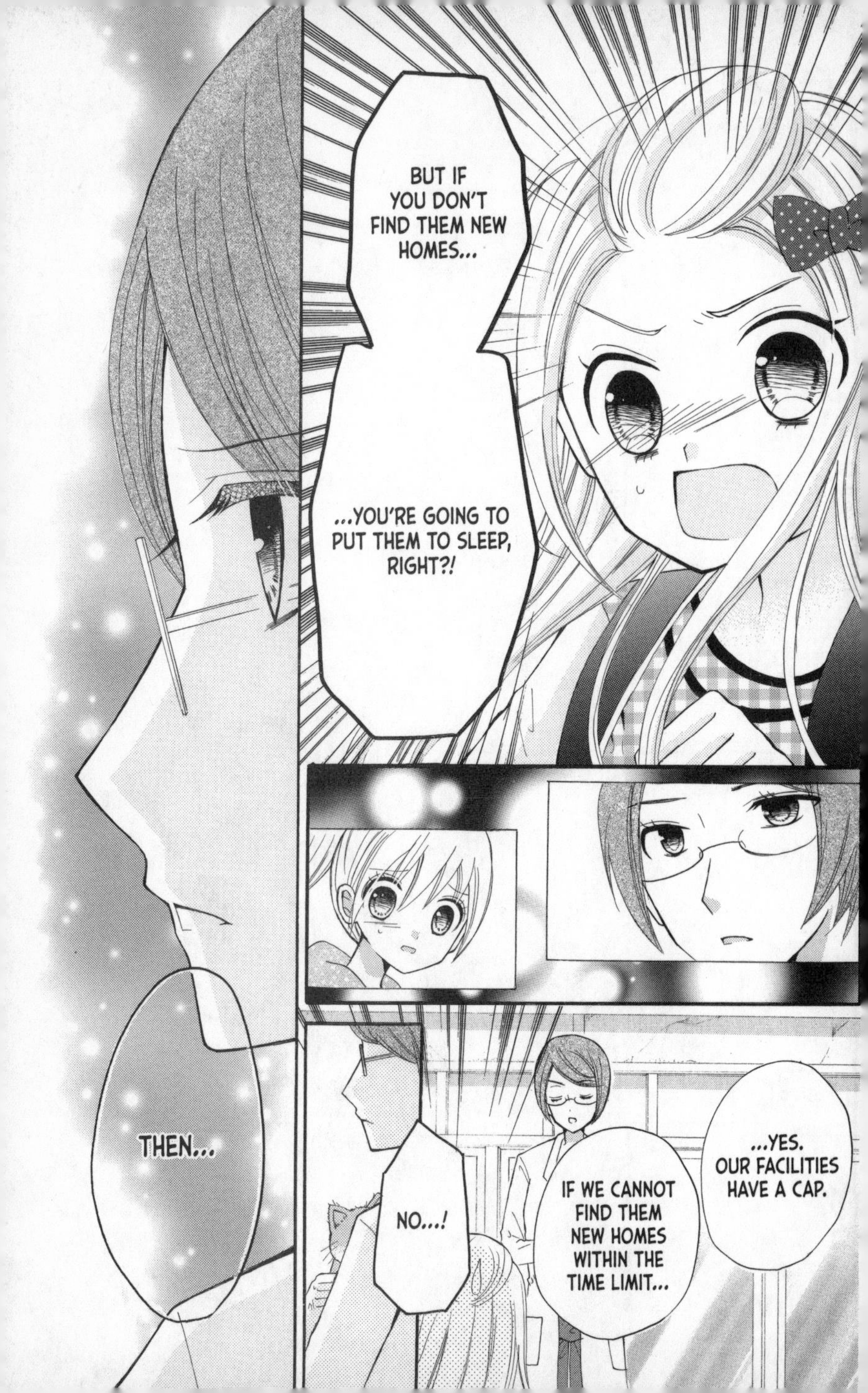
BUT IF YOU DON'T FIND THEM NEW HOMES...
...YOU'RE GOING TO PUT THEM TO SLEEP, RIGHT?!
...YES. OUR FACILITIES HAVE A CAP.
IF WE CANNOT FIND THEM NEW HOMES WITHIN THE TIME LIMIT...
NO...!
THEN...

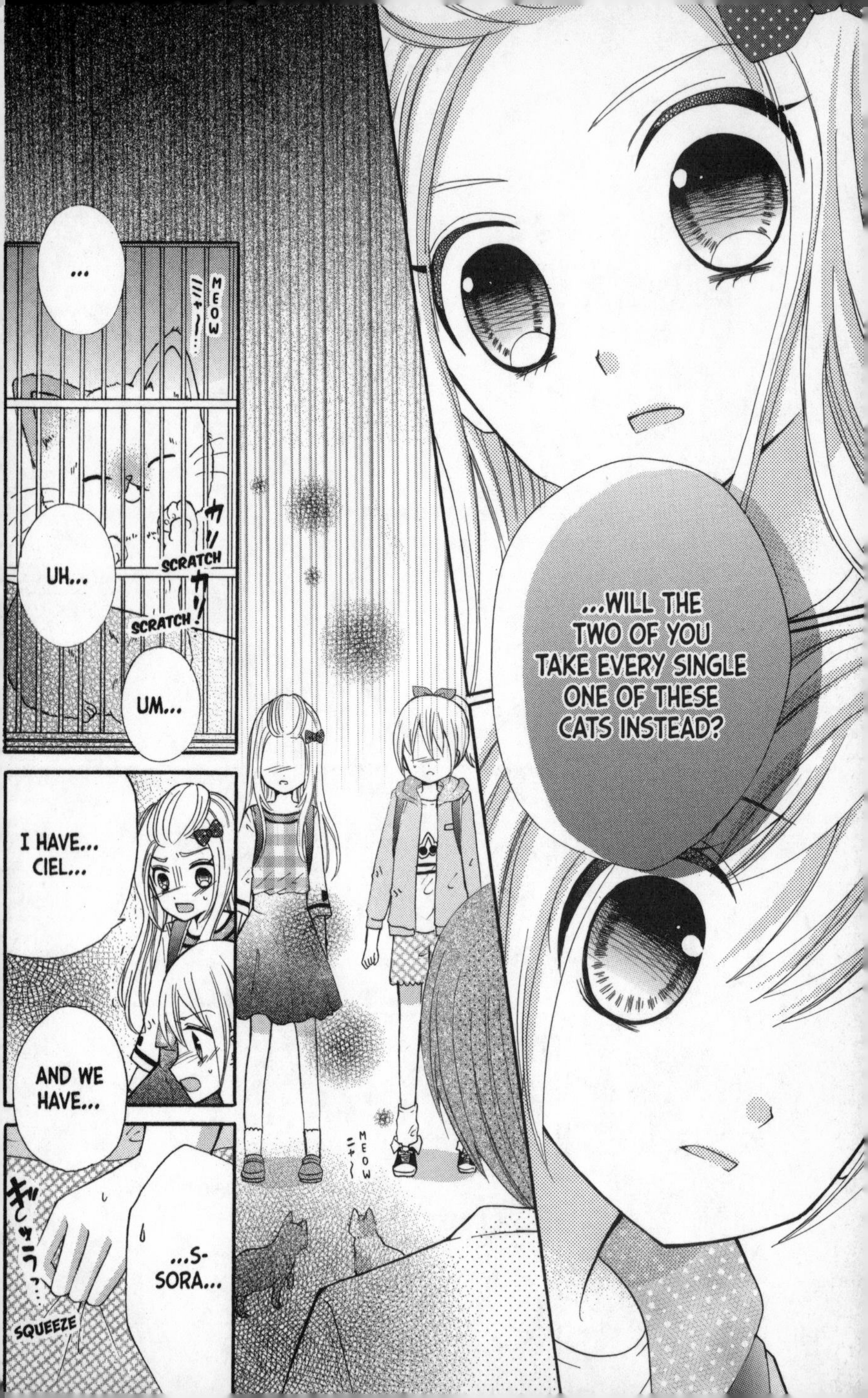
...WILL THE TWO OF YOU TAKE EVERY SINGLE ONE OF THESE CATS INSTEAD?
MEOW
...
MEOW
SCRATCH
SCRATCH
UH...
UM...
I HAVE... CIEL...
AND WE HAVE...
...S-SORA...
SQUEEZE

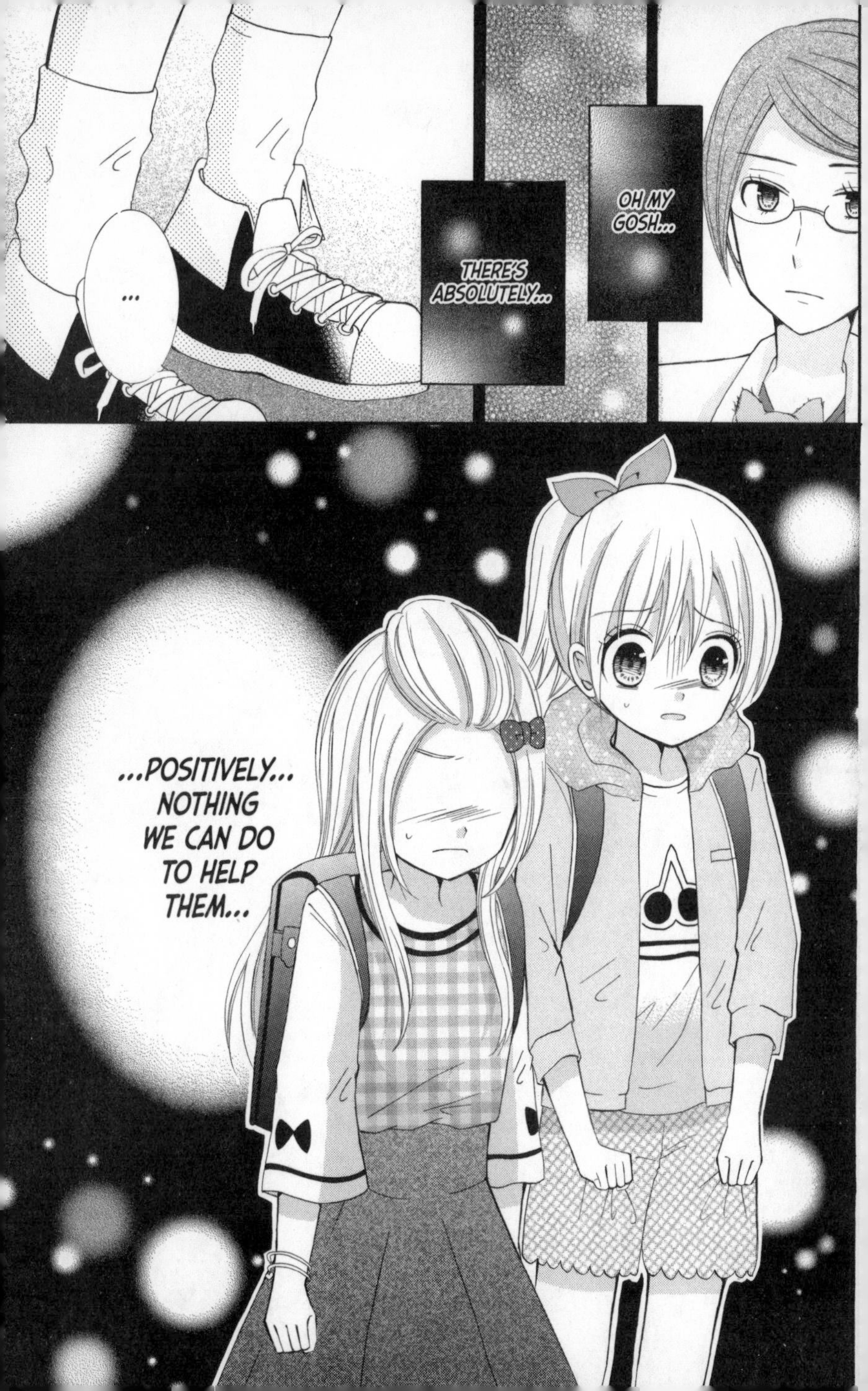
OH MY GOSH...
THERE'S ABSOLUTELY...
...
...POSITIVELY... NOTHING WE CAN DO TO HELP THEM...

YUZU THE PET VET

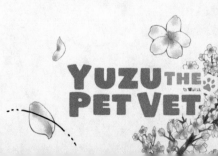

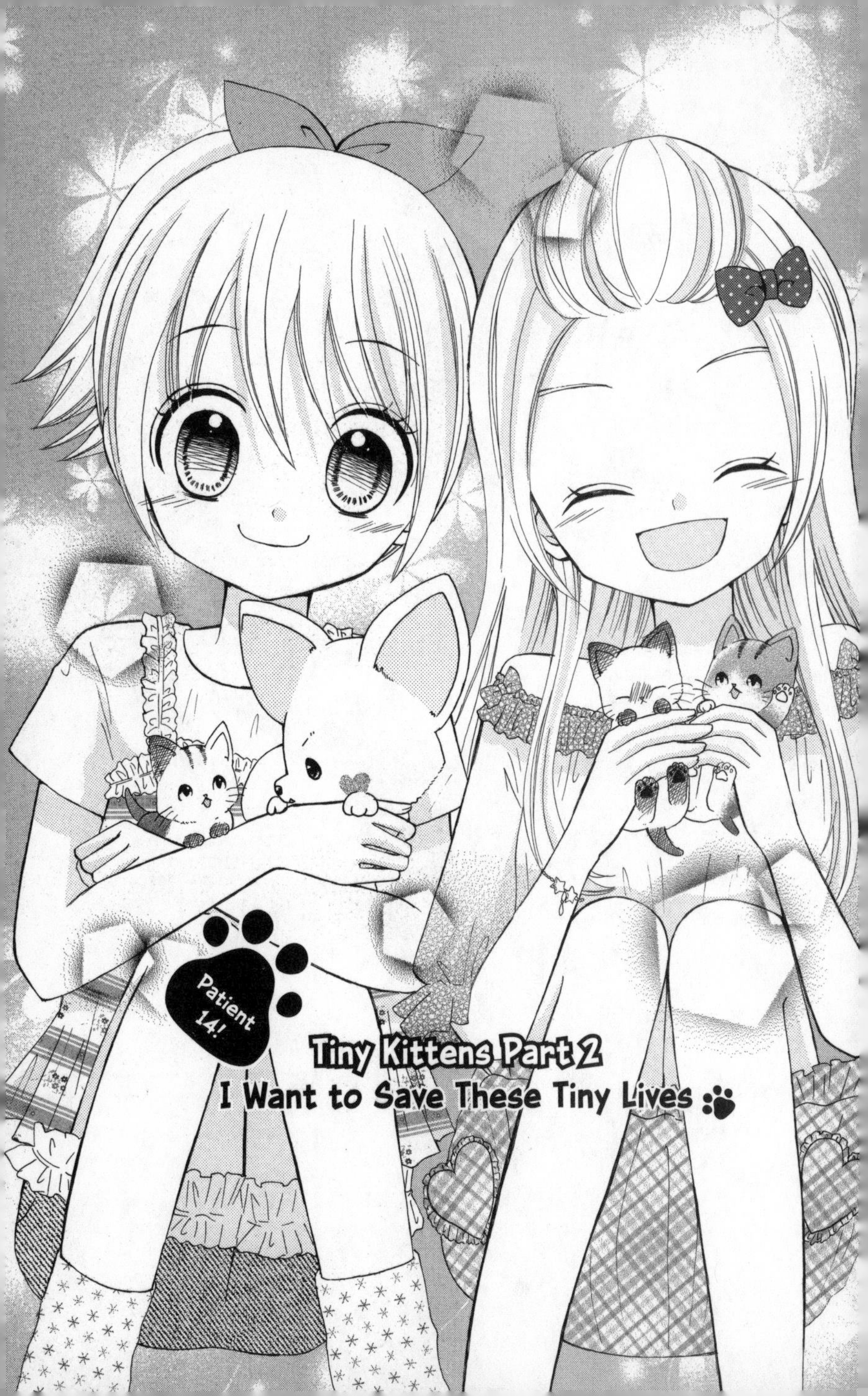
Patient 14!
Tiny Kittens Part 2
I Want to Save These Tiny Lives

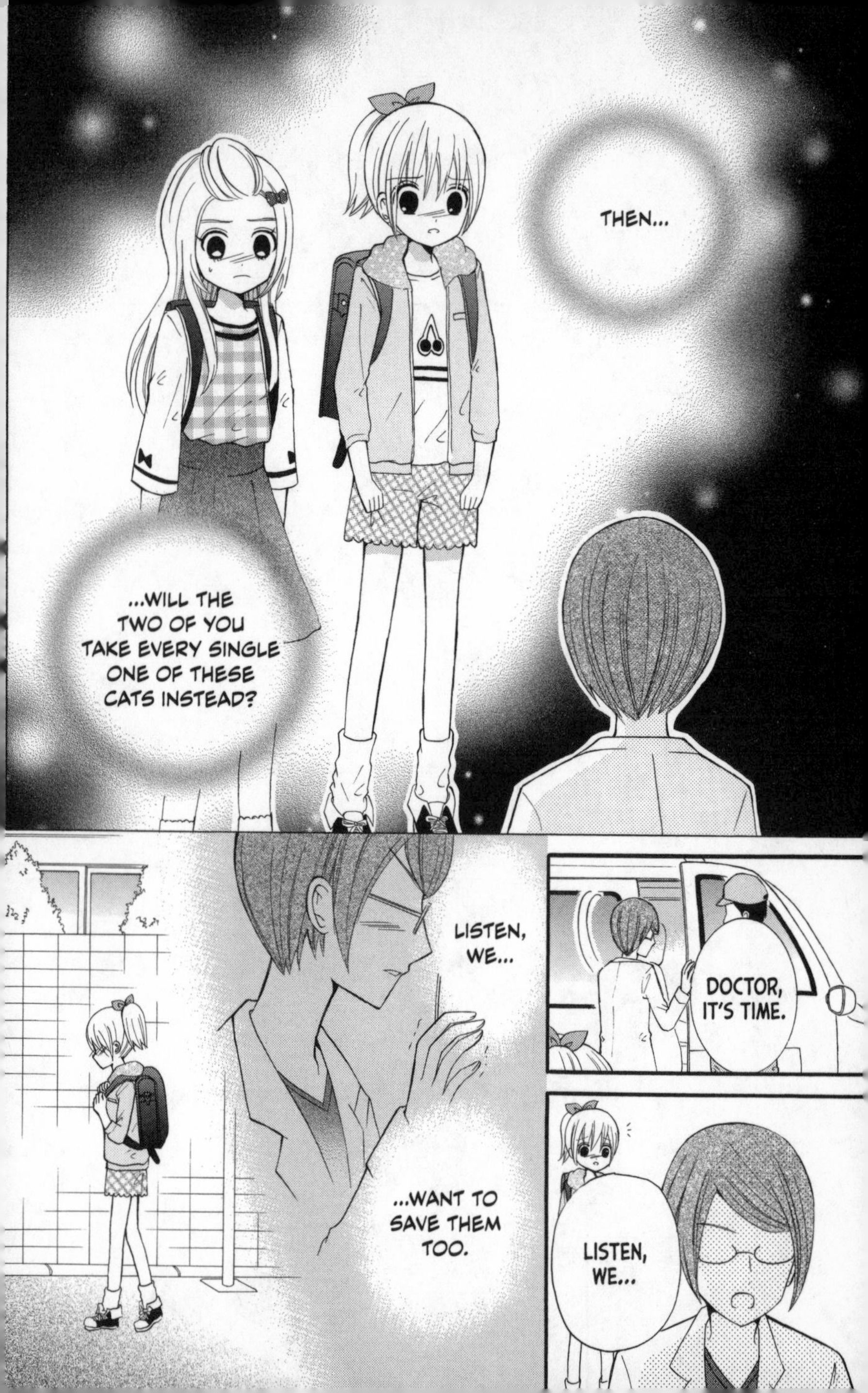
THEN...
...WILL THE TWO OF YOU TAKE EVERY SINGLE ONE OF THESE CATS INSTEAD?
DOCTOR, IT'S TIME.
LISTEN, WE...
LISTEN, WE...
...WANT TO SAVE THEM TOO.

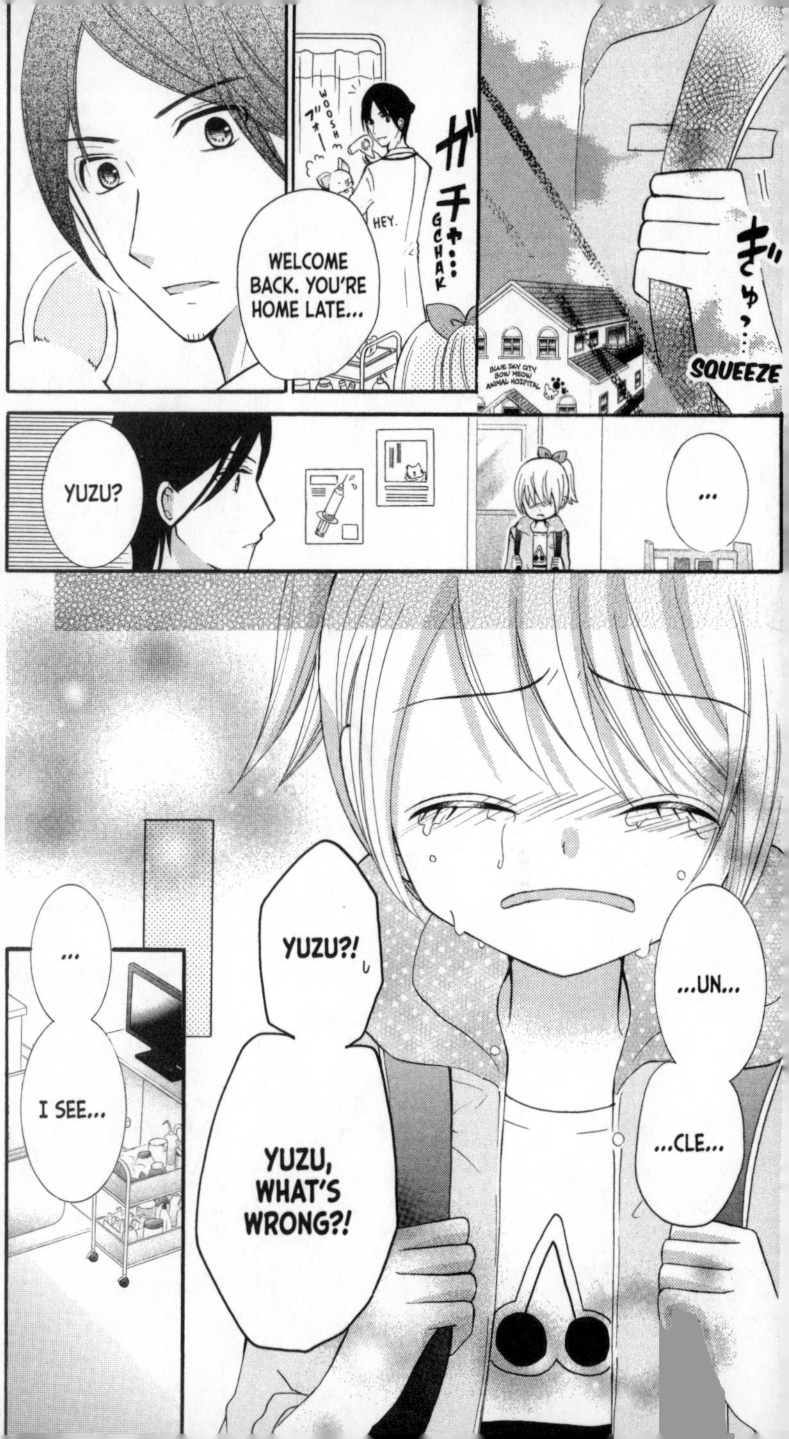
ぎゅっ…
SQUEEZE
BLUE SKY CITY BOW MEOW ANIMAL HOSPITAL
ガチャ…
GCHAK
ブォー
WOOSH
HEY.
WELCOME BACK. YOU'RE HOME LATE...
...
YUZU?
...UN...
...CLE...
YUZU?!
YUZU, WHAT'S WRONG?!
...
I SEE...

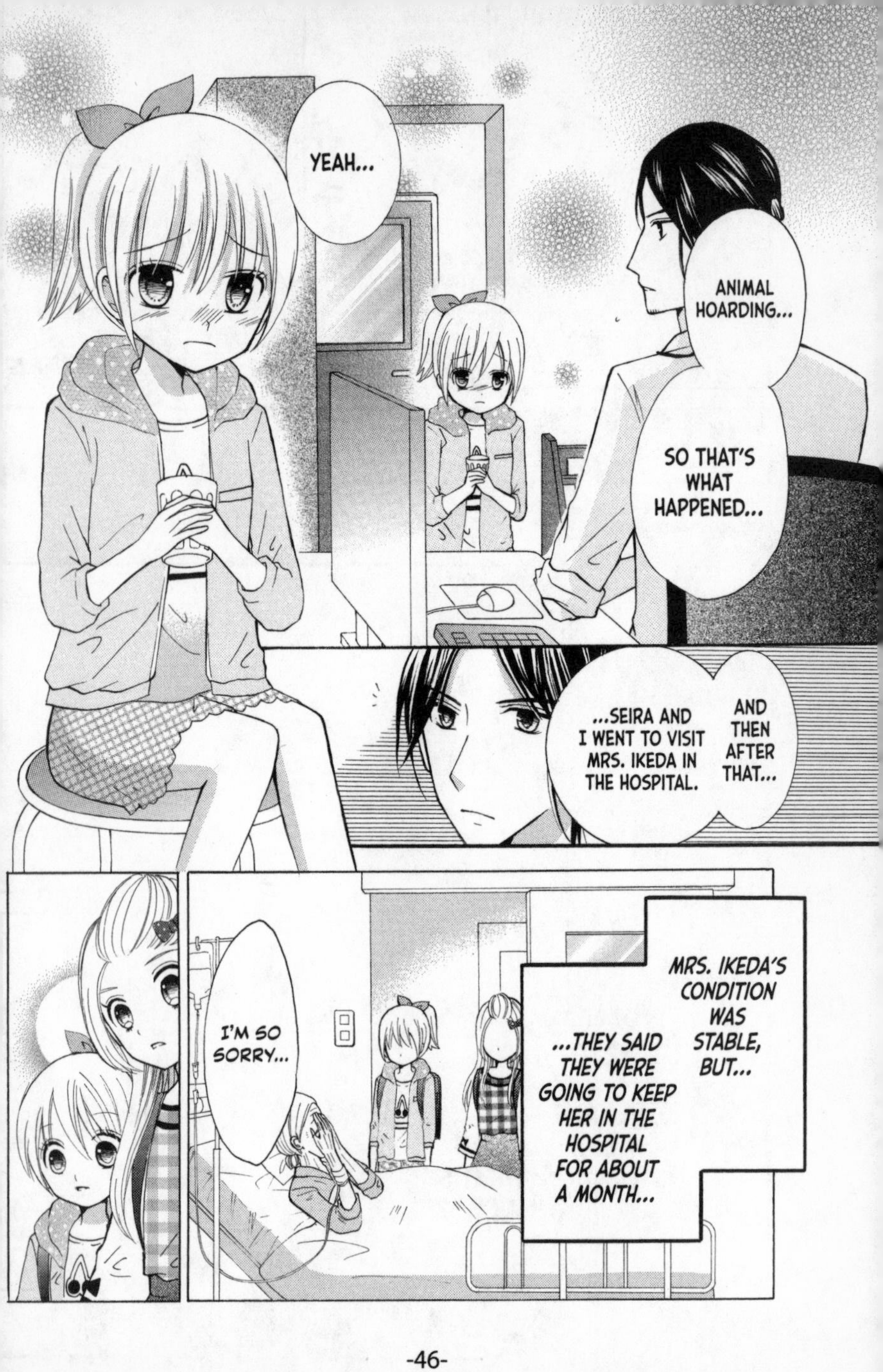
ANIMAL HOARDING...
SO THAT'S WHAT HAPPENED...
YEAH...
AND THEN AFTER THAT...
...SEIRA AND I WENT TO VISIT MRS. IKEDA IN THE HOSPITAL.
MRS. IKEDA'S CONDITION WAS STABLE, BUT...
...THEY SAID THEY WERE GOING TO KEEP HER IN THE HOSPITAL FOR ABOUT A MONTH...
I'M SO SORRY...

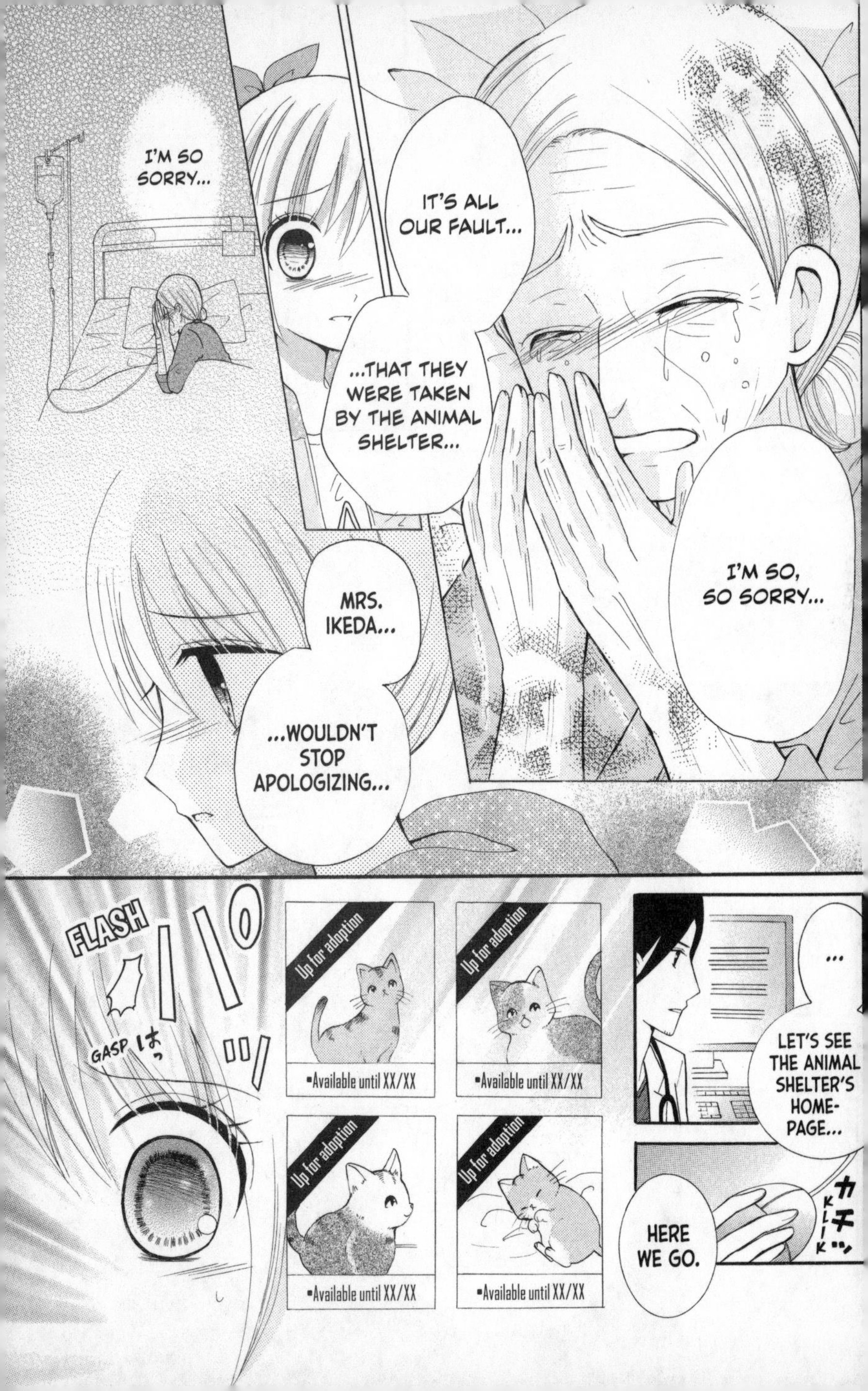
IT'S ALL OUR FAULT...
...THAT THEY WERE TAKEN BY THE ANIMAL SHELTER...
I'M SO, SO SORRY...
I'M SO SORRY...
MRS. IKEDA...
...WOULDN'T STOP APOLOGIZING...
...
LET'S SEE THE ANIMAL SHELTER'S HOME-PAGE...
KLIK
HERE WE GO.
Up for adoption
•Available until XX/XX
Up for adoption
•Available until XX/XX
Up for adoption
•Available until XX/XX
Up for adoption
•Available until XX/XX
FLASH
GASP

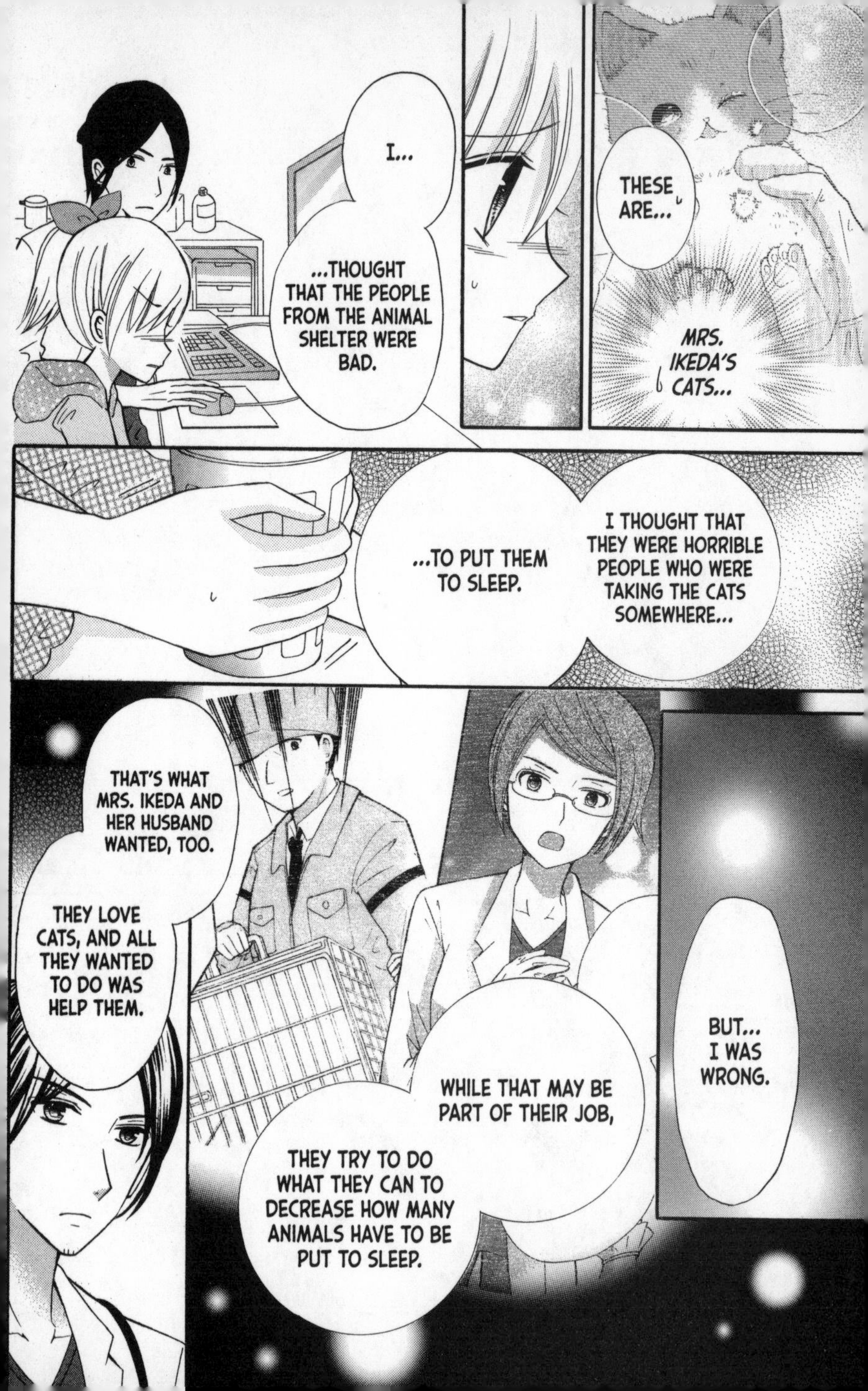
THESE ARE...
MRS. IKEDA'S CATS...
I...
...THOUGHT THAT THE PEOPLE FROM THE ANIMAL SHELTER WERE BAD.
I THOUGHT THAT THEY WERE HORRIBLE PEOPLE WHO WERE TAKING THE CATS SOMEWHERE...
...TO PUT THEM TO SLEEP.
BUT... I WAS WRONG.
WHILE THAT MAY BE PART OF THEIR JOB,
THEY TRY TO DO WHAT THEY CAN TO DECREASE HOW MANY ANIMALS HAVE TO BE PUT TO SLEEP.
THAT'S WHAT MRS. IKEDA AND HER HUSBAND WANTED, TOO.
THEY LOVE CATS, AND ALL THEY WANTED TO DO WAS HELP THEM.

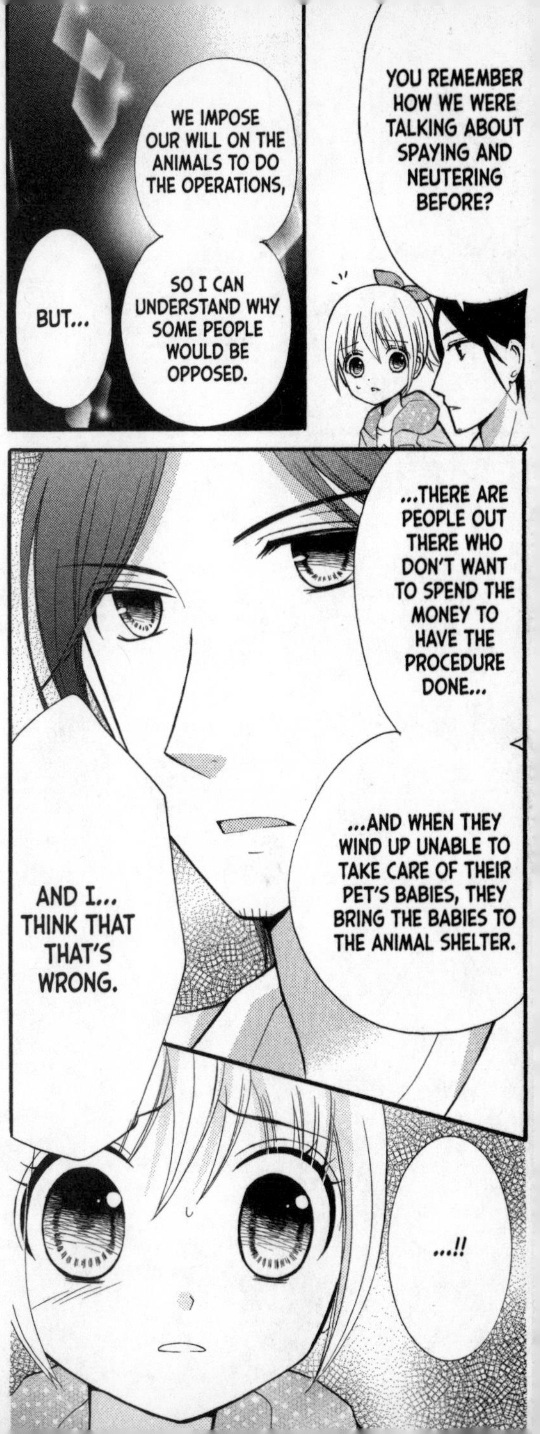
YOU REMEMBER HOW WE WERE TALKING ABOUT SPAYING AND NEUTERING BEFORE?
WE IMPOSE OUR WILL ON THE ANIMALS TO DO THE OPERATIONS,
SO I CAN UNDERSTAND WHY SOME PEOPLE WOULD BE OPPOSED.
BUT...
...THERE ARE PEOPLE OUT THERE WHO DON'T WANT TO SPEND THE MONEY TO HAVE THE PROCEDURE DONE...
...AND WHEN THEY WIND UP UNABLE TO TAKE CARE OF THEIR PET'S BABIES, THEY BRING THE BABIES TO THE ANIMAL SHELTER.
AND I... THINK THAT THAT'S WRONG.
...!!

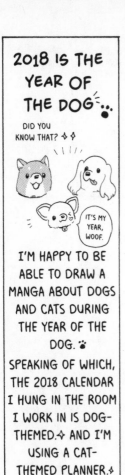

2018 IS THE YEAR OF THE DOG

DID YOU KNOW THAT?

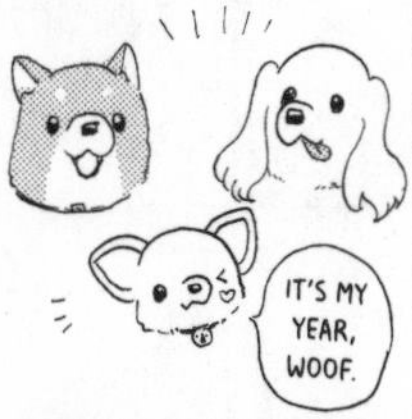
IT'S MY YEAR, WOOF.

I'M HAPPY TO BE ABLE TO DRAW A MANGA ABOUT DOGS AND CATS DURING THE YEAR OF THE DOG.

SPEAKING OF WHICH, THE 2018 CALENDAR I HUNG IN THE ROOM I WORK IN IS DOG-THEMED. AND I'M USING A CAT-THEMED PLANNER.

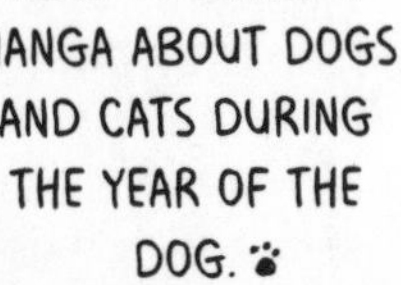

I HOPE THAT I'LL BE ABLE TO DRAW LOTS OF DOGS AND CATS THIS YEAR AS WELL.

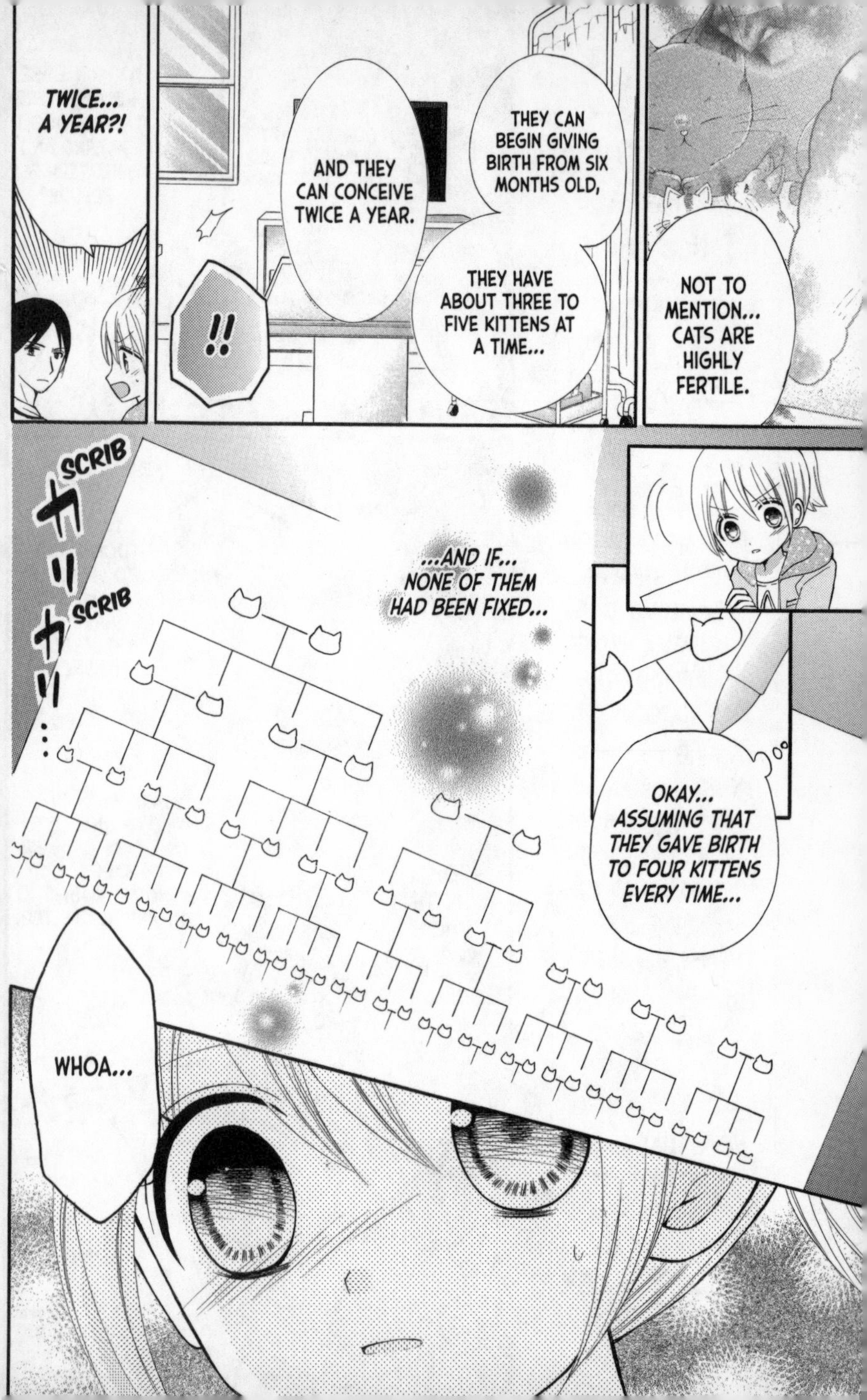

NOT TO MENTION... CATS ARE HIGHLY FERTILE.
THEY CAN BEGIN GIVING BIRTH FROM SIX MONTHS OLD,
THEY HAVE ABOUT THREE TO FIVE KITTENS AT A TIME...
AND THEY CAN CONCEIVE TWICE A YEAR.
!!
TWICE... A YEAR?!
OKAY... ASSUMING THAT THEY GAVE BIRTH TO FOUR KITTENS EVERY TIME...
...AND IF... NONE OF THEM HAD BEEN FIXED...
SCRIB
SCRIB
カリカリ…
WHOA...

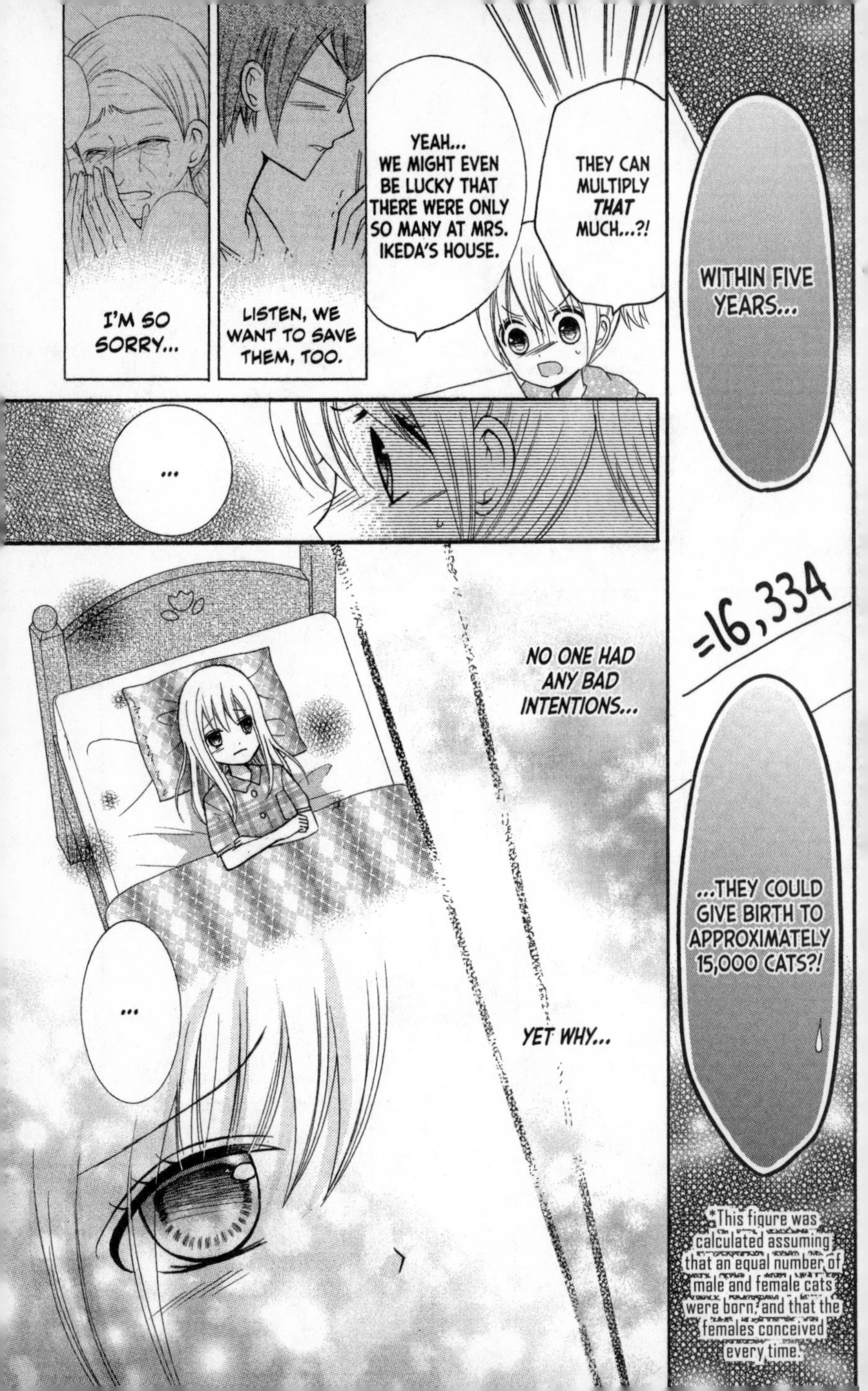
WITHIN FIVE YEARS...
=16,334
...THEY COULD GIVE BIRTH TO APPROXIMATELY 15,000 CATS?!
*This figure was calculated assuming that an equal number of male and female cats were born, and that the females conceived every time.
THEY CAN MULTIPLY *THAT* MUCH...?!
YEAH... WE MIGHT EVEN BE LUCKY THAT THERE WERE ONLY SO MANY AT MRS. IKEDA'S HOUSE.
LISTEN, WE WANT TO SAVE THEM, TOO.
I'M SO SORRY...
...
NO ONE HAD ANY BAD INTENTIONS...
YET WHY...
...

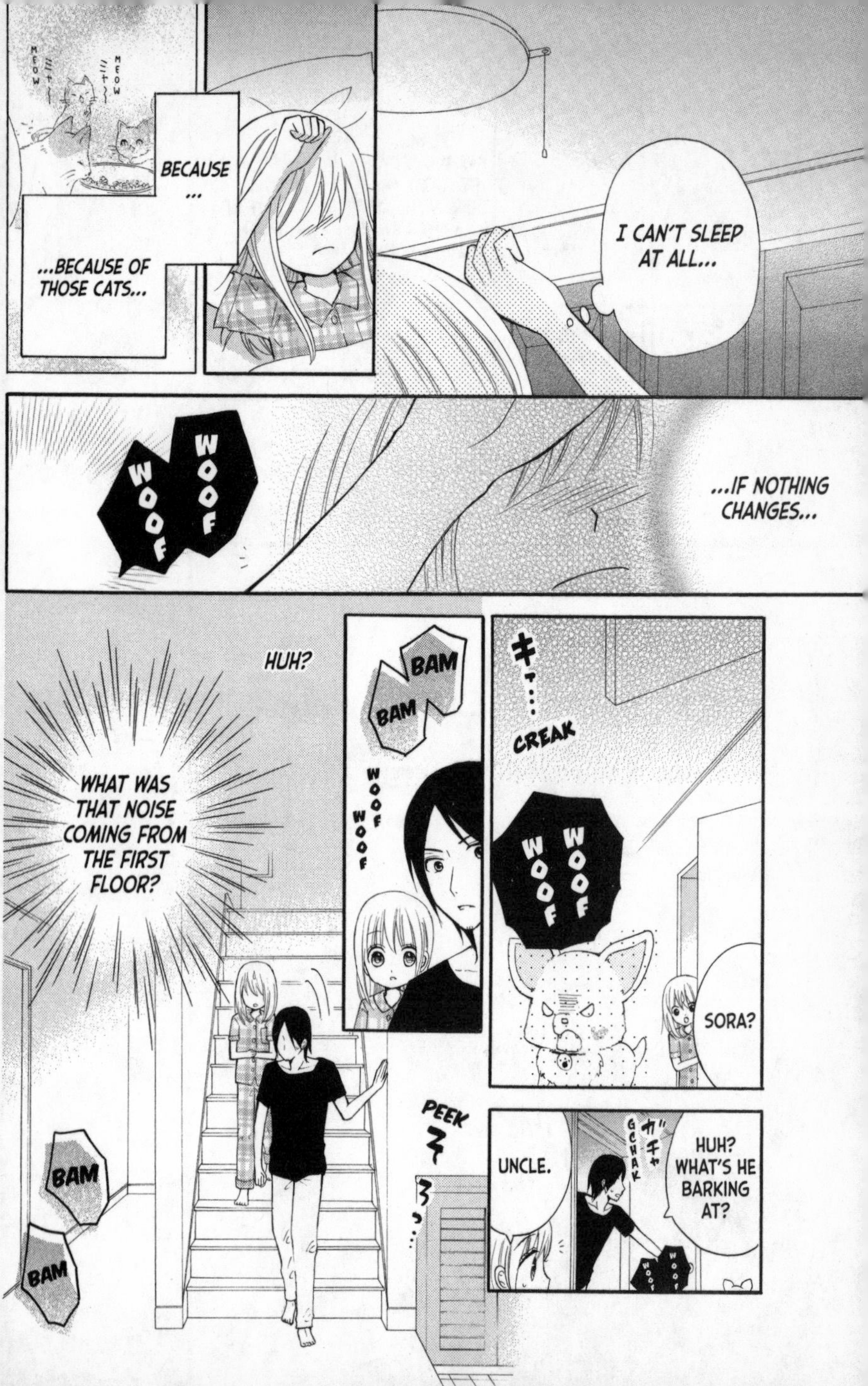
I CAN'T SLEEP AT ALL...
BECAUSE ...
...BECAUSE OF THOSE CATS...
MEOW
MEOW
...IF NOTHING CHANGES...
WOOF WOOF
CREAK
WOOF WOOF
SORA?
HUH? WHAT'S HE BARKING AT?
GCHAK
UNCLE.
BAM BAM
WOOF WOOF
HUH?
WHAT WAS THAT NOISE COMING FROM THE FIRST FLOOR?
PEEK
BAM
BAM

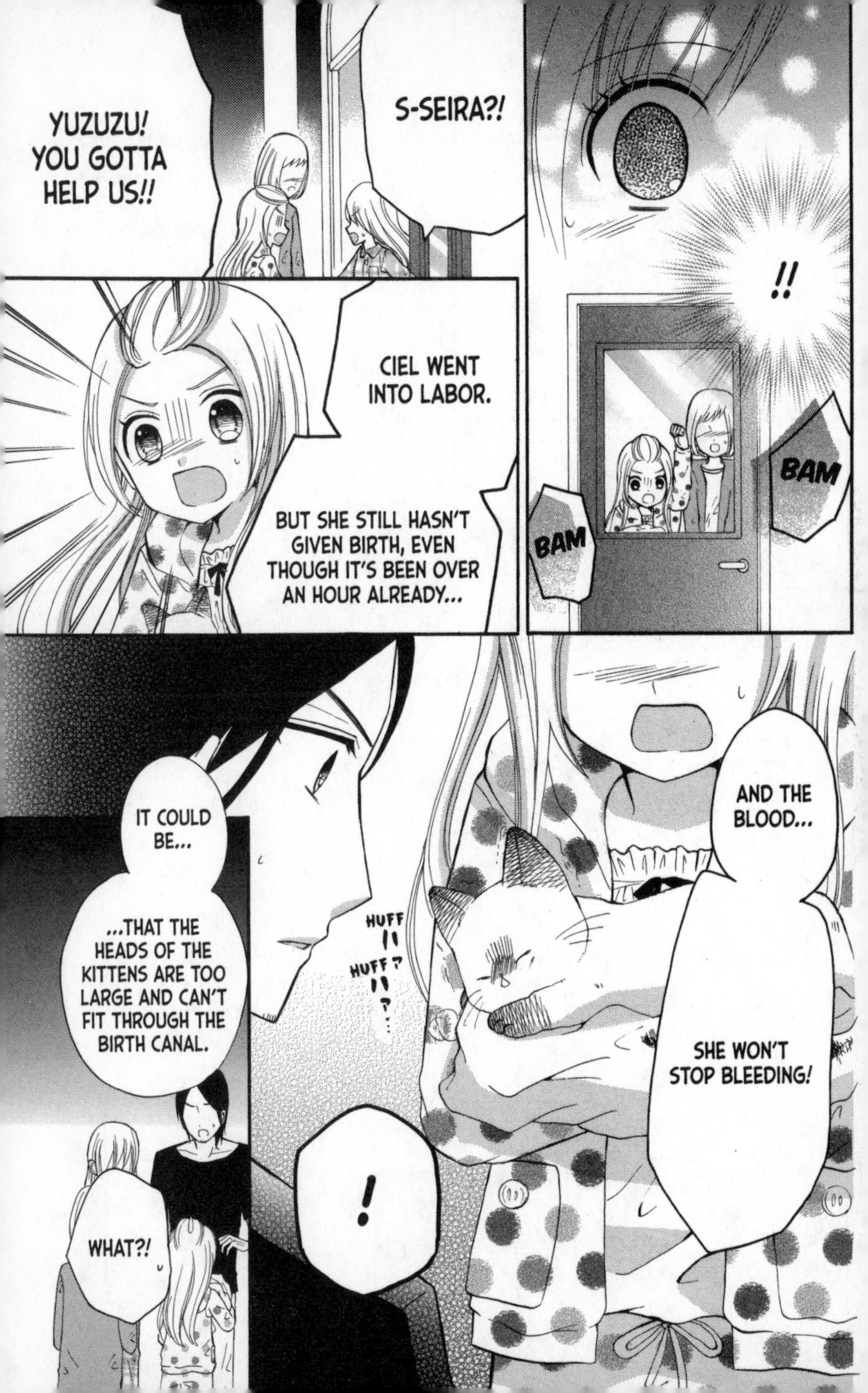
!!
BAM
BAM
S-SEIRA?!
YUZUZU! YOU GOTTA HELP US!!
CIEL WENT INTO LABOR.
BUT SHE STILL HASN'T GIVEN BIRTH, EVEN THOUGH IT'S BEEN OVER AN HOUR ALREADY...
AND THE BLOOD...
SHE WON'T STOP BLEEDING!
HUFF
HUFF
!
IT COULD BE...
...THAT THE HEADS OF THE KITTENS ARE TOO LARGE AND CAN'T FIT THROUGH THE BIRTH CANAL.
WHAT?!

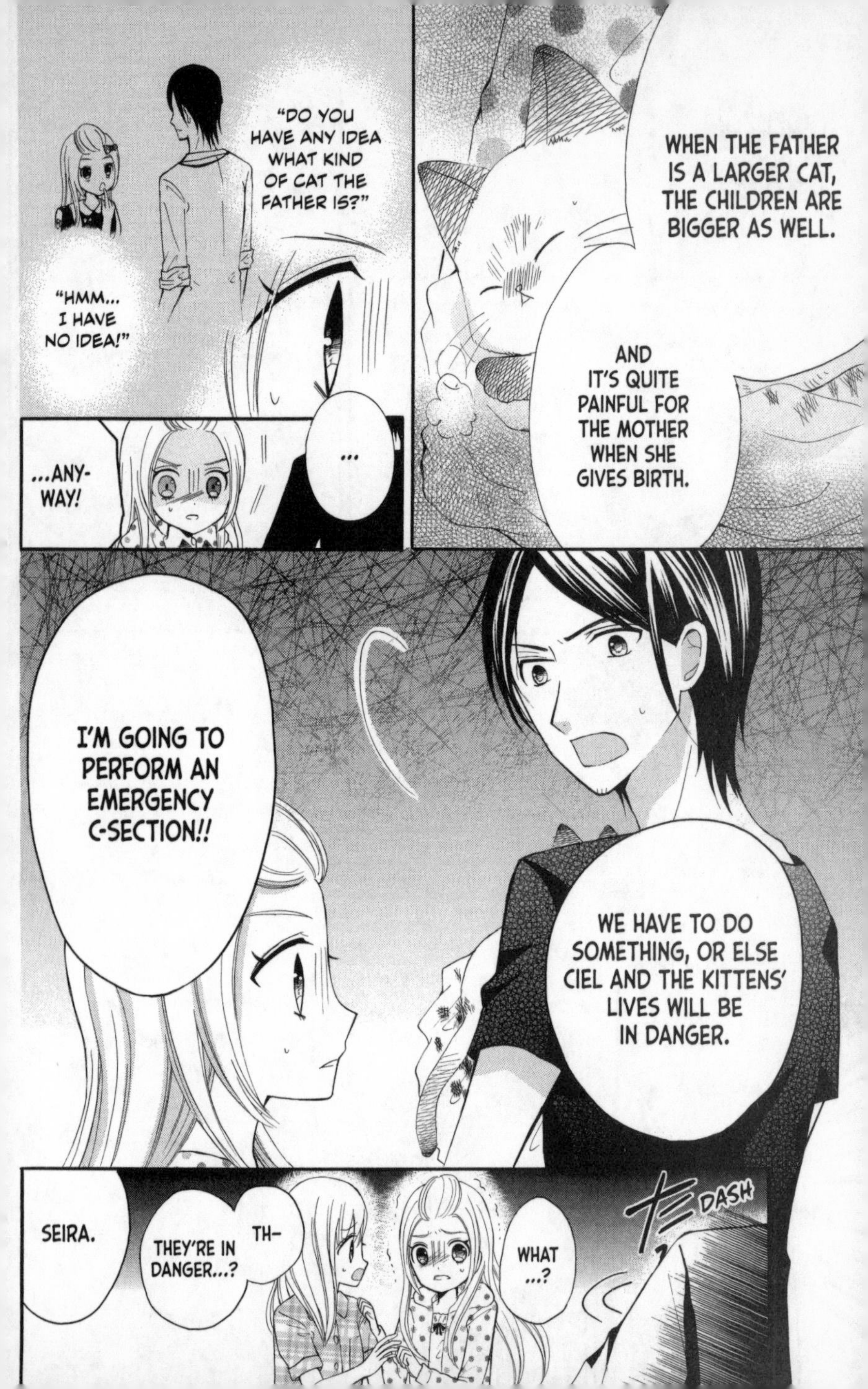
WHEN THE FATHER IS A LARGER CAT, THE CHILDREN ARE BIGGER AS WELL.
AND IT'S QUITE PAINFUL FOR THE MOTHER WHEN SHE GIVES BIRTH.
"DO YOU HAVE ANY IDEA WHAT KIND OF CAT THE FATHER IS?"
"HMM... I HAVE NO IDEA!"
...
...ANY-WAY!
WE HAVE TO DO SOMETHING, OR ELSE CIEL AND THE KITTENS' LIVES WILL BE IN DANGER.
I'M GOING TO PERFORM AN EMERGENCY C-SECTION!!
DASH
WHAT ...?
TH-
THEY'RE IN DANGER...?
SEIRA.

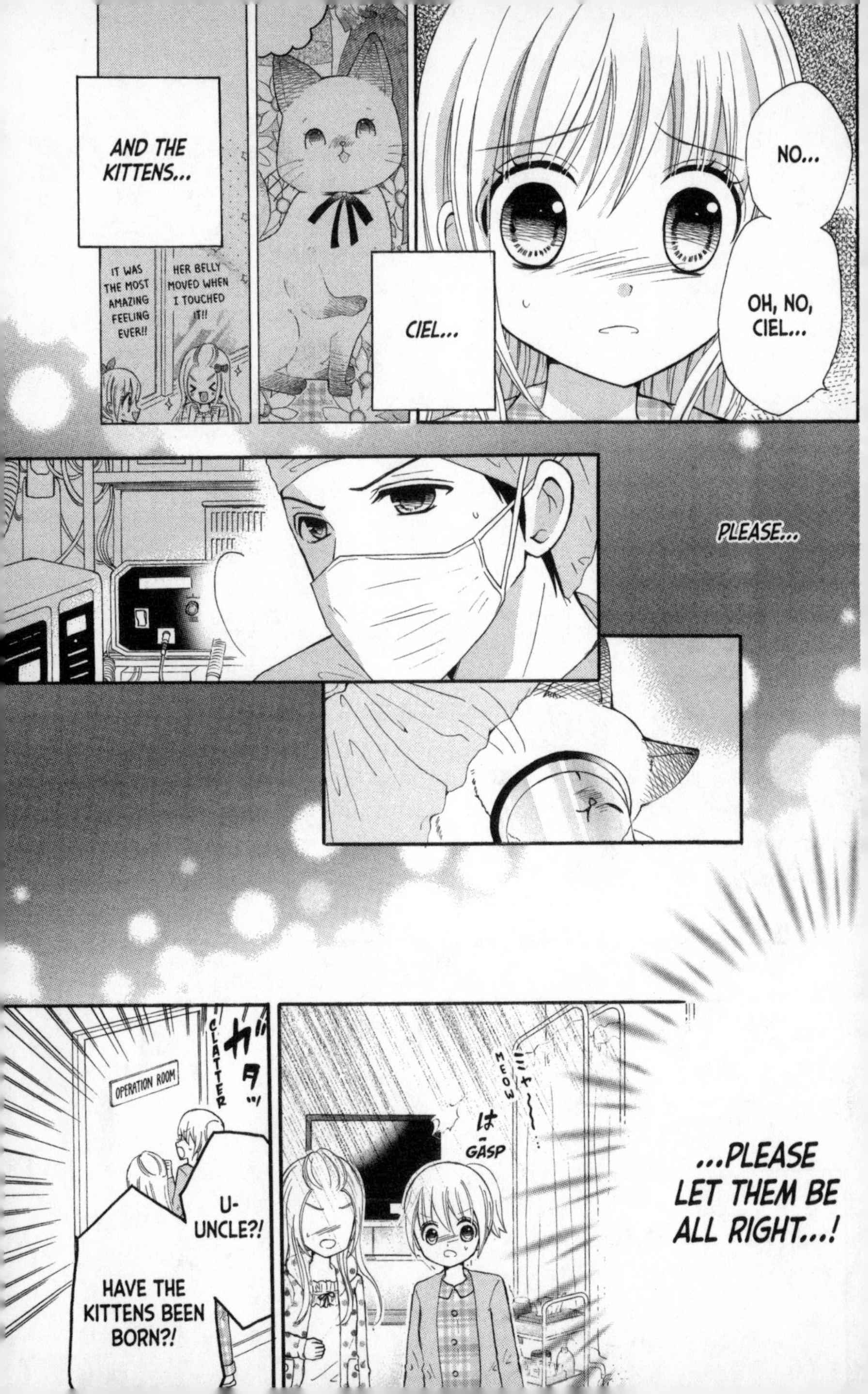
NO...
OH, NO, CIEL...
CIEL...
AND THE KITTENS...
HER BELLY MOVED WHEN I TOUCHED IT!!
IT WAS THE MOST AMAZING FEELING EVER!!
PLEASE...
...PLEASE LET THEM BE ALL RIGHT...!
ニャ〜
MEOW
は
GASP
カタッ
CLATTER
OPERATION ROOM
U-UNCLE?!
HAVE THE KITTENS BEEN BORN?!

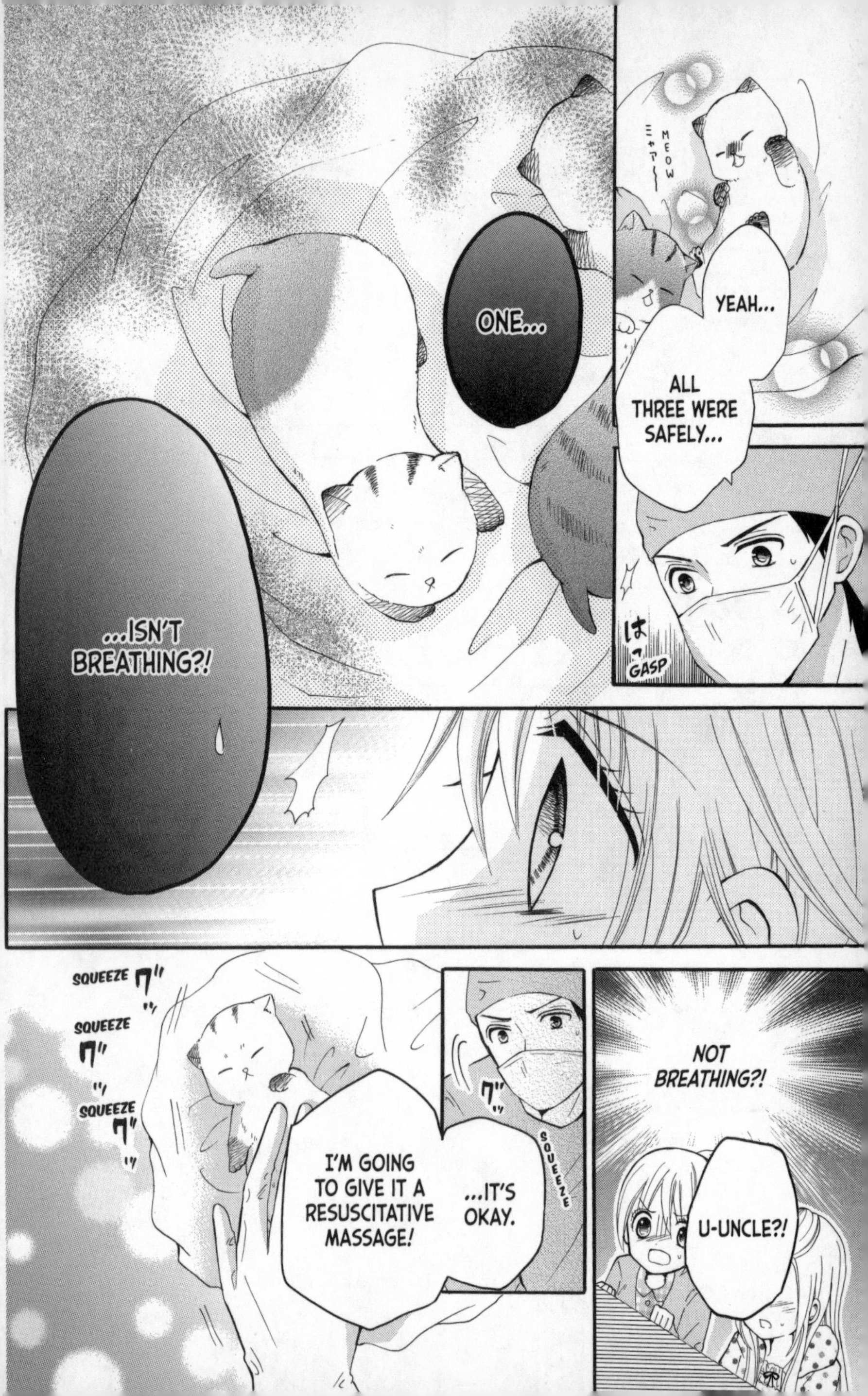
MEOW
ミャア～
YEAH...
ALL THREE WERE SAFELY...
はっ
GASP
ONE...
...ISN'T BREATHING?!
NOT BREATHING?!
U-UNCLE?!
...IT'S OKAY.
SQUEEZE
I'M GOING TO GIVE IT A RESUSCITATIVE MASSAGE!
SQUEEZE
SQUEEZE
SQUEEZE

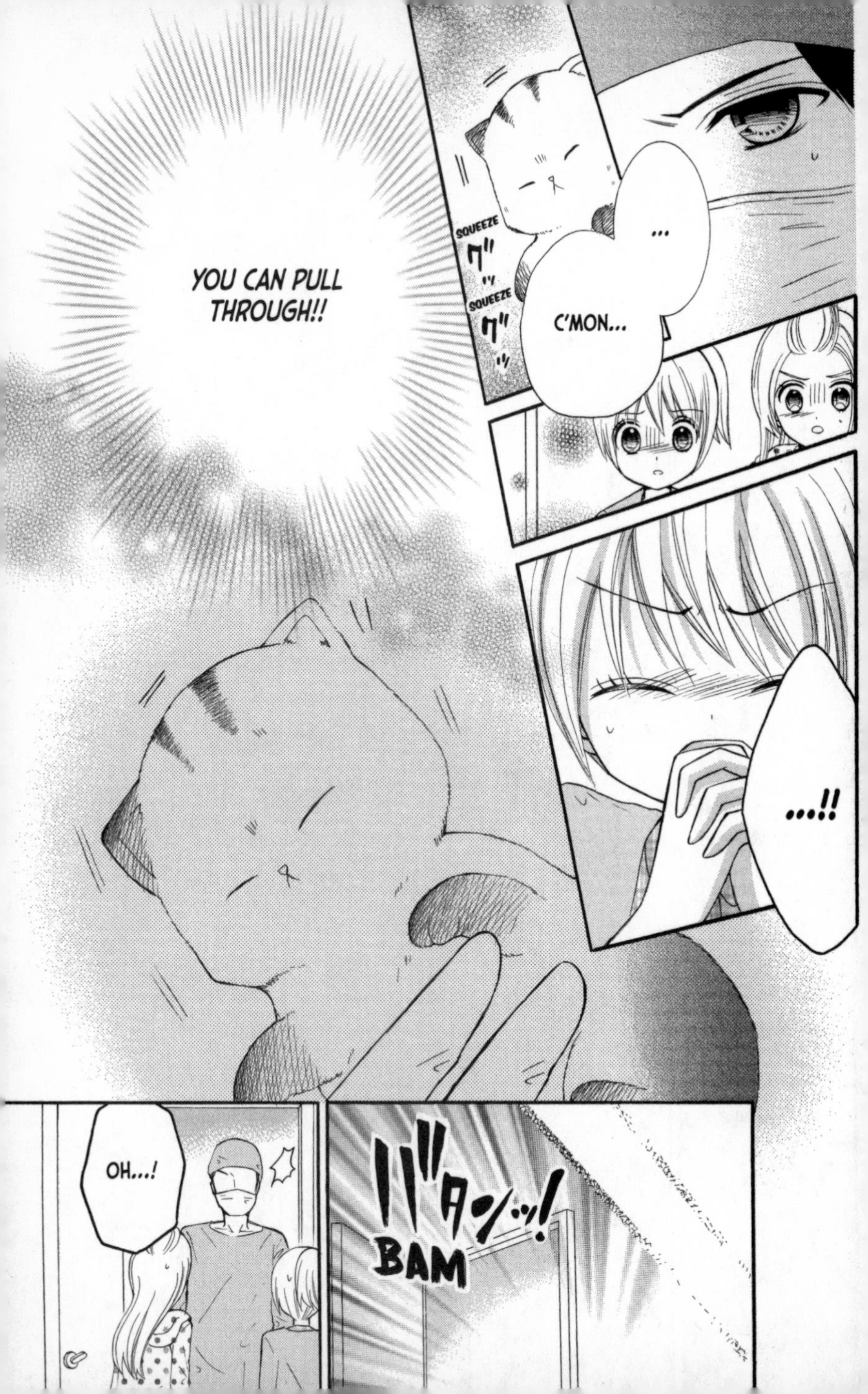

...
C'MON...
SQUEEZE
SQUEEZE
...!!
YOU CAN PULL THROUGH!!
BAM
OH...!

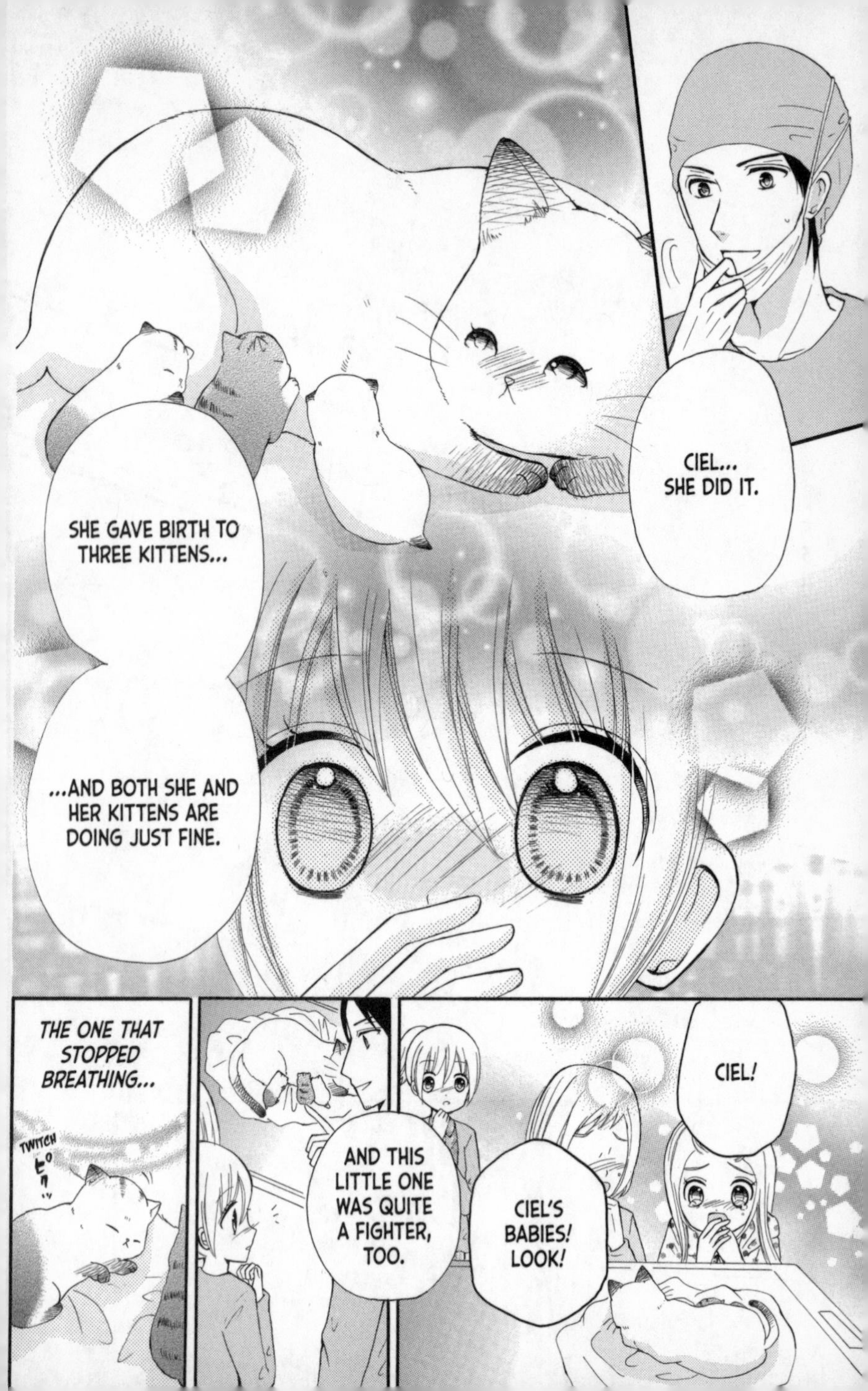
CIEL... SHE DID IT.
SHE GAVE BIRTH TO THREE KITTENS...
...AND BOTH SHE AND HER KITTENS ARE DOING JUST FINE.
CIEL!
CIEL'S BABIES! LOOK!
AND THIS LITTLE ONE WAS QUITE A FIGHTER, TOO.
THE ONE THAT STOPPED BREATHING...
TWITCH

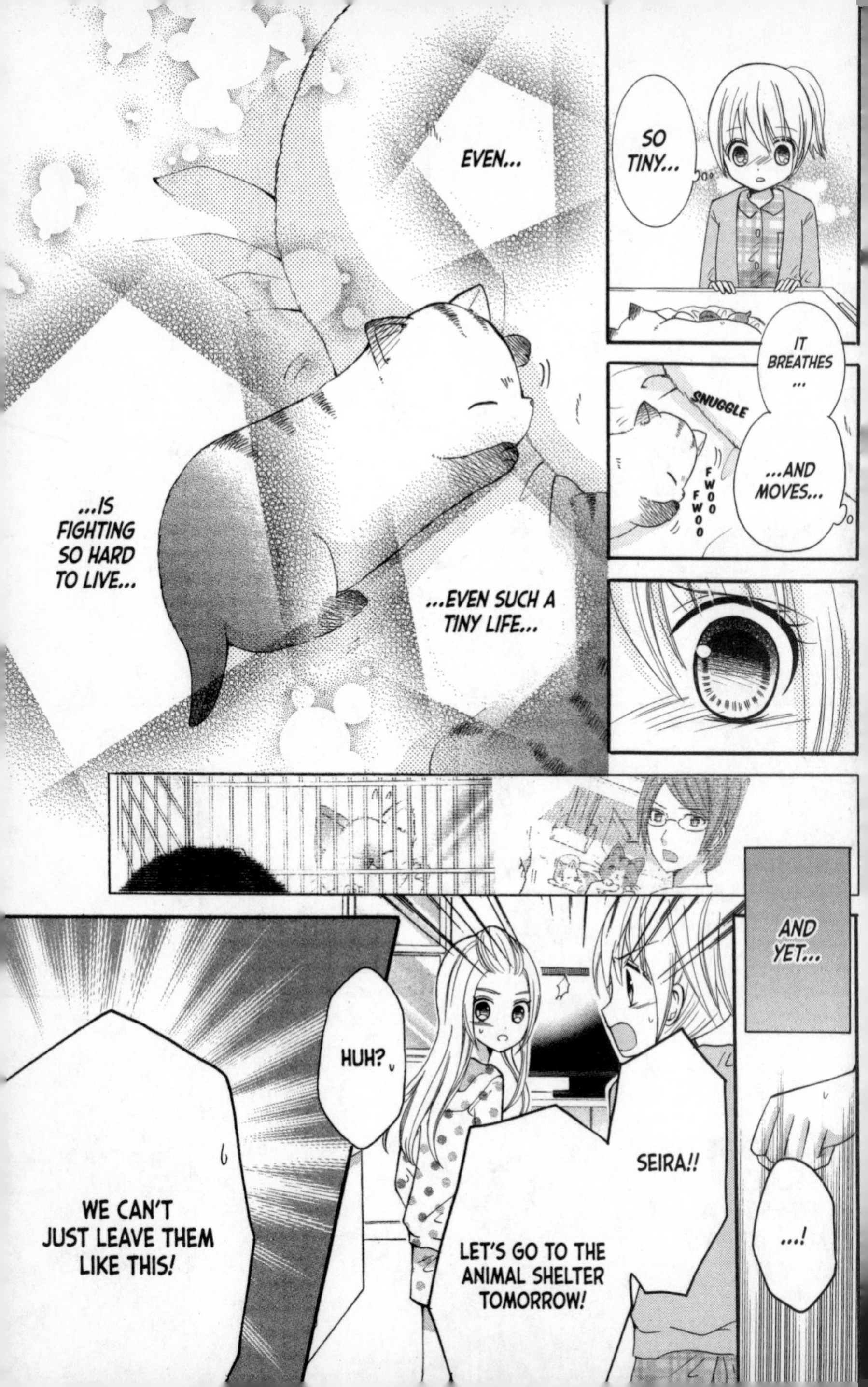
SO TINY...
IT BREATHES ...
SNUGGLE
FWOO FWOO
...AND MOVES...
EVEN...
...EVEN SUCH A TINY LIFE...
...IS FIGHTING SO HARD TO LIVE...
AND YET...
...!
SEIRA!!
LET'S GO TO THE ANIMAL SHELTER TOMORROW!
HUH?
WE CAN'T JUST LEAVE THEM LIKE THIS!

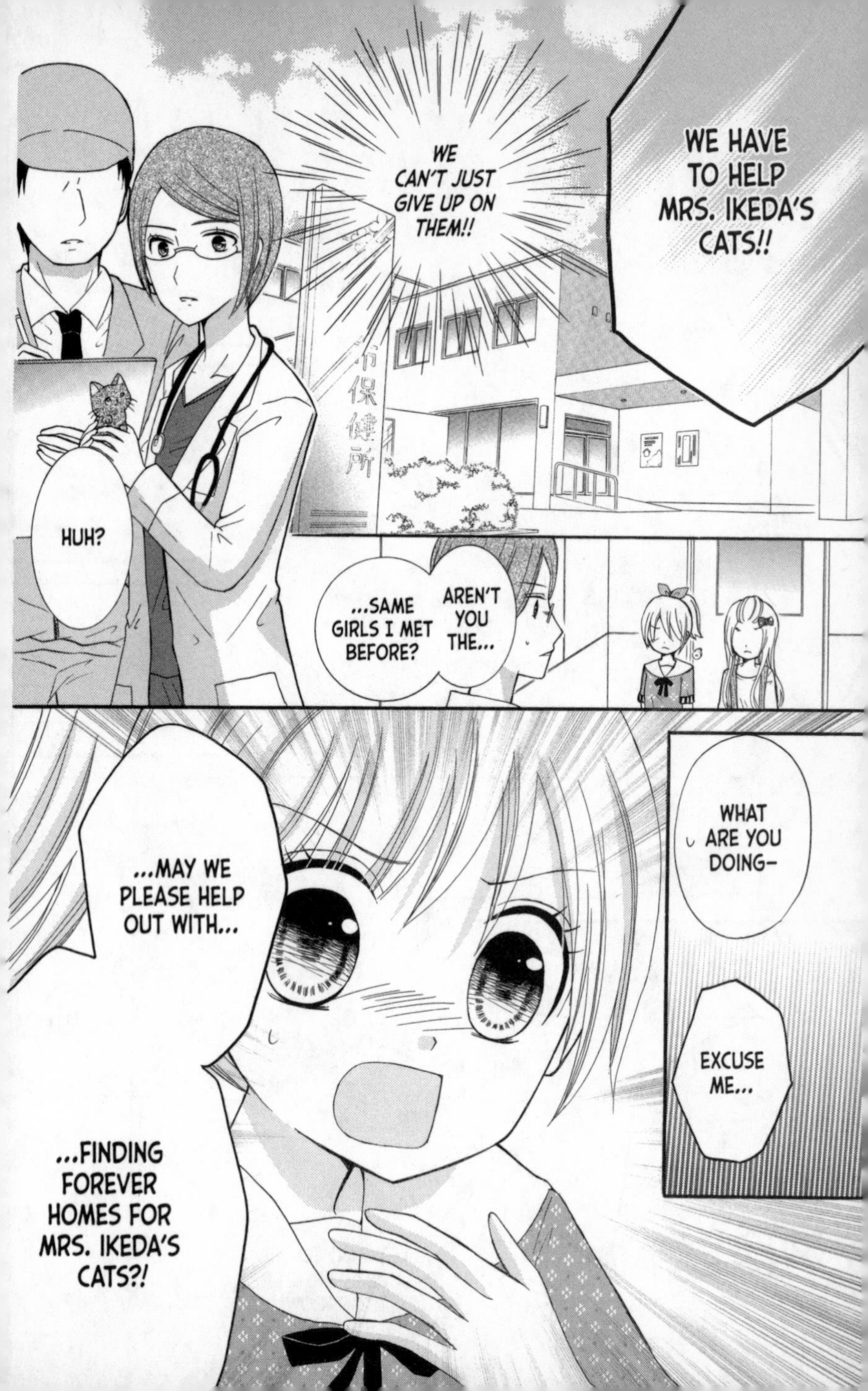
WE HAVE TO HELP MRS. IKEDA'S CATS!!
WE CAN'T JUST GIVE UP ON THEM!!
AREN'T YOU THE...
...SAME GIRLS I MET BEFORE?
HUH?
WHAT ARE YOU DOING–
EXCUSE ME...
...MAY WE PLEASE HELP OUT WITH...
...FINDING FOREVER HOMES FOR MRS. IKEDA'S CATS?!

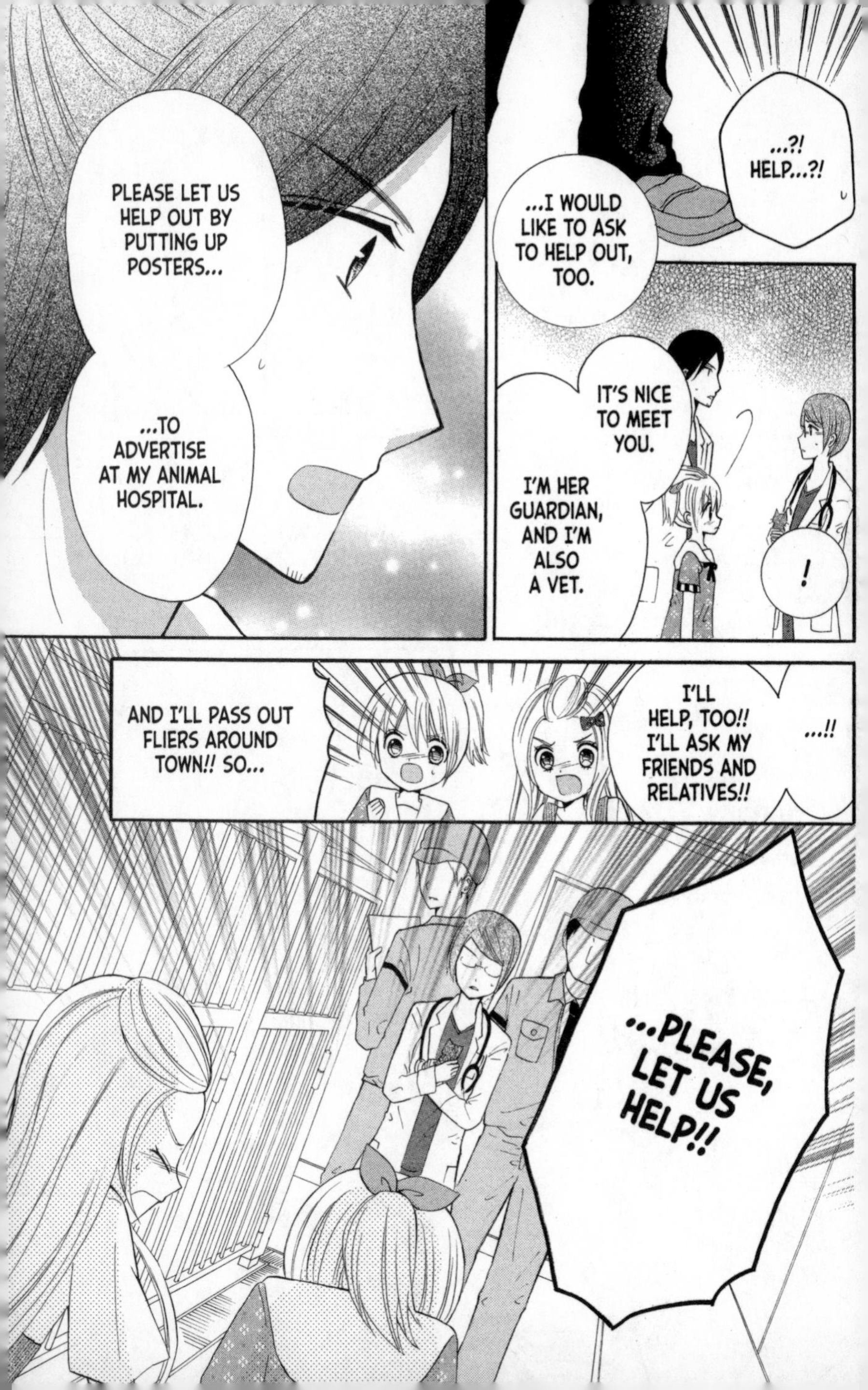
...?! HELP...?!
...I WOULD LIKE TO ASK TO HELP OUT, TOO.
IT'S NICE TO MEET YOU.
I'M HER GUARDIAN, AND I'M ALSO A VET.
!
PLEASE LET US HELP OUT BY PUTTING UP POSTERS...
...TO ADVERTISE AT MY ANIMAL HOSPITAL.
...!!
I'LL HELP, TOO!! I'LL ASK MY FRIENDS AND RELATIVES!!
AND I'LL PASS OUT FLIERS AROUND TOWN!! SO...
...PLEASE, LET US HELP!!

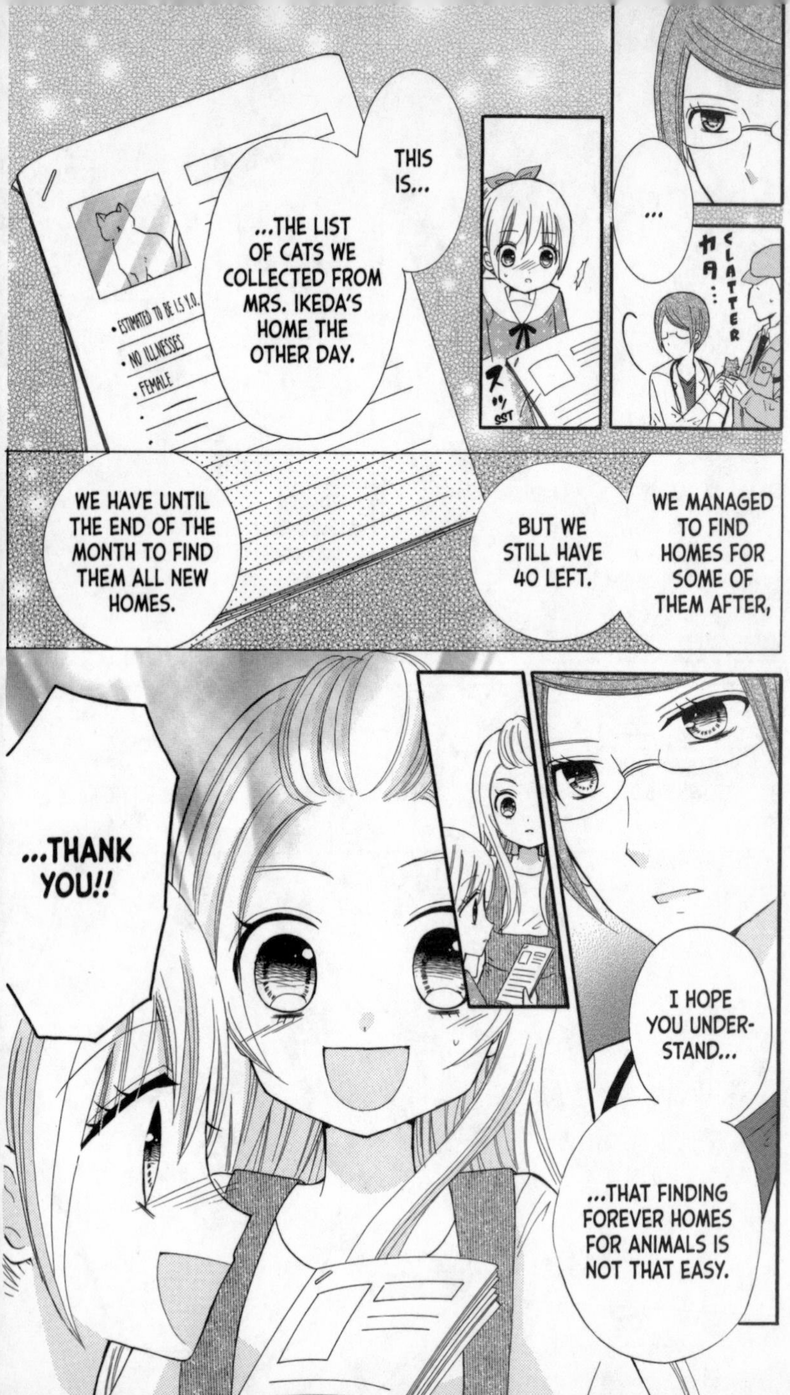
...
カタ…
CLATTER
スッ
SST
THIS IS...
...THE LIST OF CATS WE COLLECTED FROM MRS. IKEDA'S HOME THE OTHER DAY.
• ESTIMATED TO BE 1.5 Y.O.
• NO ILLNESSES
• FEMALE
WE MANAGED TO FIND HOMES FOR SOME OF THEM AFTER,
BUT WE STILL HAVE 40 LEFT.
WE HAVE UNTIL THE END OF THE MONTH TO FIND THEM ALL NEW HOMES.
I HOPE YOU UNDER-STAND...
...THAT FINDING FOREVER HOMES FOR ANIMALS IS NOT THAT EASY.
...THANK YOU!!

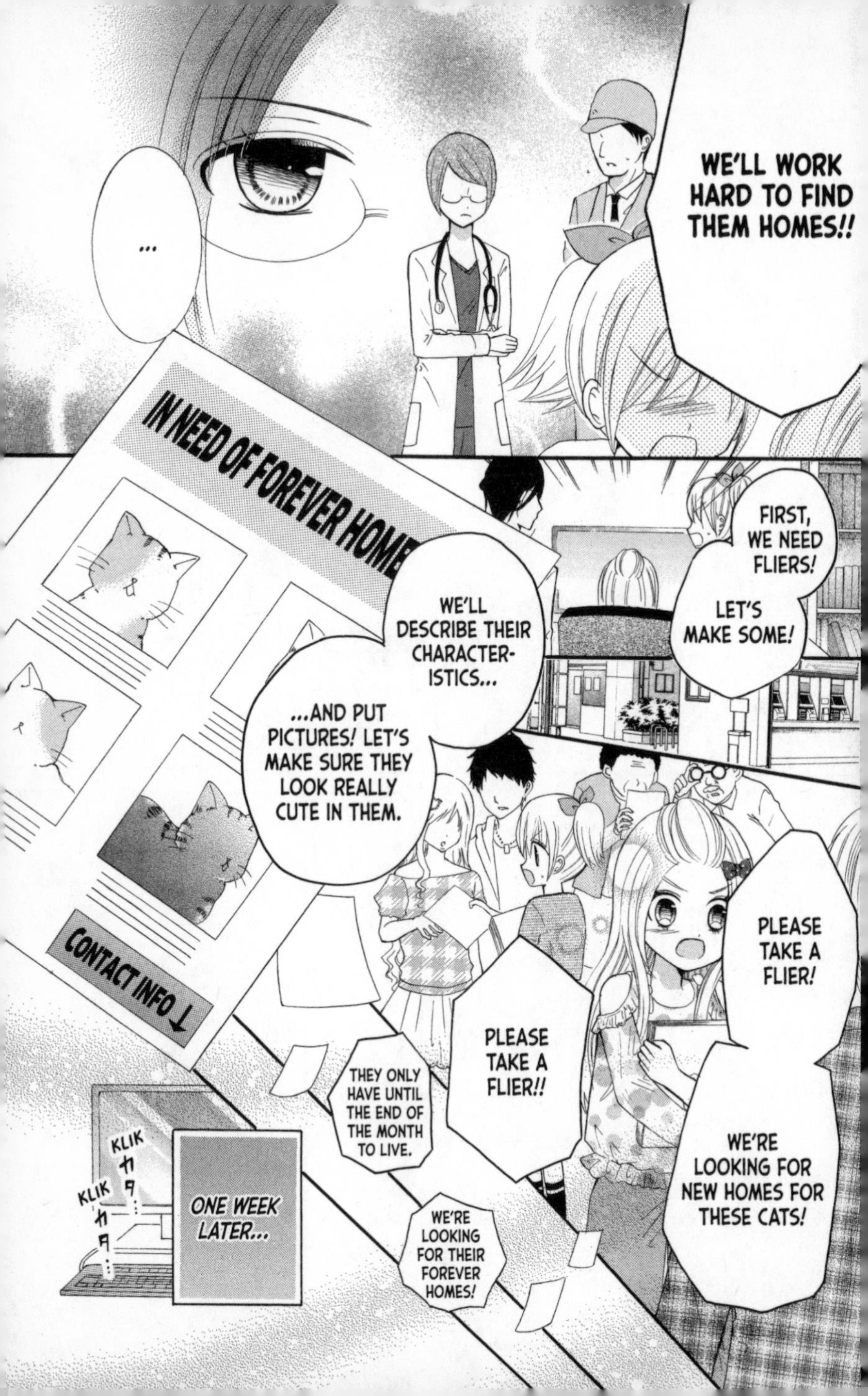
WE'LL WORK HARD TO FIND THEM HOMES!!
...
FIRST, WE NEED FLIERS!
LET'S MAKE SOME!
IN NEED OF FOREVER HOME
WE'LL DESCRIBE THEIR CHARACTER-ISTICS...
...AND PUT PICTURES! LET'S MAKE SURE THEY LOOK REALLY CUTE IN THEM.
CONTACT INFO ↓
PLEASE TAKE A FLIER!
WE'RE LOOKING FOR NEW HOMES FOR THESE CATS!
PLEASE TAKE A FLIER!!
THEY ONLY HAVE UNTIL THE END OF THE MONTH TO LIVE.
WE'RE LOOKING FOR THEIR FOREVER HOMES!
ONE WEEK LATER...
KLIK カタ…
KLIK カタ…

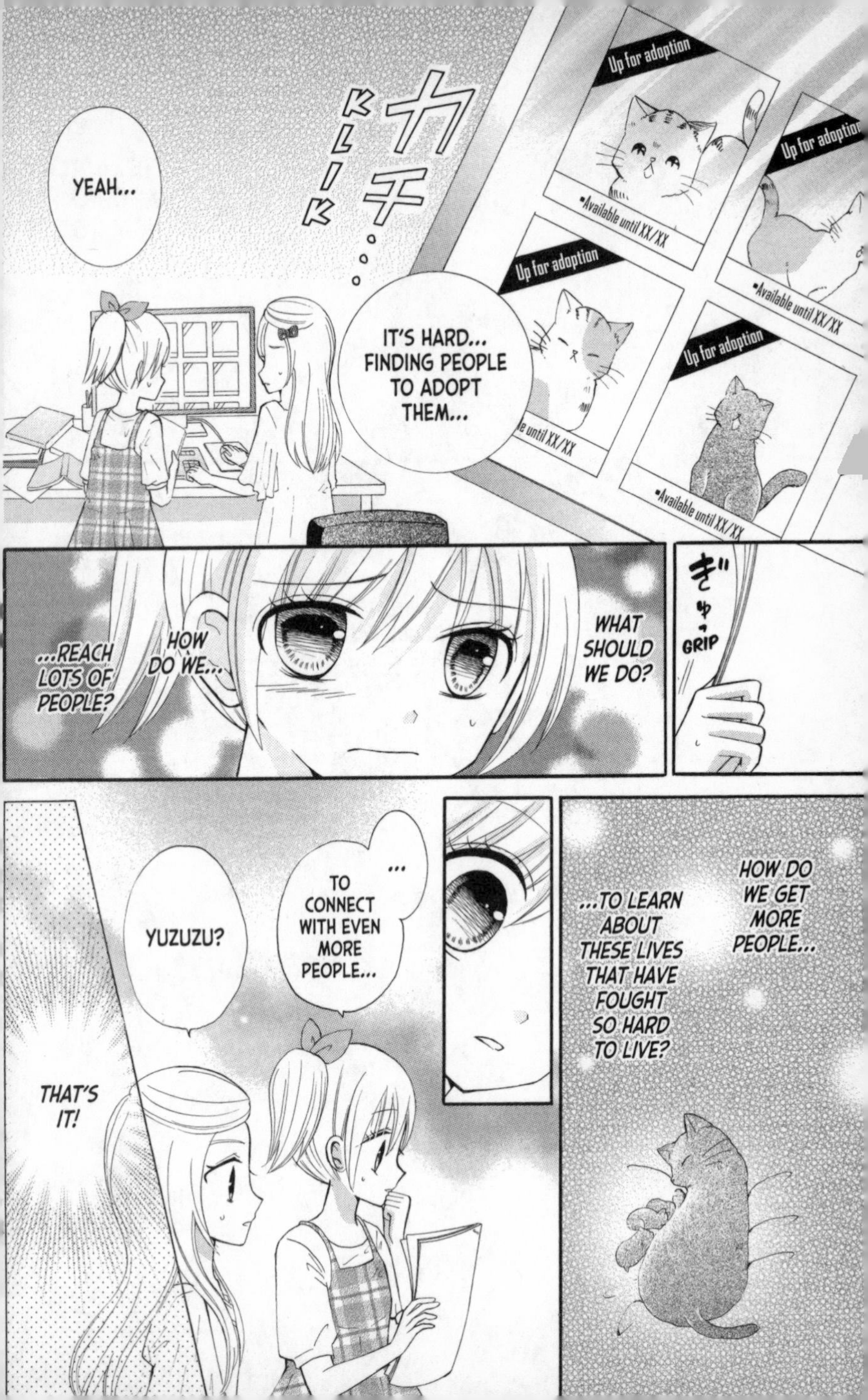
Up for adoption
•Available until XX/XX
Up for adoption
•Available until XX/XX
Up for adoption
Up for adoption
•Available until XX/XX
カチ
KLIK
IT'S HARD... FINDING PEOPLE TO ADOPT THEM...
YEAH...
ぎゅっ
GRIP
WHAT SHOULD WE DO?
HOW DO WE...
...REACH LOTS OF PEOPLE?
HOW DO WE GET MORE PEOPLE...
...TO LEARN ABOUT THESE LIVES THAT HAVE FOUGHT SO HARD TO LIVE?
... TO CONNECT WITH EVEN MORE PEOPLE...
YUZUZU?
THAT'S IT!

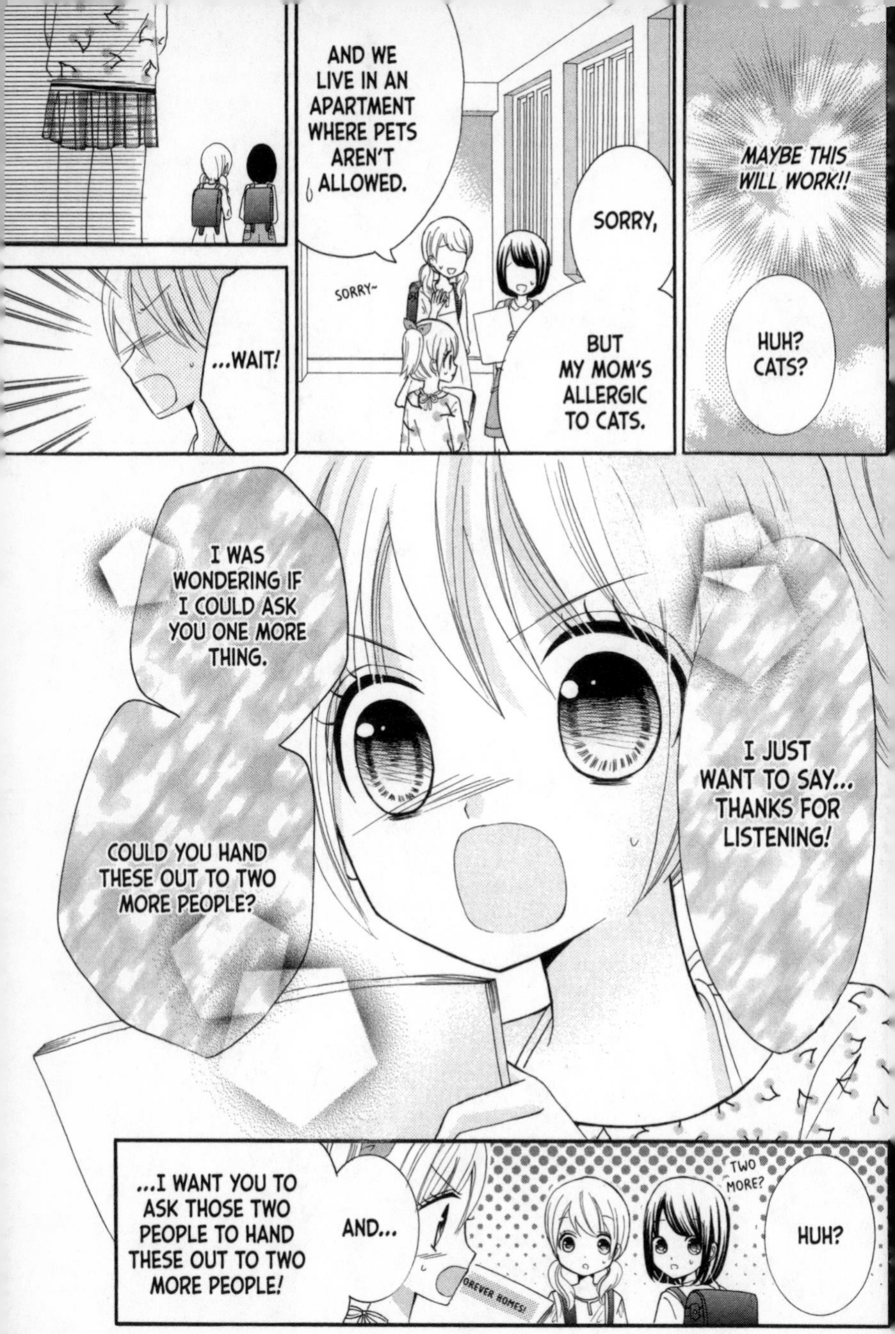
MAYBE THIS WILL WORK!!
HUH? CATS?
SORRY,
BUT MY MOM'S ALLERGIC TO CATS.
AND WE LIVE IN AN APARTMENT WHERE PETS AREN'T ALLOWED.
SORRY~
...WAIT!
I JUST WANT TO SAY... THANKS FOR LISTENING!
I WAS WONDERING IF I COULD ASK YOU ONE MORE THING.
COULD YOU HAND THESE OUT TO TWO MORE PEOPLE?
HUH?
TWO MORE?
AND...
...I WANT YOU TO ASK THOSE TWO PEOPLE TO HAND THESE OUT TO TWO MORE PEOPLE!

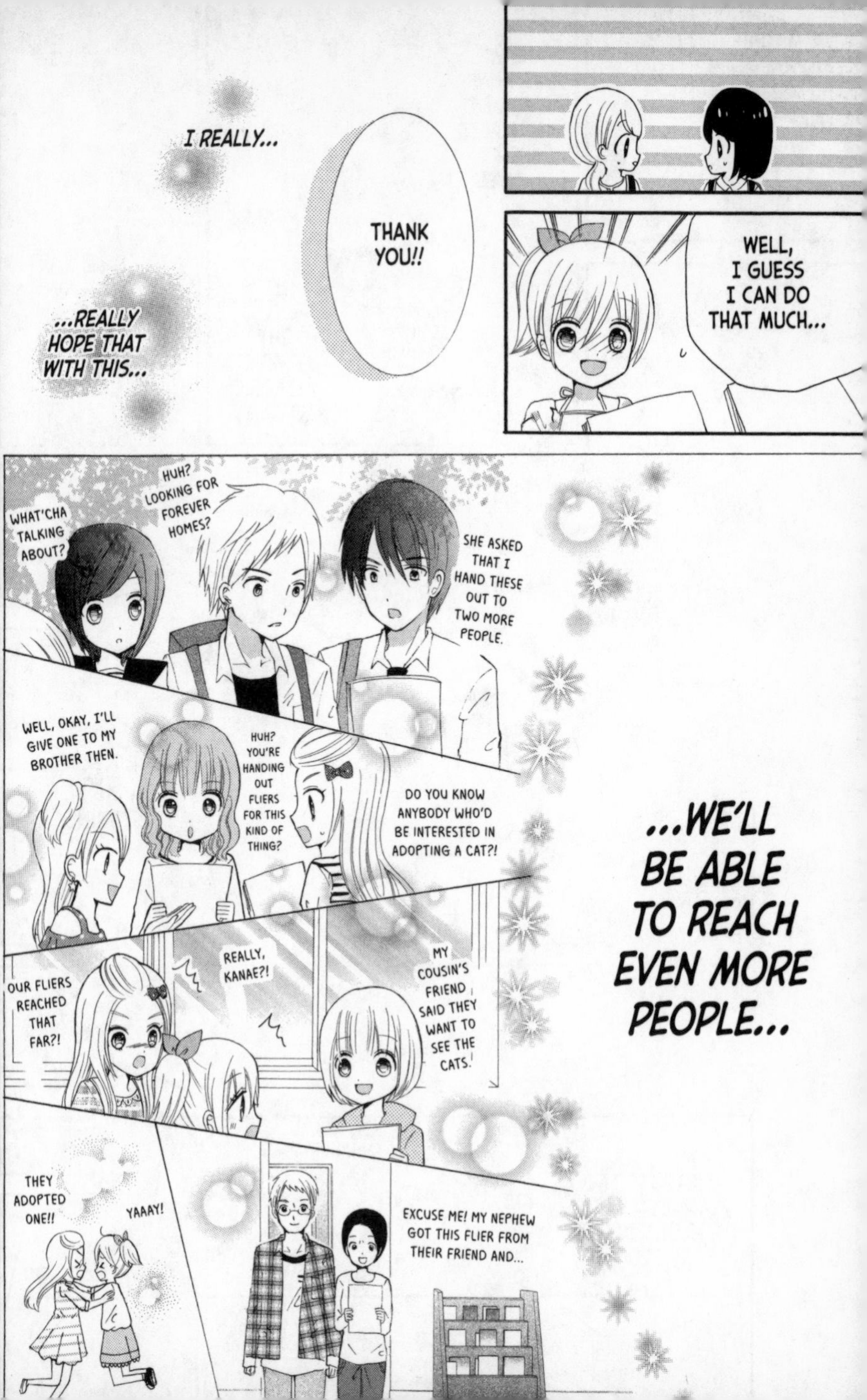
WELL, I GUESS I CAN DO THAT MUCH...
THANK YOU!!
I REALLY...
...REALLY HOPE THAT WITH THIS...
...WE'LL BE ABLE TO REACH EVEN MORE PEOPLE...
SHE ASKED THAT I HAND THESE OUT TO TWO MORE PEOPLE.
HUH? LOOKING FOR FOREVER HOMES?
WHAT'CHA TALKING ABOUT?
DO YOU KNOW ANYBODY WHO'D BE INTERESTED IN ADOPTING A CAT?!
HUH? YOU'RE HANDING OUT FLIERS FOR THIS KIND OF THING?
WELL, OKAY, I'LL GIVE ONE TO MY BROTHER THEN.
MY COUSIN'S FRIEND SAID THEY WANT TO SEE THE CATS.
REALLY, KANAE?!
OUR FLIERS REACHED THAT FAR?!
EXCUSE ME! MY NEPHEW GOT THIS FLIER FROM THEIR FRIEND AND...
YAAAY!
THEY ADOPTED ONE!!

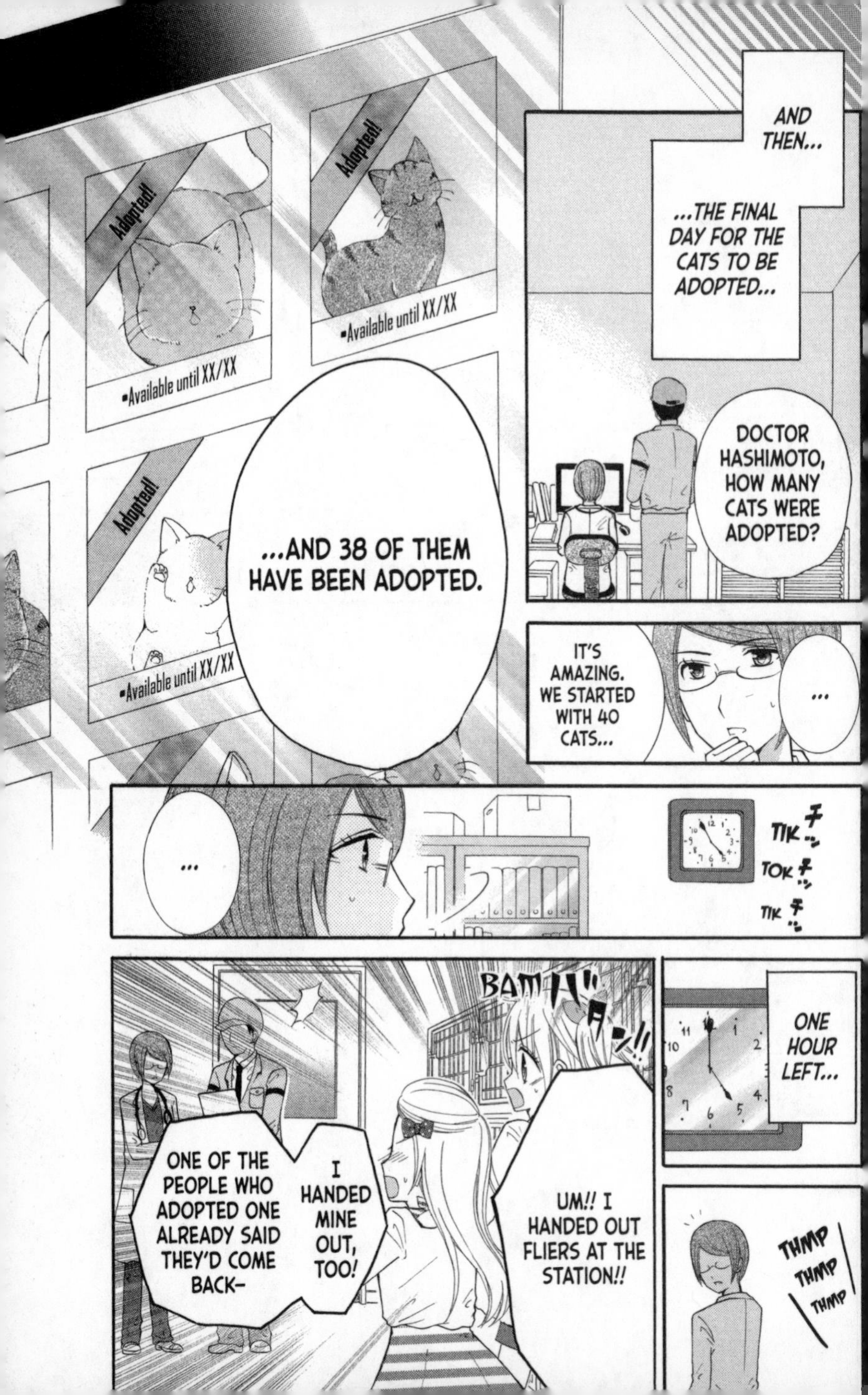
AND THEN...
...THE FINAL DAY FOR THE CATS TO BE ADOPTED...
DOCTOR HASHIMOTO, HOW MANY CATS WERE ADOPTED?
...
IT'S AMAZING. WE STARTED WITH 40 CATS...
Adopted!
Adopted!
■Available until XX/XX
■Available until XX/XX
Adopted!
■Available until XX/XX
...AND 38 OF THEM HAVE BEEN ADOPTED.
TIK
TOK
TIK
...
ONE HOUR LEFT...
THMP
THMP
THMP
BAM
UM!! I HANDED OUT FLIERS AT THE STATION!!
I HANDED MINE OUT, TOO!
ONE OF THE PEOPLE WHO ADOPTED ONE ALREADY SAID THEY'D COME BACK–

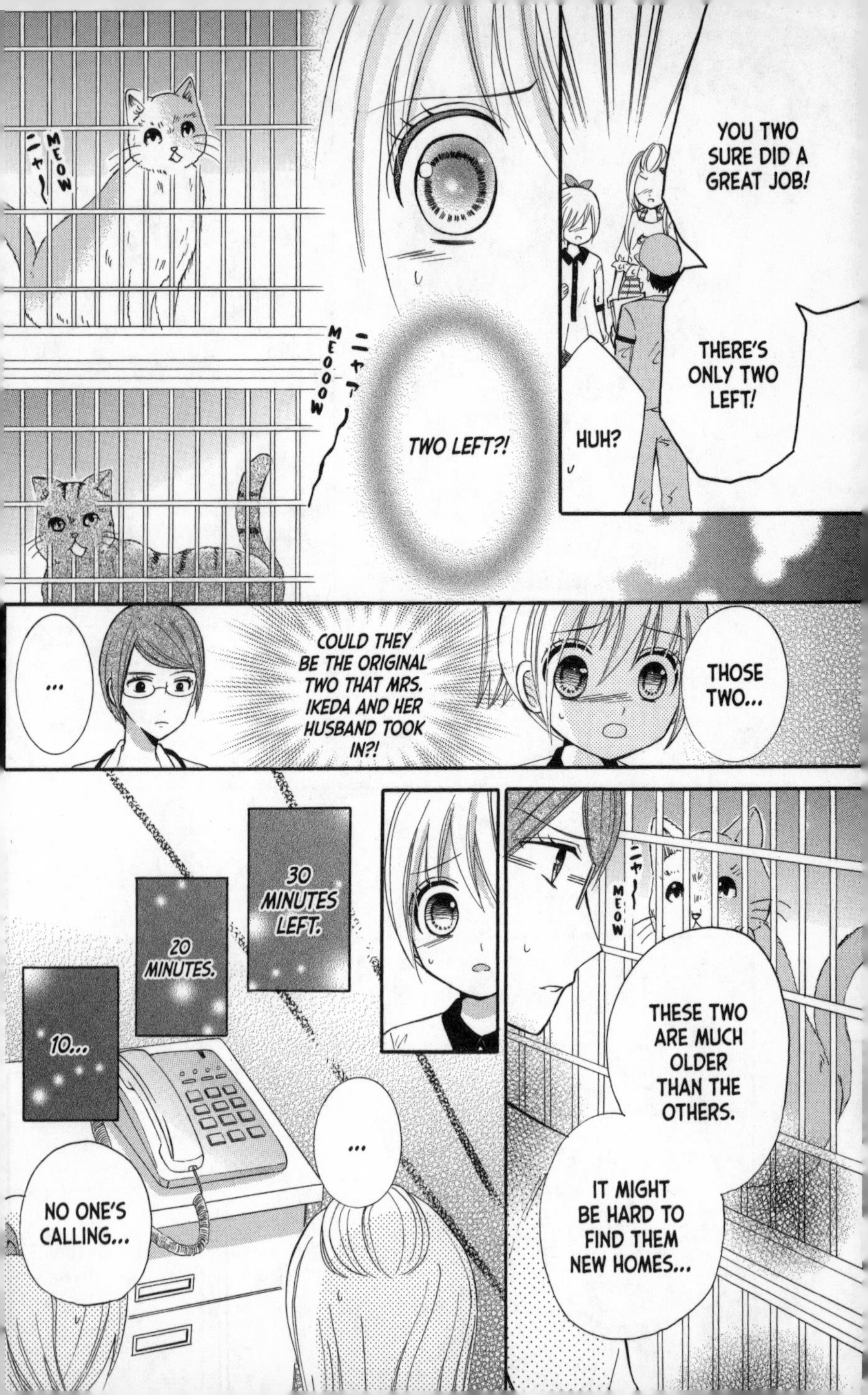
YOU TWO SURE DID A GREAT JOB!
THERE'S ONLY TWO LEFT!
HUH?
TWO LEFT?!
ニャ〜
MEOW
ニャア
MEOOOOW
THOSE TWO...
COULD THEY BE THE ORIGINAL TWO THAT MRS. IKEDA AND HER HUSBAND TOOK IN?!
...
ニャ〜
MEOW
THESE TWO ARE MUCH OLDER THAN THE OTHERS.
IT MIGHT BE HARD TO FIND THEM NEW HOMES...
30 MINUTES LEFT.
20 MINUTES.
10...
...
NO ONE'S CALLING...

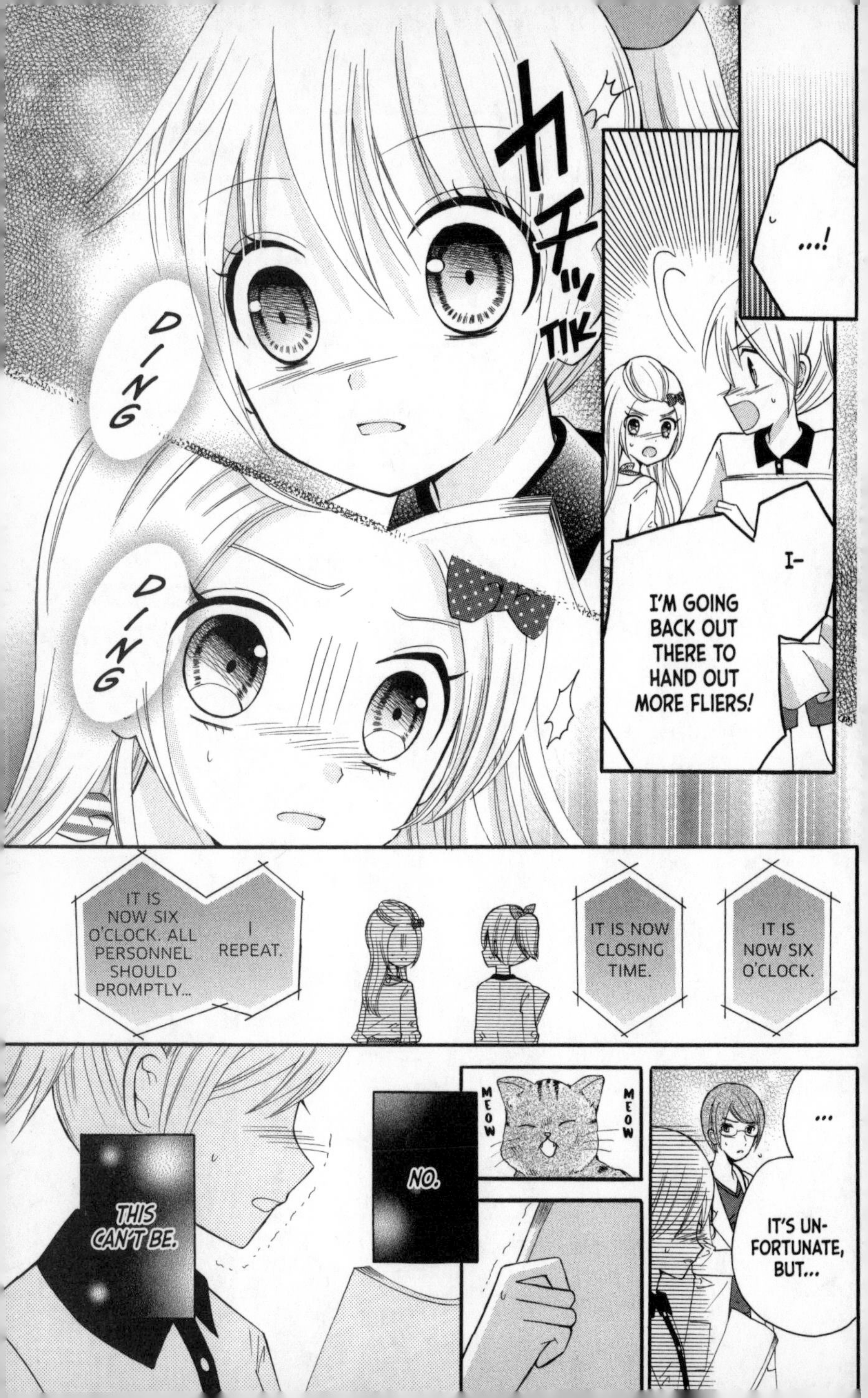
...!
I-
I'M GOING BACK OUT THERE TO HAND OUT MORE FLIERS!
カチッ
TIK
DING
DING
IT IS NOW SIX O'CLOCK.
IT IS NOW CLOSING TIME.
I REPEAT.
IT IS NOW SIX O'CLOCK. ALL PERSONNEL SHOULD PROMPTLY...
...
IT'S UN-FORTUNATE, BUT...
MEOW
MEOW
NO.
THIS CAN'T BE.

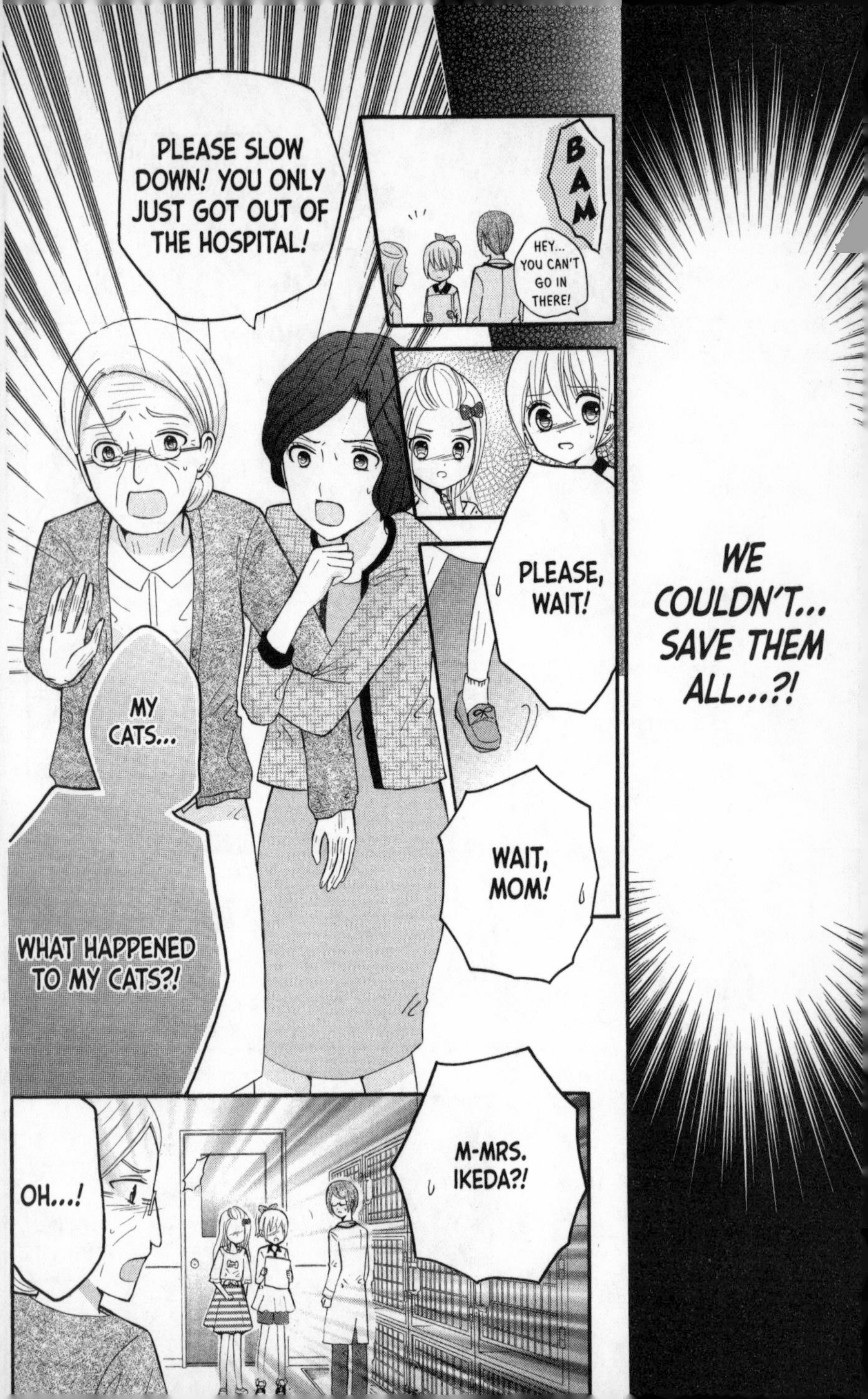
WE COULDN'T... SAVE THEM ALL...?!
BAM
HEY... YOU CAN'T GO IN THERE!
PLEASE, WAIT!
WAIT, MOM!
PLEASE SLOW DOWN! YOU ONLY JUST GOT OUT OF THE HOSPITAL!
MY CATS...
WHAT HAPPENED TO MY CATS?!
M-MRS. IKEDA?!
OH...!

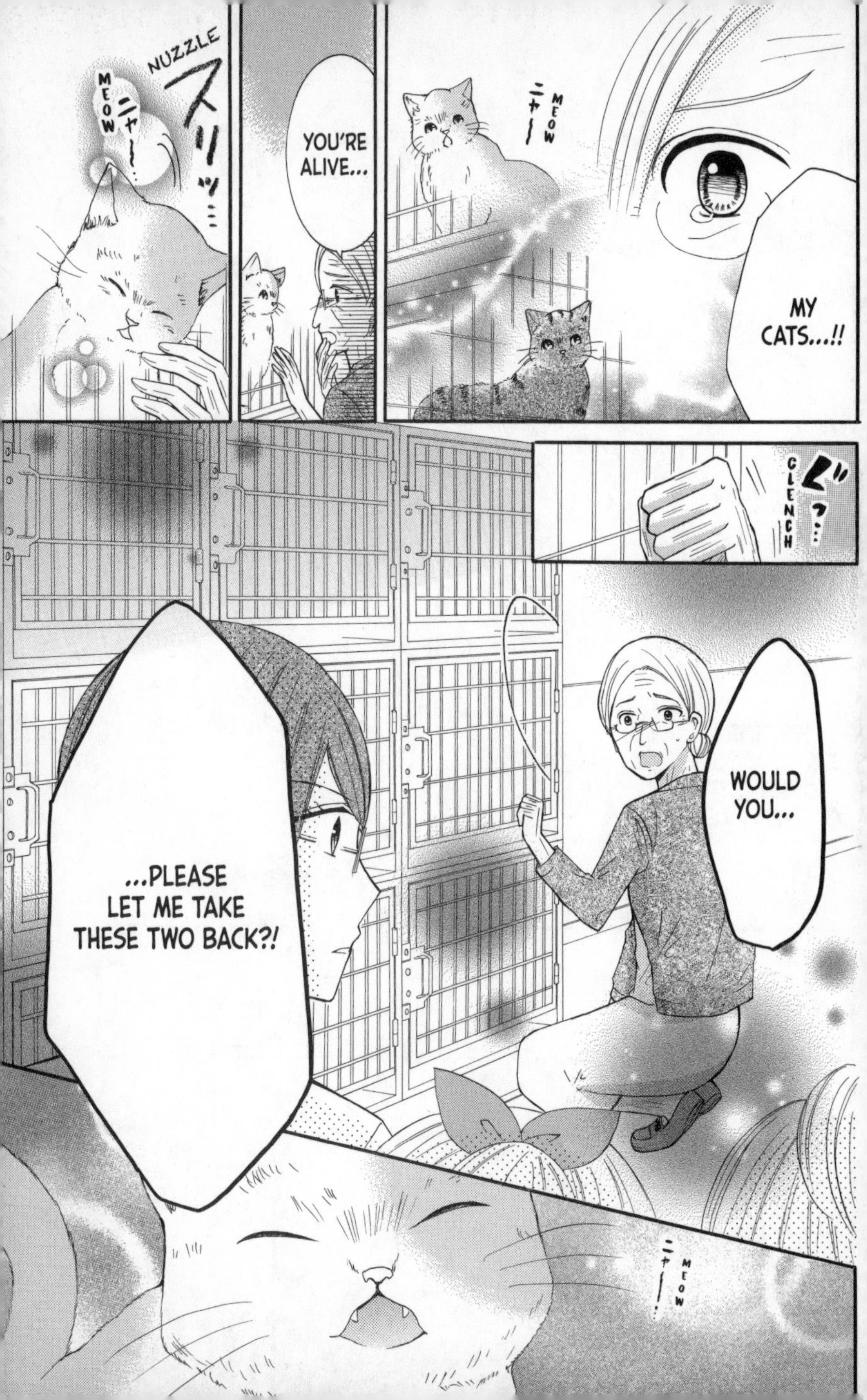
MY CATS...!!
MEOW
ニャー
YOU'RE ALIVE...
NUZZLE
スリッ
MEOW
ニャー...
CLENCH
ぐっ...
WOULD YOU...
...PLEASE LET ME TAKE THESE TWO BACK?!
MEOW
ニャー!

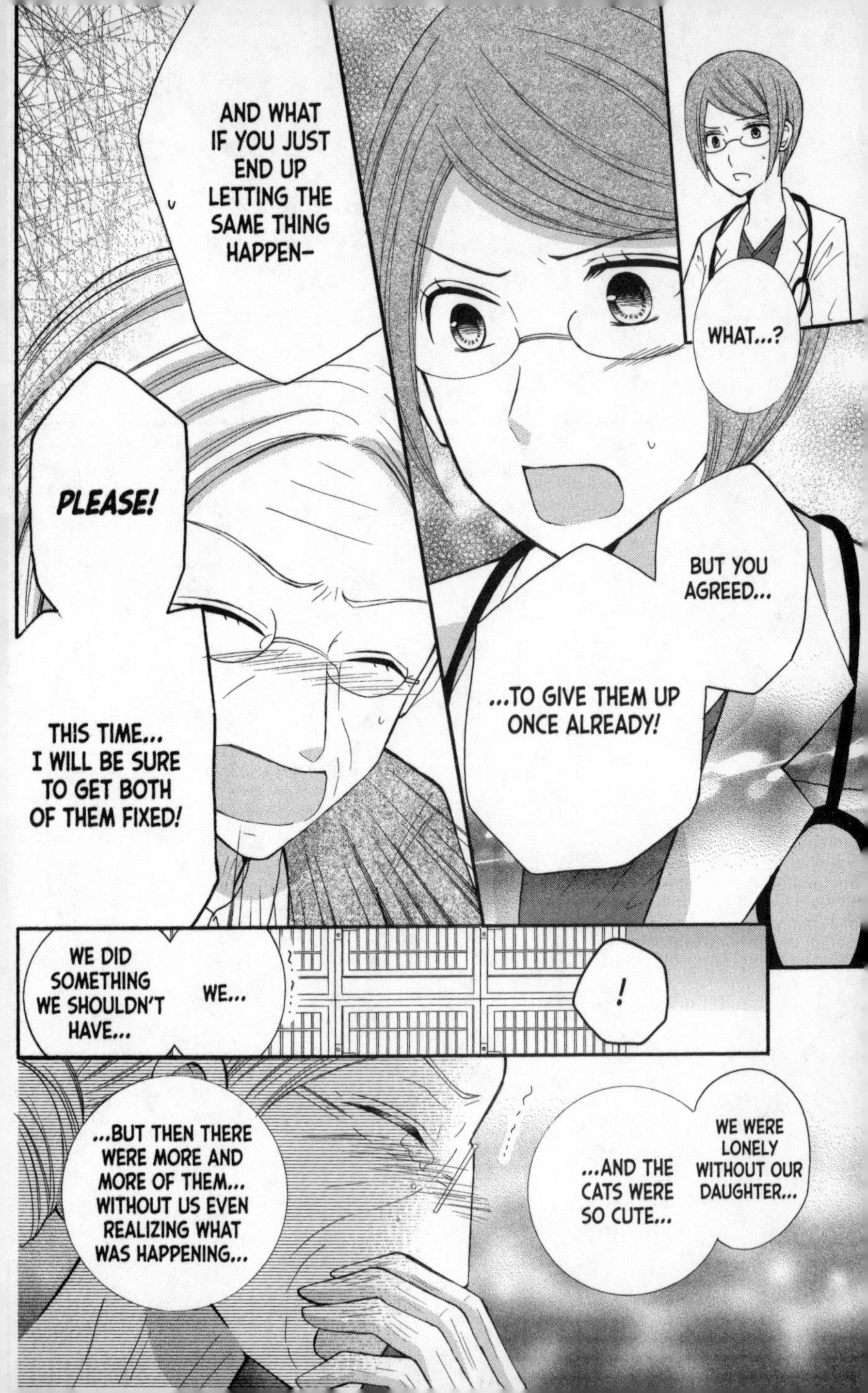
WHAT...?
BUT YOU AGREED...
...TO GIVE THEM UP ONCE ALREADY!
AND WHAT IF YOU JUST END UP LETTING THE SAME THING HAPPEN–
PLEASE!
THIS TIME... I WILL BE SURE TO GET BOTH OF THEM FIXED!
!
WE...
WE DID SOMETHING WE SHOULDN'T HAVE...
WE WERE LONELY WITHOUT OUR DAUGHTER...
...AND THE CATS WERE SO CUTE...
...BUT THEN THERE WERE MORE AND MORE OF THEM... WITHOUT US EVEN REALIZING WHAT WAS HAPPENING...

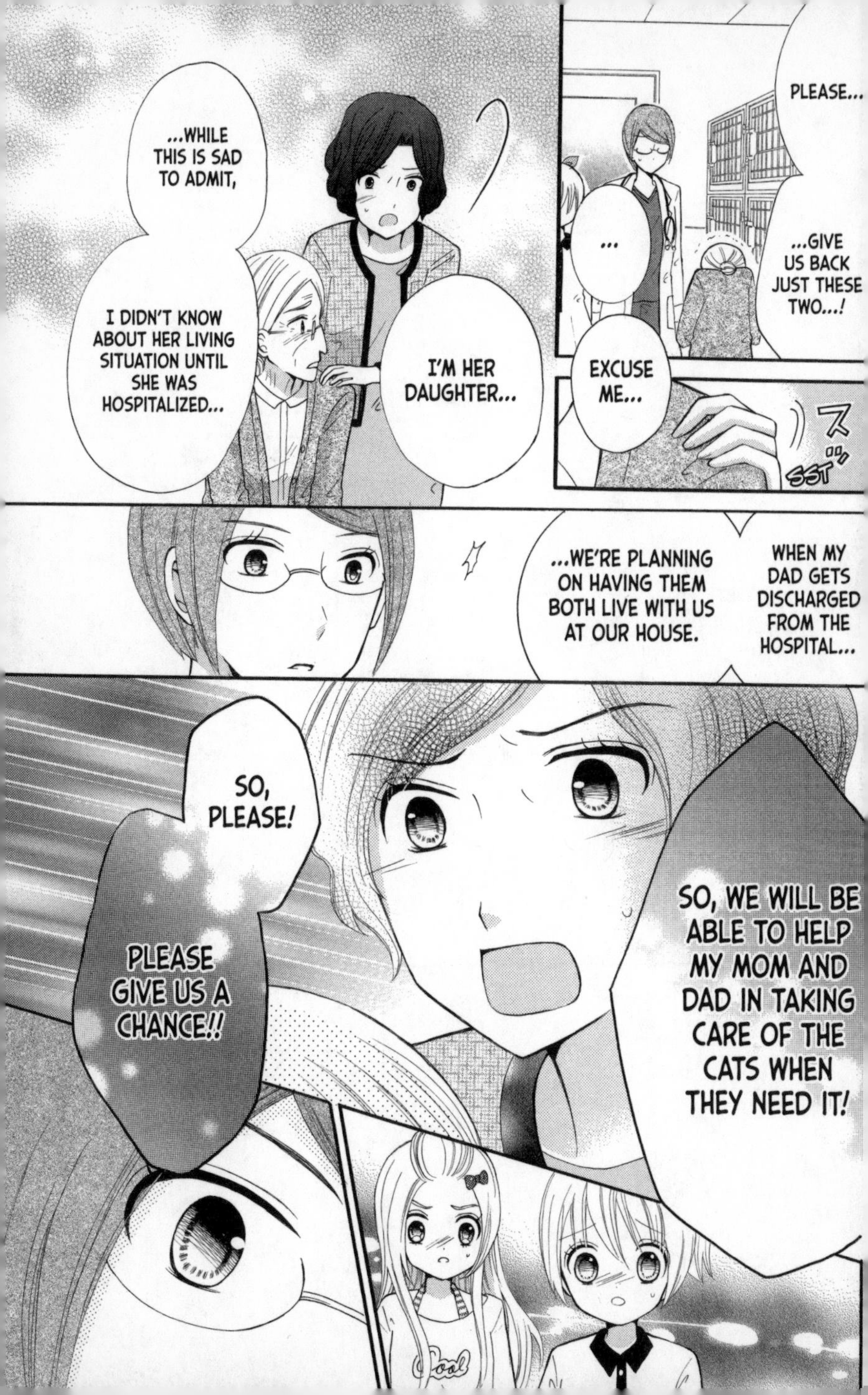
PLEASE...
...GIVE US BACK JUST THESE TWO...!
...
EXCUSE ME...
SST
I'M HER DAUGHTER...
...WHILE THIS IS SAD TO ADMIT,
I DIDN'T KNOW ABOUT HER LIVING SITUATION UNTIL SHE WAS HOSPITALIZED...
WHEN MY DAD GETS DISCHARGED FROM THE HOSPITAL...
...WE'RE PLANNING ON HAVING THEM BOTH LIVE WITH US AT OUR HOUSE.
SO, WE WILL BE ABLE TO HELP MY MOM AND DAD IN TAKING CARE OF THE CATS WHEN THEY NEED IT!
SO, PLEASE!
PLEASE GIVE US A CHANCE!!

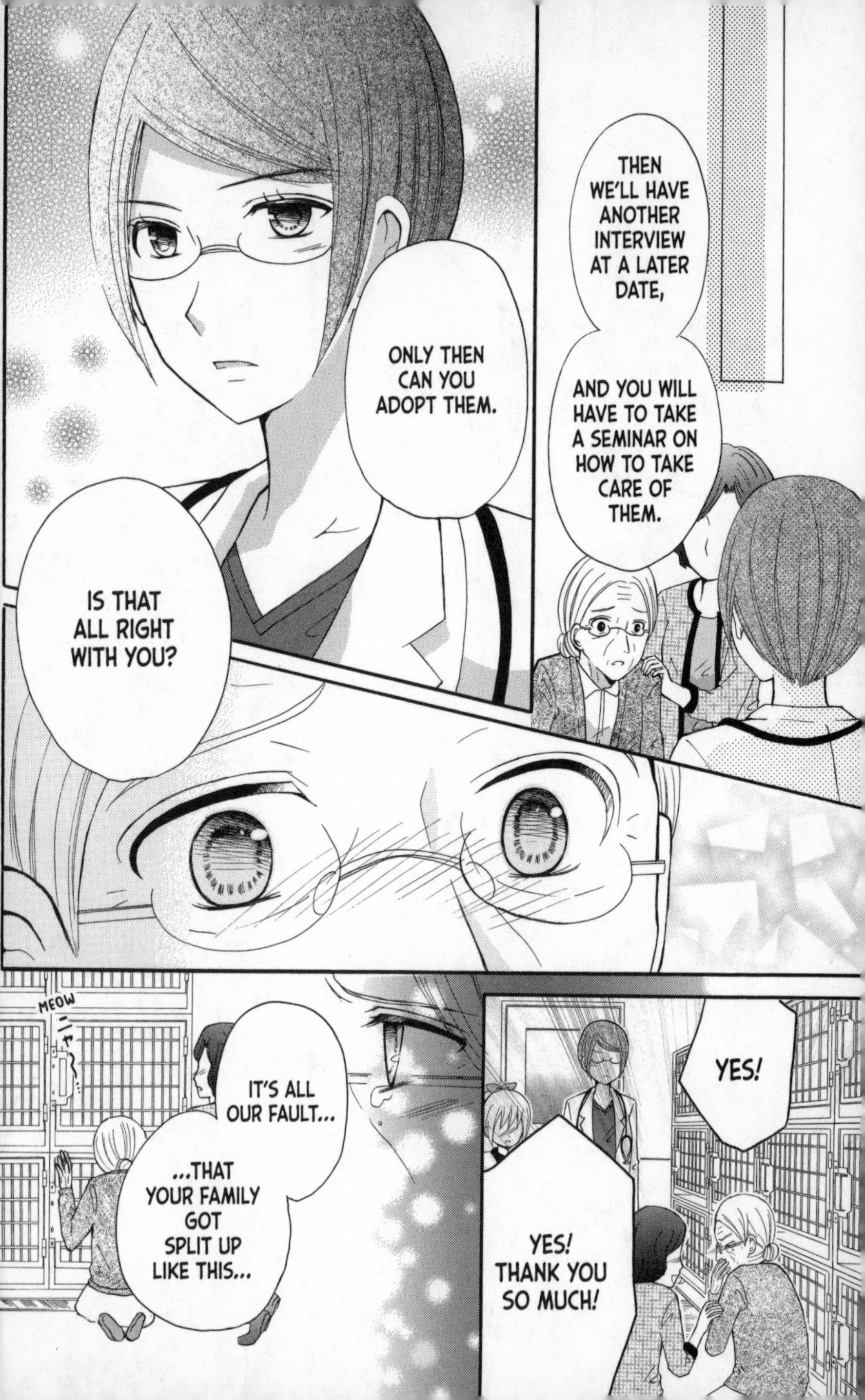
THEN WE'LL HAVE ANOTHER INTERVIEW AT A LATER DATE,
AND YOU WILL HAVE TO TAKE A SEMINAR ON HOW TO TAKE CARE OF THEM.
ONLY THEN CAN YOU ADOPT THEM.
IS THAT ALL RIGHT WITH YOU?
YES!
YES! THANK YOU SO MUCH!
MEOW
ニャ～…
IT'S ALL OUR FAULT...
...THAT YOUR FAMILY GOT SPLIT UP LIKE THIS...

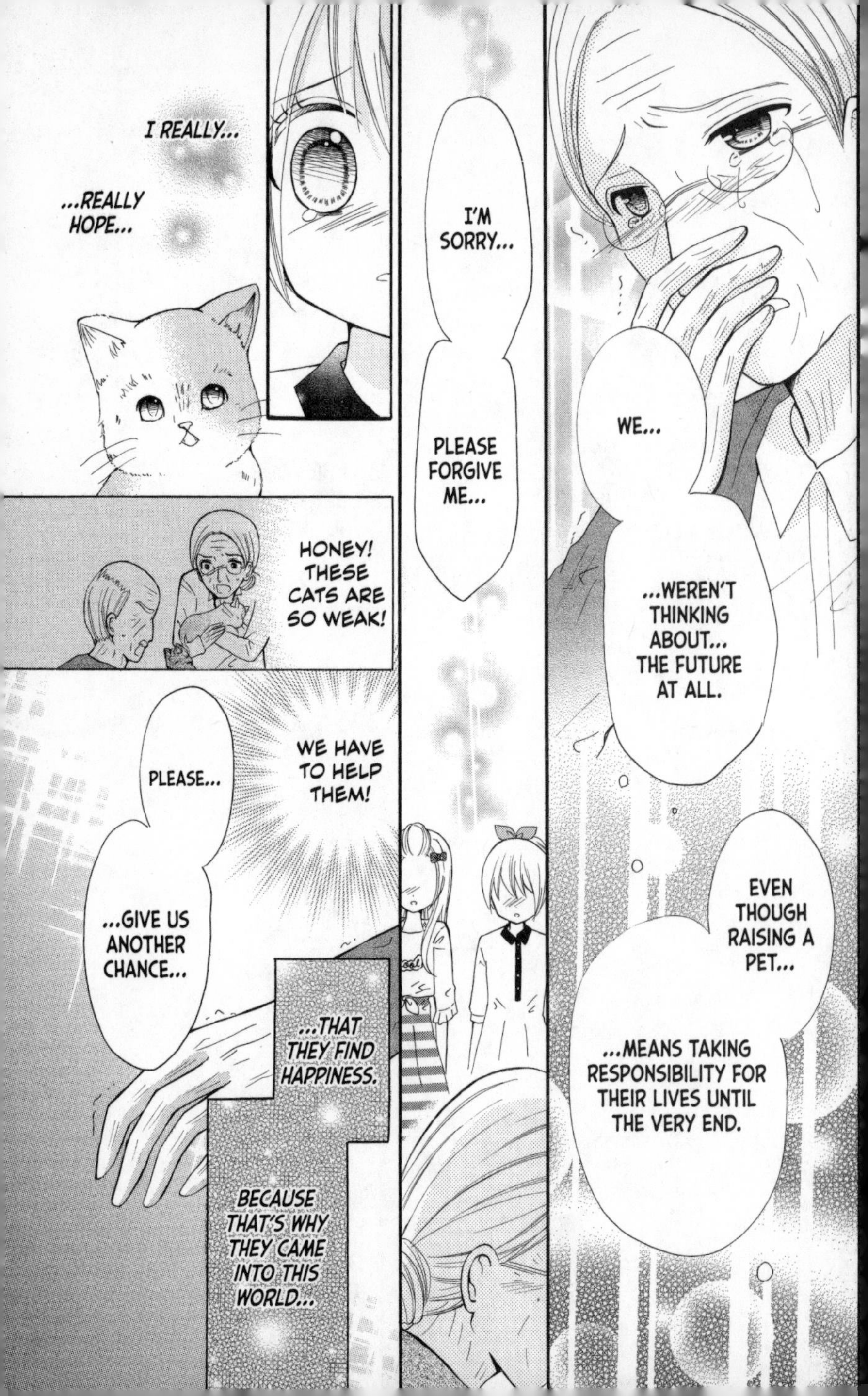
WE...
...WEREN'T THINKING ABOUT... THE FUTURE AT ALL.
EVEN THOUGH RAISING A PET...
...MEANS TAKING RESPONSIBILITY FOR THEIR LIVES UNTIL THE VERY END.
I'M SORRY...
PLEASE FORGIVE ME...
I REALLY...
...REALLY HOPE...
HONEY! THESE CATS ARE SO WEAK!
WE HAVE TO HELP THEM!
PLEASE...
...GIVE US ANOTHER CHANCE...
...THAT THEY FIND HAPPINESS.
BECAUSE THAT'S WHY THEY CAME INTO THIS WORLD...

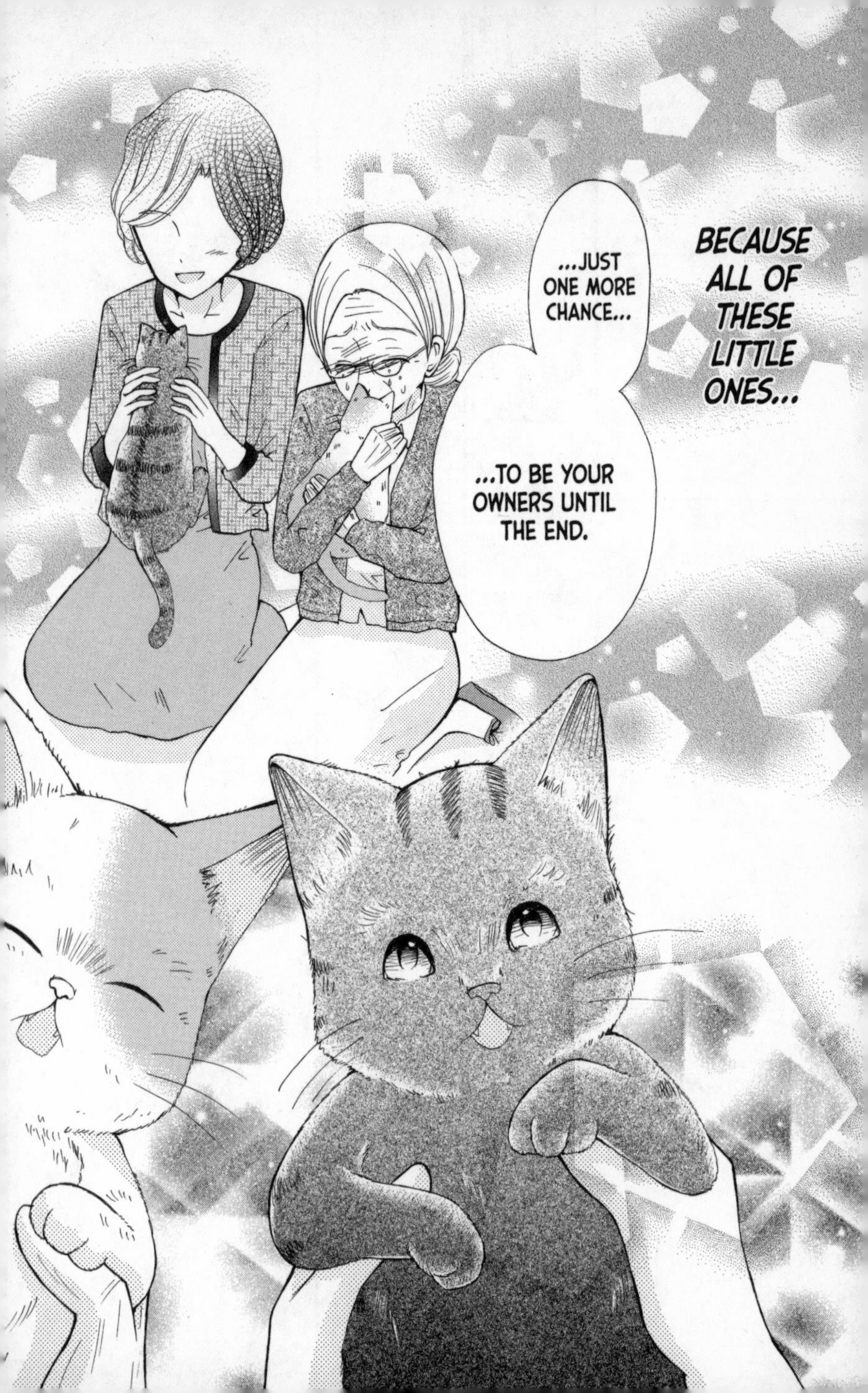
BECAUSE ALL OF THESE LITTLE ONES...
...JUST ONE MORE CHANCE...
...TO BE YOUR OWNERS UNTIL THE END.

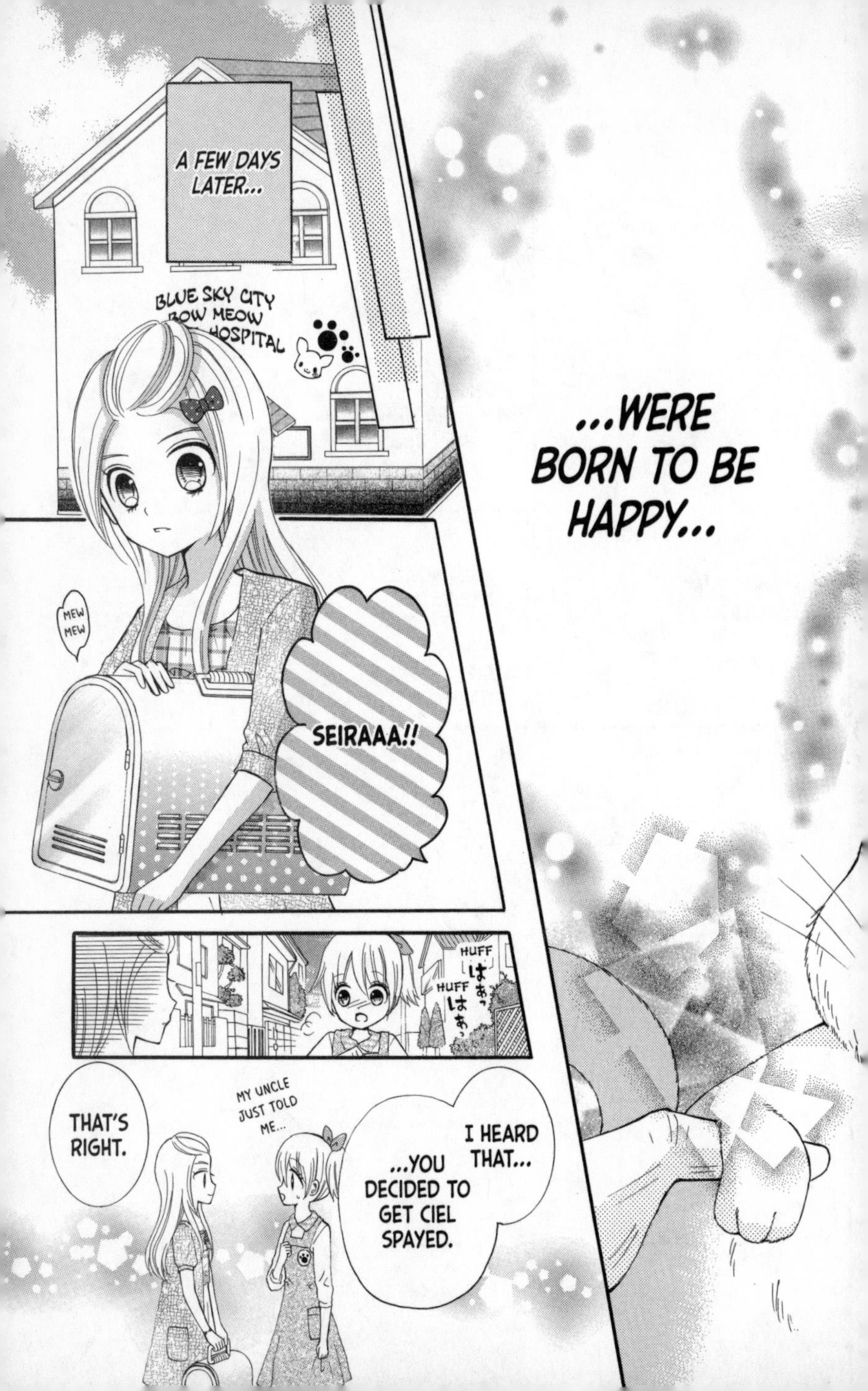
...WERE BORN TO BE HAPPY...
A FEW DAYS LATER...
BLUE SKY CITY BOW MEOW
HOSPITAL
SEIRAAA!!
MEW MEW
HUFF はあっ
HUFF はあっ
I HEARD THAT...
...YOU DECIDED TO GET CIEL SPAYED.
MY UNCLE JUST TOLD ME...
THAT'S RIGHT.

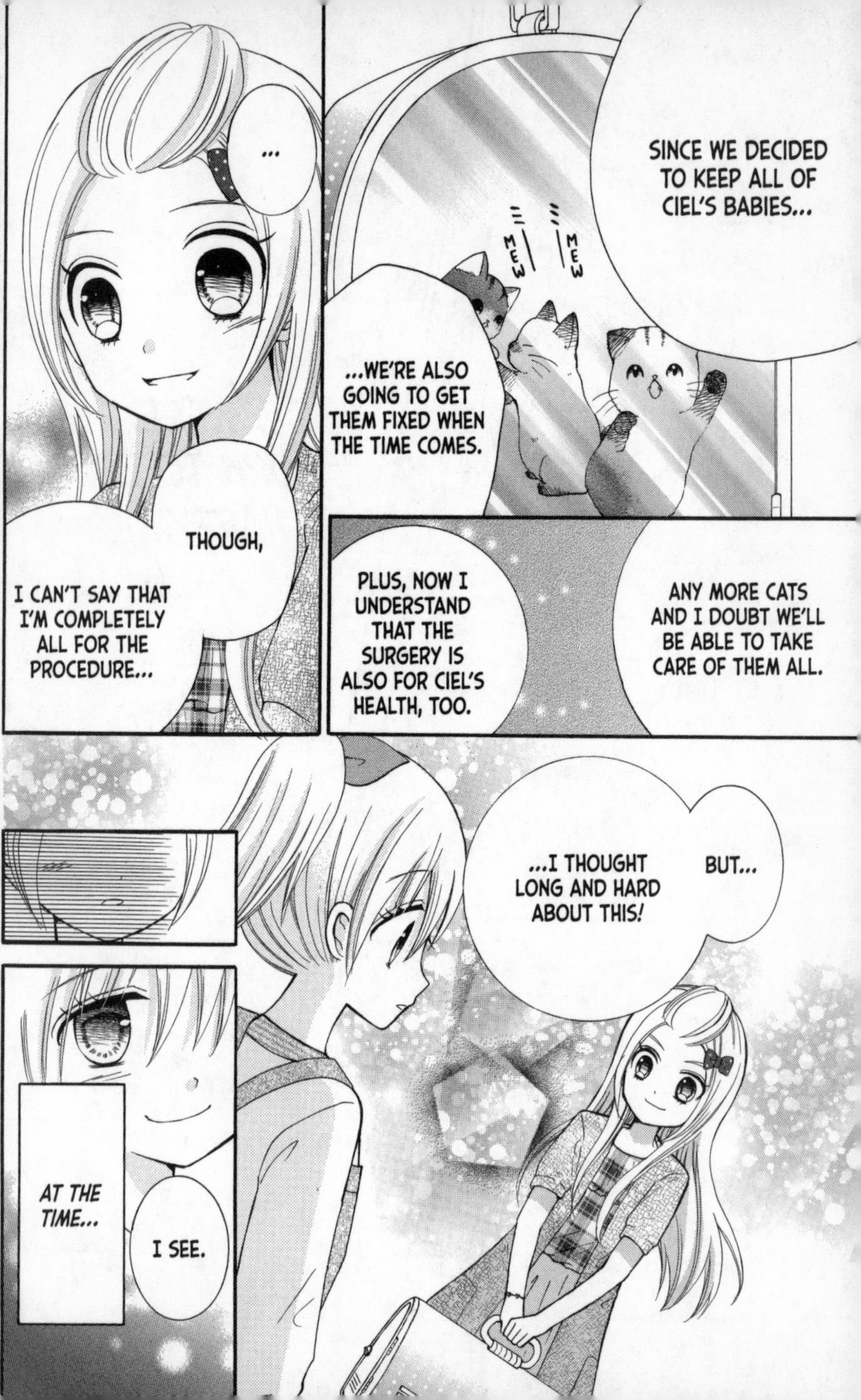
SINCE WE DECIDED TO KEEP ALL OF CIEL'S BABIES...
MEW
MEW
...WE'RE ALSO GOING TO GET THEM FIXED WHEN THE TIME COMES.
ANY MORE CATS AND I DOUBT WE'LL BE ABLE TO TAKE CARE OF THEM ALL.
PLUS, NOW I UNDERSTAND THAT THE SURGERY IS ALSO FOR CIEL'S HEALTH, TOO.
...
THOUGH,
I CAN'T SAY THAT I'M COMPLETELY ALL FOR THE PROCEDURE...
BUT...
...I THOUGHT LONG AND HARD ABOUT THIS!
I SEE.
AT THE TIME...

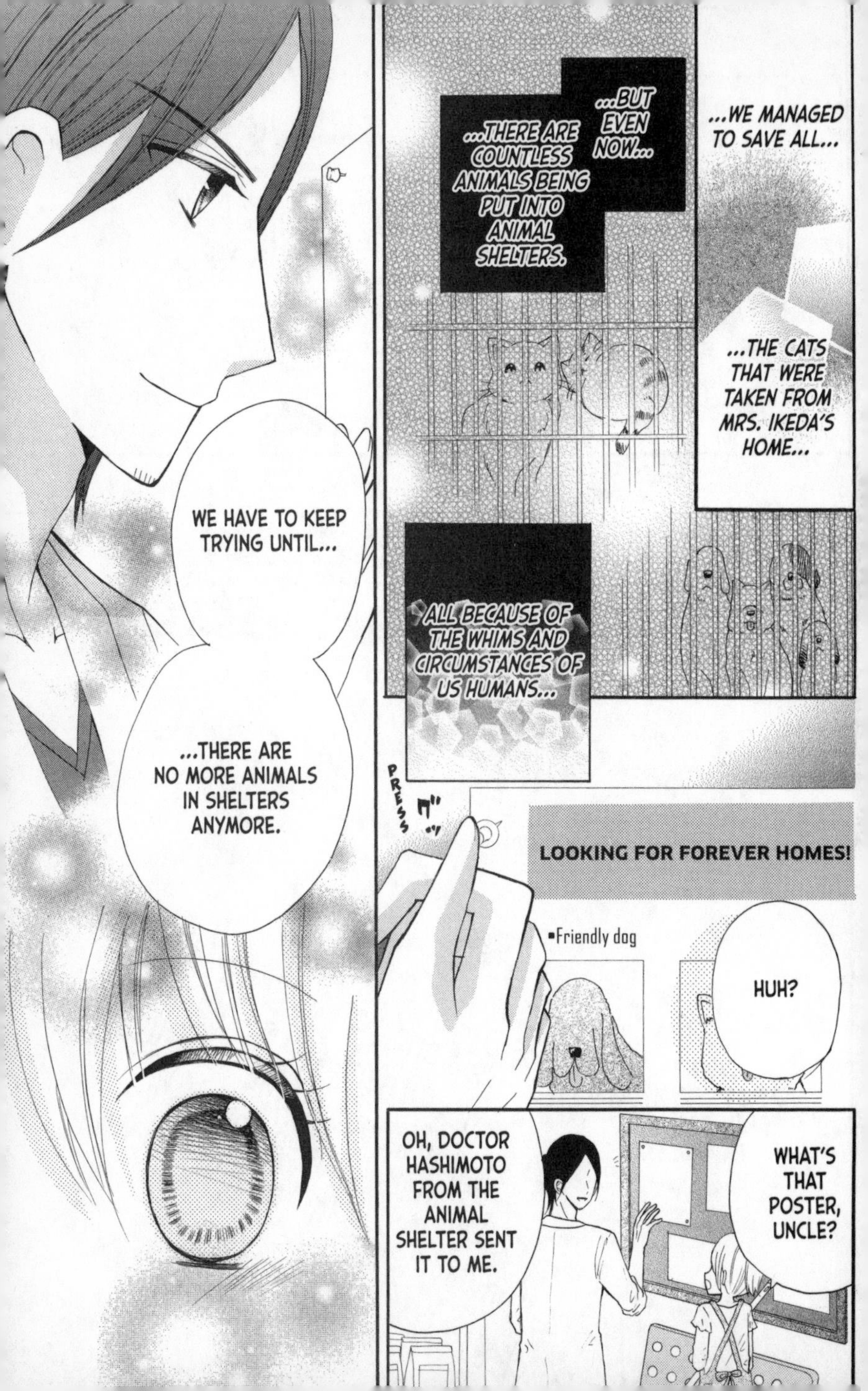
...WE MANAGED TO SAVE ALL...
...THE CATS THAT WERE TAKEN FROM MRS. IKEDA'S HOME...
...BUT EVEN NOW...
...THERE ARE COUNTLESS ANIMALS BEING PUT INTO ANIMAL SHELTERS.
ALL BECAUSE OF THE WHIMS AND CIRCUMSTANCES OF US HUMANS...
WE HAVE TO KEEP TRYING UNTIL...
...THERE ARE NO MORE ANIMALS IN SHELTERS ANYMORE.
PRESS
LOOKING FOR FOREVER HOMES!
•Friendly dog
HUH?
WHAT'S THAT POSTER, UNCLE?
OH, DOCTOR HASHIMOTO FROM THE ANIMAL SHELTER SENT IT TO ME.

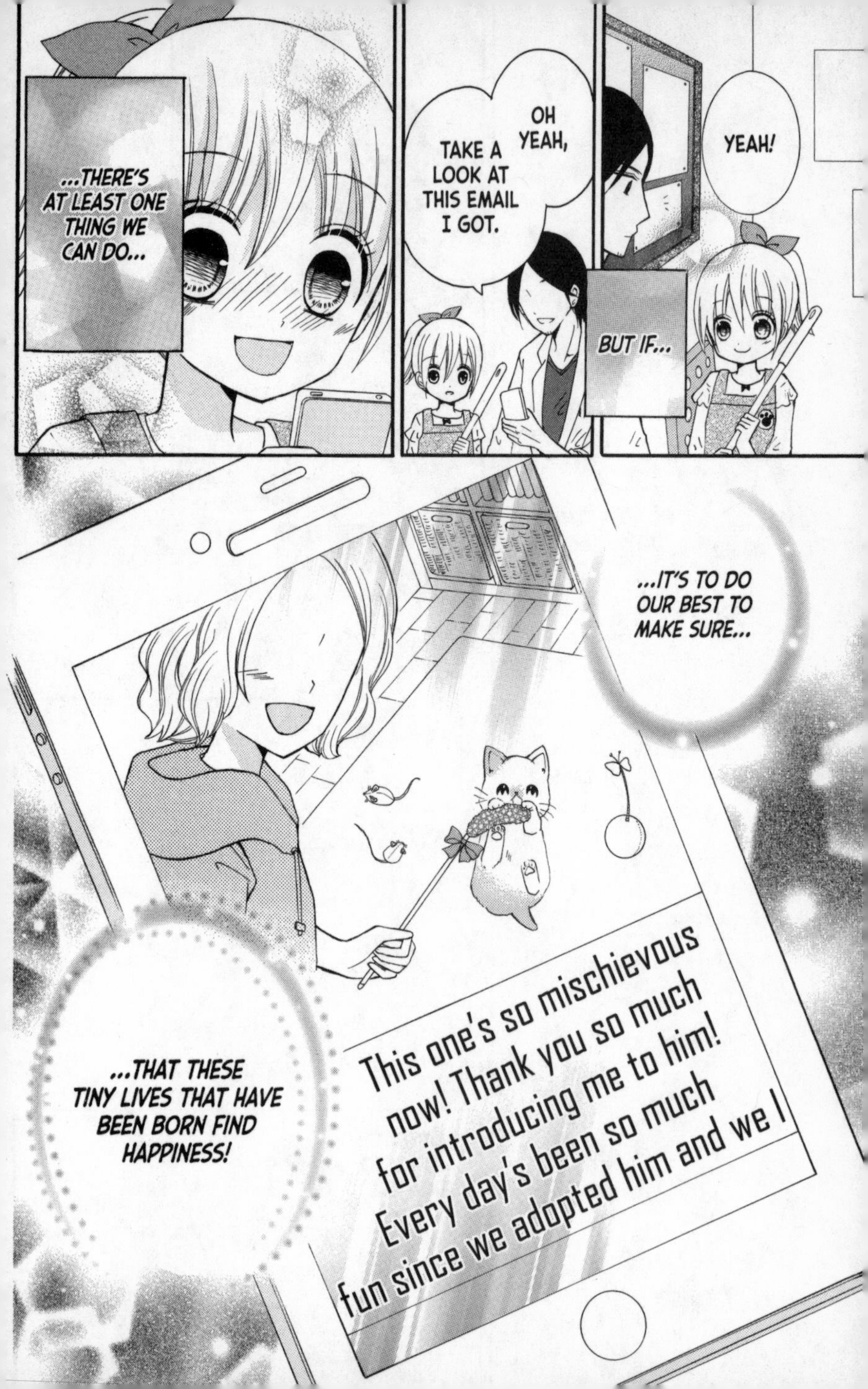
YEAH!
BUT IF...
OH YEAH, TAKE A LOOK AT THIS EMAIL I GOT.
...THERE'S AT LEAST ONE THING WE CAN DO...
...IT'S TO DO OUR BEST TO MAKE SURE...
...THAT THESE TINY LIVES THAT HAVE BEEN BORN FIND HAPPINESS!
This one's so mischievous now! Thank you so much for introducing me to him! Every day's been so much fun since we adopted him and we l

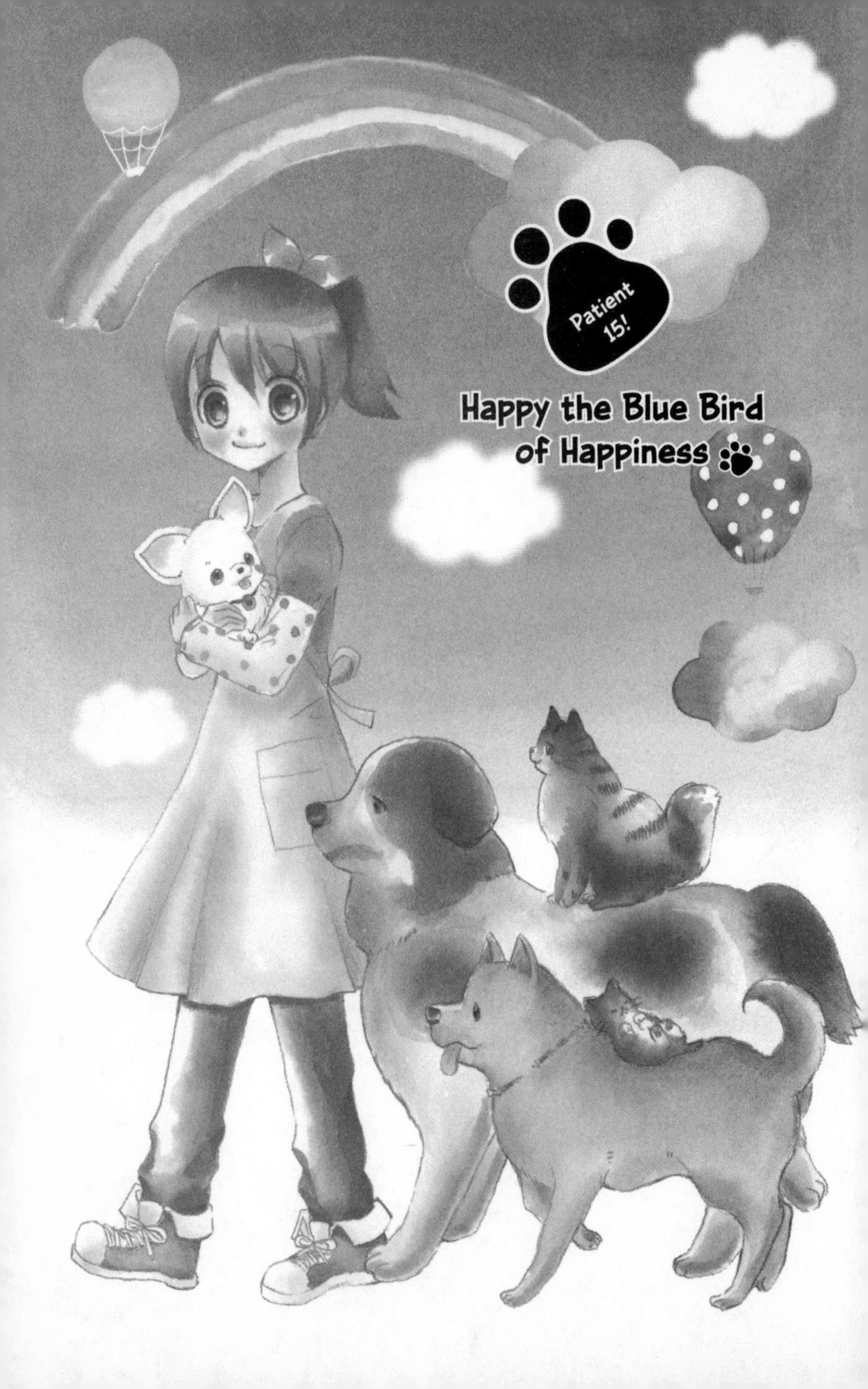
Patient 15!
Happy the Blue Bird of Happiness

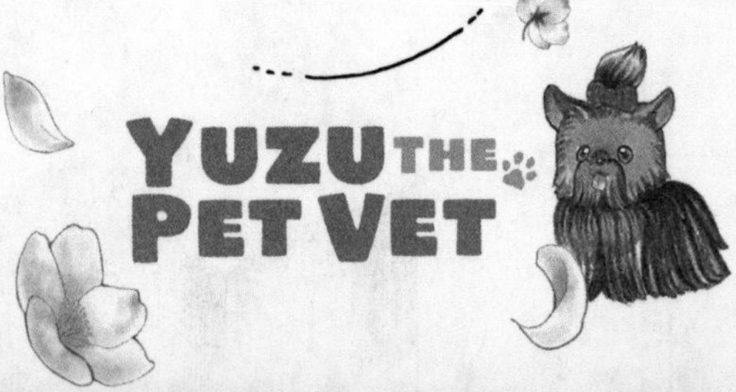
YUZU THE PET VET

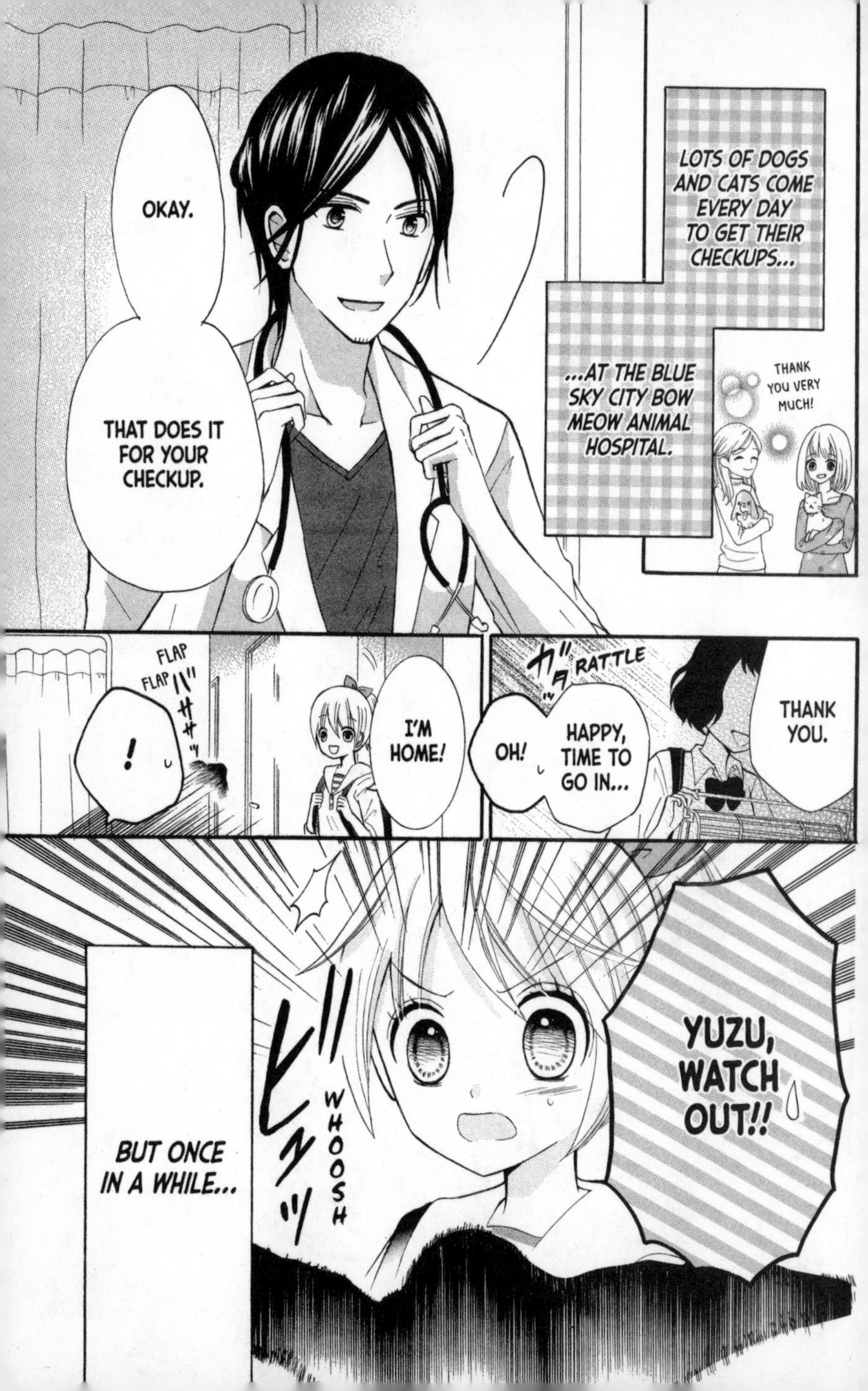

LOTS OF DOGS AND CATS COME EVERY DAY TO GET THEIR CHECKUPS...
...AT THE BLUE SKY CITY BOW MEOW ANIMAL HOSPITAL.
THANK YOU VERY MUCH!
OKAY.
THAT DOES IT FOR YOUR CHECKUP.
RATTLE
THANK YOU.
HAPPY, TIME TO GO IN...
OH!
I'M HOME!
FLAP FLAP
!
YUZU, WATCH OUT!!
WHOOSH
BUT ONCE IN A WHILE...

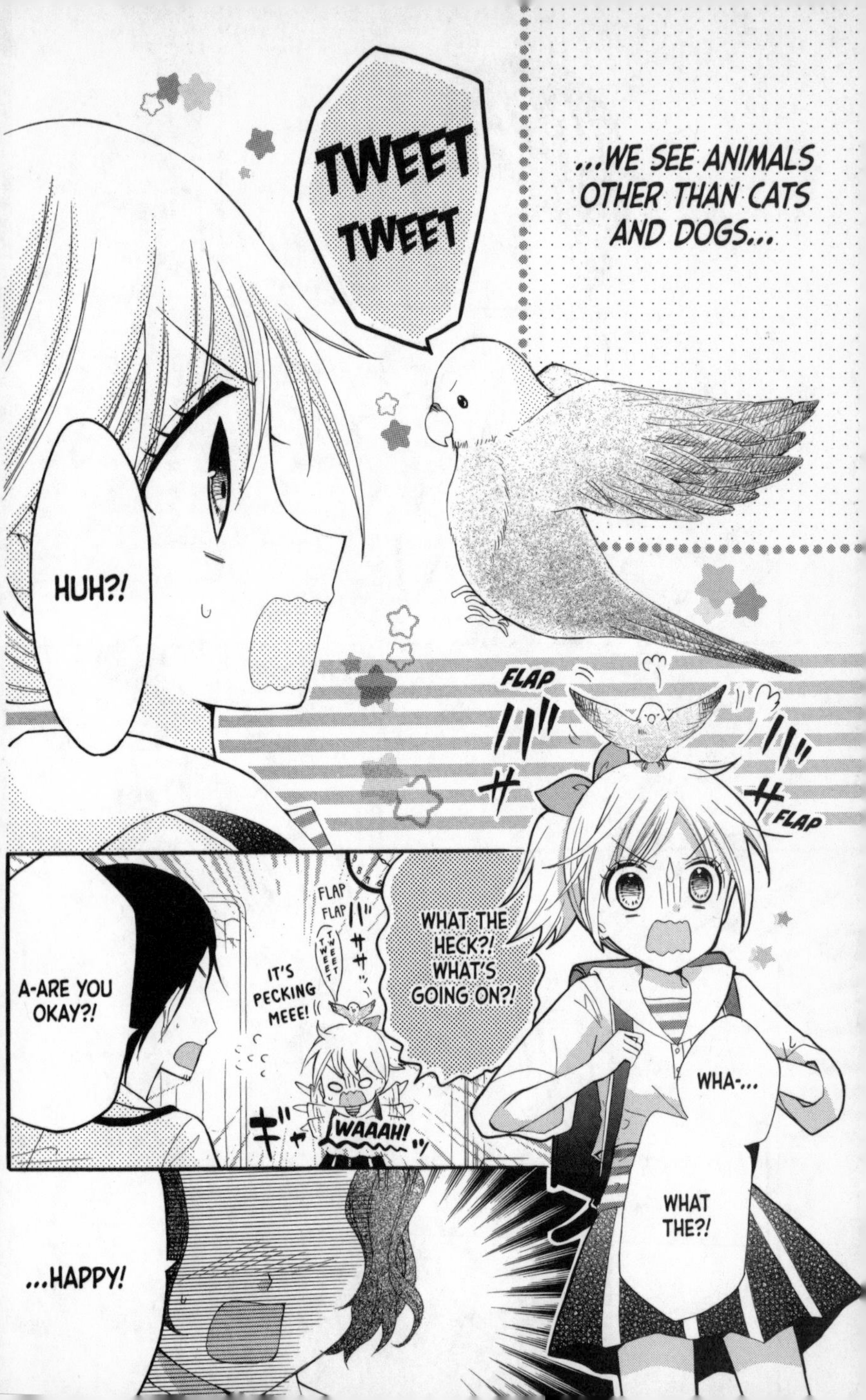
...WE SEE ANIMALS OTHER THAN CATS AND DOGS...
TWEET TWEET
HUH?!
FLAP
FLAP
WHA-...
WHAT THE?!
WHAT THE HECK?! WHAT'S GOING ON?!
FLAP FLAP
TWEET TWEET
IT'S PECKING MEEE!
WAAAH!
A-ARE YOU OKAY?!
...HAPPY!

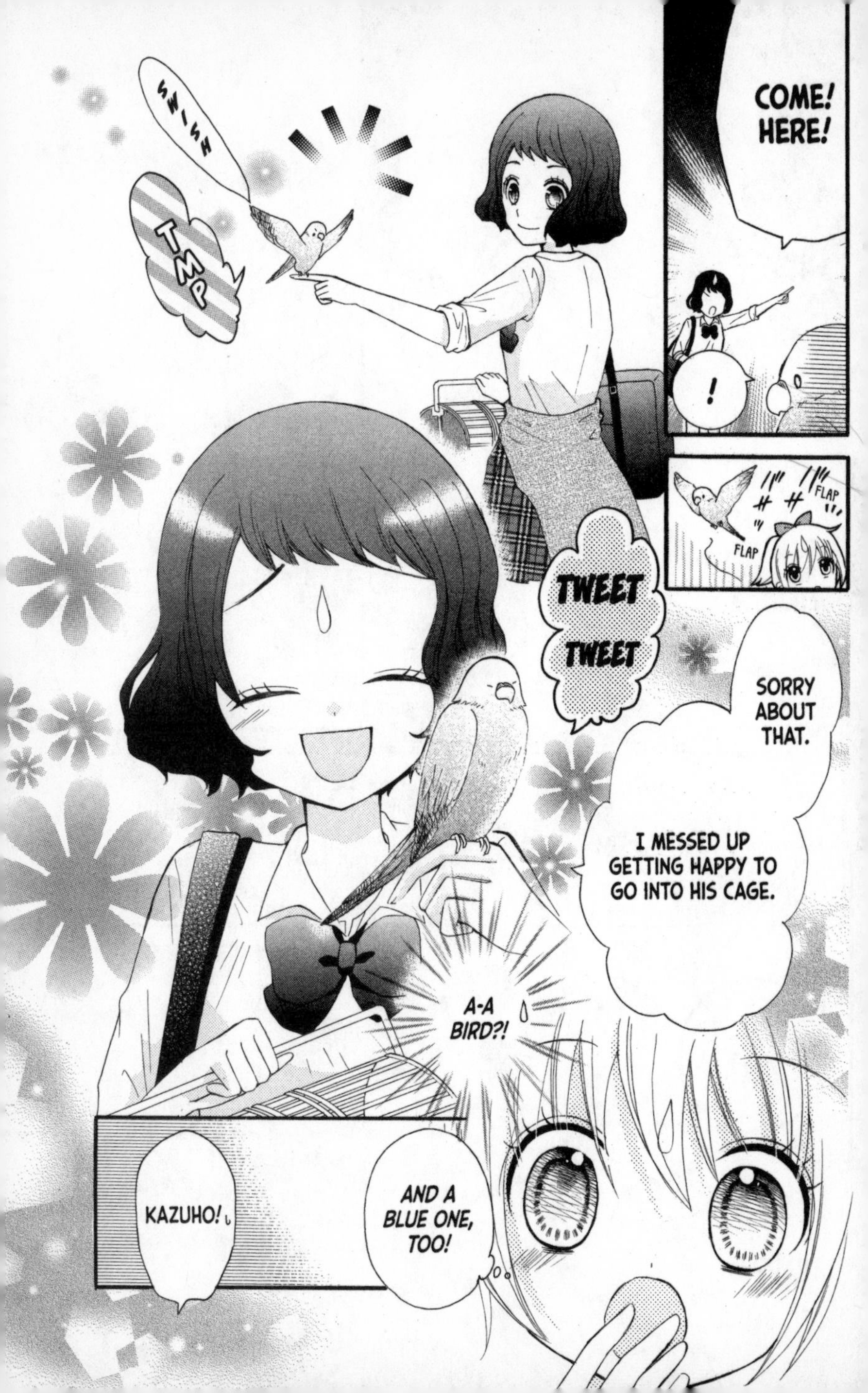

COME! HERE!
!
FLAP
FLAP
SWISH
TMP
TWEET TWEET
SORRY ABOUT THAT.
I MESSED UP GETTING HAPPY TO GO INTO HIS CAGE.
A-A BIRD?!
AND A BLUE ONE, TOO!
KAZUHO!

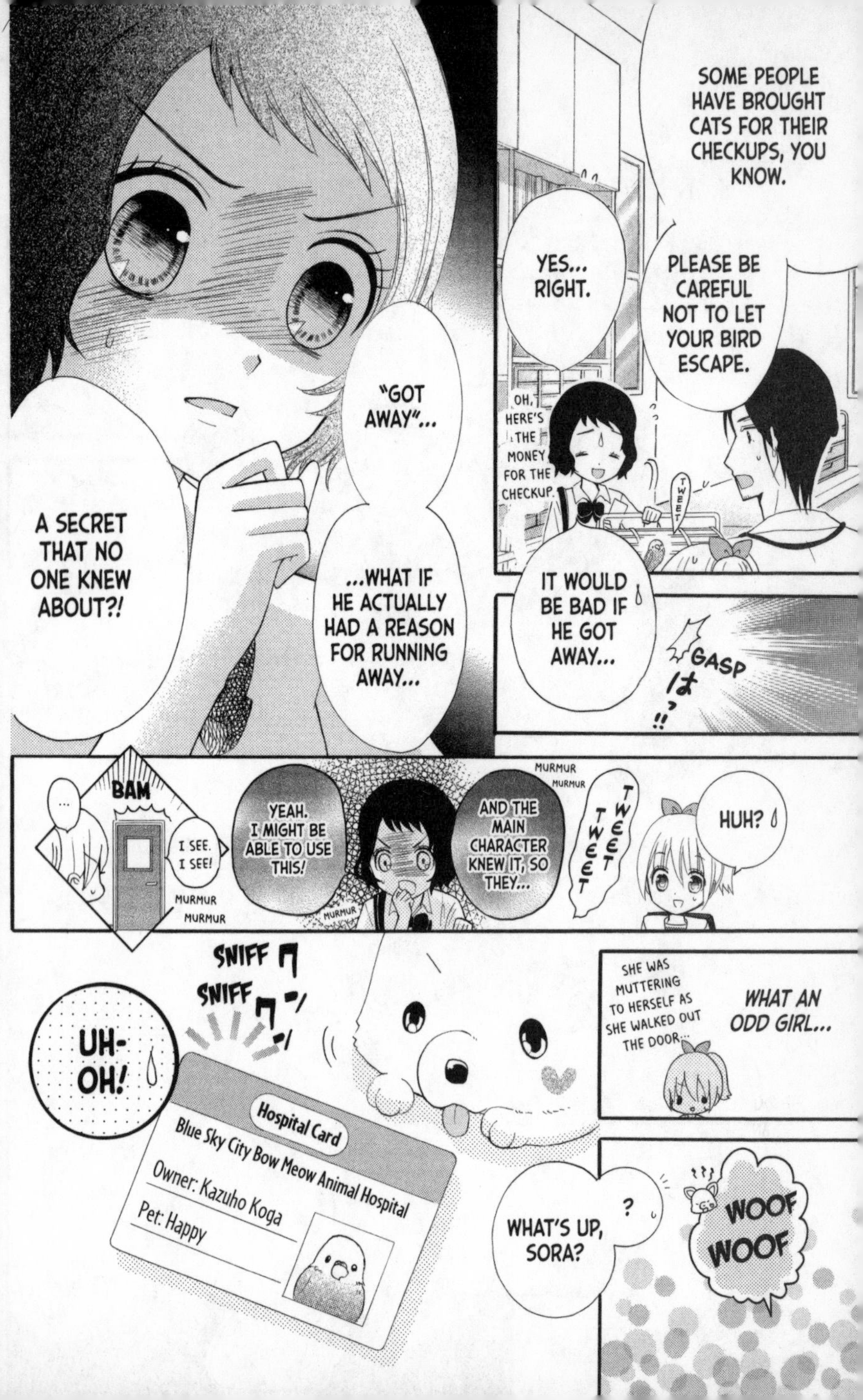
SOME PEOPLE HAVE BROUGHT CATS FOR THEIR CHECKUPS, YOU KNOW.
PLEASE BE CAREFUL NOT TO LET YOUR BIRD ESCAPE.
YES... RIGHT.
OH, HERE'S THE MONEY FOR THE CHECKUP.
TWEET
IT WOULD BE BAD IF HE GOT AWAY...
GASP
はっ!!
"GOT AWAY"...
...WHAT IF HE ACTUALLY HAD A REASON FOR RUNNING AWAY...
A SECRET THAT NO ONE KNEW ABOUT?!
HUH?
TWEET TWEET
MURMUR MURMUR
AND THE MAIN CHARACTER KNEW IT, SO THEY...
YEAH. I MIGHT BE ABLE TO USE THIS!
MURMUR
BAM
I SEE. I SEE!
MURMUR MURMUR
...
SHE WAS MUTTERING TO HERSELF AS SHE WALKED OUT THE DOOR...
WHAT AN ODD GIRL...
WOOF WOOF
?
WHAT'S UP, SORA?
SNIFF SNIFF
UH-OH!
Hospital Card
Blue Sky City Bow Meow Animal Hospital
Owner: Kazuho Koga
Pet: Happy

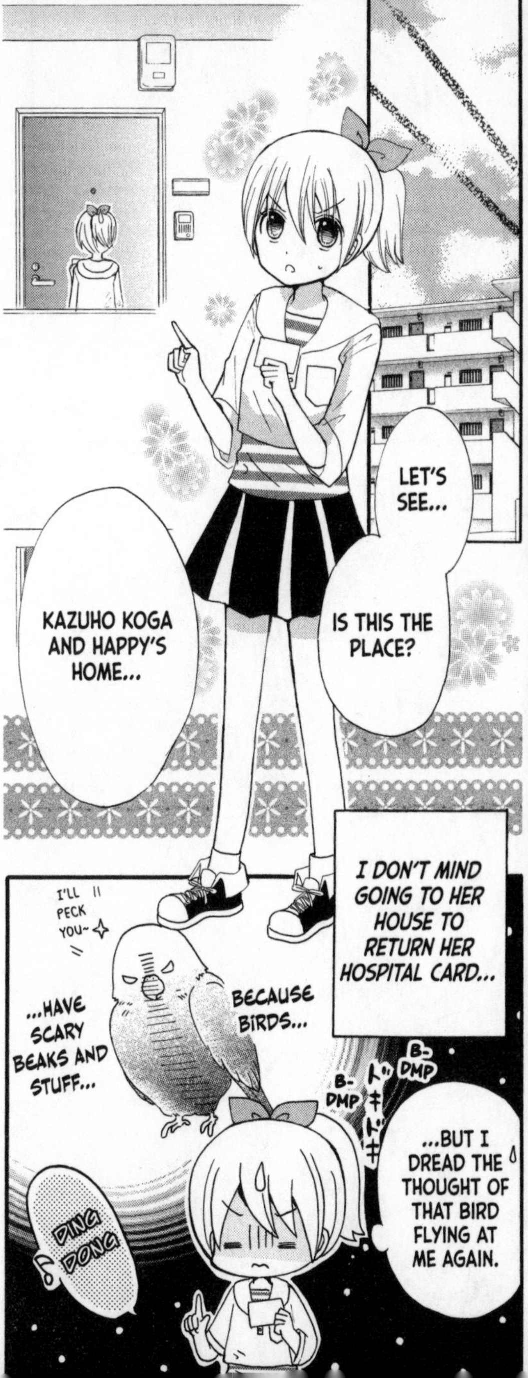
LET'S SEE...
IS THIS THE PLACE?
KAZUHO KOGA AND HAPPY'S HOME...
I DON'T MIND GOING TO HER HOUSE TO RETURN HER HOSPITAL CARD...
BECAUSE BIRDS...
I'LL PECK YOU~
...HAVE SCARY BEAKS AND STUFF...
B-DMP
ドキドキ
B-DMP
...BUT I DREAD THE THOUGHT OF THAT BIRD FLYING AT ME AGAIN.
DING DONG

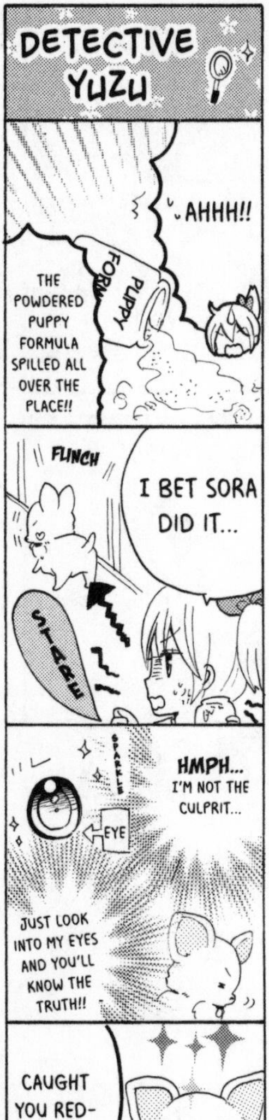
DETECTIVE YUZU
AHHH!!
PUPPY FORM
THE POWDERED PUPPY FORMULA SPILLED ALL OVER THE PLACE!!
I BET SORA DID IT...
FLINCH
STARE
HMPH... I'M NOT THE CULPRIT...
SPARKLE
EYE
JUST LOOK INTO MY EYES AND YOU'LL KNOW THE TRUTH!!
CAUGHT YOU RED-HANDED!!
COVERED IN POWDER

SORA DIDN'T KNOW HOW YUZU COULD TELL.

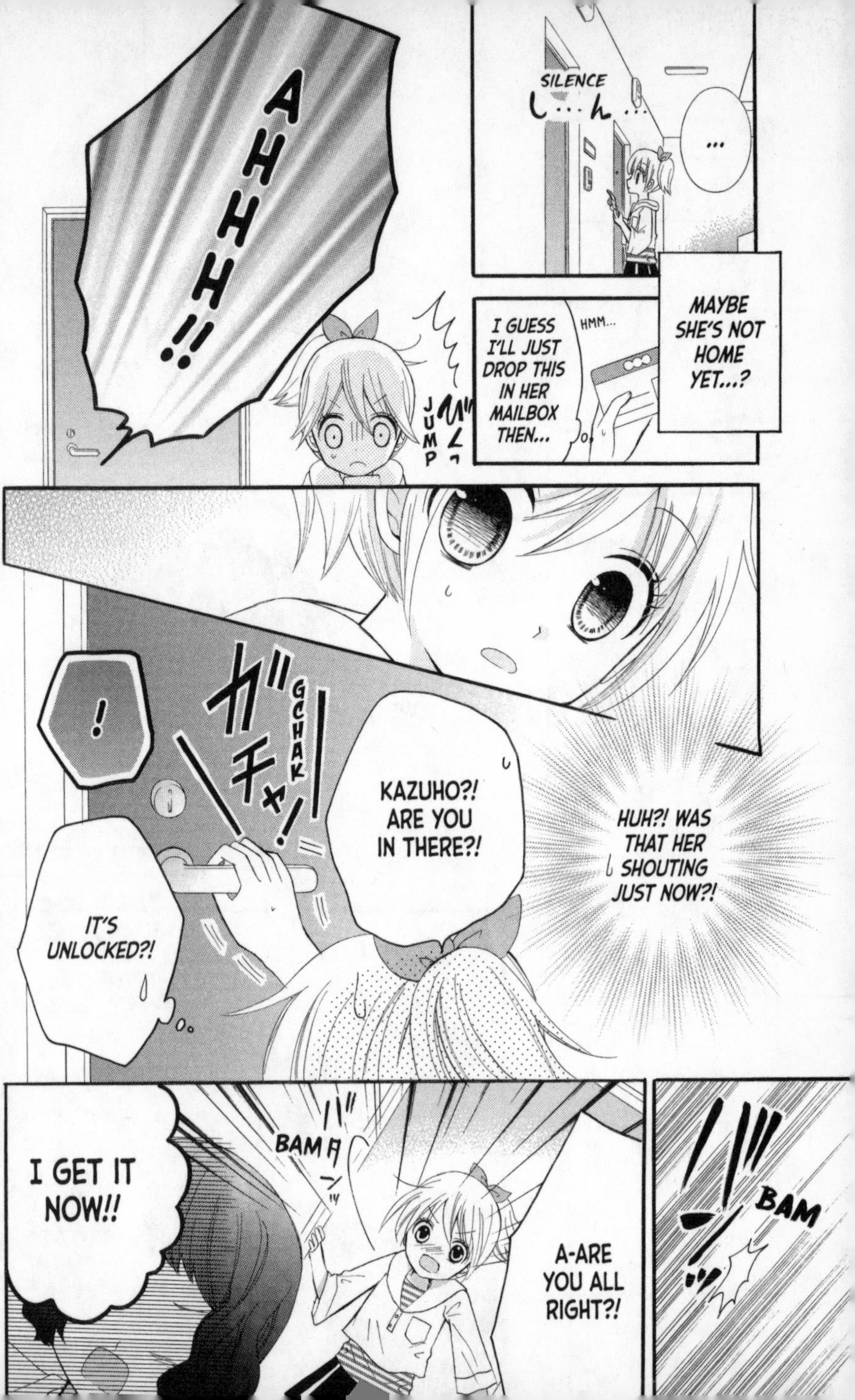
SILENCE
し…ん…
...
MAYBE SHE'S NOT HOME YET...?
HMM...
I GUESS I'LL JUST DROP THIS IN HER MAILBOX THEN...
AHHHH!!
びくっ
JUMP
HUH?! WAS THAT HER SHOUTING JUST NOW?!
KAZUHO?! ARE YOU IN THERE?!
ガチャ
GCHAK
!
IT'S UNLOCKED?!
BAM
A-ARE YOU ALL RIGHT?!
バン
BAM
I GET IT NOW!!

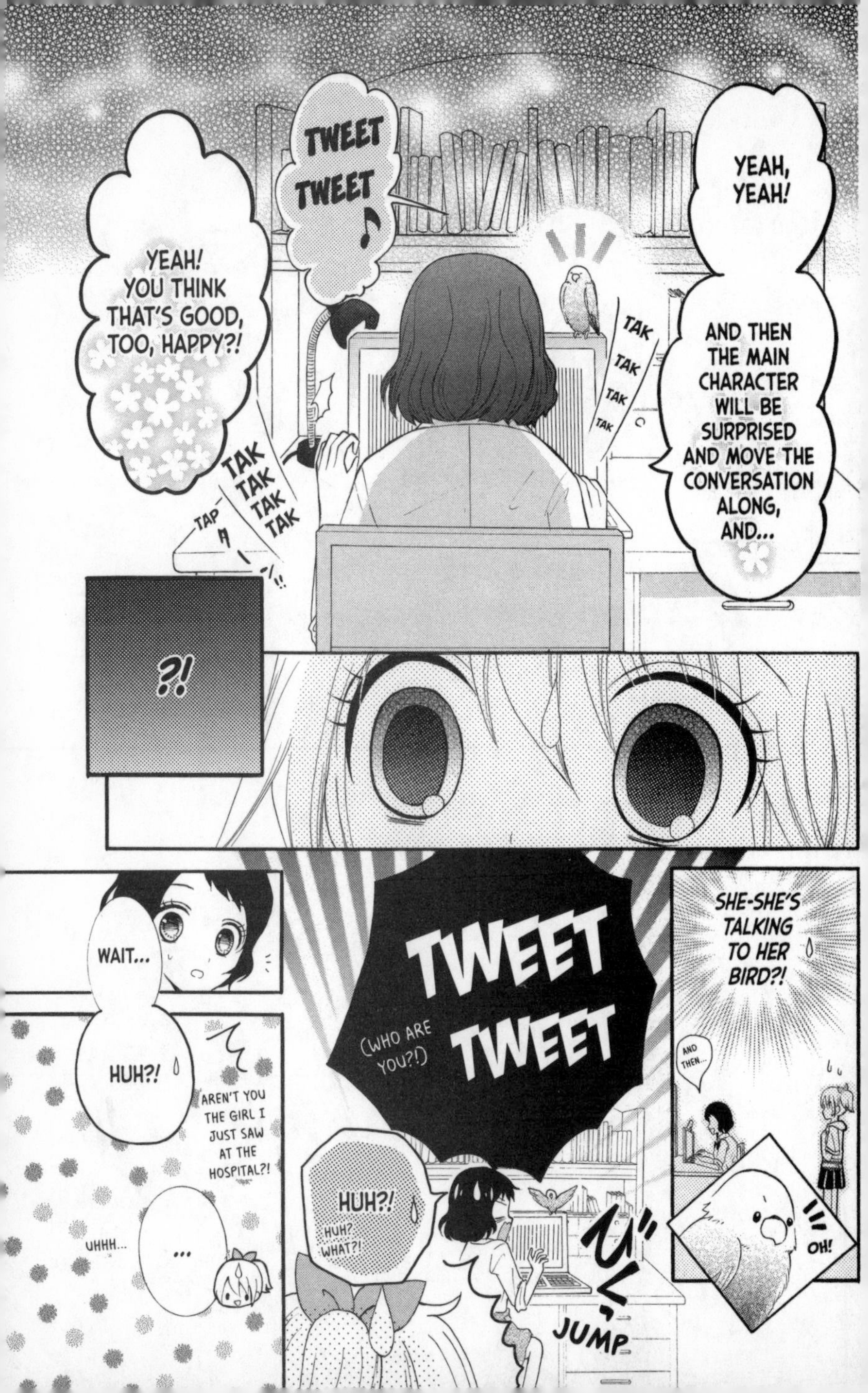
YEAH, YEAH!
AND THEN THE MAIN CHARACTER WILL BE SURPRISED AND MOVE THE CONVERSATION ALONG, AND...
TAK TAK TAK TAK
TWEET TWEET ♪
YEAH! YOU THINK THAT'S GOOD, TOO, HAPPY?!
TAK TAK TAK TAK
TAP
?!
SHE-SHE'S TALKING TO HER BIRD?!
AND THEN...
OH!
TWEET TWEET
(WHO ARE YOU?!)
HUH?!
HUH? WHAT?!
JUMP
WAIT...
HUH?!
AREN'T YOU THE GIRL I JUST SAW AT THE HOSPITAL?!
...
UHHH...

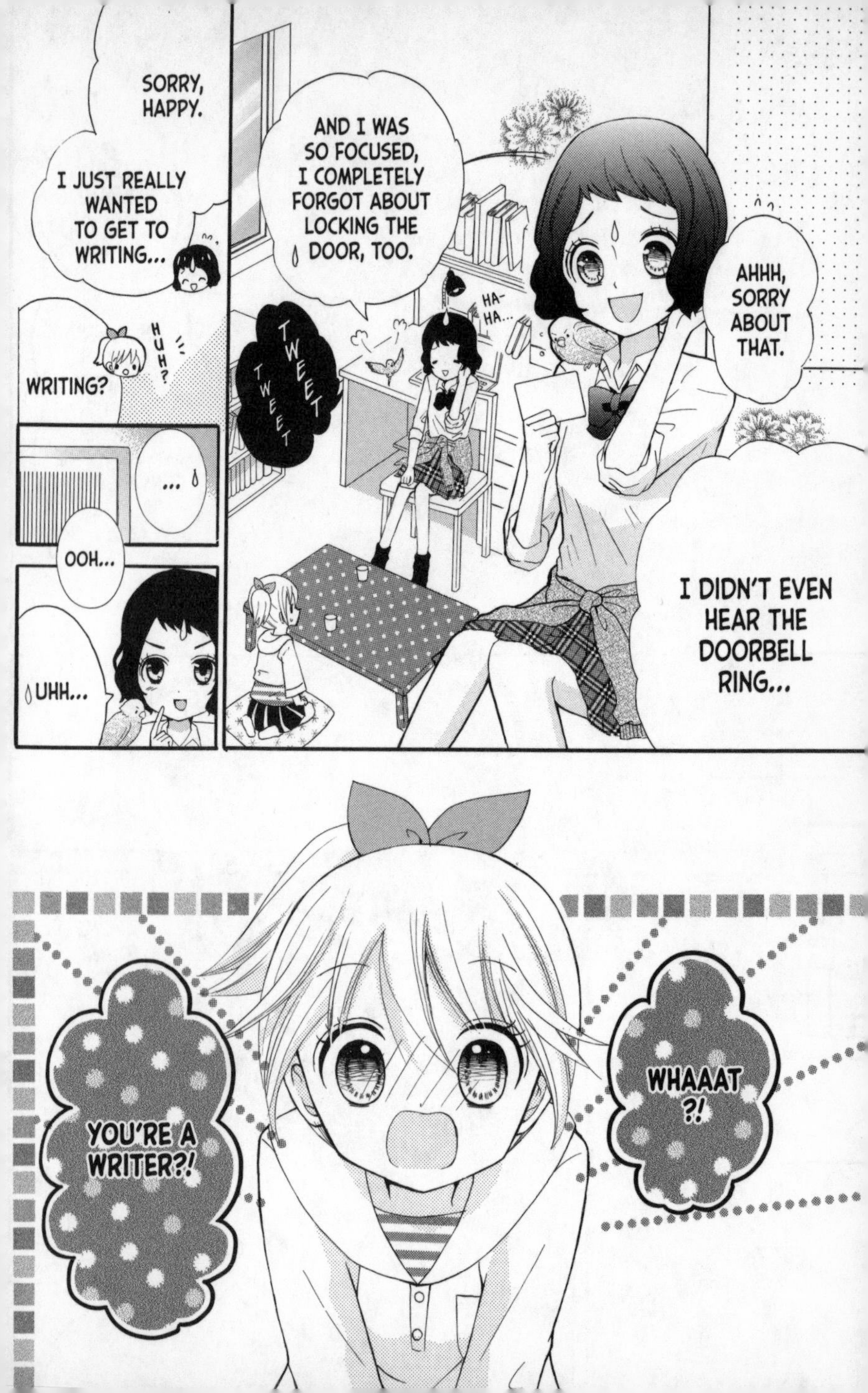
AHHH, SORRY ABOUT THAT.
I DIDN'T EVEN HEAR THE DOORBELL RING...
HA-HA...
AND I WAS SO FOCUSED, I COMPLETELY FORGOT ABOUT LOCKING THE DOOR, TOO.
TWEET TWEET
SORRY, HAPPY.
I JUST REALLY WANTED TO GET TO WRITING...
HUH?
WRITING?
...
OOH...
UHH...
WHAAAT?!
YOU'RE A WRITER?!

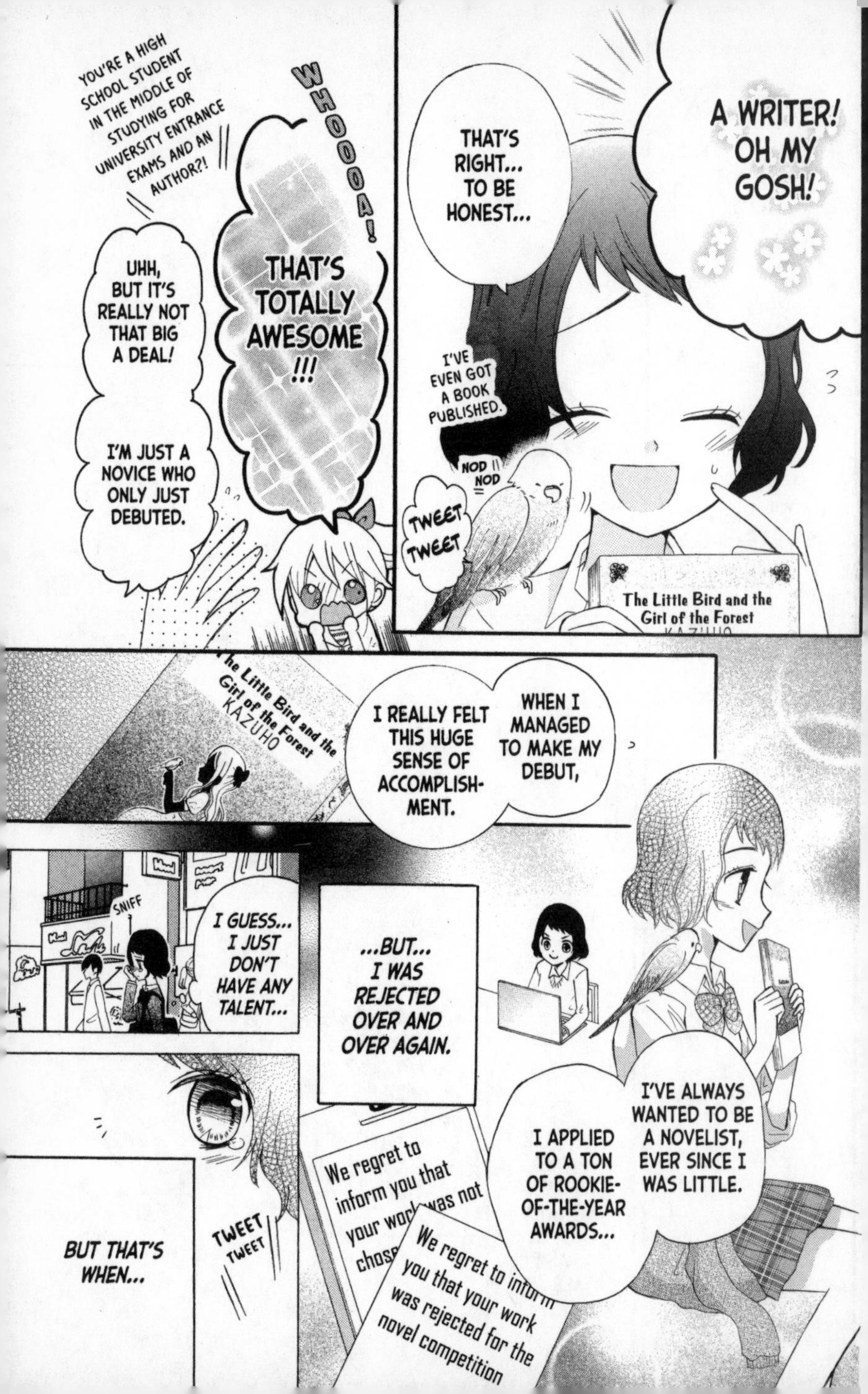
A WRITER! OH MY GOSH!
THAT'S RIGHT... TO BE HONEST...
I'VE EVEN GOT A BOOK PUBLISHED.
NOD NOD
TWEET TWEET
The Little Bird and the Girl of the Forest
WHOOOA!
THAT'S TOTALLY AWESOME!!!
YOU'RE A HIGH SCHOOL STUDENT IN THE MIDDLE OF STUDYING FOR UNIVERSITY ENTRANCE EXAMS AND AN AUTHOR?!
UHH, BUT IT'S REALLY NOT THAT BIG A DEAL!
I'M JUST A NOVICE WHO ONLY JUST DEBUTED.
I'VE ALWAYS WANTED TO BE A NOVELIST, EVER SINCE I WAS LITTLE.
I APPLIED TO A TON OF ROOKIE-OF-THE-YEAR AWARDS...
The Little Bird and the Girl of the Forest KAZUHO
WHEN I MANAGED TO MAKE MY DEBUT,
I REALLY FELT THIS HUGE SENSE OF ACCOMPLISH-MENT.
...BUT... I WAS REJECTED OVER AND OVER AGAIN.
I GUESS... I JUST DON'T HAVE ANY TALENT...
SNIFF
We regret to inform you that your work was not
We regret to inform you that your work was rejected for the novel competition
TWEET TWEET
BUT THAT'S WHEN...

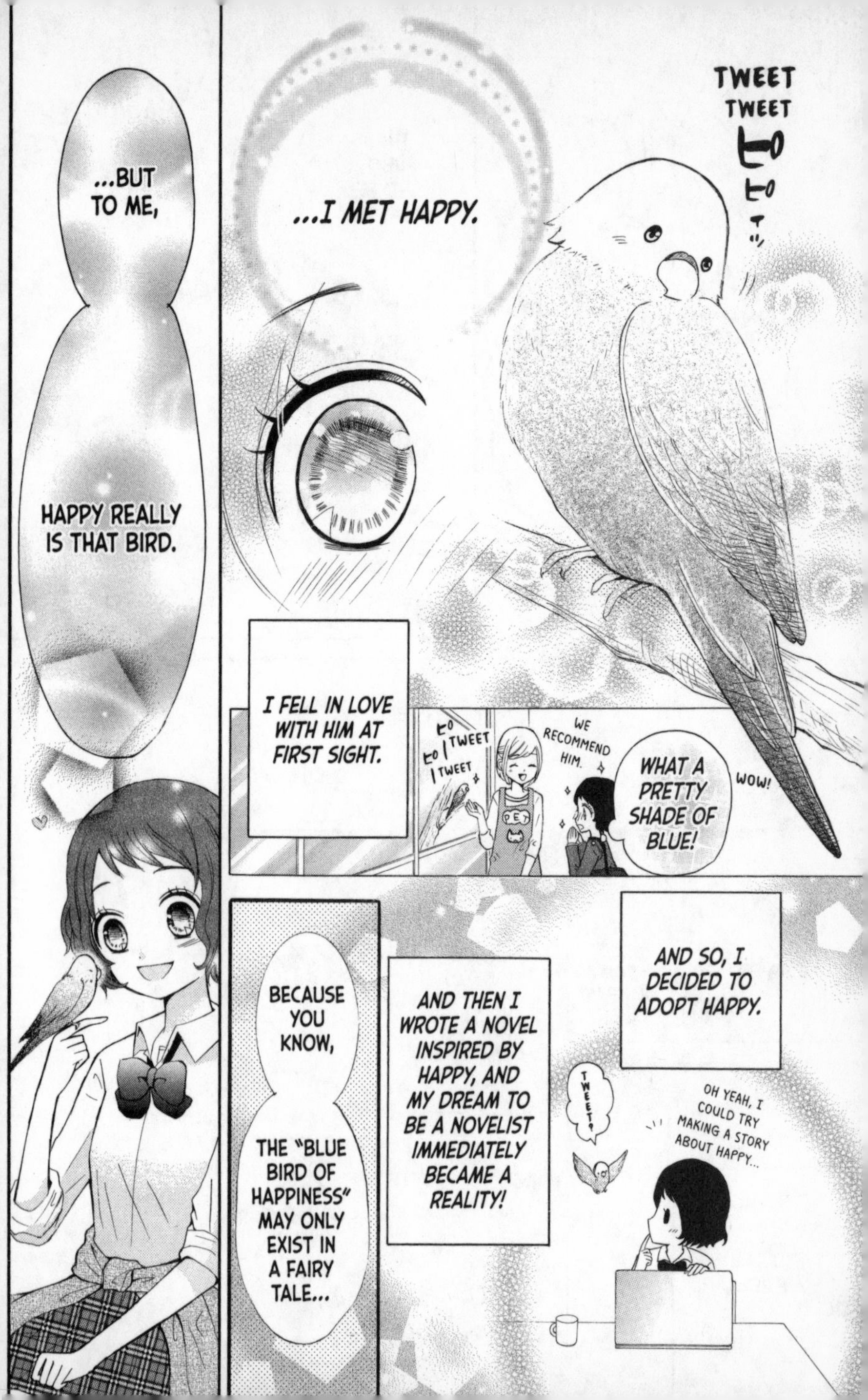
TWEET TWEET
...I MET HAPPY.
I FELL IN LOVE WITH HIM AT FIRST SIGHT.
WOW!
WHAT A PRETTY SHADE OF BLUE!
WE RECOMMEND HIM.
TWEET TWEET
AND SO, I DECIDED TO ADOPT HAPPY.
OH YEAH, I COULD TRY MAKING A STORY ABOUT HAPPY...
TWEET?
AND THEN I WROTE A NOVEL INSPIRED BY HAPPY, AND MY DREAM TO BE A NOVELIST IMMEDIATELY BECAME A REALITY!
BECAUSE YOU KNOW,
THE "BLUE BIRD OF HAPPINESS" MAY ONLY EXIST IN A FAIRY TALE...
...BUT TO ME,
HAPPY REALLY IS THAT BIRD.

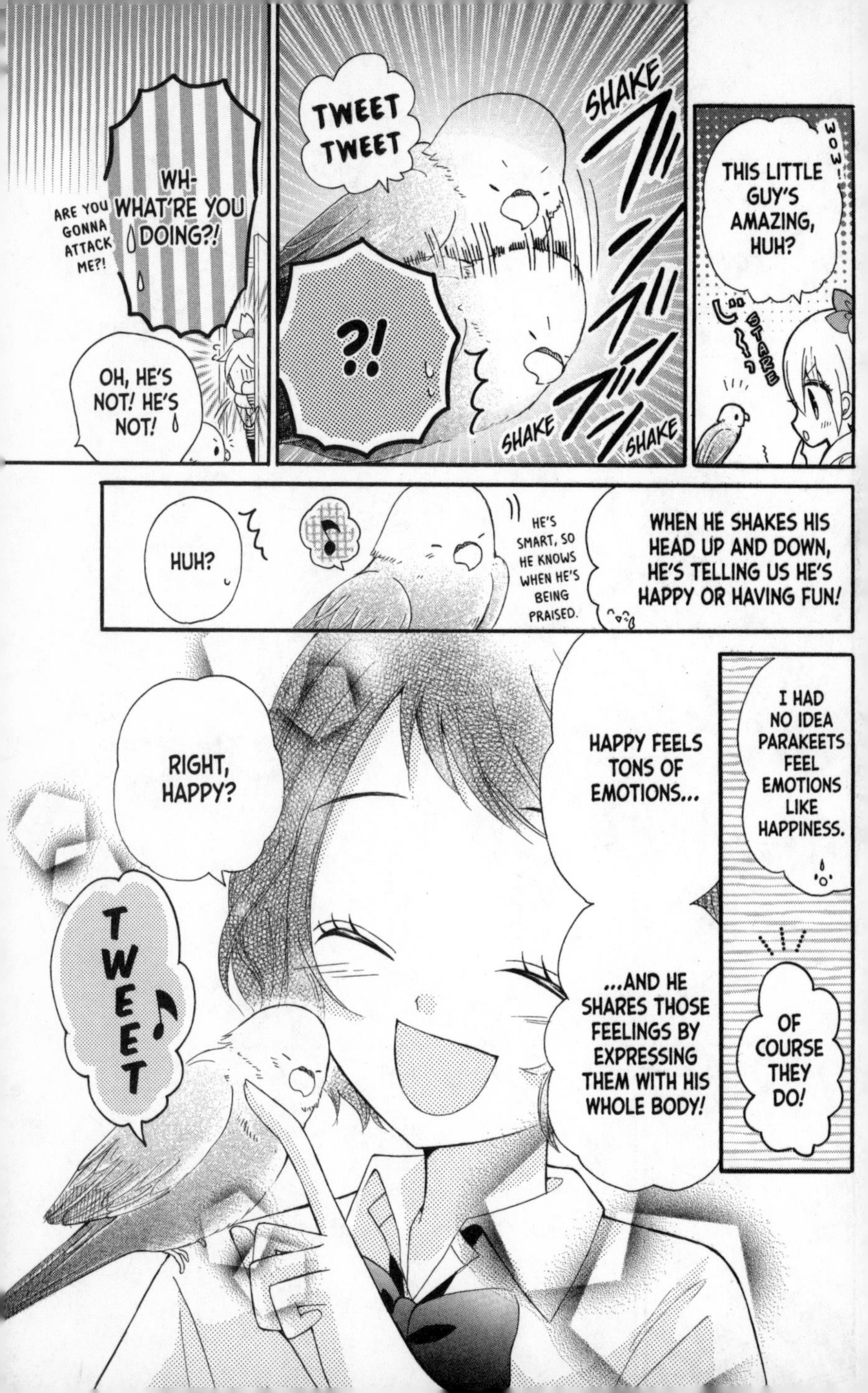
WOW!
THIS LITTLE GUY'S AMAZING, HUH?
STARE
TWEET TWEET
SHAKE
?!
SHAKE
SHAKE
WH- WHAT'RE YOU DOING?!
ARE YOU GONNA ATTACK ME?!
OH, HE'S NOT! HE'S NOT!
WHEN HE SHAKES HIS HEAD UP AND DOWN, HE'S TELLING US HE'S HAPPY OR HAVING FUN!
HE'S SMART, SO HE KNOWS WHEN HE'S BEING PRAISED.
HUH?
I HAD NO IDEA PARAKEETS FEEL EMOTIONS LIKE HAPPINESS.
OF COURSE THEY DO!
HAPPY FEELS TONS OF EMOTIONS...
...AND HE SHARES THOSE FEELINGS BY EXPRESSING THEM WITH HIS WHOLE BODY!
RIGHT, HAPPY?
TWEET

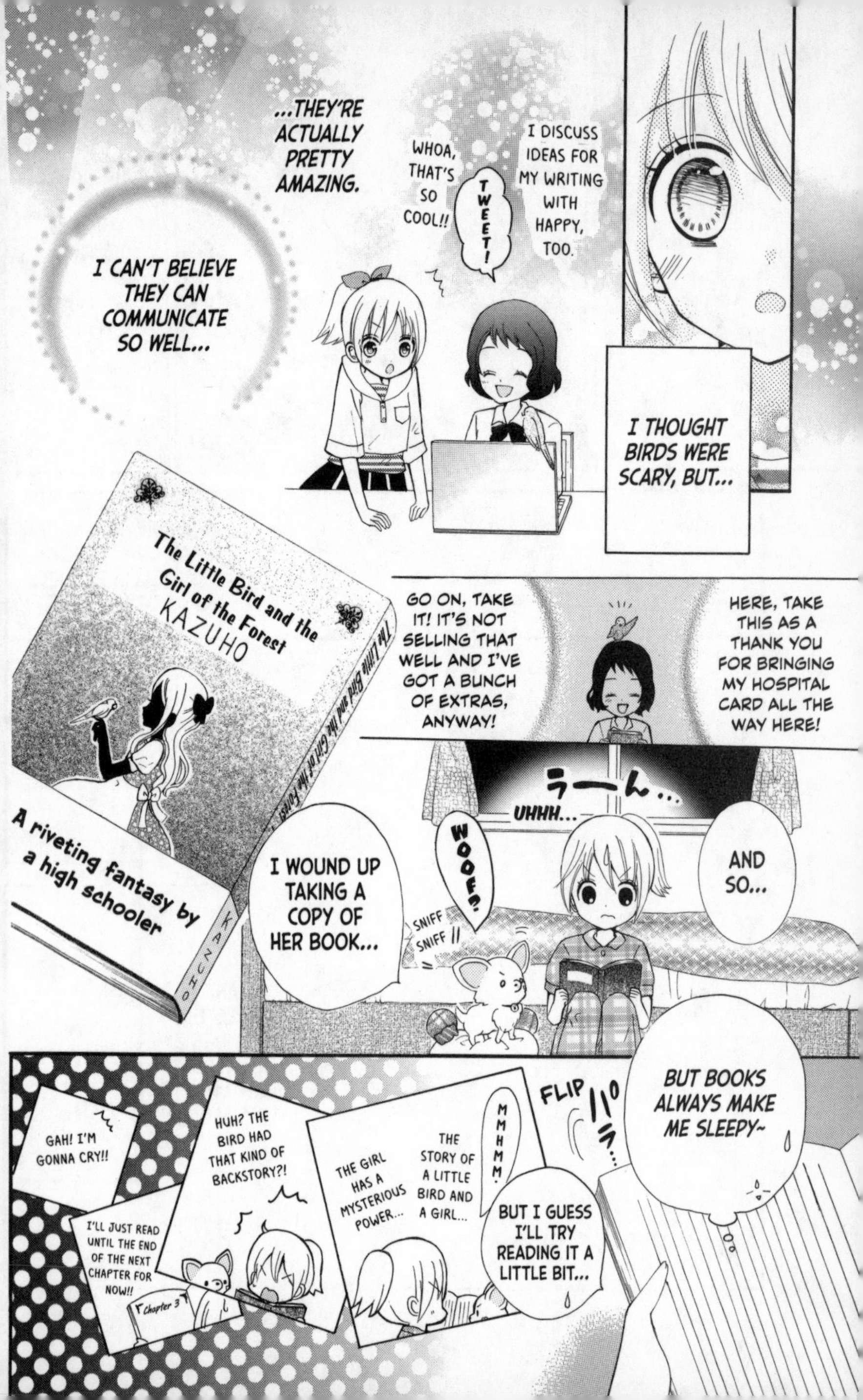
I THOUGHT BIRDS WERE SCARY, BUT...
I DISCUSS IDEAS FOR MY WRITING WITH HAPPY, TOO.
TWEET!
WHOA, THAT'S SO COOL!!
...THEY'RE ACTUALLY PRETTY AMAZING.
I CAN'T BELIEVE THEY CAN COMMUNICATE SO WELL...
HERE, TAKE THIS AS A THANK YOU FOR BRINGING MY HOSPITAL CARD ALL THE WAY HERE!
GO ON, TAKE IT! IT'S NOT SELLING THAT WELL AND I'VE GOT A BUNCH OF EXTRAS, ANYWAY!
AND SO...
ラーん…
UHHH...
WOOF?
SNIFF SNIFF
I WOUND UP TAKING A COPY OF HER BOOK...
The Little Bird and the Girl of the Forest
KAZUHO
The Little Bird and the Girl of the Forest
KAZUHO
A riveting fantasy by a high schooler
BUT BOOKS ALWAYS MAKE ME SLEEPY~
FLIP
パラ…
BUT I GUESS I'LL TRY READING IT A LITTLE BIT...
MMHMM.
THE STORY OF A LITTLE BIRD AND A GIRL...
THE GIRL HAS A MYSTERIOUS POWER...
HUH? THE BIRD HAD THAT KIND OF BACKSTORY?!
GAH! I'M GONNA CRY!!
I'LL JUST READ UNTIL THE END OF THE NEXT CHAPTER FOR NOW!!
Chapter 3

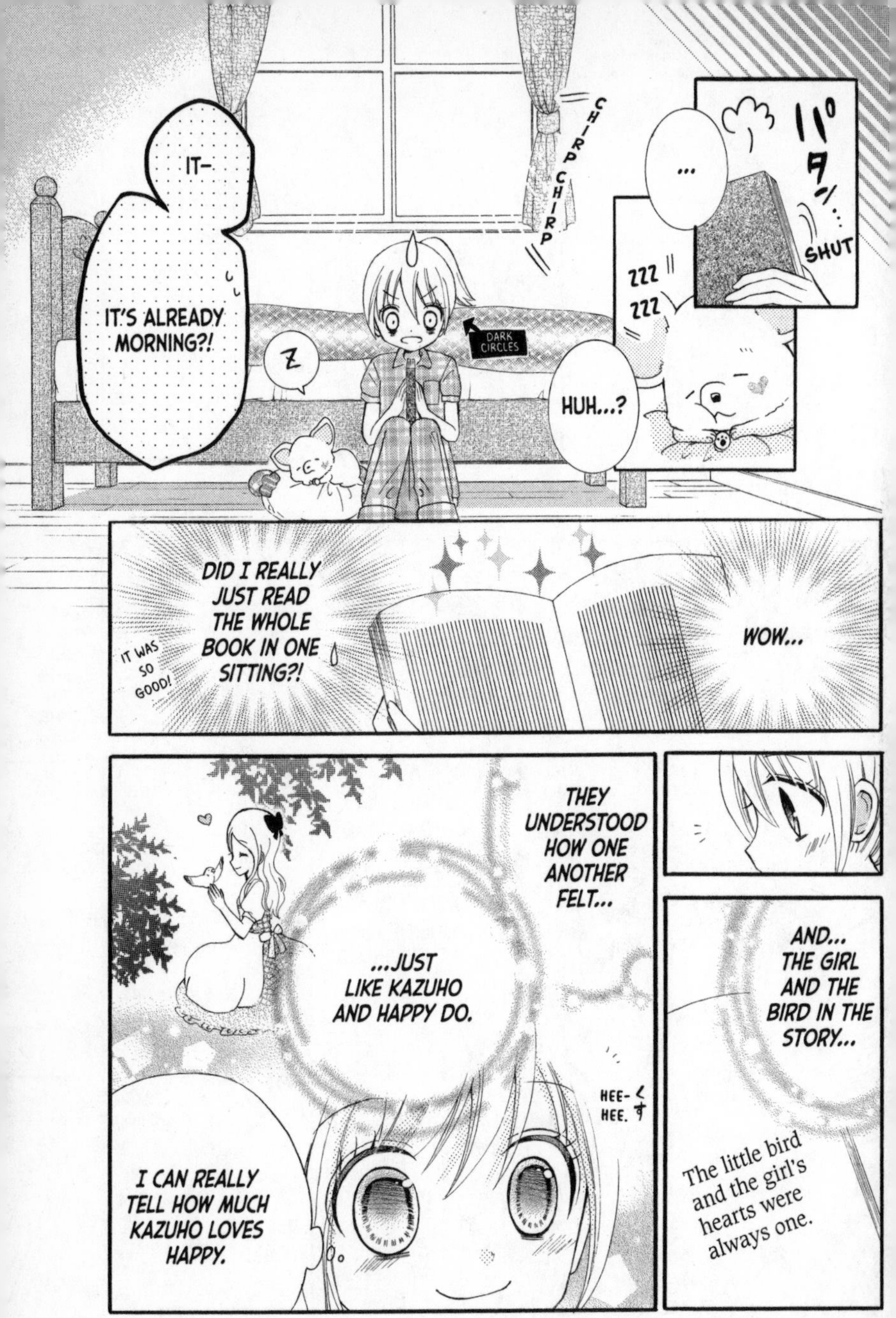
パタン…
SHUT
...
ZZZ
ZZZ
HUH...?
CHIRP CHIRP CHIRP
DARK CIRCLES
Z
IT—
IT'S ALREADY MORNING?!
WOW...
DID I REALLY JUST READ THE WHOLE BOOK IN ONE SITTING?!
IT WAS SO GOOD!
AND... THE GIRL AND THE BIRD IN THE STORY...
The little bird and the girl's hearts were always one.
THEY UNDERSTOOD HOW ONE ANOTHER FELT...
...JUST LIKE KAZUHO AND HAPPY DO.
HEE-HEE. くす
I CAN REALLY TELL HOW MUCH KAZUHO LOVES HAPPY.

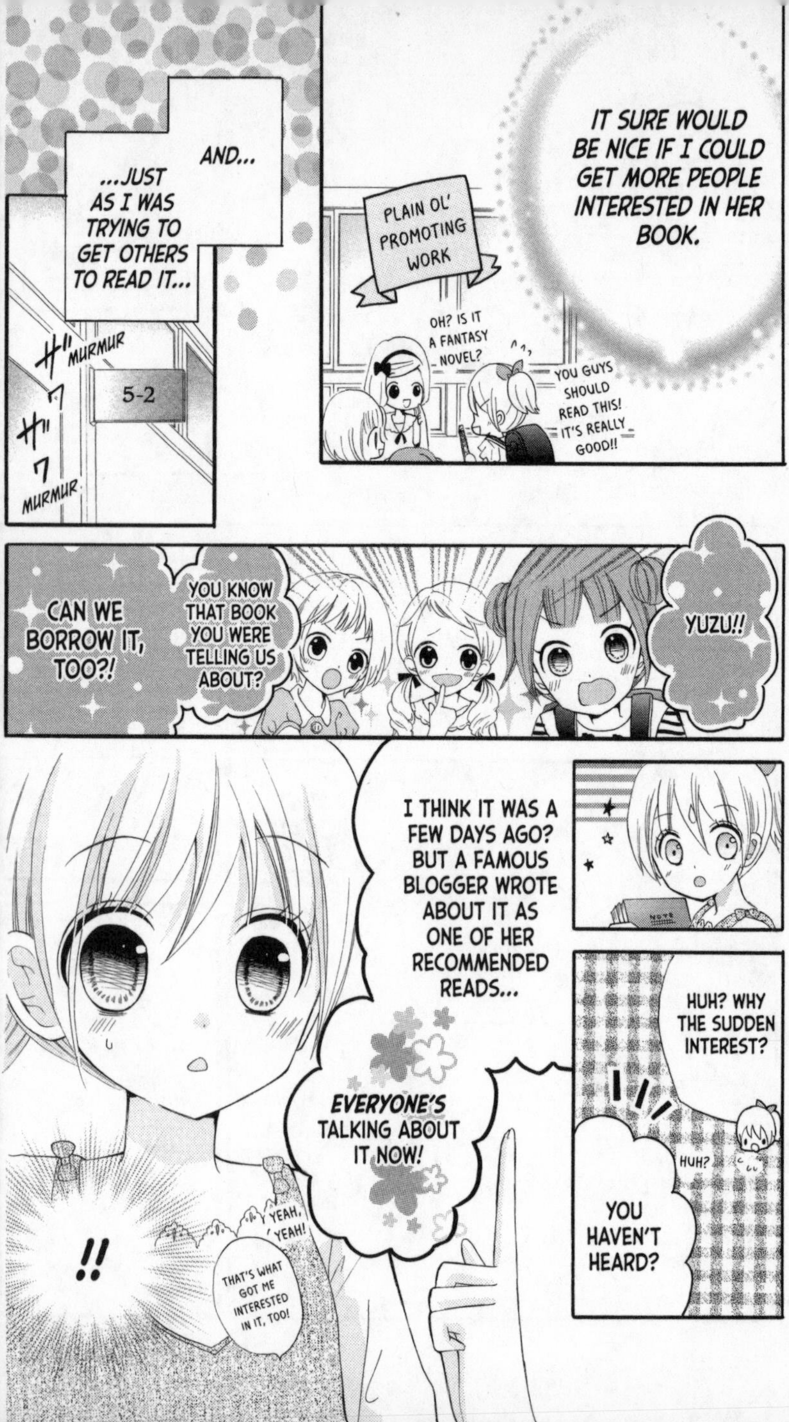

IT SURE WOULD BE NICE IF I COULD GET MORE PEOPLE INTERESTED IN HER BOOK.
PLAIN OL' PROMOTING WORK
YOU GUYS SHOULD READ THIS! IT'S REALLY GOOD!!
OH? IS IT A FANTASY NOVEL?
AND...
...JUST AS I WAS TRYING TO GET OTHERS TO READ IT...
5-2
ザワ MURMUR
ザワ MURMUR
YUZU!!
YOU KNOW THAT BOOK YOU WERE TELLING US ABOUT?
CAN WE BORROW IT, TOO?!
HUH? WHY THE SUDDEN INTEREST?
HUH?
YOU HAVEN'T HEARD?
I THINK IT WAS A FEW DAYS AGO? BUT A FAMOUS BLOGGER WROTE ABOUT IT AS ONE OF HER RECOMMENDED READS...
EVERYONE'S TALKING ABOUT IT NOW!
YEAH, YEAH!
THAT'S WHAT GOT ME INTERESTED IN IT, TOO!
!!

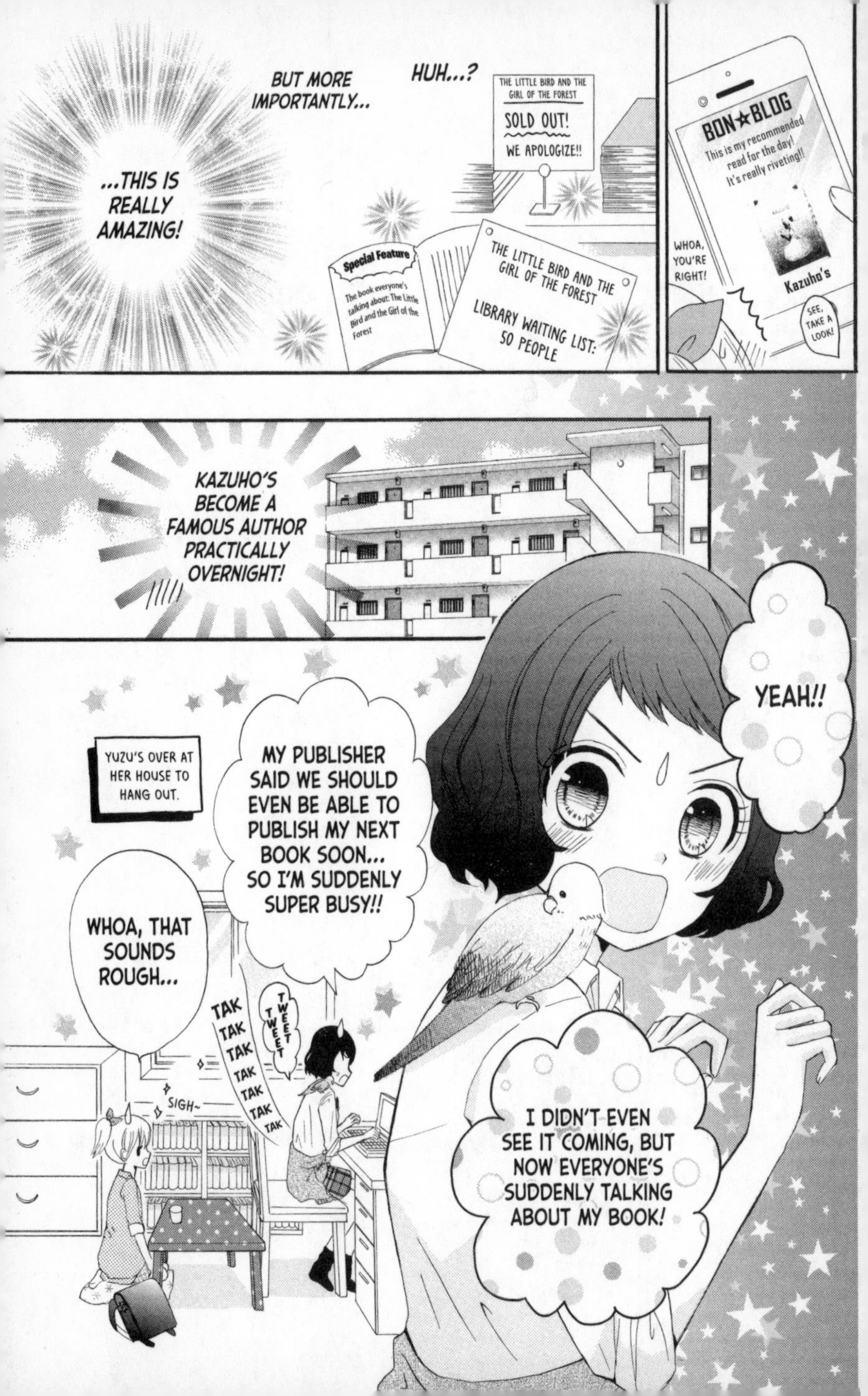
BON☆BLOG
This is my recommended read for the day! It's really riveting!!
Kazuho's
WHOA, YOU'RE RIGHT!
SEE, TAKE A LOOK!
HUH...?
THE LITTLE BIRD AND THE GIRL OF THE FOREST
SOLD OUT!
WE APOLOGIZE!!
BUT MORE IMPORTANTLY...
...THIS IS REALLY AMAZING!
THE LITTLE BIRD AND THE GIRL OF THE FOREST
LIBRARY WAITING LIST: 50 PEOPLE
Special Feature
The book everyone's talking about: The Little Bird and the Girl of the Forest
KAZUHO'S BECOME A FAMOUS AUTHOR PRACTICALLY OVERNIGHT!
YEAH!!
I DIDN'T EVEN SEE IT COMING, BUT NOW EVERYONE'S SUDDENLY TALKING ABOUT MY BOOK!
YUZU'S OVER AT HER HOUSE TO HANG OUT.
MY PUBLISHER SAID WE SHOULD EVEN BE ABLE TO PUBLISH MY NEXT BOOK SOON... SO I'M SUDDENLY SUPER BUSY!!
WHOA, THAT SOUNDS ROUGH...
TWEET TWEET
TAK TAK TAK TAK TAK TAK TAK
SIGH~

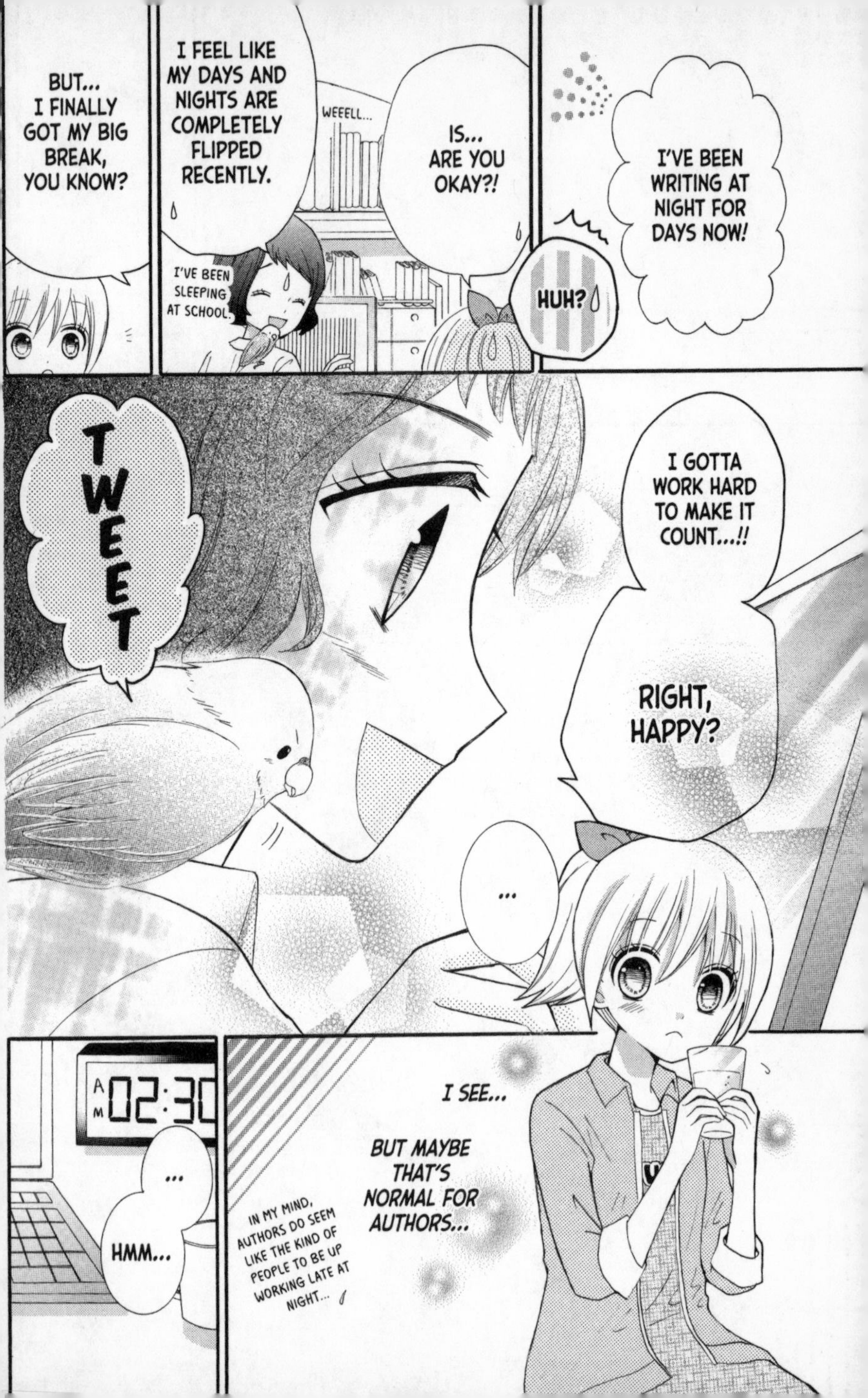
I'VE BEEN WRITING AT NIGHT FOR DAYS NOW!
HUH?
IS... ARE YOU OKAY?!
WEEELL...
I FEEL LIKE MY DAYS AND NIGHTS ARE COMPLETELY FLIPPED RECENTLY.
I'VE BEEN SLEEPING AT SCHOOL.
BUT... I FINALLY GOT MY BIG BREAK, YOU KNOW?
I GOTTA WORK HARD TO MAKE IT COUNT...!!
RIGHT, HAPPY?
TWEET
...
I SEE...
BUT MAYBE THAT'S NORMAL FOR AUTHORS...
IN MY MIND, AUTHORS DO SEEM LIKE THE KIND OF PEOPLE TO BE UP WORKING LATE AT NIGHT...
AM 02:30
...
HMM...

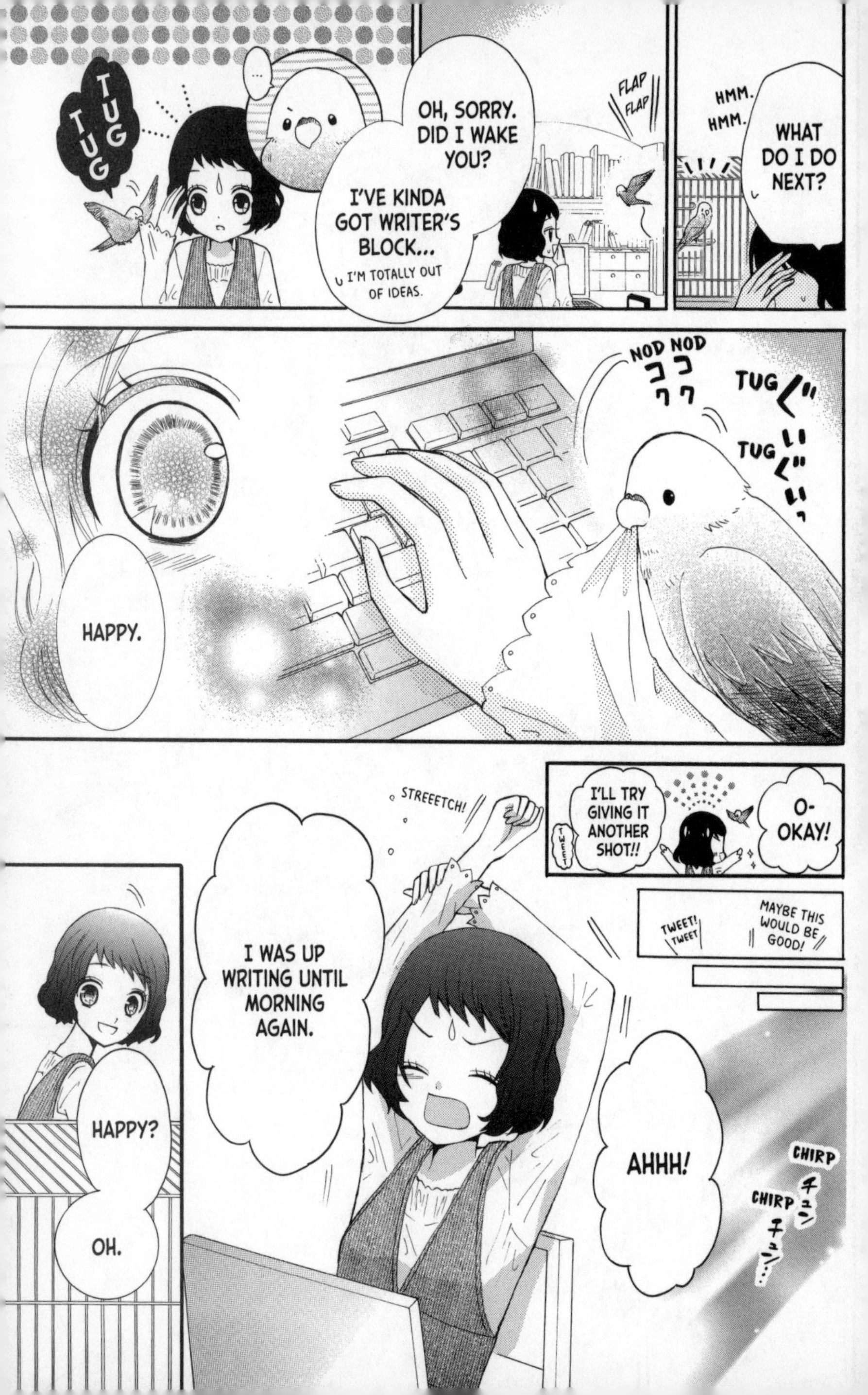
HMM. HMM.
WHAT DO I DO NEXT?
FLAP FLAP
...
OH, SORRY. DID I WAKE YOU?
I'VE KINDA GOT WRITER'S BLOCK...
I'M TOTALLY OUT OF IDEAS.
TUG TUG
NOD NOD
TUG TUG
HAPPY.
O-OKAY!
I'LL TRY GIVING IT ANOTHER SHOT!!
TWEET
MAYBE THIS WOULD BE GOOD!
TWEET! TWEET!
CHIRP CHIRP
AHHH!
STREEETCH!
I WAS UP WRITING UNTIL MORNING AGAIN.
HAPPY?
OH.

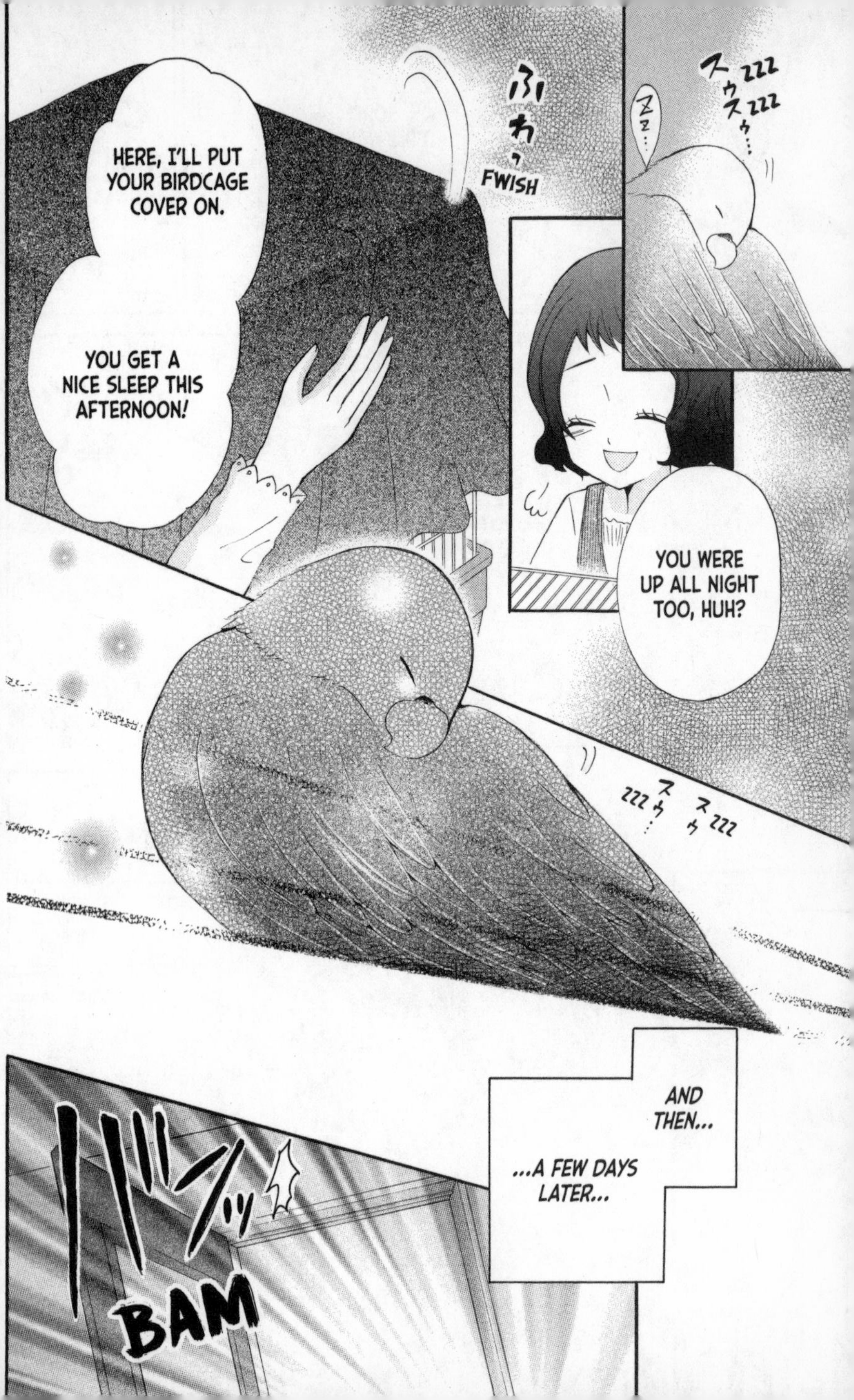

スゥ zzz スゥ… zzz
Zz…
YOU WERE UP ALL NIGHT TOO, HUH?
ふわっ
FWISH
HERE, I'LL PUT YOUR BIRDCAGE COVER ON.
YOU GET A NICE SLEEP THIS AFTERNOON!
スゥ zzz スゥ… zzz
AND THEN…
…A FEW DAYS LATER…
BAM

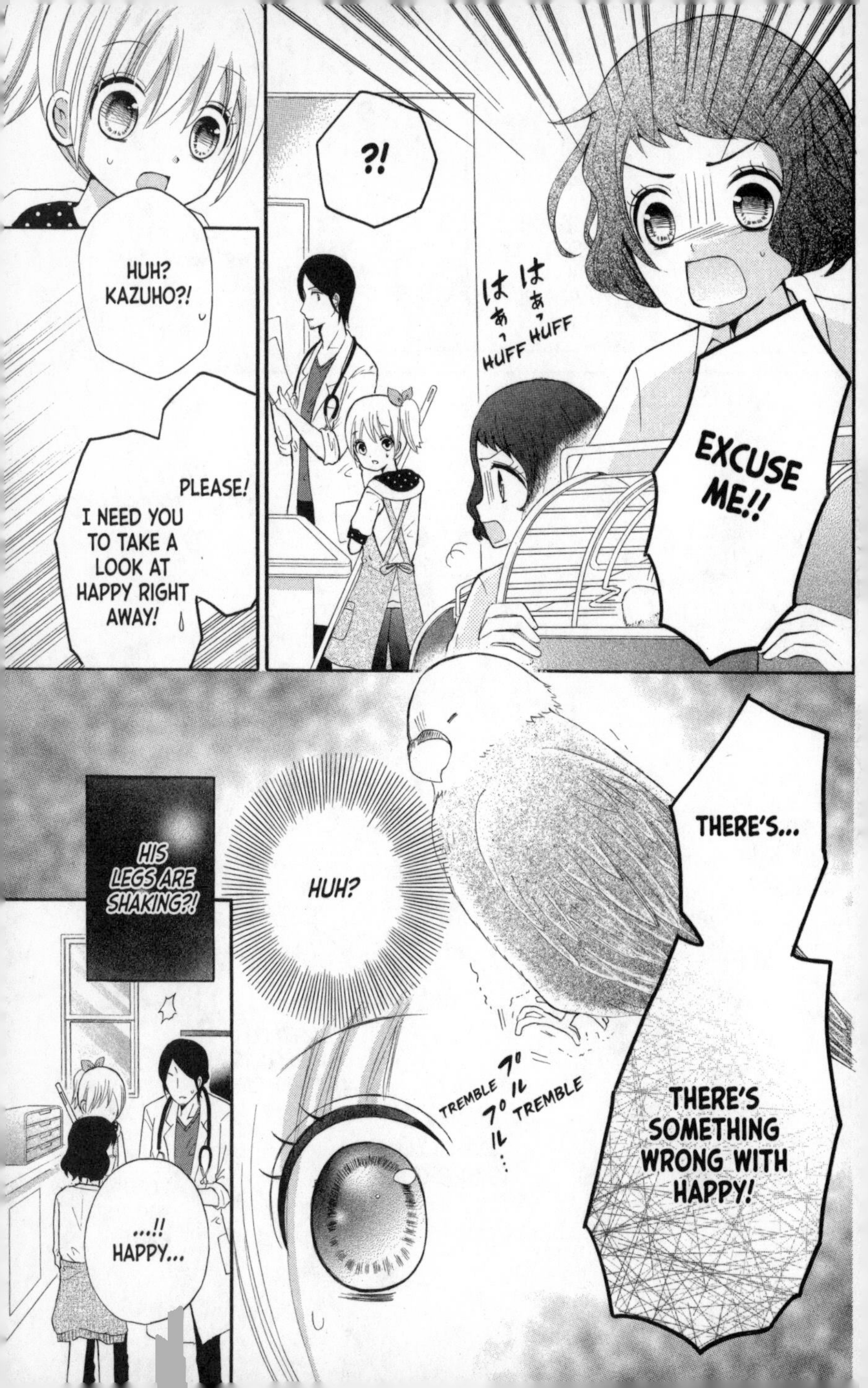

EXCUSE ME!!
はぁっ はぁっ
HUFF HUFF
?!
HUH? KAZUHO?!
PLEASE! I NEED YOU TO TAKE A LOOK AT HAPPY RIGHT AWAY!
THERE'S...
THERE'S SOMETHING WRONG WITH HAPPY!
ブルブル…
TREMBLE TREMBLE
HUH?
HIS LEGS ARE SHAKING?!
...!! HAPPY...

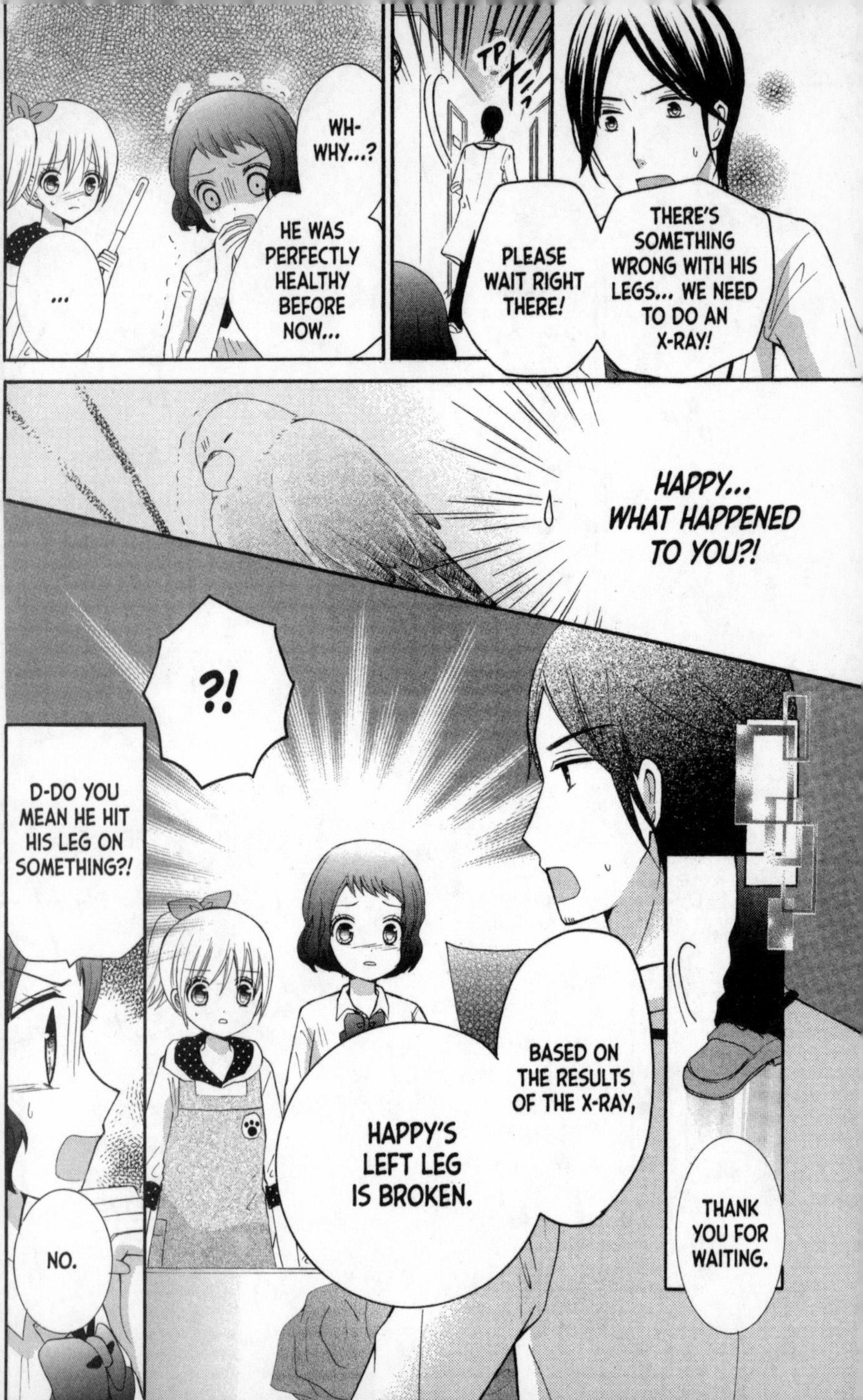
TP
THERE'S SOMETHING WRONG WITH HIS LEGS... WE NEED TO DO AN X-RAY!
PLEASE WAIT RIGHT THERE!
WH- WHY...?
HE WAS PERFECTLY HEALTHY BEFORE NOW...
...
HAPPY... WHAT HAPPENED TO YOU?!
THANK YOU FOR WAITING.
BASED ON THE RESULTS OF THE X-RAY,
HAPPY'S LEFT LEG IS BROKEN.
?!
D-DO YOU MEAN HE HIT HIS LEG ON SOMETHING?!
NO.

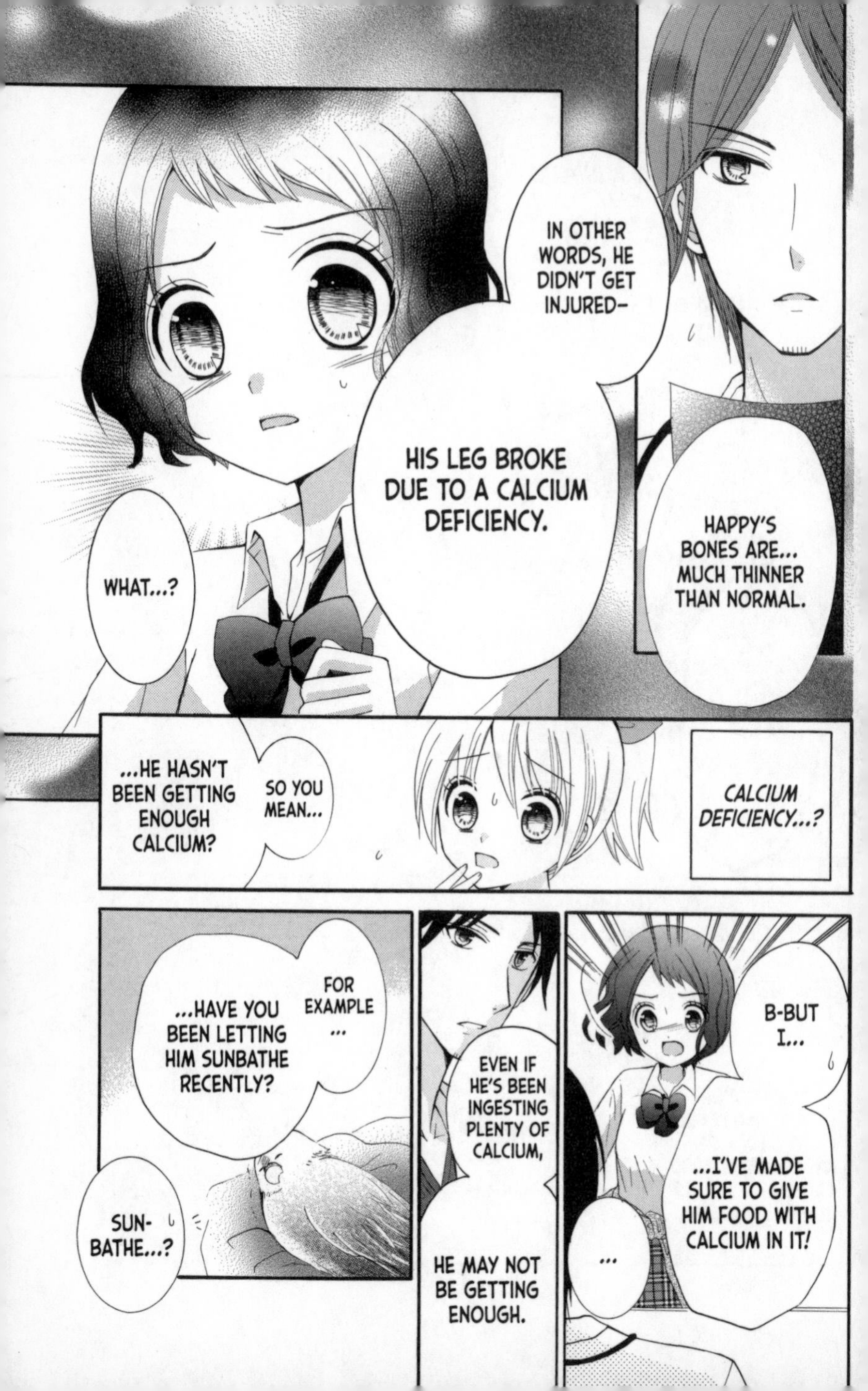
HAPPY'S BONES ARE... MUCH THINNER THAN NORMAL.
IN OTHER WORDS, HE DIDN'T GET INJURED–
HIS LEG BROKE DUE TO A CALCIUM DEFICIENCY.
WHAT...?
CALCIUM DEFICIENCY...?
SO YOU MEAN...
...HE HASN'T BEEN GETTING ENOUGH CALCIUM?
B-BUT I...
...I'VE MADE SURE TO GIVE HIM FOOD WITH CALCIUM IN IT!
...
EVEN IF HE'S BEEN INGESTING PLENTY OF CALCIUM,
HE MAY NOT BE GETTING ENOUGH.
FOR EXAMPLE...
...HAVE YOU BEEN LETTING HIM SUNBATHE RECENTLY?
SUN-BATHE...?

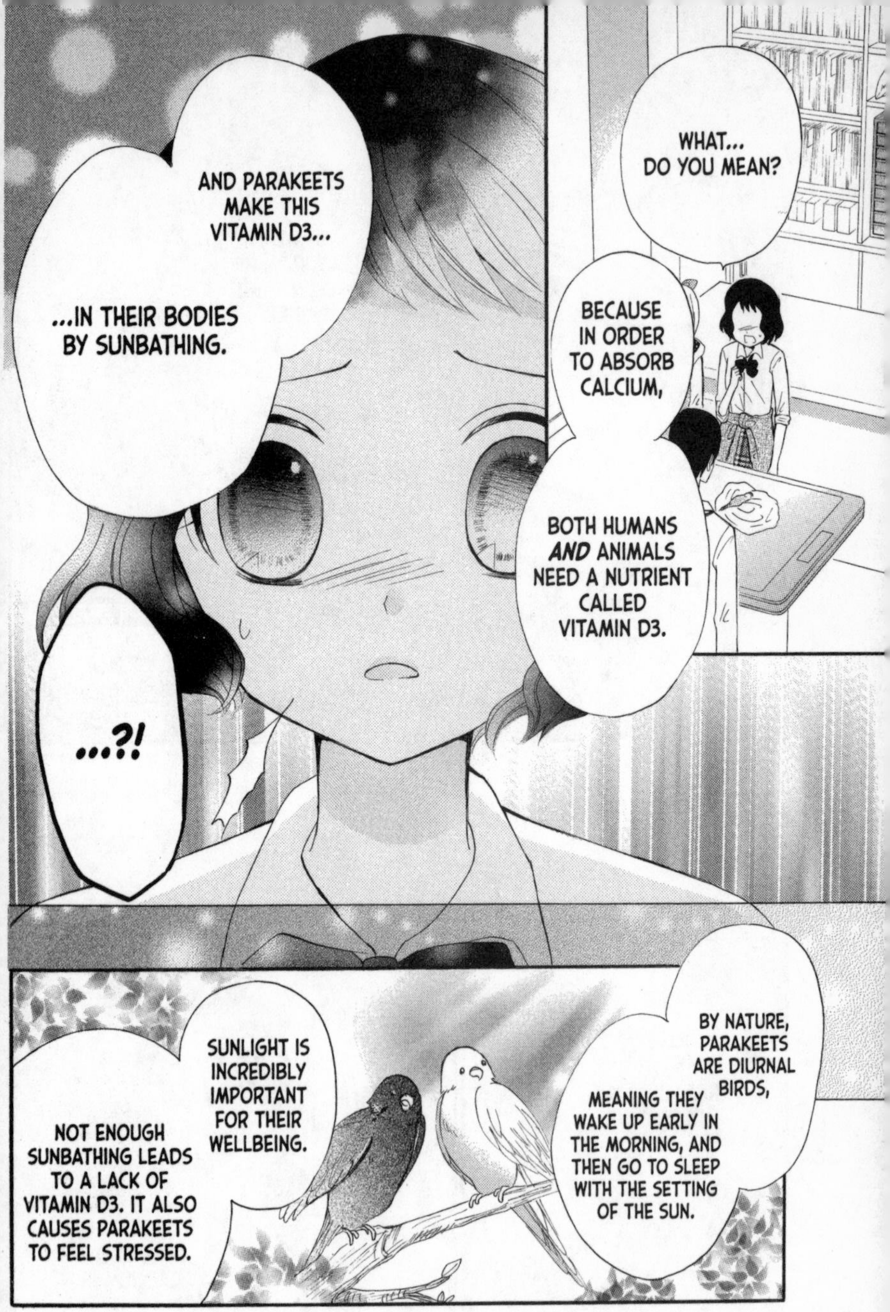
WHAT... DO YOU MEAN?
BECAUSE IN ORDER TO ABSORB CALCIUM,
BOTH HUMANS *AND* ANIMALS NEED A NUTRIENT CALLED VITAMIN D3.
AND PARAKEETS MAKE THIS VITAMIN D3...
...IN THEIR BODIES BY SUNBATHING.
...?!
BY NATURE, PARAKEETS ARE DIURNAL BIRDS,
MEANING THEY WAKE UP EARLY IN THE MORNING, AND THEN GO TO SLEEP WITH THE SETTING OF THE SUN.
SUNLIGHT IS INCREDIBLY IMPORTANT FOR THEIR WELLBEING.
NOT ENOUGH SUNBATHING LEADS TO A LACK OF VITAMIN D3. IT ALSO CAUSES PARAKEETS TO FEEL STRESSED.

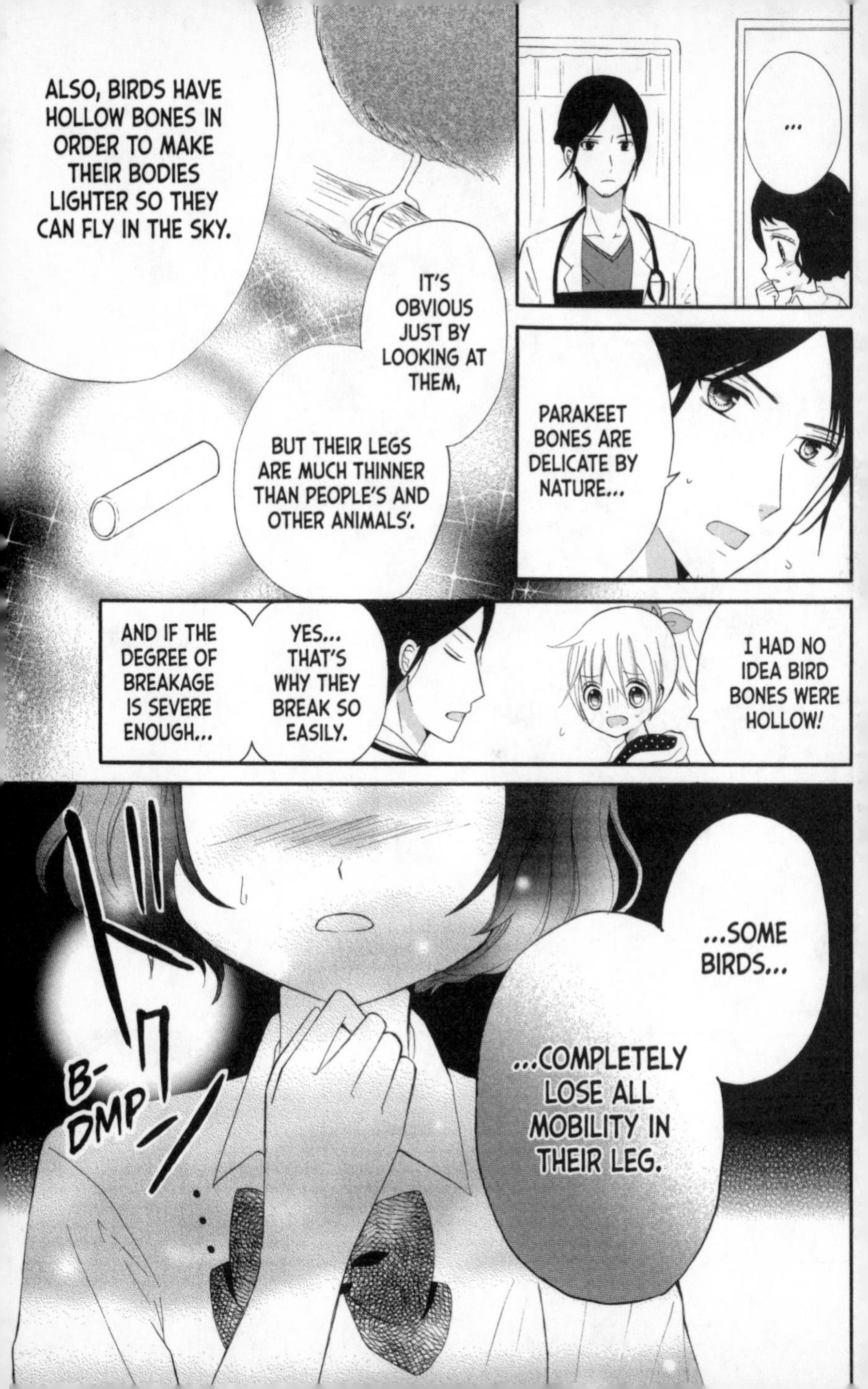
...
PARAKEET BONES ARE DELICATE BY NATURE...
IT'S OBVIOUS JUST BY LOOKING AT THEM,
BUT THEIR LEGS ARE MUCH THINNER THAN PEOPLE'S AND OTHER ANIMALS'.
ALSO, BIRDS HAVE HOLLOW BONES IN ORDER TO MAKE THEIR BODIES LIGHTER SO THEY CAN FLY IN THE SKY.
I HAD NO IDEA BIRD BONES WERE HOLLOW!
YES... THAT'S WHY THEY BREAK SO EASILY.
AND IF THE DEGREE OF BREAKAGE IS SEVERE ENOUGH...
...SOME BIRDS...
...COMPLETELY LOSE ALL MOBILITY IN THEIR LEG.
B-DMP

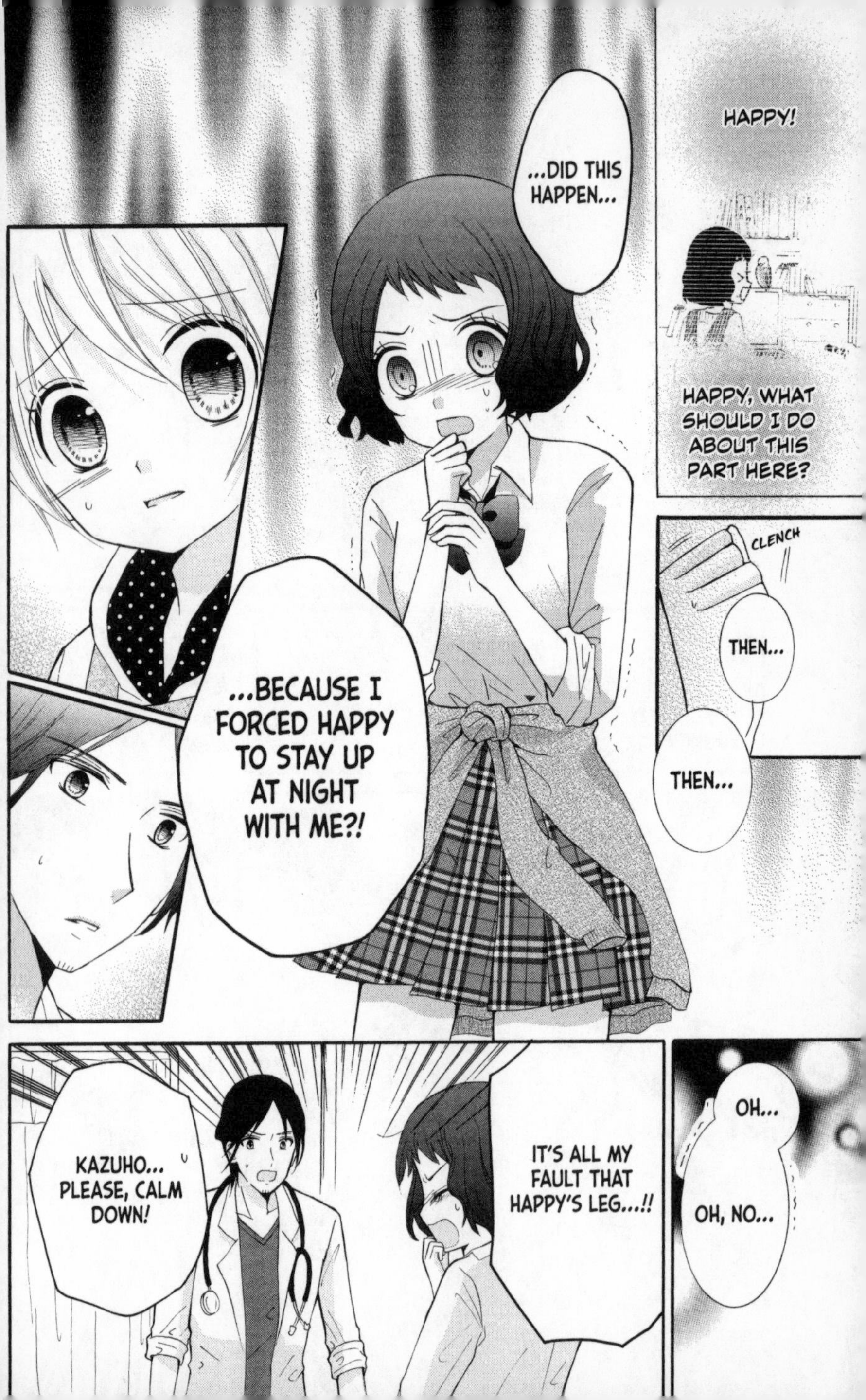
HAPPY!
HAPPY, WHAT SHOULD I DO ABOUT THIS PART HERE?
CLENCH
THEN...
THEN...
...DID THIS HAPPEN...
...BECAUSE I FORCED HAPPY TO STAY UP AT NIGHT WITH ME?!
OH...
OH, NO...
IT'S ALL MY FAULT THAT HAPPY'S LEG...!!
KAZUHO... PLEASE, CALM DOWN!

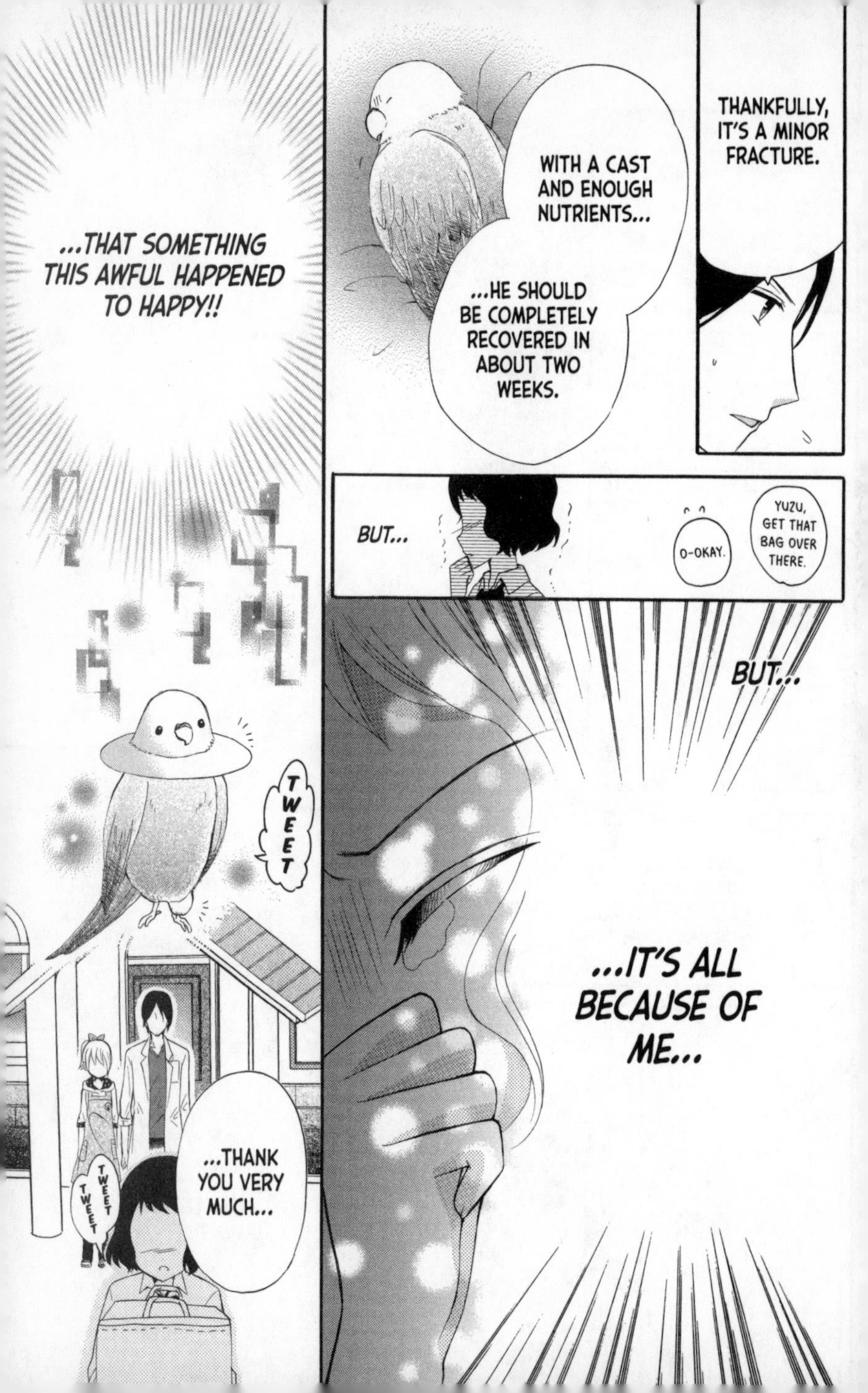
THANKFULLY, IT'S A MINOR FRACTURE.
WITH A CAST AND ENOUGH NUTRIENTS...
...HE SHOULD BE COMPLETELY RECOVERED IN ABOUT TWO WEEKS.
YUZU, GET THAT BAG OVER THERE.
O-OKAY.
BUT...
BUT...
...IT'S ALL BECAUSE OF ME...
...THAT SOMETHING THIS AWFUL HAPPENED TO HAPPY!!
TWEET
...THANK YOU VERY MUCH...
TWEET TWEET

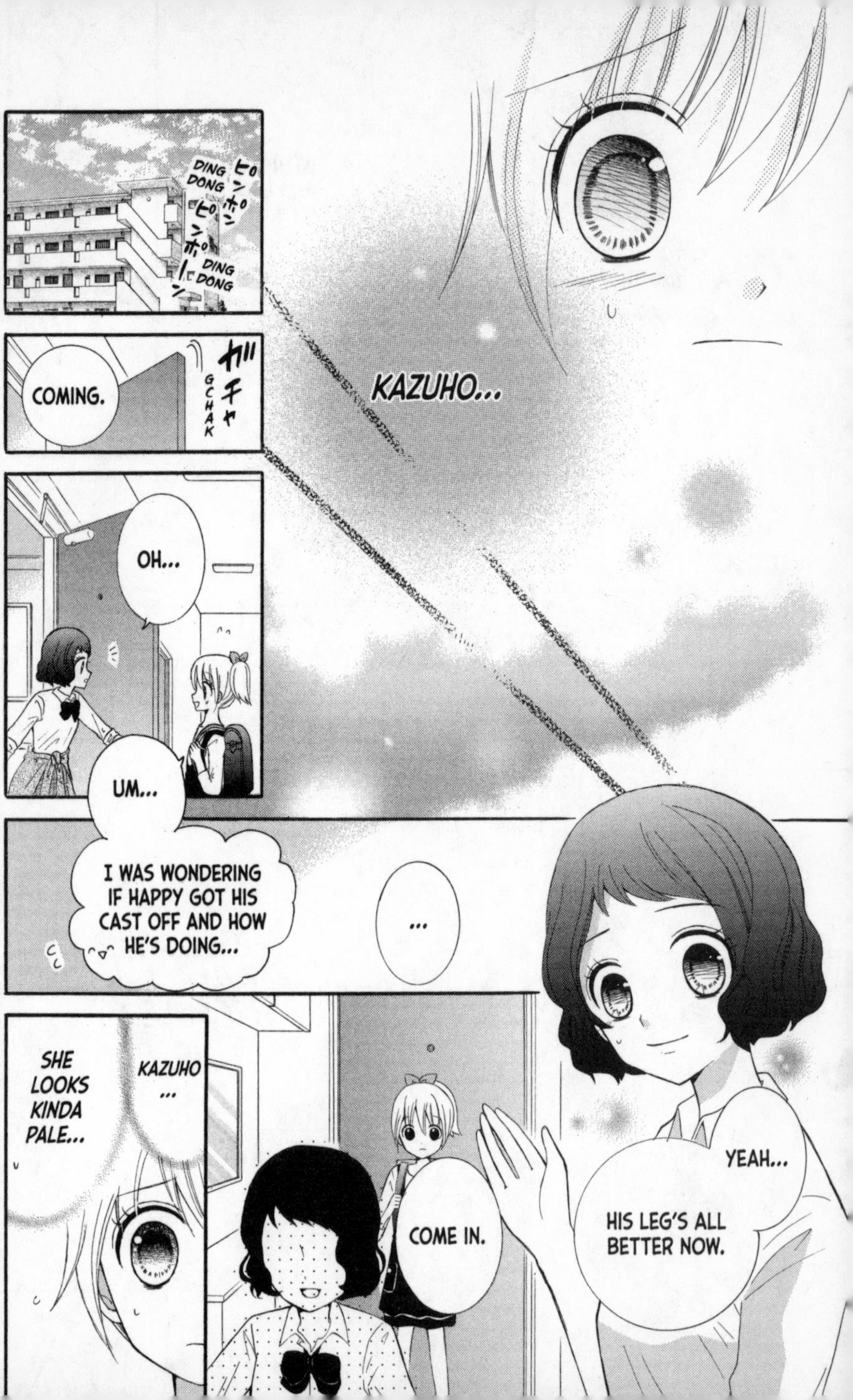
KAZUHO...
ピンポン DING DONG
ピンポーン DING DONG
COMING.
ガチャ GCHAK
OH...
UM...
I WAS WONDERING IF HAPPY GOT HIS CAST OFF AND HOW HE'S DOING...
...
YEAH...
HIS LEG'S ALL BETTER NOW.
COME IN.
KAZUHO...
SHE LOOKS KINDA PALE...

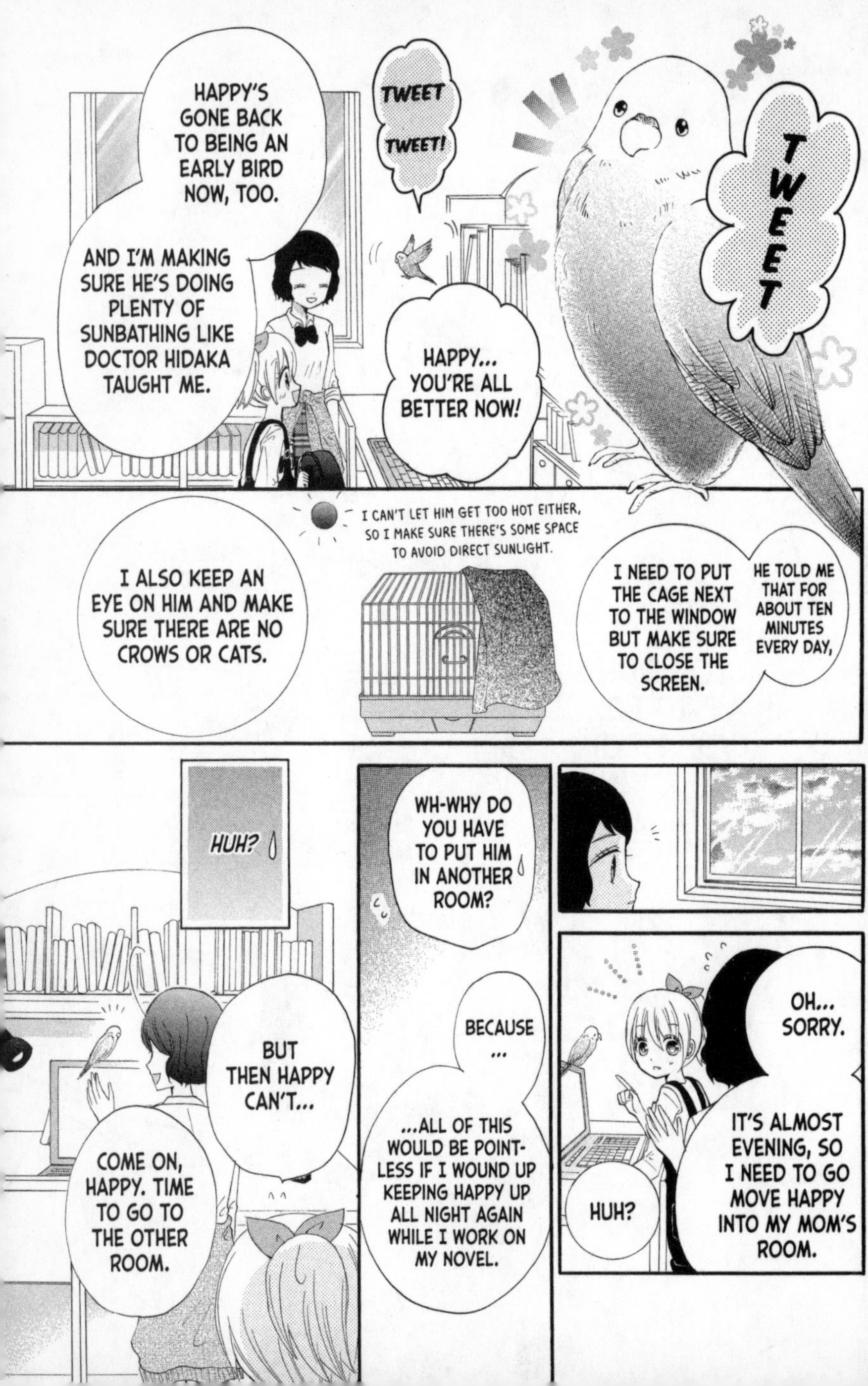
TWEET
TWEET
TWEET TWEET!
HAPPY'S GONE BACK TO BEING AN EARLY BIRD NOW, TOO.
HAPPY... YOU'RE ALL BETTER NOW!
AND I'M MAKING SURE HE'S DOING PLENTY OF SUNBATHING LIKE DOCTOR HIDAKA TAUGHT ME.
HE TOLD ME THAT FOR ABOUT TEN MINUTES EVERY DAY,
I NEED TO PUT THE CAGE NEXT TO THE WINDOW BUT MAKE SURE TO CLOSE THE SCREEN.
I CAN'T LET HIM GET TOO HOT EITHER, SO I MAKE SURE THERE'S SOME SPACE TO AVOID DIRECT SUNLIGHT.
I ALSO KEEP AN EYE ON HIM AND MAKE SURE THERE ARE NO CROWS OR CATS.
OH... SORRY.
IT'S ALMOST EVENING, SO I NEED TO GO MOVE HAPPY INTO MY MOM'S ROOM.
HUH?
WH-WHY DO YOU HAVE TO PUT HIM IN ANOTHER ROOM?
BECAUSE ...
...ALL OF THIS WOULD BE POINT-LESS IF I WOUND UP KEEPING HAPPY UP ALL NIGHT AGAIN WHILE I WORK ON MY NOVEL.
HUH?
BUT THEN HAPPY CAN'T...
COME ON, HAPPY. TIME TO GO TO THE OTHER ROOM.

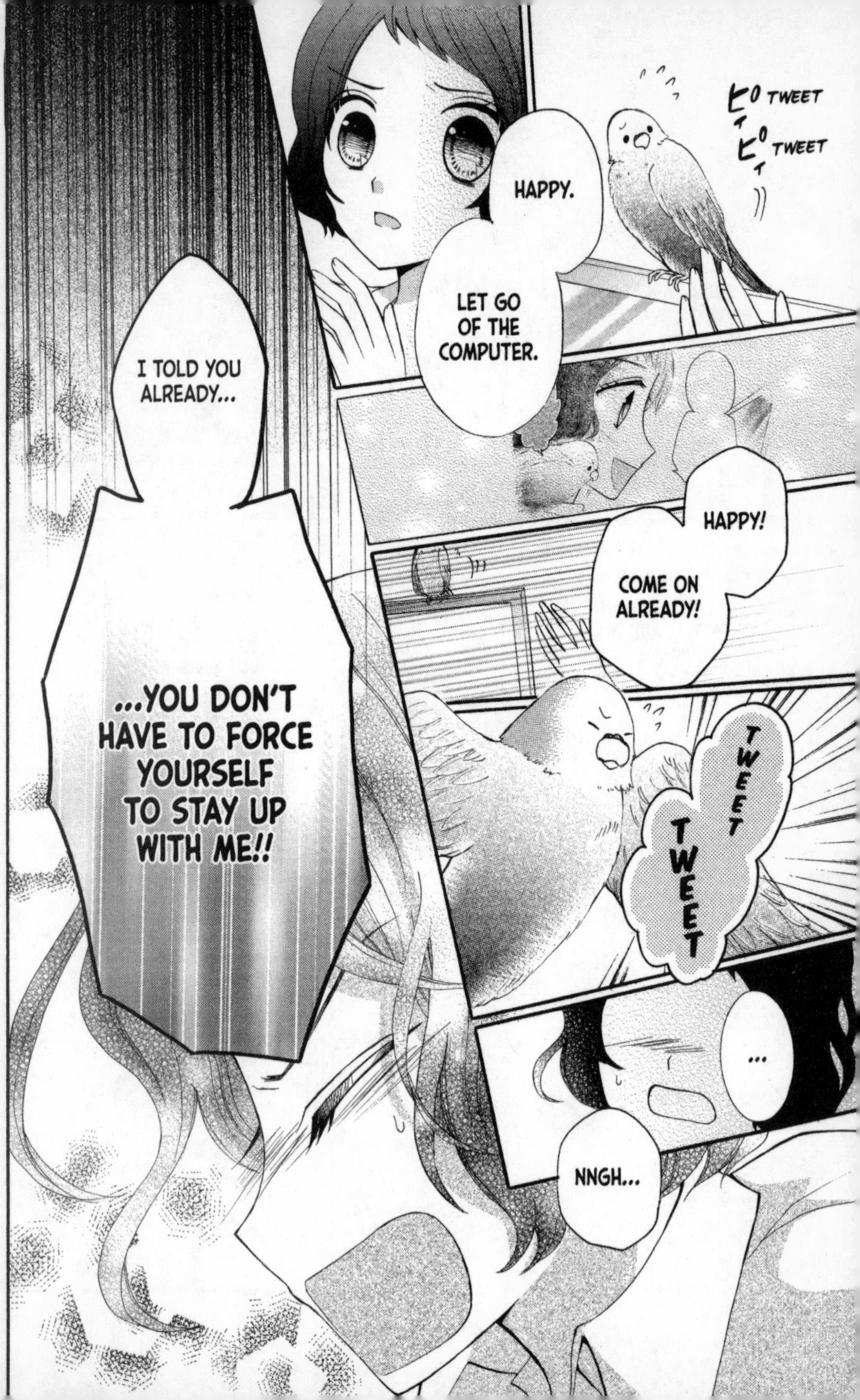

ピィ TWEET
ピィ TWEET
HAPPY.
LET GO OF THE COMPUTER.
HAPPY!
COME ON ALREADY!
TWEET TWEET
...
NNGH...
I TOLD YOU ALREADY...
...YOU DON'T HAVE TO FORCE YOURSELF TO STAY UP WITH ME!!

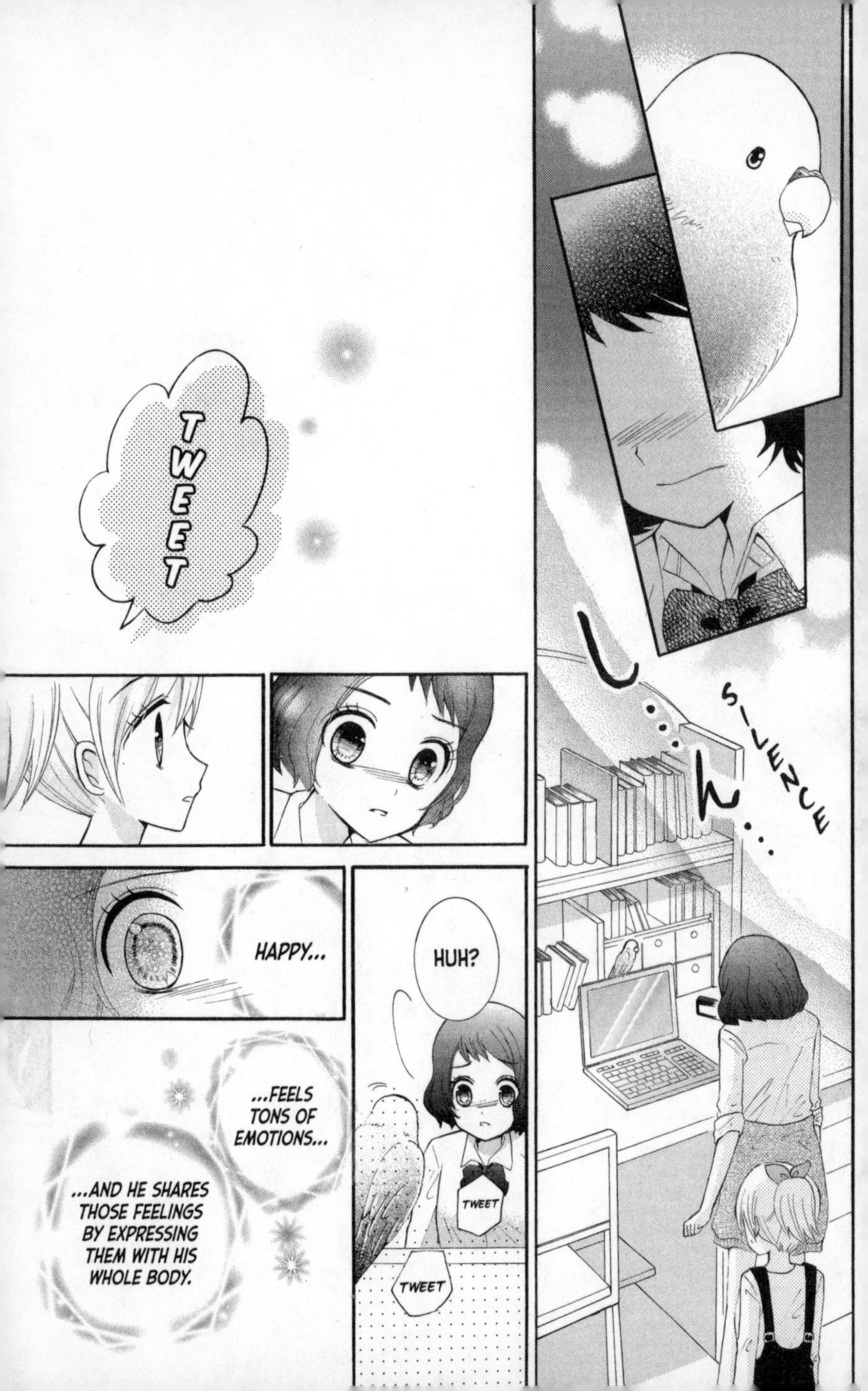
し…ん…
SILENCE
TWEET
HUH?
TWEET
TWEET
HAPPY...
...FEELS TONS OF EMOTIONS...
...AND HE SHARES THOSE FEELINGS BY EXPRESSING THEM WITH HIS WHOLE BODY.

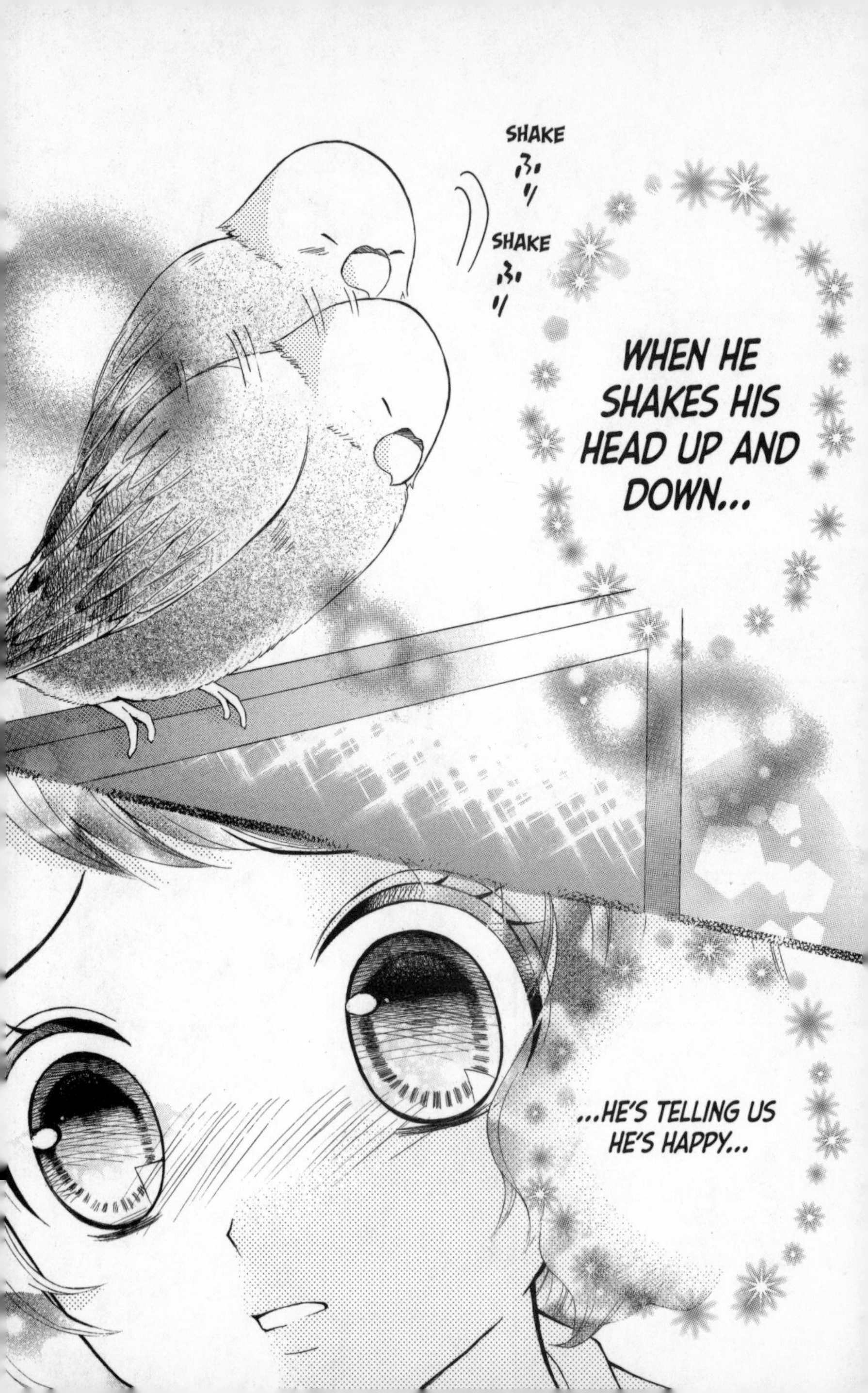
SHAKE
ふり
SHAKE
ふり
WHEN HE SHAKES HIS HEAD UP AND DOWN...
...HE'S TELLING US HE'S HAPPY...

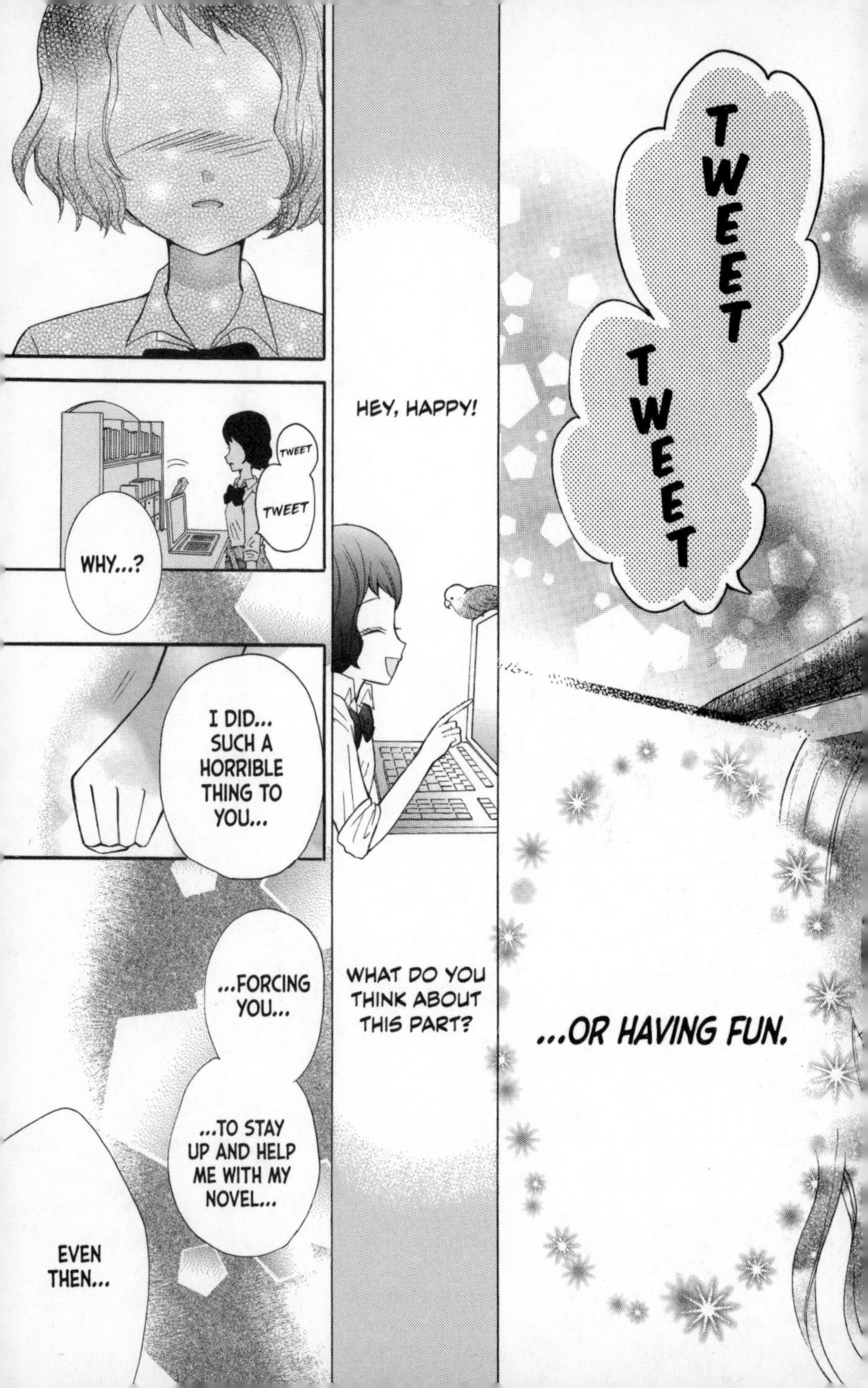
TWEET TWEET
...OR HAVING FUN.
HEY, HAPPY!
WHAT DO YOU THINK ABOUT THIS PART?
TWEET
TWEET
WHY...?
I DID... SUCH A HORRIBLE THING TO YOU...
...FORCING YOU...
...TO STAY UP AND HELP ME WITH MY NOVEL...
EVEN THEN...

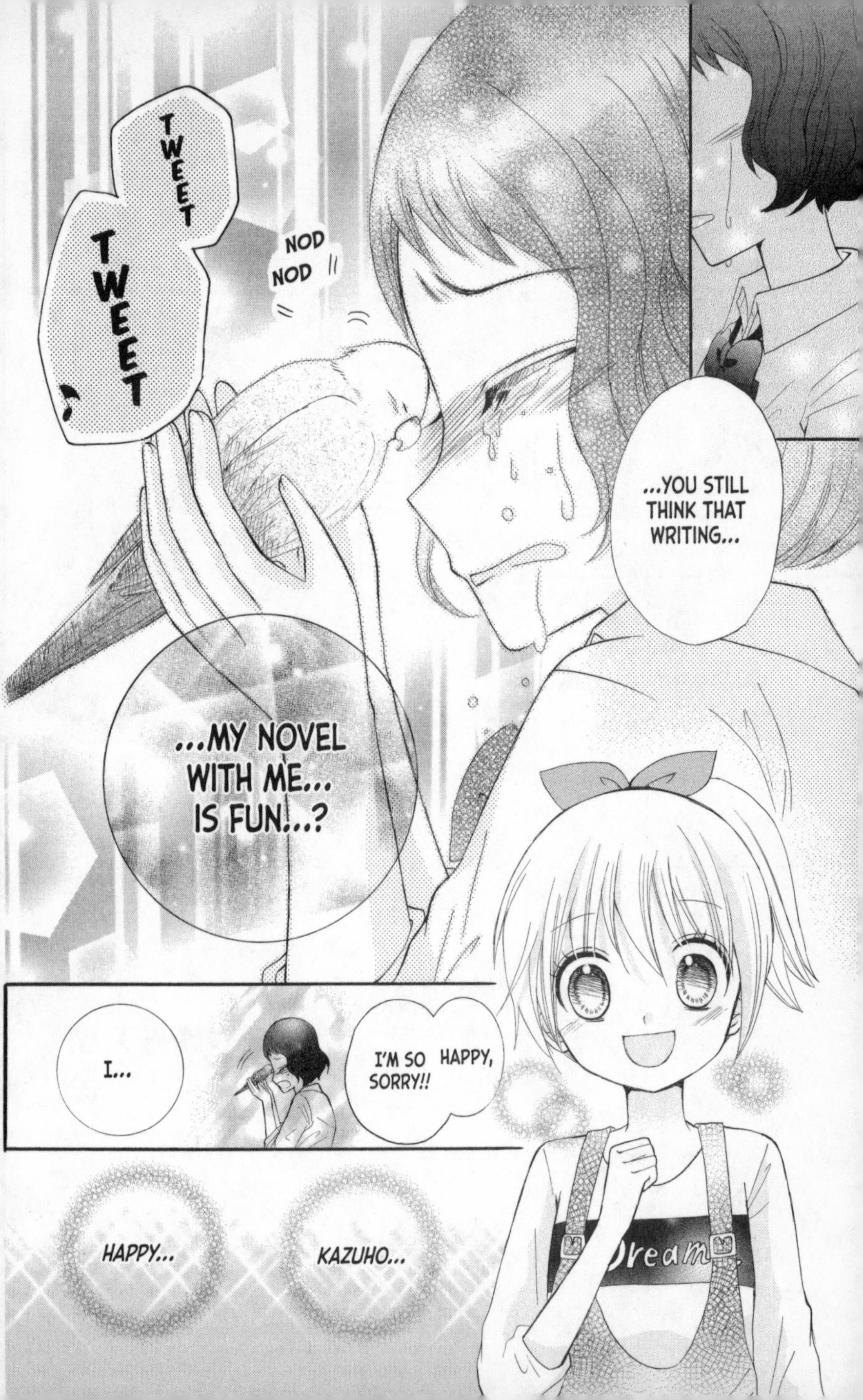
...YOU STILL THINK THAT WRITING...
...MY NOVEL WITH ME... IS FUN...?
NOD NOD
TWEET TWEET
I'M SO HAPPY, SORRY!!
I...
Dream
KAZUHO...
HAPPY...

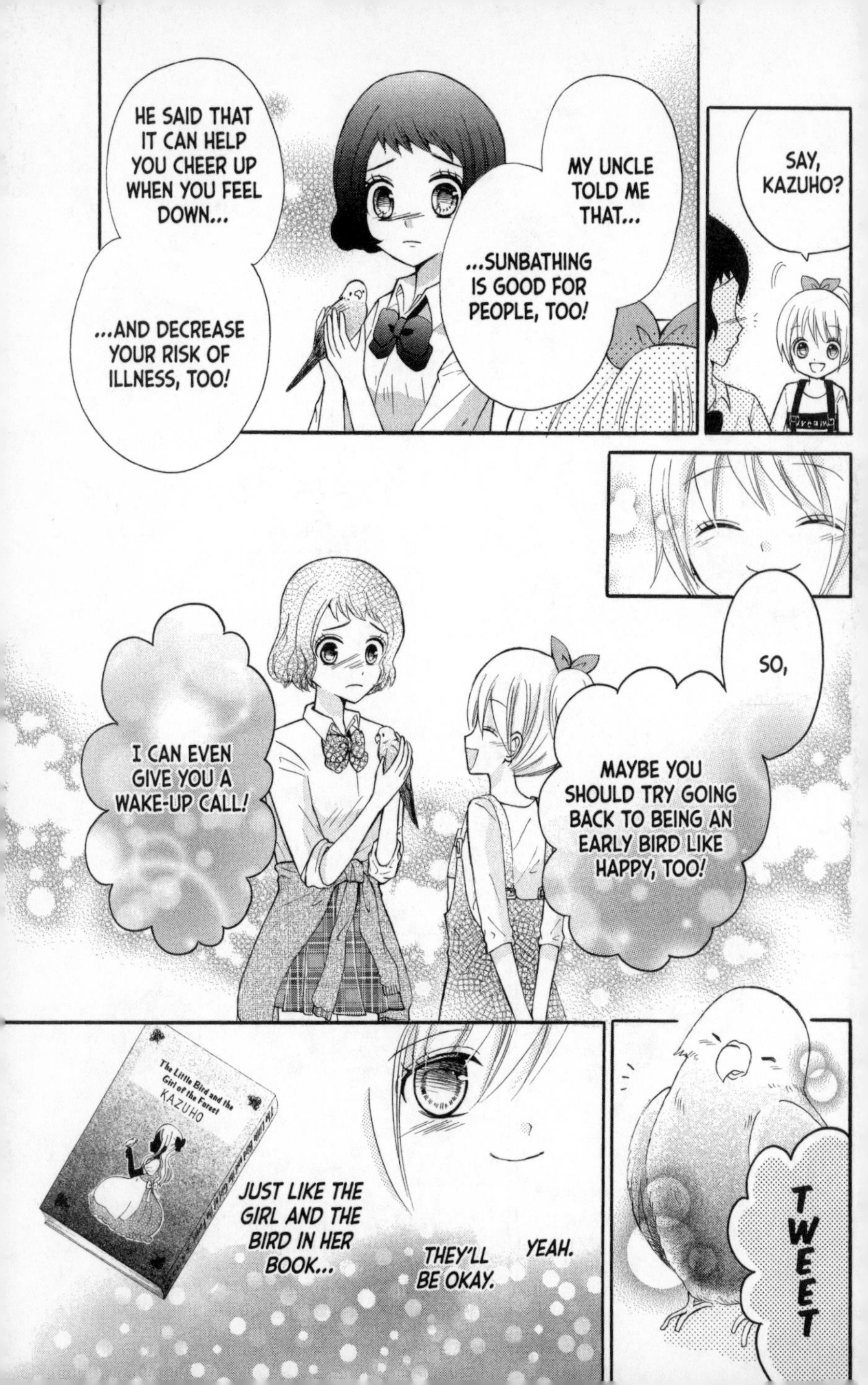
SAY, KAZUHO?
MY UNCLE TOLD ME THAT...
...SUNBATHING IS GOOD FOR PEOPLE, TOO!
HE SAID THAT IT CAN HELP YOU CHEER UP WHEN YOU FEEL DOWN...
...AND DECREASE YOUR RISK OF ILLNESS, TOO!
SO,
MAYBE YOU SHOULD TRY GOING BACK TO BEING AN EARLY BIRD LIKE HAPPY, TOO!
I CAN EVEN GIVE YOU A WAKE-UP CALL!
TWEET
YEAH.
THEY'LL BE OKAY.
JUST LIKE THE GIRL AND THE BIRD IN HER BOOK...
The Little Bird and the Girl of the Forest
KAZUHO

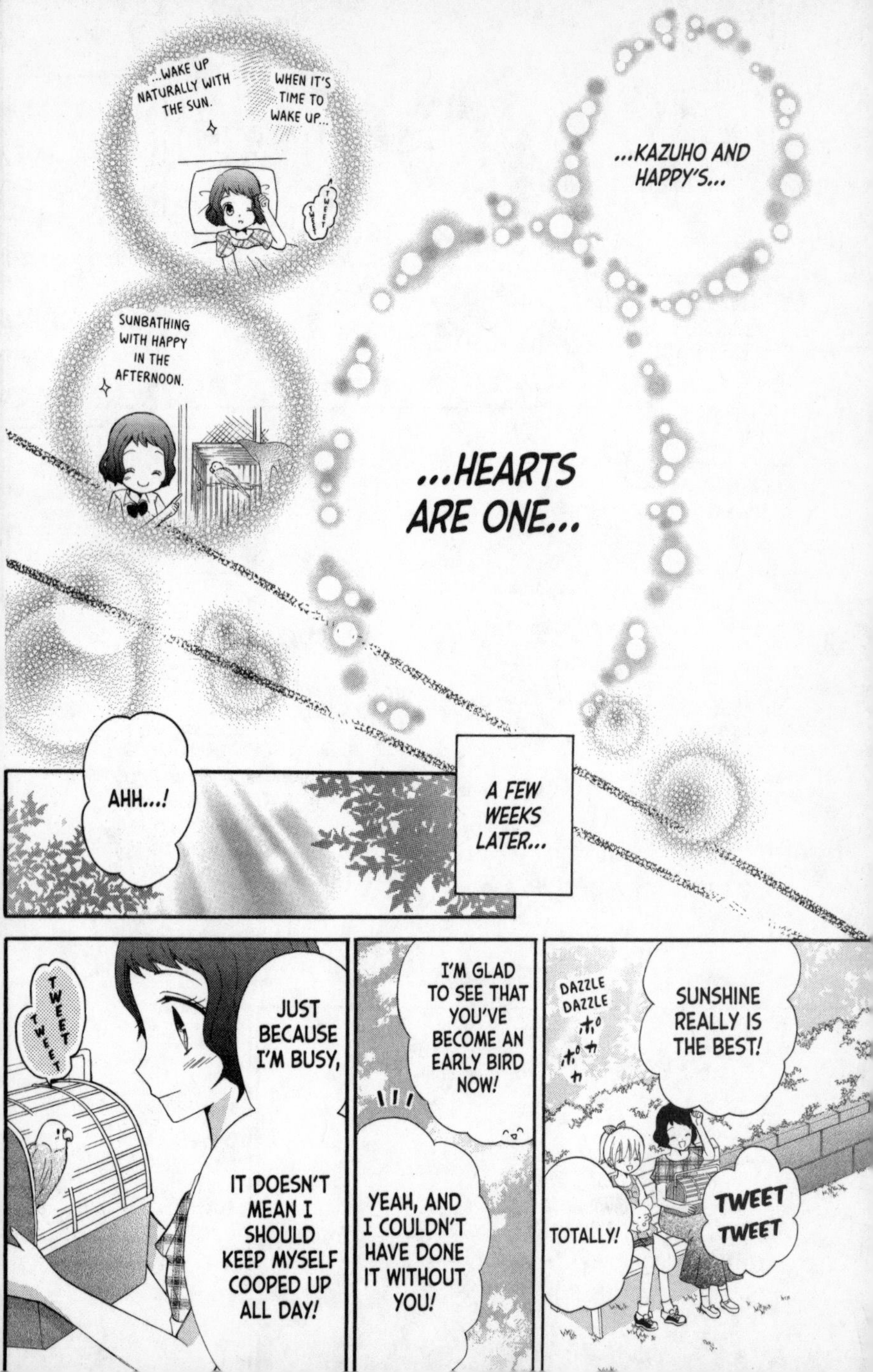
...KAZUHO AND HAPPY'S...
...HEARTS ARE ONE...
WHEN IT'S TIME TO WAKE UP...
...WAKE UP NATURALLY WITH THE SUN.
TWEET TWEET
SUNBATHING WITH HAPPY IN THE AFTERNOON.
A FEW WEEKS LATER...
AHH...!
DAZZLE DAZZLE
SUNSHINE REALLY IS THE BEST!
TWEET TWEET
TOTALLY!
I'M GLAD TO SEE THAT YOU'VE BECOME AN EARLY BIRD NOW!
YEAH, AND I COULDN'T HAVE DONE IT WITHOUT YOU!
TWEET TWEET
JUST BECAUSE I'M BUSY,
IT DOESN'T MEAN I SHOULD KEEP MYSELF COOPED UP ALL DAY!

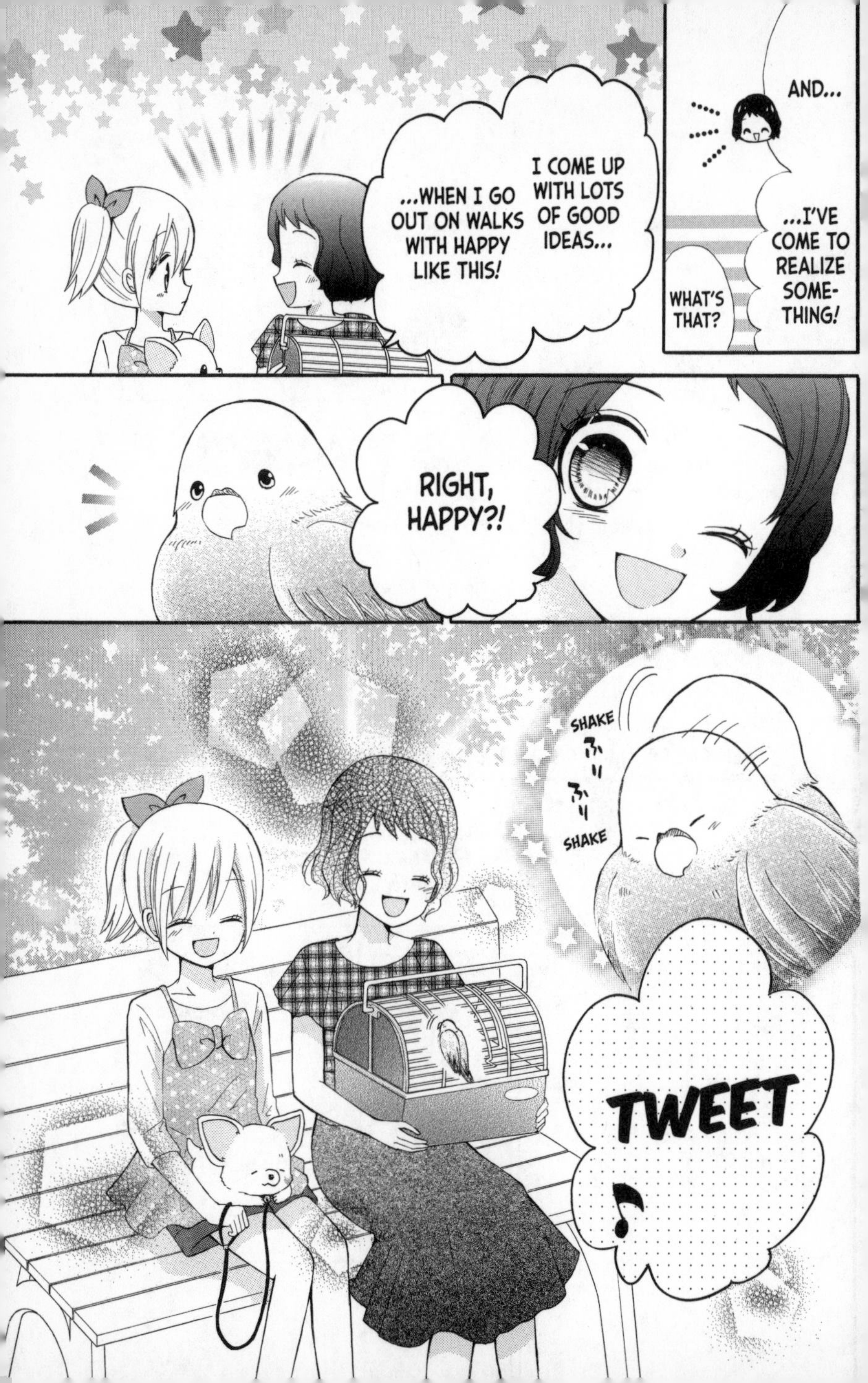
AND...
...I'VE COME TO REALIZE SOMETHING!
WHAT'S THAT?
I COME UP WITH LOTS OF GOOD IDEAS...
...WHEN I GO OUT ON WALKS WITH HAPPY LIKE THIS!
RIGHT, HAPPY?!
SHAKE ふり
ふり SHAKE
TWEET ♪

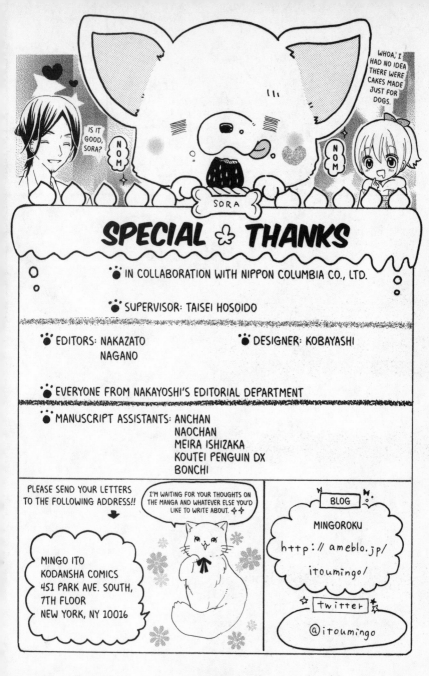

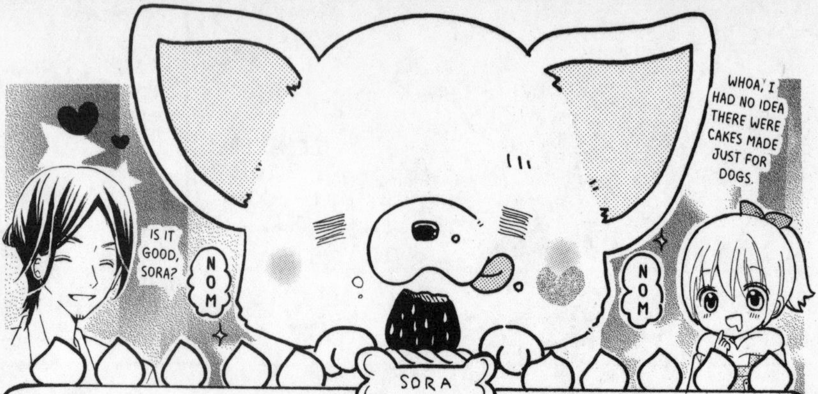
WHOA, I HAD NO IDEA THERE WERE CAKES MADE JUST FOR DOGS.
NOM
NOM
IS IT GOOD, SORA?
SORA

SPECIAL ✿ THANKS

- IN COLLABORATION WITH NIPPON COLUMBIA CO., LTD.
- SUPERVISOR: TAISEI HOSOIDO

- EDITORS: NAKAZATO
  NAGANO
- DESIGNER: KOBAYASHI
- EVERYONE FROM NAKAYOSHI'S EDITORIAL DEPARTMENT

- MANUSCRIPT ASSISTANTS: ANCHAN
  NAOCHAN
  MEIRA ISHIZAKA
  KOUTEI PENGUIN DX
  BONCHI

PLEASE SEND YOUR LETTERS TO THE FOLLOWING ADDRESS!!

MINGO ITO
KODANSHA COMICS
451 PARK AVE. SOUTH,
7TH FLOOR
NEW YORK, NY 10016

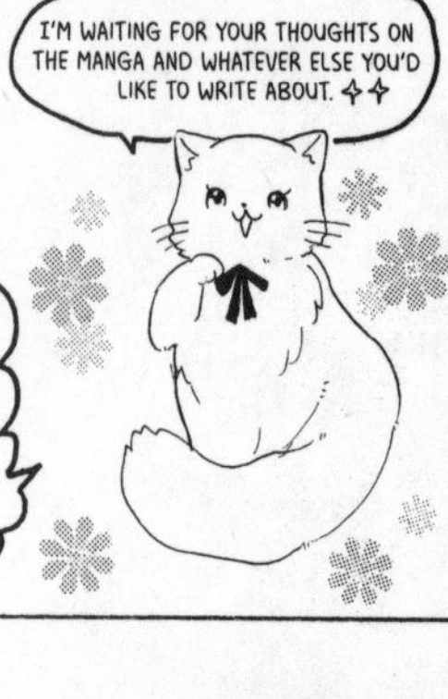
I'M WAITING FOR YOUR THOUGHTS ON THE MANGA AND WHATEVER ELSE YOU'D LIKE TO WRITE ABOUT. ✧✧

BLOG

MINGOROKU

http://ameblo.jp/itoumingo/

twitter

@itoumingo

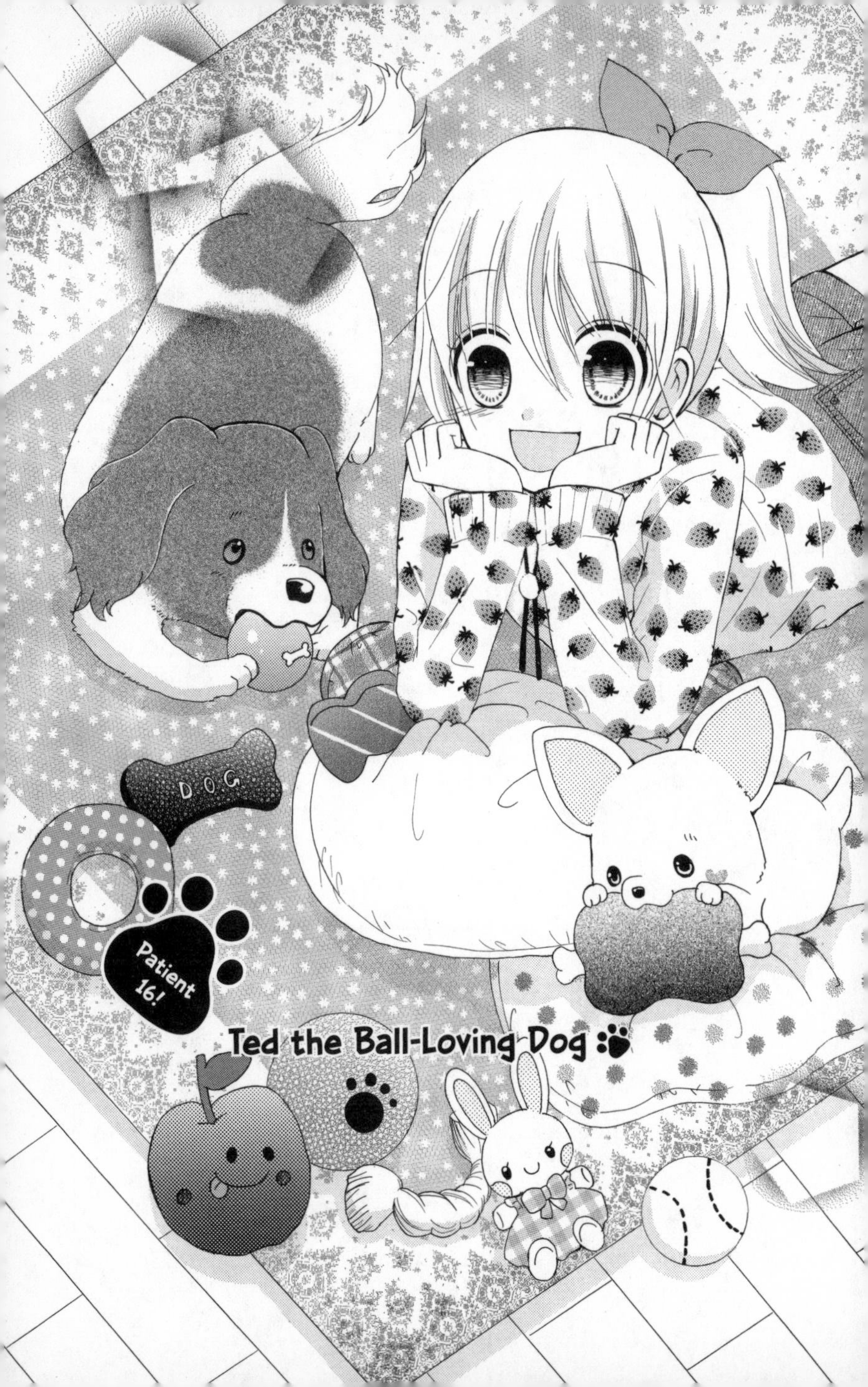
DOG
Patient 16!
Ted the Ball-Loving Dog

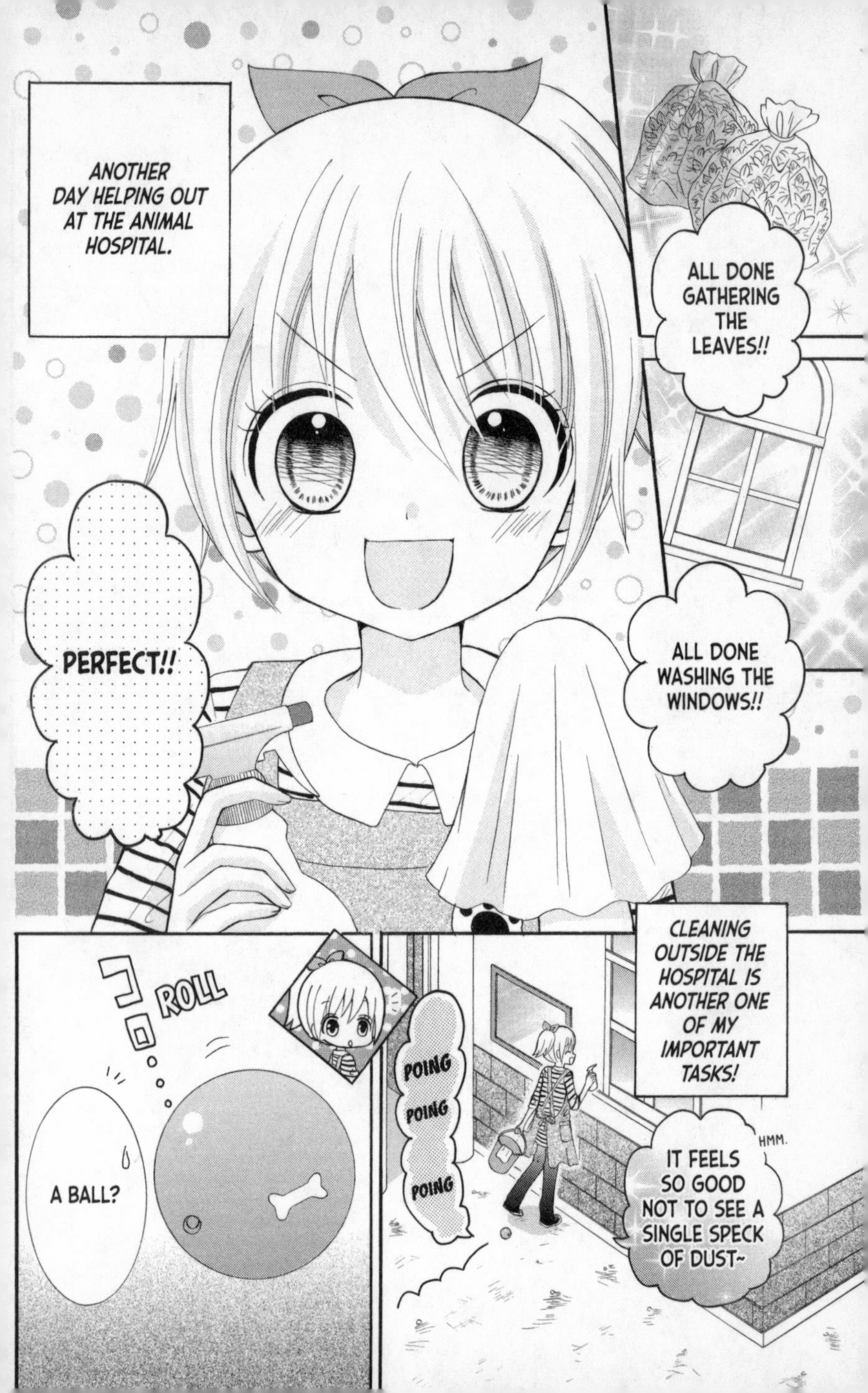

ALL DONE GATHERING THE LEAVES!!
ALL DONE WASHING THE WINDOWS!!
ANOTHER DAY HELPING OUT AT THE ANIMAL HOSPITAL.
PERFECT!!
CLEANING OUTSIDE THE HOSPITAL IS ANOTHER ONE OF MY IMPORTANT TASKS!
HMM.
IT FEELS SO GOOD NOT TO SEE A SINGLE SPECK OF DUST~
POING
POING
POING
コロ
ROLL
A BALL?

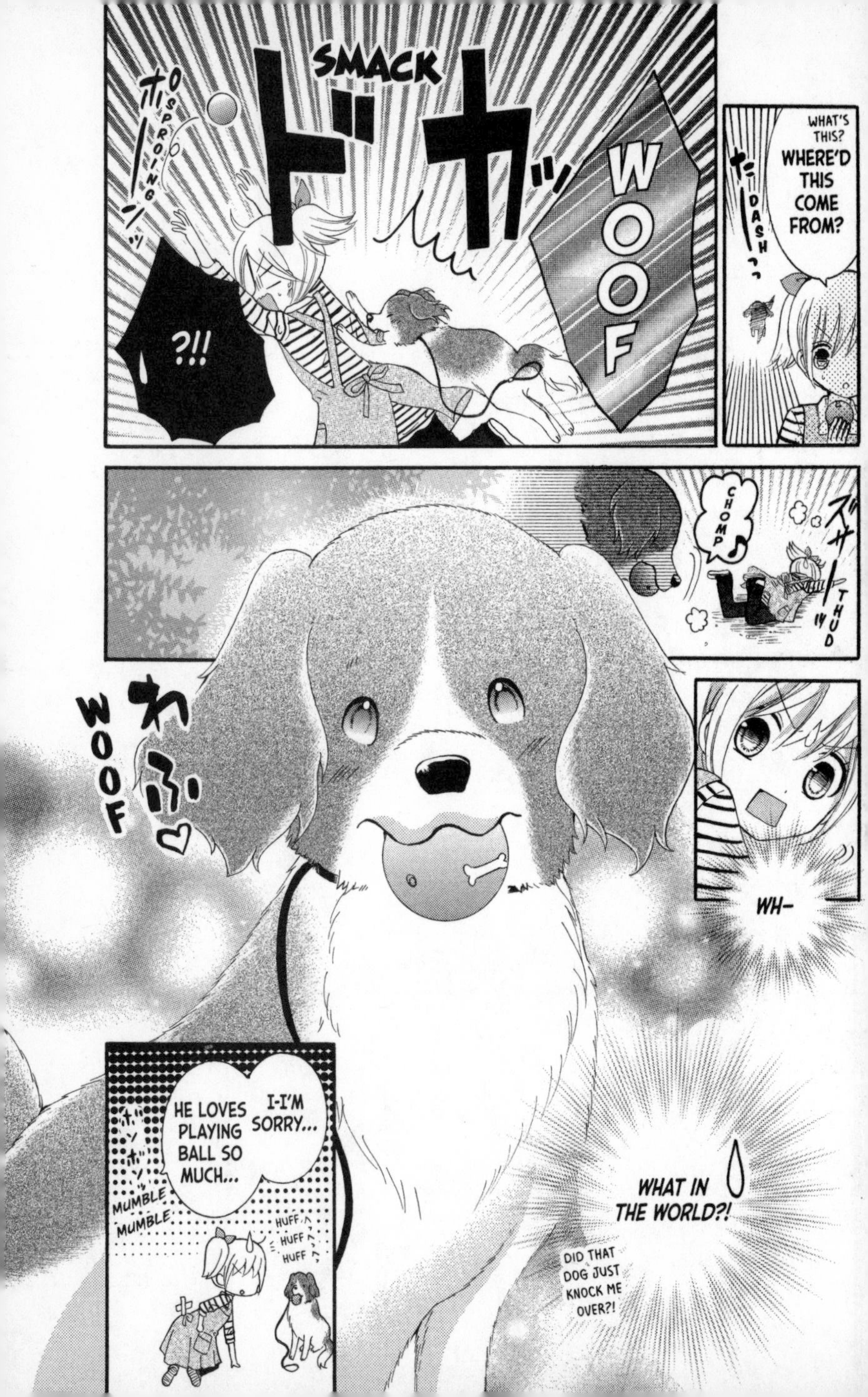

WHAT'S THIS? WHERE'D THIS COME FROM?
DASH
SMACK
SPROING
WOOF
?!!
CHOMP
THUD
WH-
WOOF
WHAT IN THE WORLD?!
DID THAT DOG JUST KNOCK ME OVER?!
I-I'M SORRY...
HE LOVES PLAYING BALL SO MUCH...
MUMBLE MUMBLE
HUFF HUFF HUFF

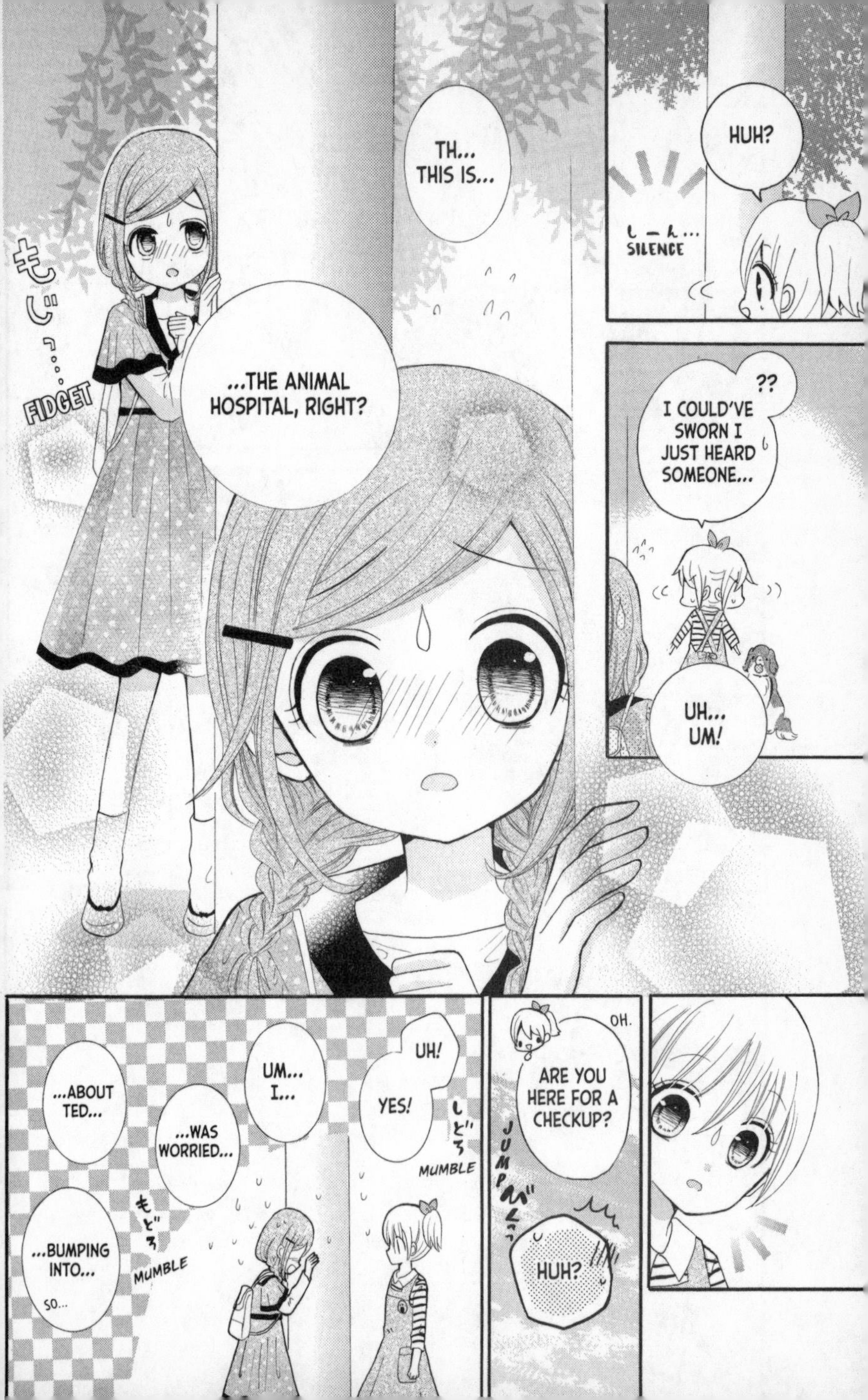
HUH?
しーん…
SILENCE
??
I COULD'VE SWORN I JUST HEARD SOMEONE...
UH... UM!
TH... THIS IS...
...THE ANIMAL HOSPITAL, RIGHT?
もじっ…
FIDGET
OH.
ARE YOU HERE FOR A CHECKUP?
びくっ
JUMP
HUH?
UH!
YES!
しどろ
MUMBLE
UM... I...
...WAS WORRIED...
...ABOUT TED...
もどろ
MUMBLE
...BUMPING INTO...
SO...

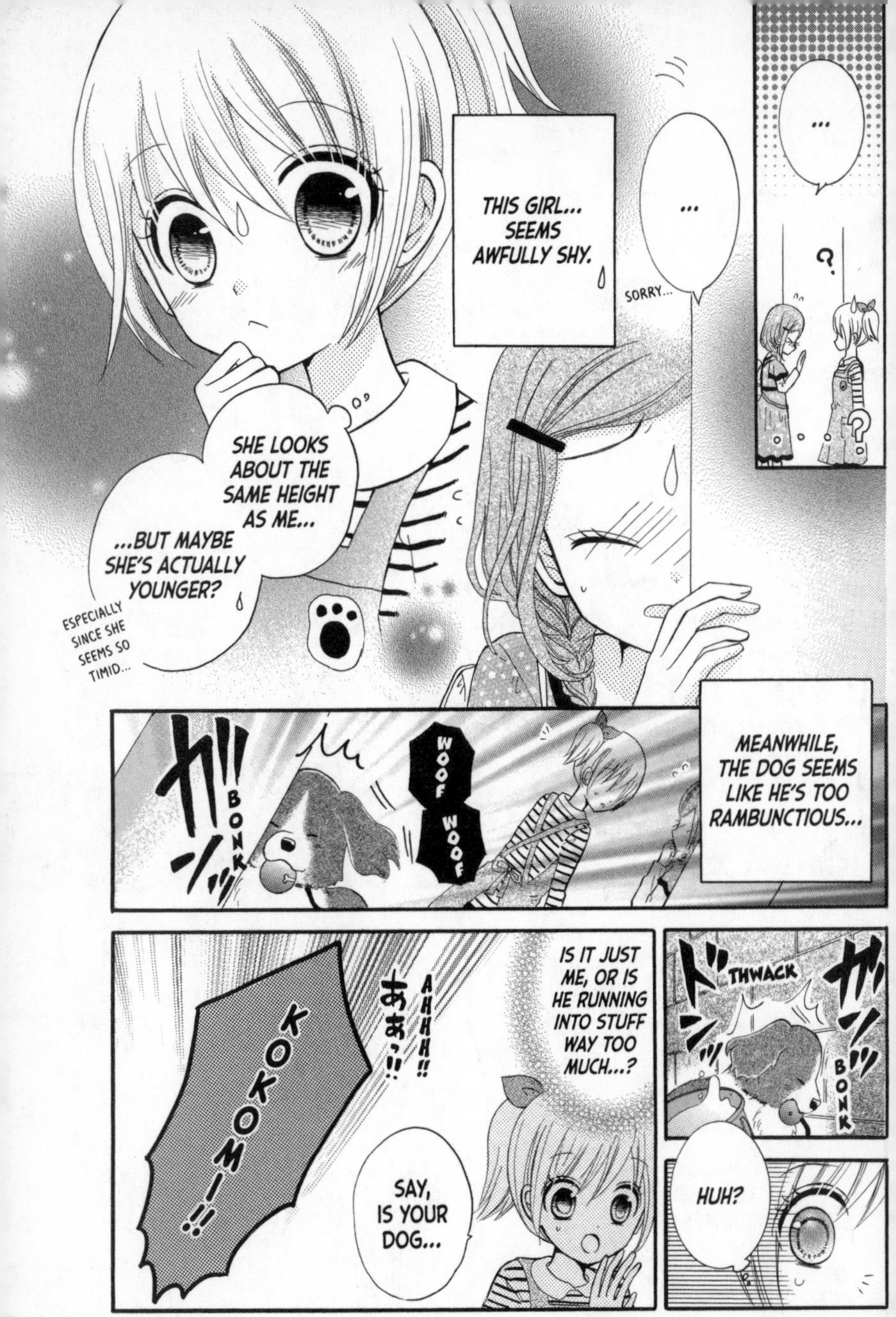
...
?
...
THIS GIRL... SEEMS AWFULLY SHY.
SORRY...
SHE LOOKS ABOUT THE SAME HEIGHT AS ME...
...BUT MAYBE SHE'S ACTUALLY YOUNGER?
ESPECIALLY SINCE SHE SEEMS SO TIMID...
MEANWHILE, THE DOG SEEMS LIKE HE'S TOO RAMBUNCTIOUS...
WOOF
WOOF
BONK
THWACK
BONK
HUH?
IS IT JUST ME, OR IS HE RUNNING INTO STUFF WAY TOO MUCH...?
SAY, IS YOUR DOG...
AHHH!!
あぁっ!!
KOKOMI—!!

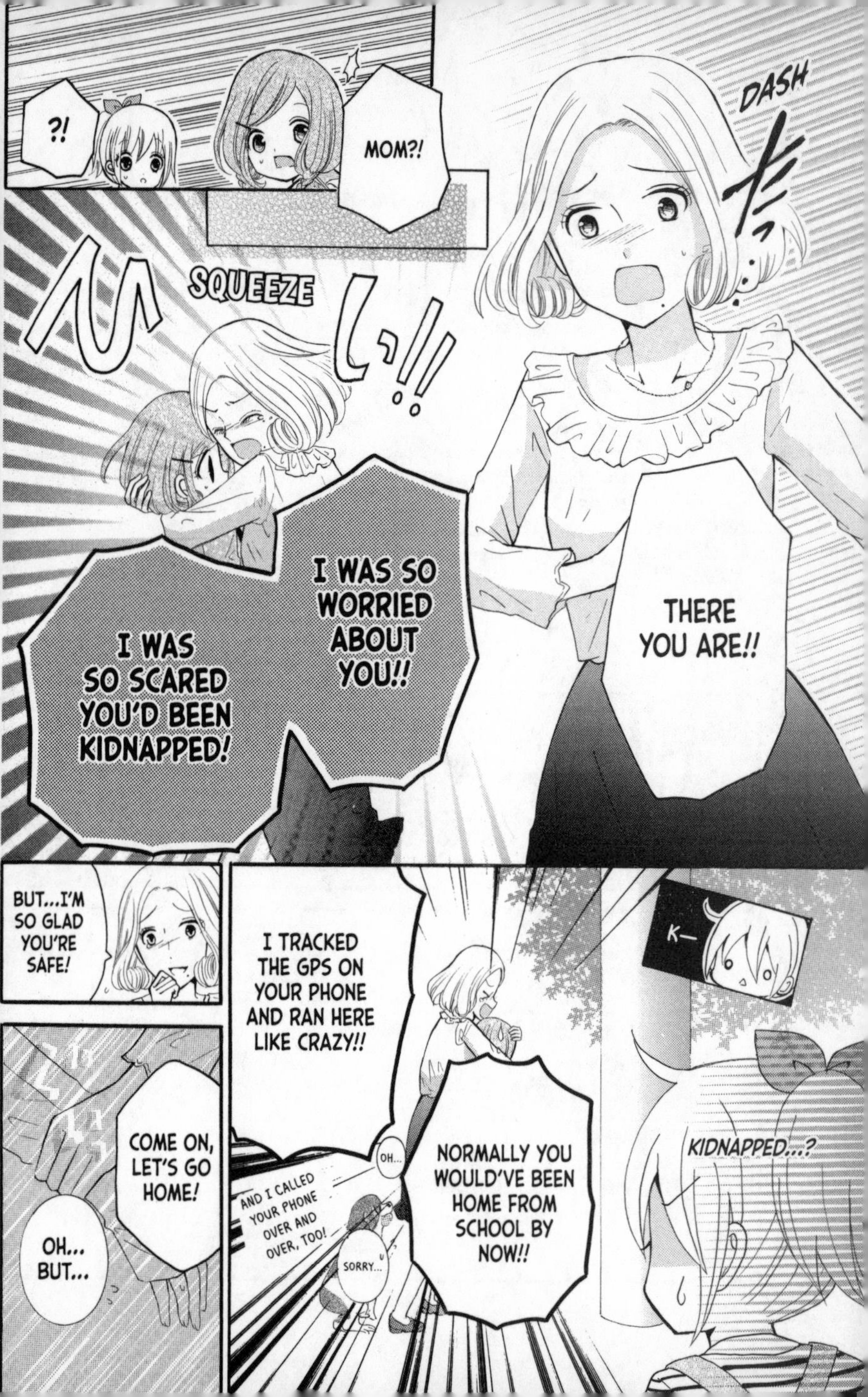
DASH
THERE YOU ARE!!
MOM?!
?!
SQUEEZE
I WAS SO WORRIED ABOUT YOU!!
I WAS SO SCARED YOU'D BEEN KIDNAPPED!
K—
KIDNAPPED...?
I TRACKED THE GPS ON YOUR PHONE AND RAN HERE LIKE CRAZY!!
NORMALLY YOU WOULD'VE BEEN HOME FROM SCHOOL BY NOW!!
OH...
AND I CALLED YOUR PHONE OVER AND OVER, TOO!
SORRY...
BUT...I'M SO GLAD YOU'RE SAFE!
COME ON, LET'S GO HOME!
OH... BUT...

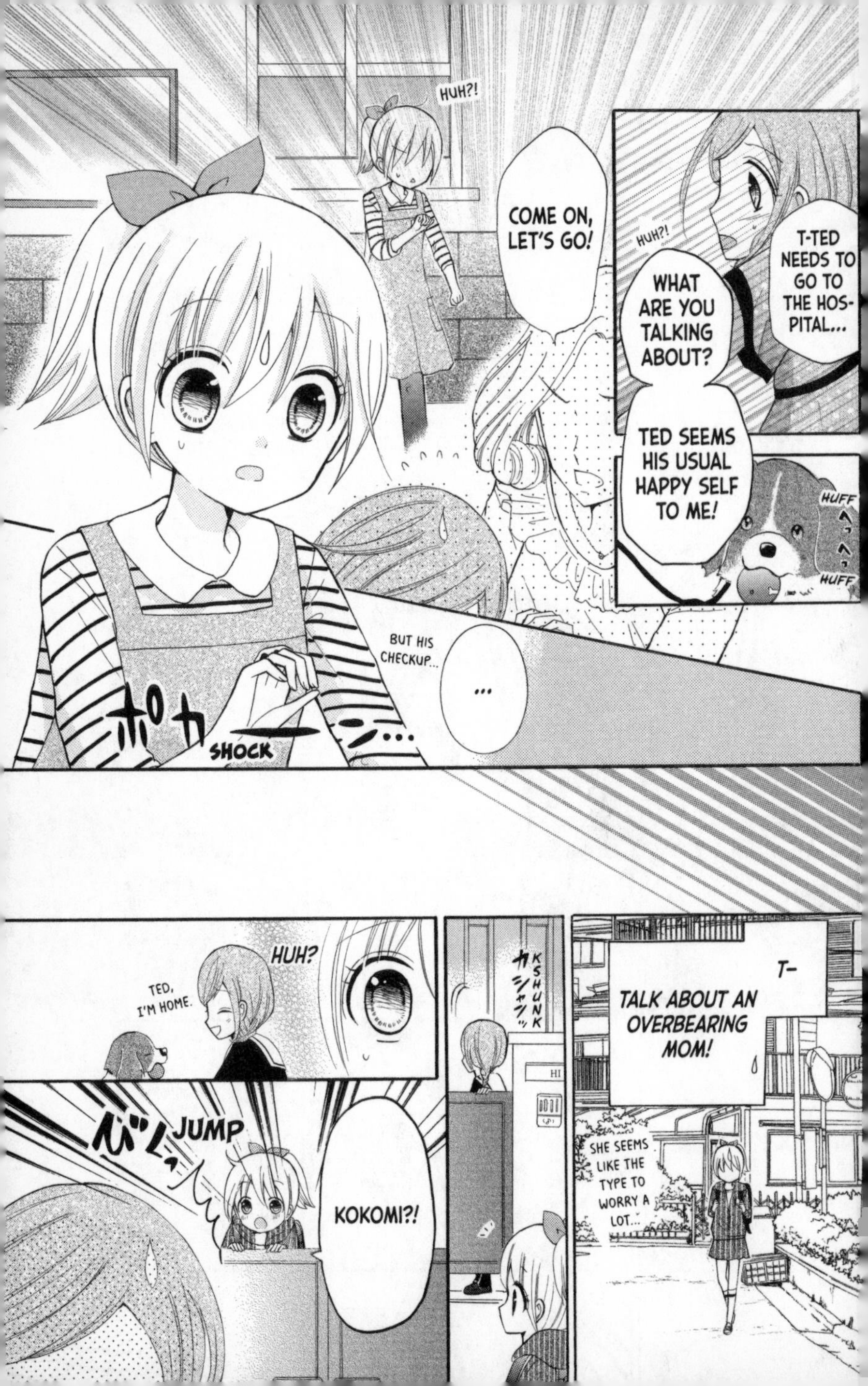

T-TED NEEDS TO GO TO THE HOS-PITAL...
HUH?!
WHAT ARE YOU TALKING ABOUT?
TED SEEMS HIS USUAL HAPPY SELF TO ME!
HUFF HUFF
COME ON, LET'S GO!
HUH?!
BUT HIS CHECKUP...
...
SHOCK
T-
TALK ABOUT AN OVERBEARING MOM!
SHE SEEMS LIKE THE TYPE TO WORRY A LOT...
KSHUNK
HI
HUH?
TED, I'M HOME.
JUMP
KOKOMI?!

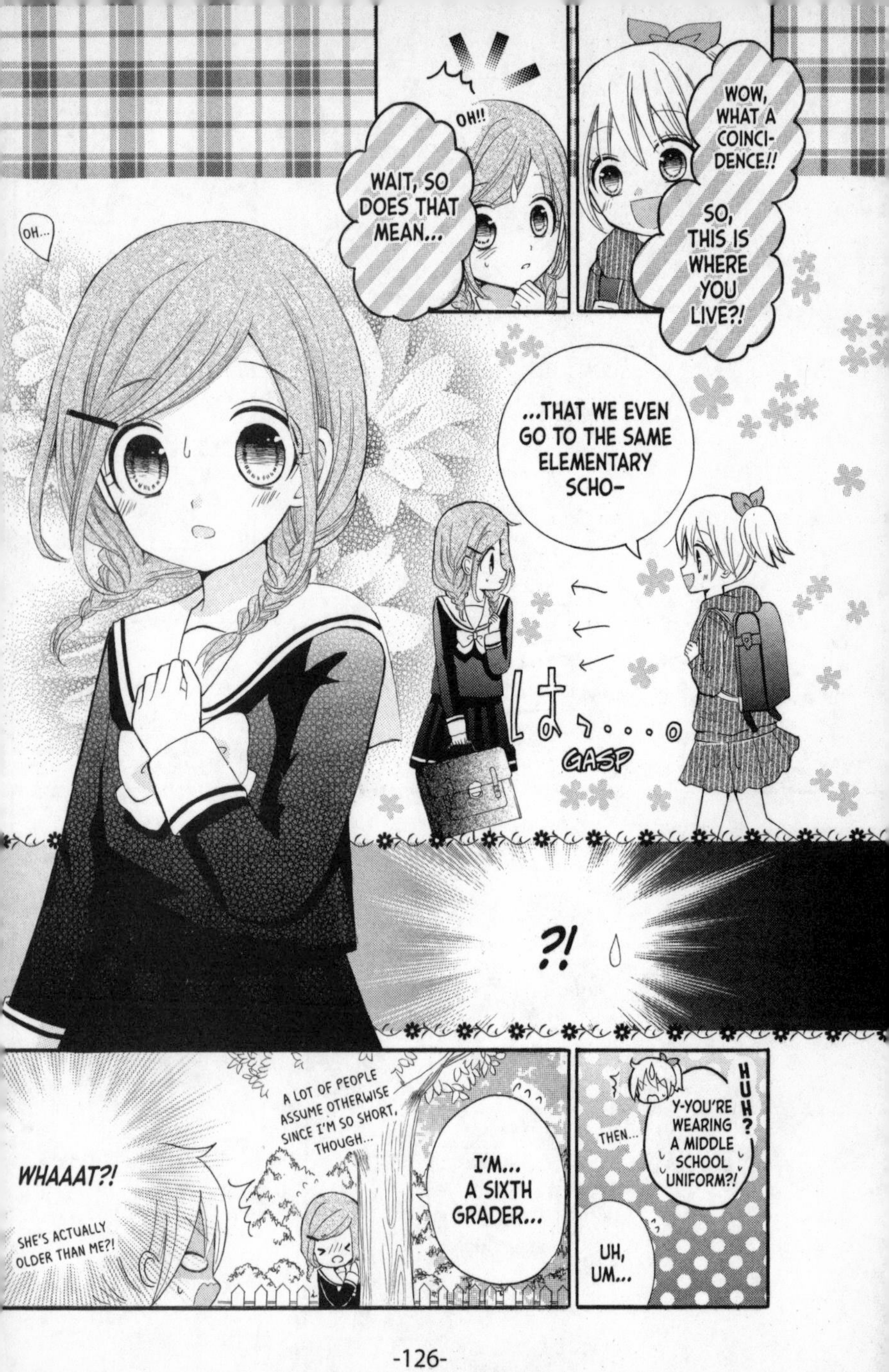
WOW, WHAT A COINCI-DENCE!!
SO, THIS IS WHERE YOU LIVE?!
OH!!
WAIT, SO DOES THAT MEAN...
...THAT WE EVEN GO TO THE SAME ELEMENTARY SCHO-
はっ。。。
GASP
?!
OH...
HUH?
Y-YOU'RE WEARING A MIDDLE SCHOOL UNIFORM?!
THEN...
UH, UM...
I'M... A SIXTH GRADER...
A LOT OF PEOPLE ASSUME OTHERWISE SINCE I'M SO SHORT, THOUGH...
WHAAAT?!
SHE'S ACTUALLY OLDER THAN ME?!

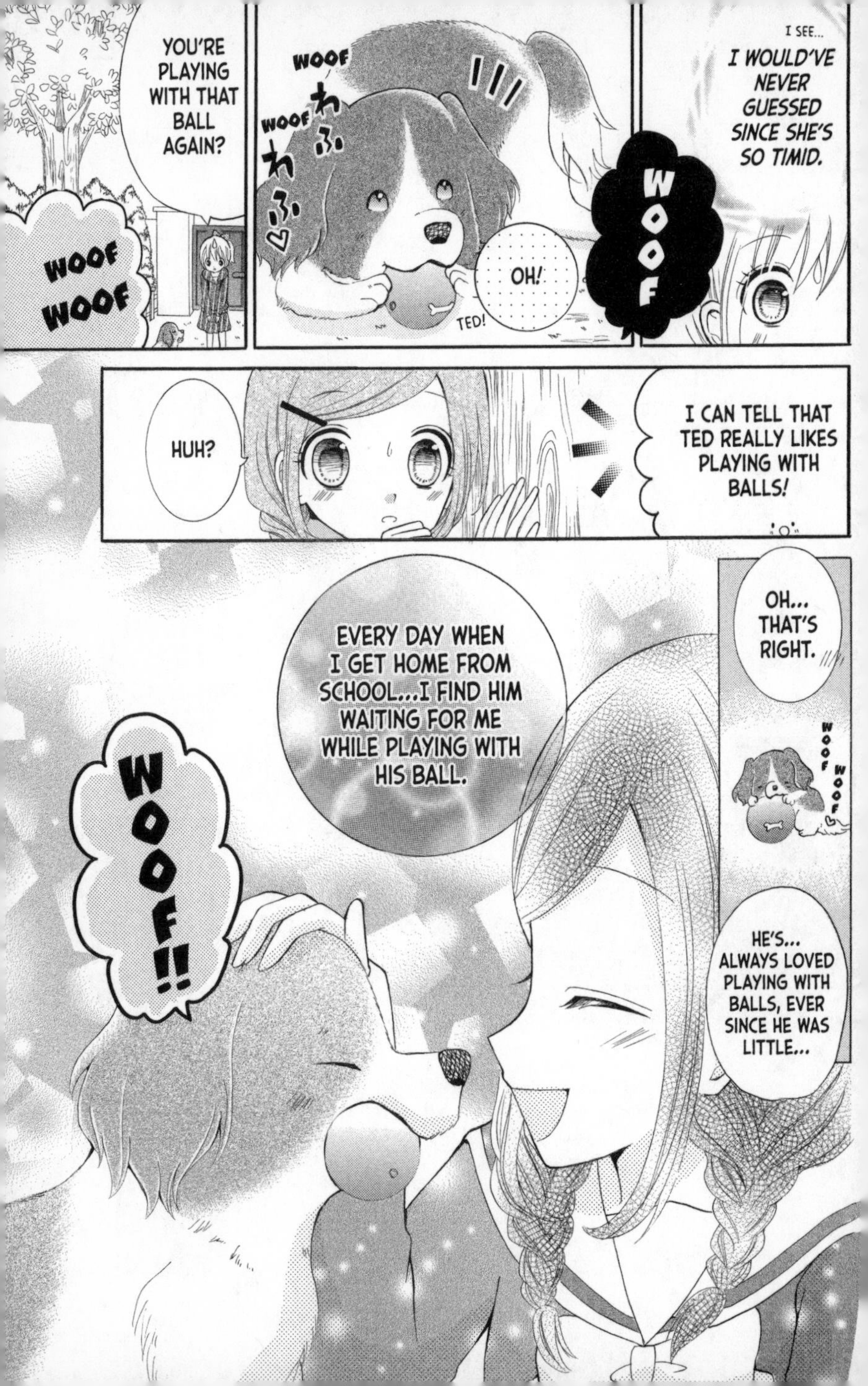
I SEE...
I WOULD'VE NEVER GUESSED SINCE SHE'S SO TIMID.
WOOF WOOF
WOOF わふ
WOOF わふ
OH!
TED!
YOU'RE PLAYING WITH THAT BALL AGAIN?
WOOF WOOF
I CAN TELL THAT TED REALLY LIKES PLAYING WITH BALLS!
HUH?
OH... THAT'S RIGHT.
WOOF WOOF
HE'S... ALWAYS LOVED PLAYING WITH BALLS, EVER SINCE HE WAS LITTLE...
EVERY DAY WHEN I GET HOME FROM SCHOOL...I FIND HIM WAITING FOR ME WHILE PLAYING WITH HIS BALL.
WOOF!!

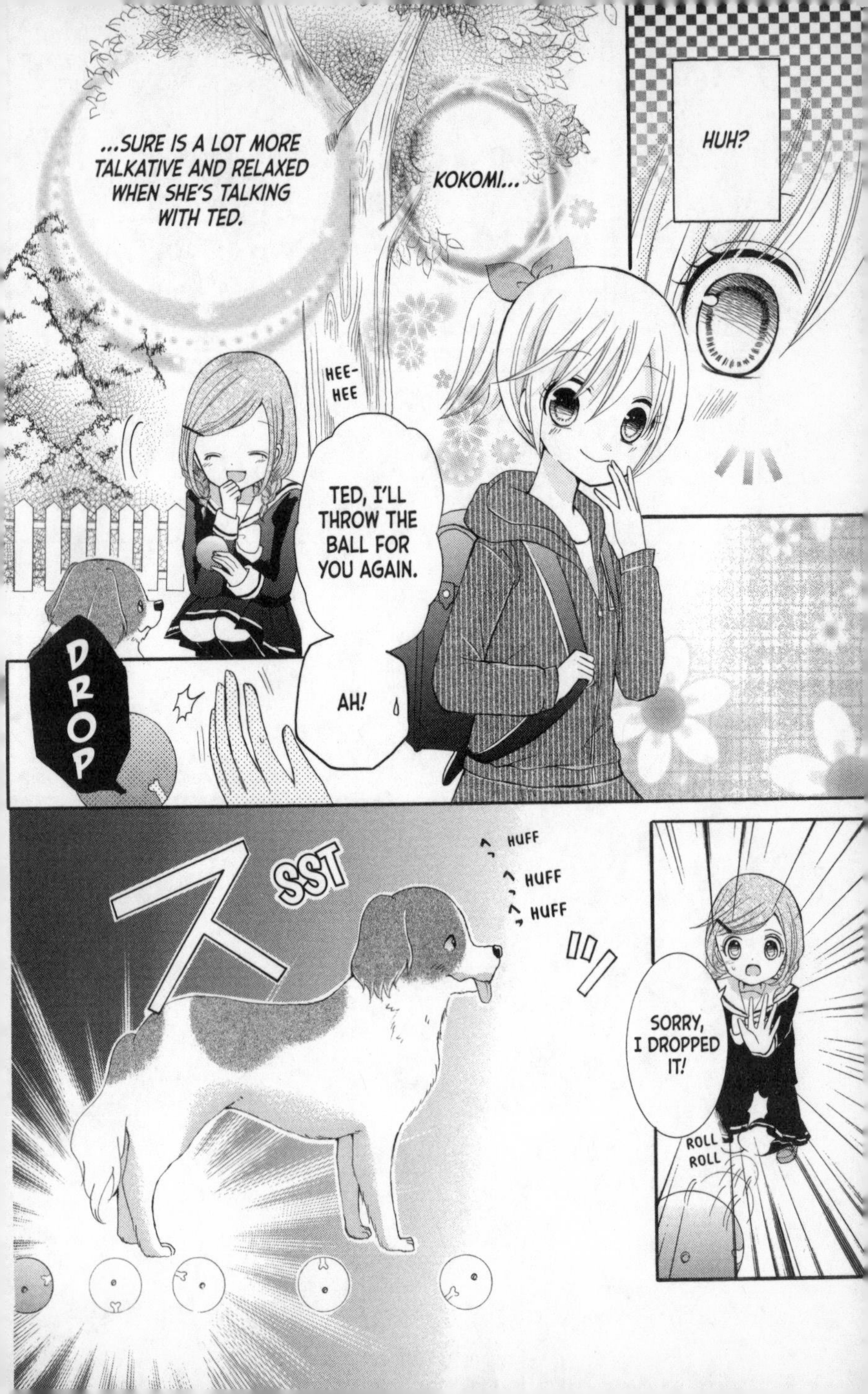
HUH?
KOKOMI...
...SURE IS A LOT MORE TALKATIVE AND RELAXED WHEN SHE'S TALKING WITH TED.
HEE-HEE
TED, I'LL THROW THE BALL FOR YOU AGAIN.
AH!
DROP
SORRY, I DROPPED IT!
ROLL ROLL
HUFF
HUFF
HUFF
SST

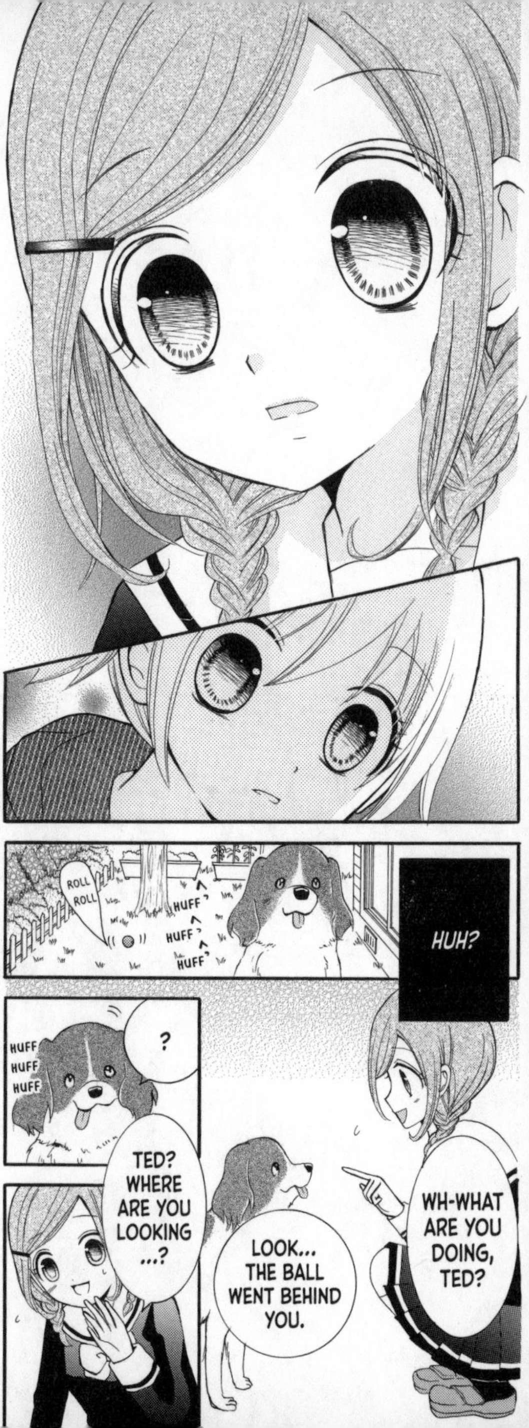
HUH?
ROLL
ROLL
HUFF
HUFF
HUFF
WH-WHAT ARE YOU DOING, TED?
?
HUFF
HUFF
HUFF
LOOK... THE BALL WENT BEHIND YOU.
TED? WHERE ARE YOU LOOKING ...?

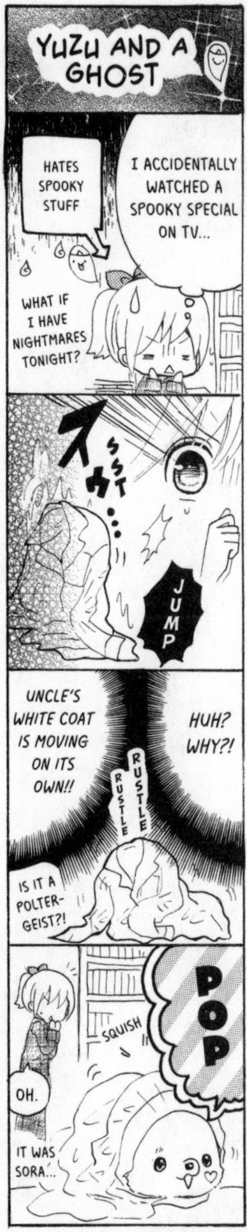
YUZU AND A GHOST
I ACCIDENTALLY WATCHED A SPOOKY SPECIAL ON TV...
HATES SPOOKY STUFF
WHAT IF I HAVE NIGHTMARES TONIGHT?
SSST...
JUMP
HUH? WHY?!
UNCLE'S WHITE COAT IS MOVING ON ITS OWN!!
RUSTLE
RUSTLE
IS IT A POLTER-GEIST?!
POP
SQUISH
OH.
IT WAS SORA...

SORA LIKES TO PLAY WITH DOCTOR HIDAKA'S WHITE COAT.

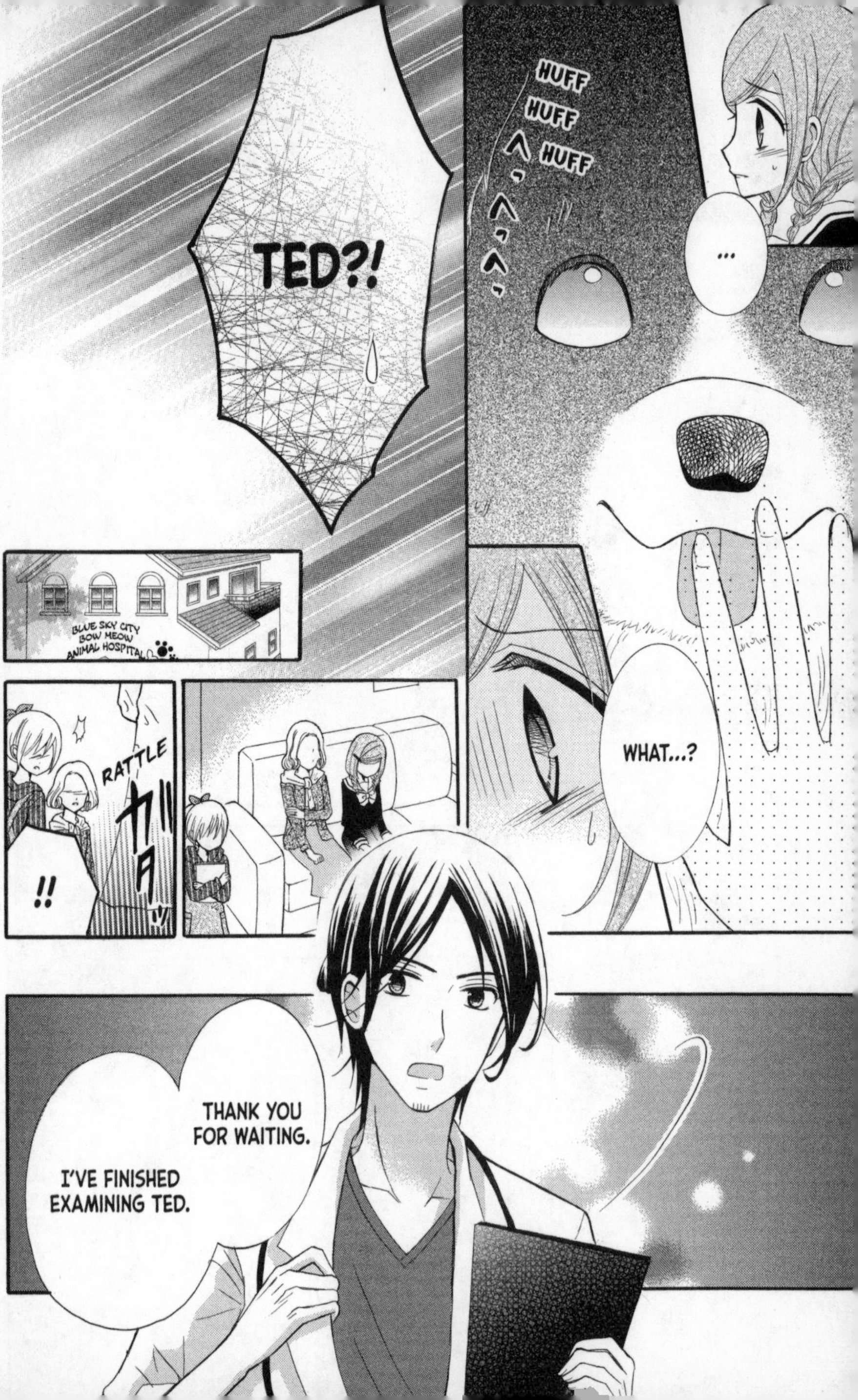
HUFF
HUFF
HUFF
...
WHAT...?
TED?!
BLUE SKY CITY BOW MEOW ANIMAL HOSPITAL
RATTLE
カタ
!!
THANK YOU FOR WAITING.
I'VE FINISHED EXAMINING TED.

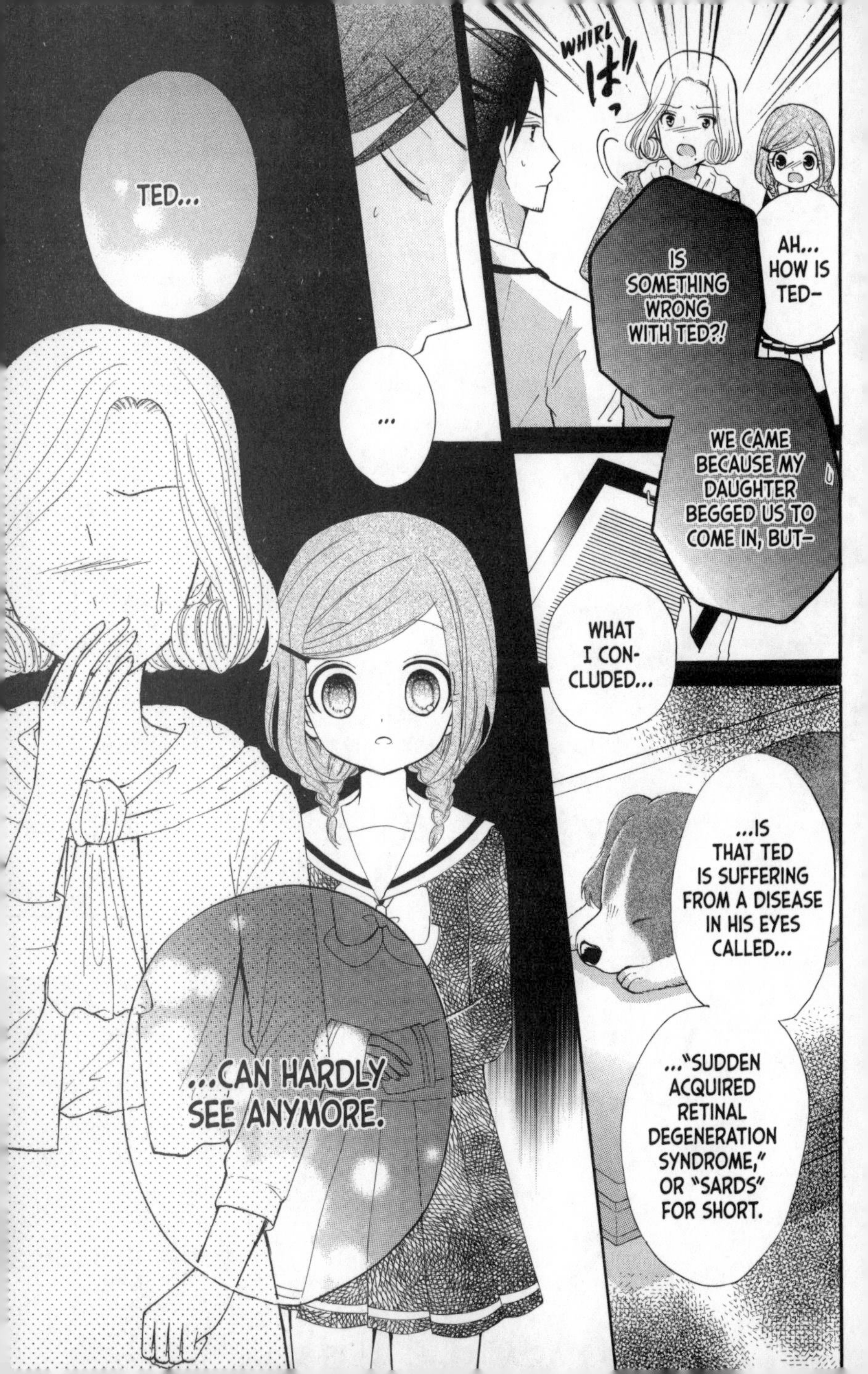
WHIRL
はっ
AH... HOW IS TED—
IS SOMETHING WRONG WITH TED?!
WE CAME BECAUSE MY DAUGHTER BEGGED US TO COME IN, BUT—
...
WHAT I CON-CLUDED...
...IS THAT TED IS SUFFERING FROM A DISEASE IN HIS EYES CALLED...
..."SUDDEN ACQUIRED RETINAL DEGENERATION SYNDROME," OR "SARDS" FOR SHORT.
TED...
...CAN HARDLY SEE ANYMORE.

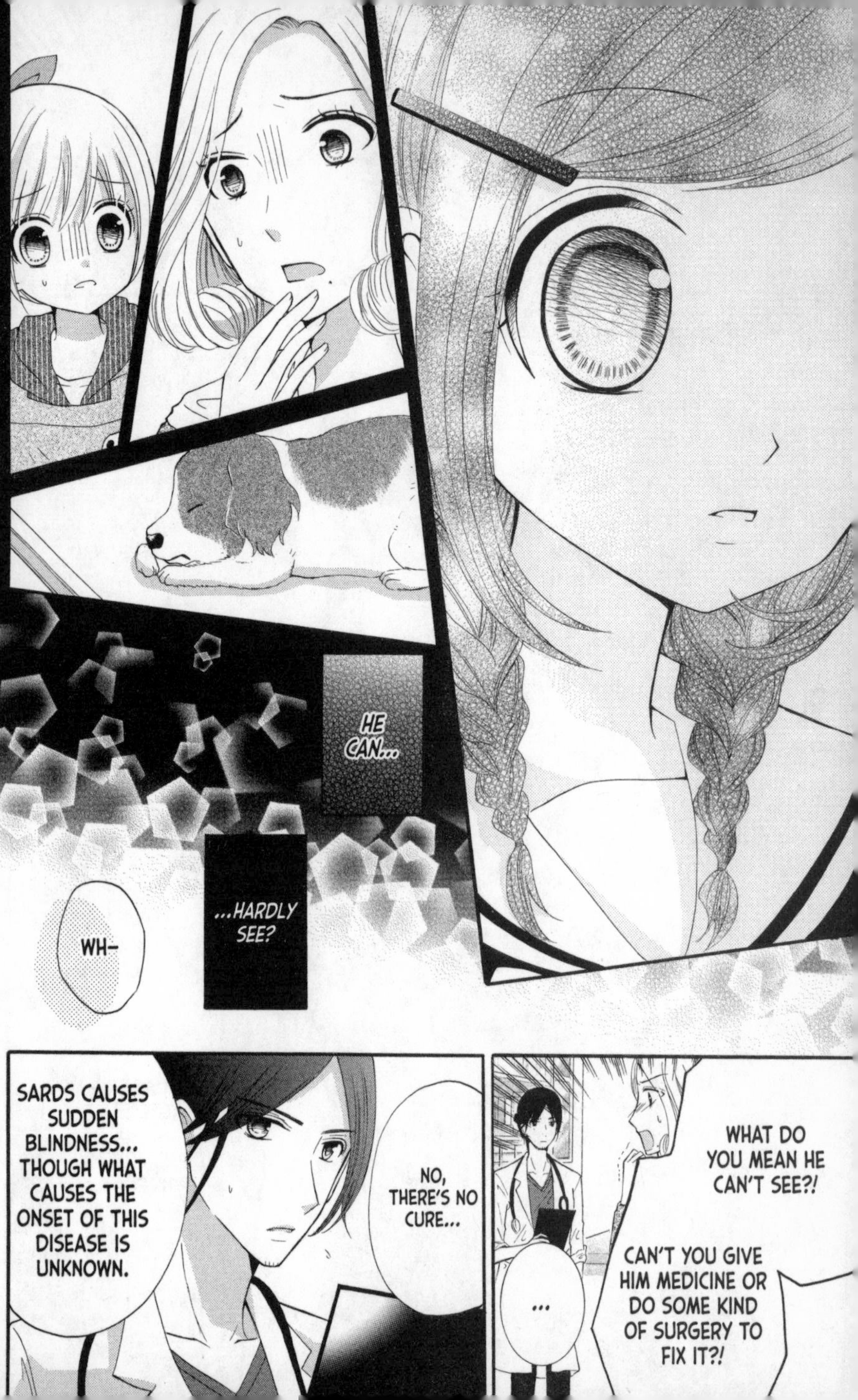
HE CAN...
...HARDLY SEE?
WH-
WHAT DO YOU MEAN HE CAN'T SEE?!
CAN'T YOU GIVE HIM MEDICINE OR DO SOME KIND OF SURGERY TO FIX IT?!
...
NO, THERE'S NO CURE...
SARDS CAUSES SUDDEN BLINDNESS... THOUGH WHAT CAUSES THE ONSET OF THIS DISEASE IS UNKNOWN.

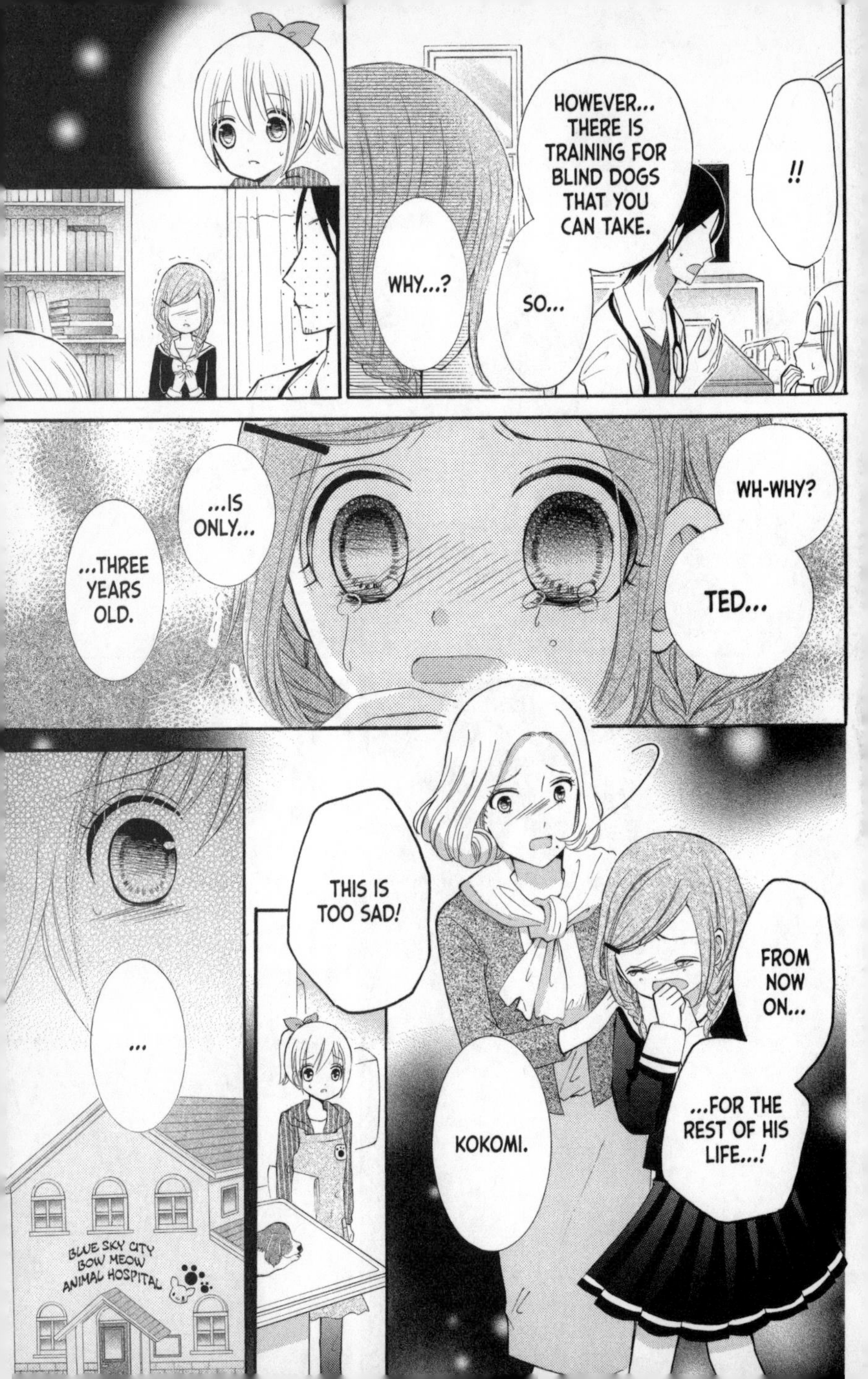
!!
HOWEVER... THERE IS TRAINING FOR BLIND DOGS THAT YOU CAN TAKE.
SO...
WHY...?
WH-WHY?
TED...
...IS ONLY...
...THREE YEARS OLD.
FROM NOW ON...
...FOR THE REST OF HIS LIFE...!
KOKOMI.
THIS IS TOO SAD!
...
BLUE SKY CITY BOW MEOW ANIMAL HOSPITAL

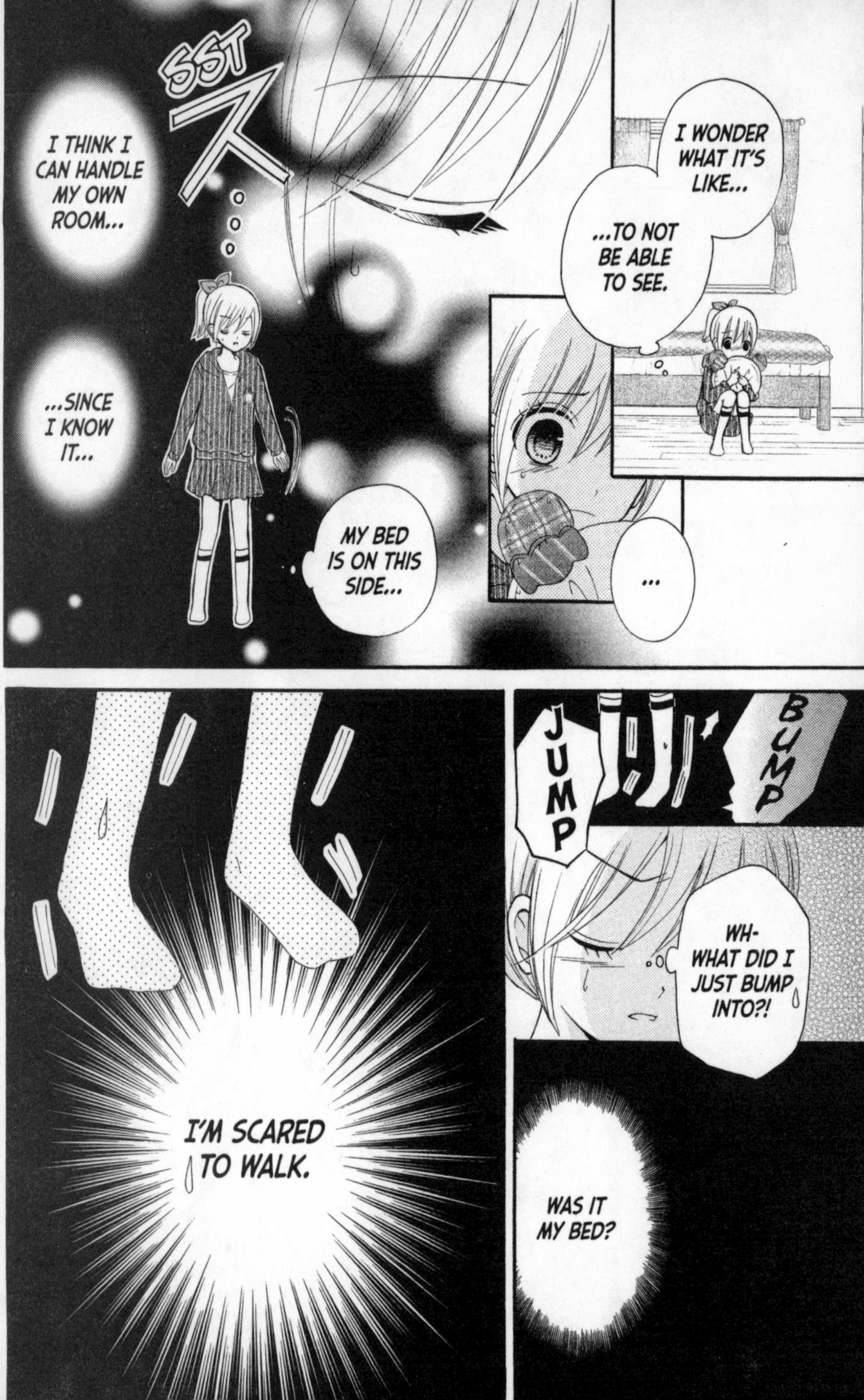
I WONDER WHAT IT'S LIKE...
...TO NOT BE ABLE TO SEE.
...
SST
I THINK I CAN HANDLE MY OWN ROOM...
...SINCE I KNOW IT...
MY BED IS ON THIS SIDE...
BUMP
JUMP
WH- WHAT DID I JUST BUMP INTO?!
WAS IT MY BED?
I'M SCARED TO WALK.

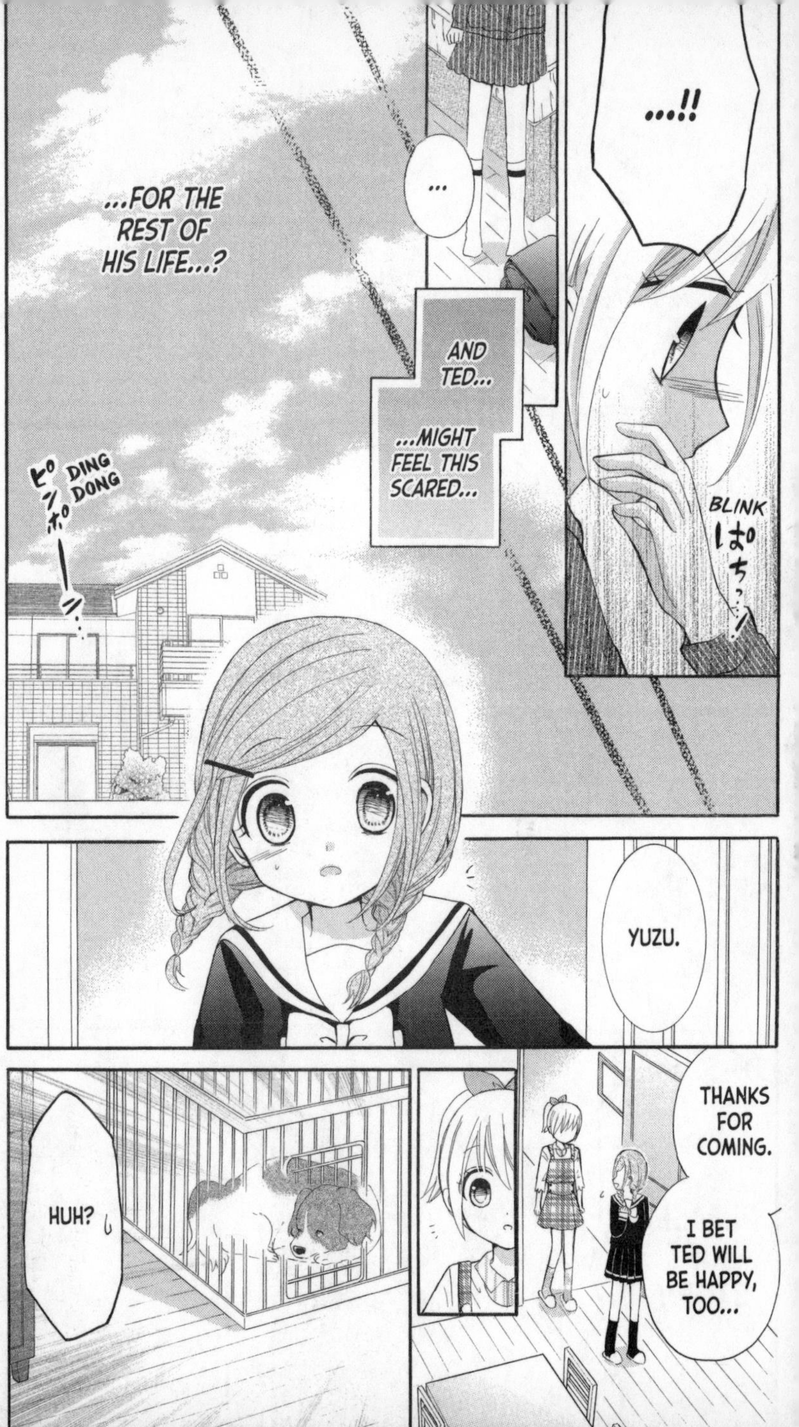

...!!
BLINK
ぱちっ
...
AND TED...
...MIGHT FEEL THIS SCARED...
...FOR THE REST OF HIS LIFE...?
ピンポーン
DING DONG
YUZU.
THANKS FOR COMING.
I BET TED WILL BE HAPPY, TOO...
HUH?

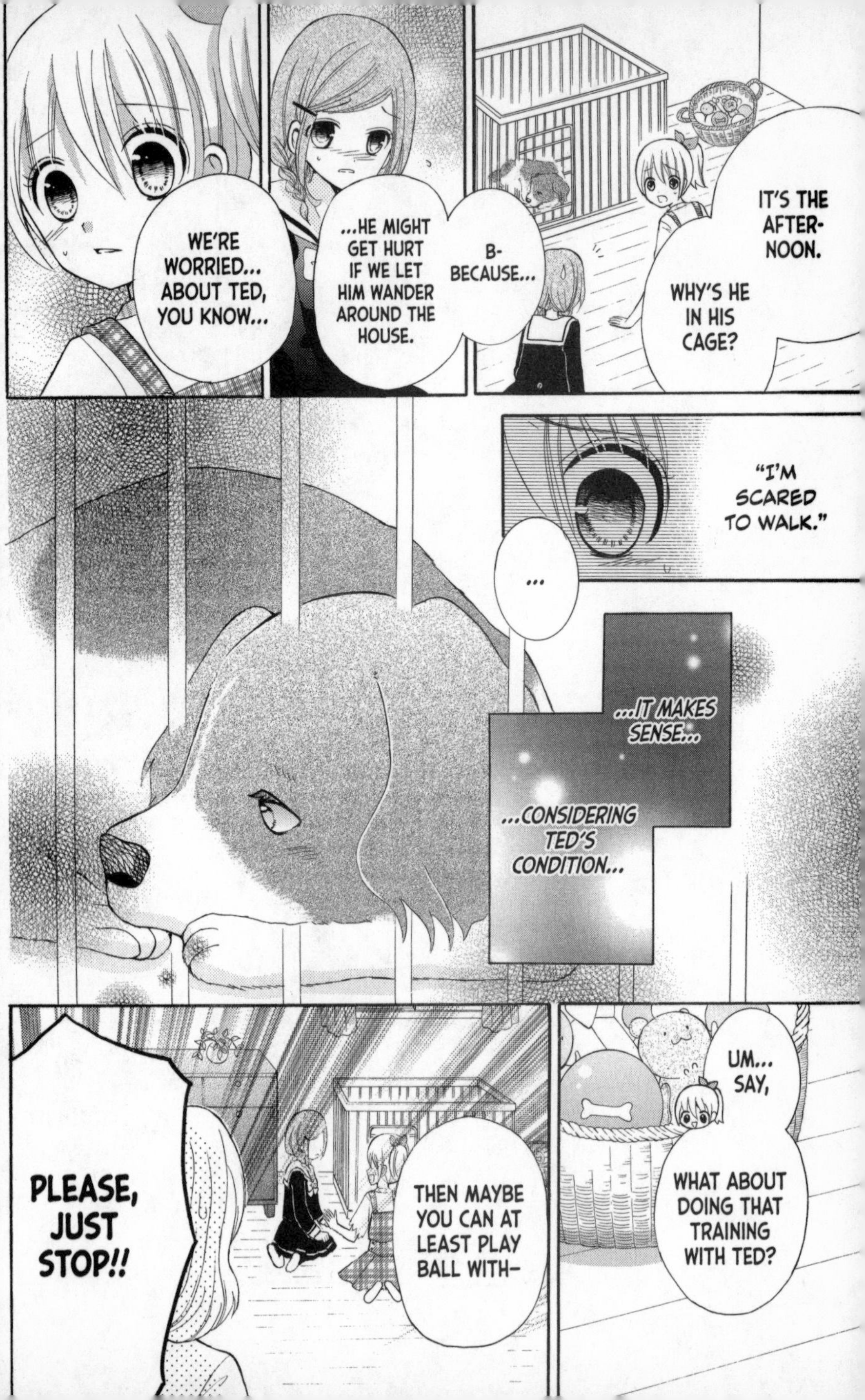
IT'S THE AFTERNOON.
WHY'S HE IN HIS CAGE?
B-BECAUSE...
...HE MIGHT GET HURT IF WE LET HIM WANDER AROUND THE HOUSE.
WE'RE WORRIED... ABOUT TED, YOU KNOW...
"I'M SCARED TO WALK."
...
...IT MAKES SENSE...
...CONSIDERING TED'S CONDITION...
UM... SAY,
WHAT ABOUT DOING THAT TRAINING WITH TED?
THEN MAYBE YOU CAN AT LEAST PLAY BALL WITH–
PLEASE, JUST STOP!!

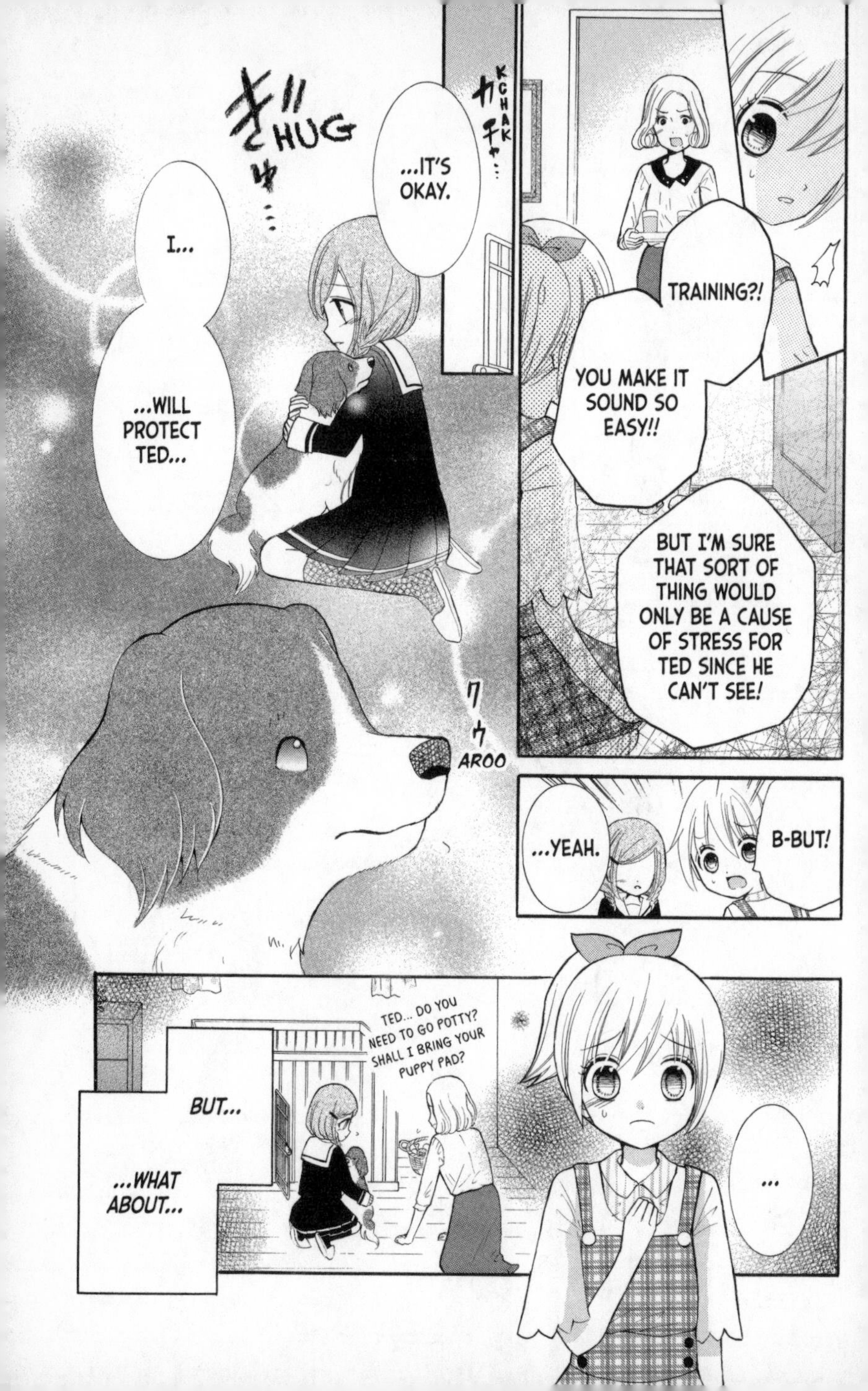
TRAINING?!
YOU MAKE IT SOUND SO EASY!!
BUT I'M SURE THAT SORT OF THING WOULD ONLY BE A CAUSE OF STRESS FOR TED SINCE HE CAN'T SEE!
B-BUT!
...YEAH.
KCHAK
...IT'S OKAY.
HUG
I...
...WILL PROTECT TED...
AROO
...
TED... DO YOU NEED TO GO POTTY? SHALL I BRING YOUR PUPPY PAD?
BUT...
...WHAT ABOUT...

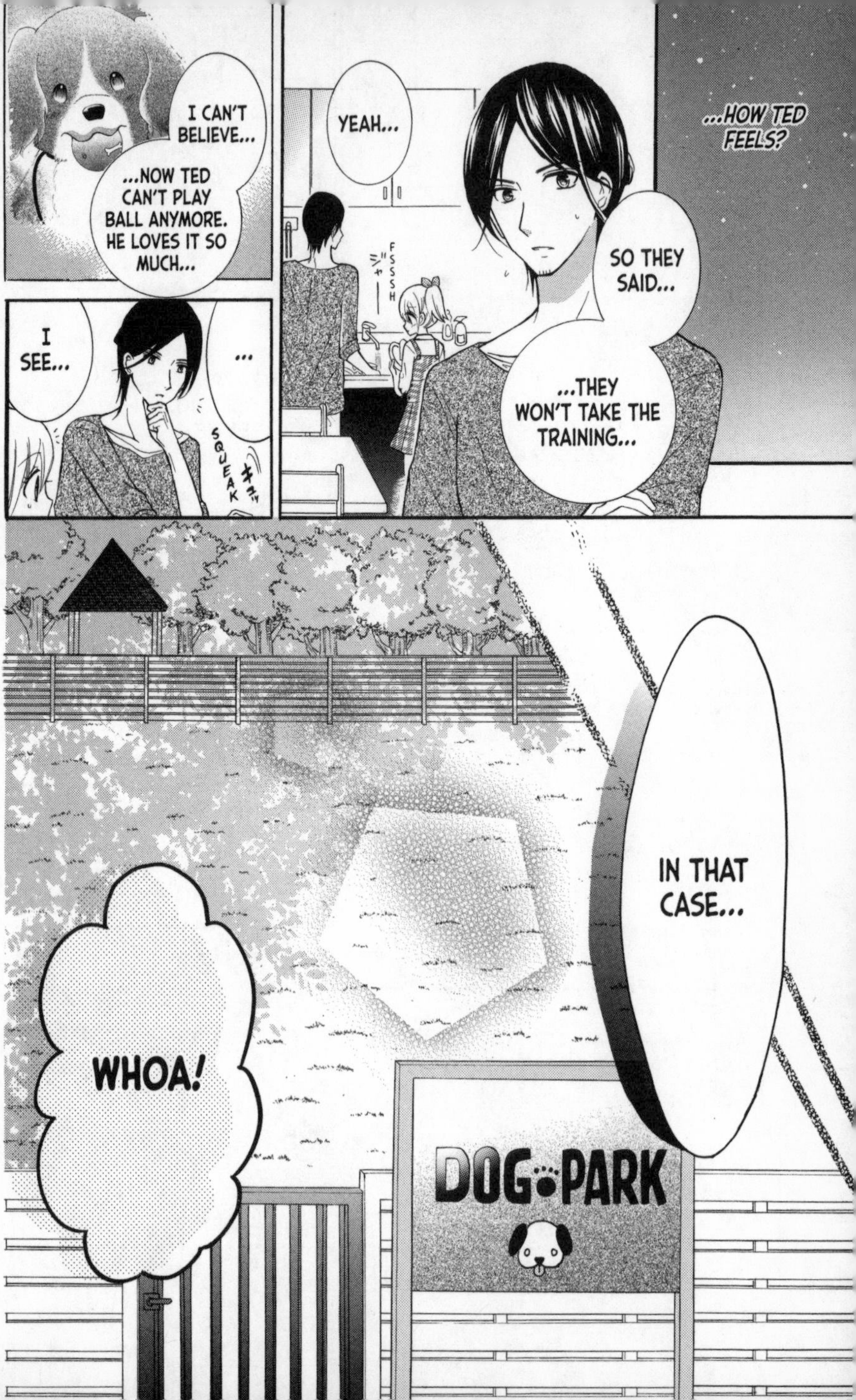

...HOW TED FEELS?
SO THEY SAID...
...THEY WON'T TAKE THE TRAINING...
YEAH...
FSSSH
I CAN'T BELIEVE...
...NOW TED CAN'T PLAY BALL ANYMORE. HE LOVES IT SO MUCH...
...
SQUEAK
I SEE...
IN THAT CASE...
DOG PARK
WHOA!

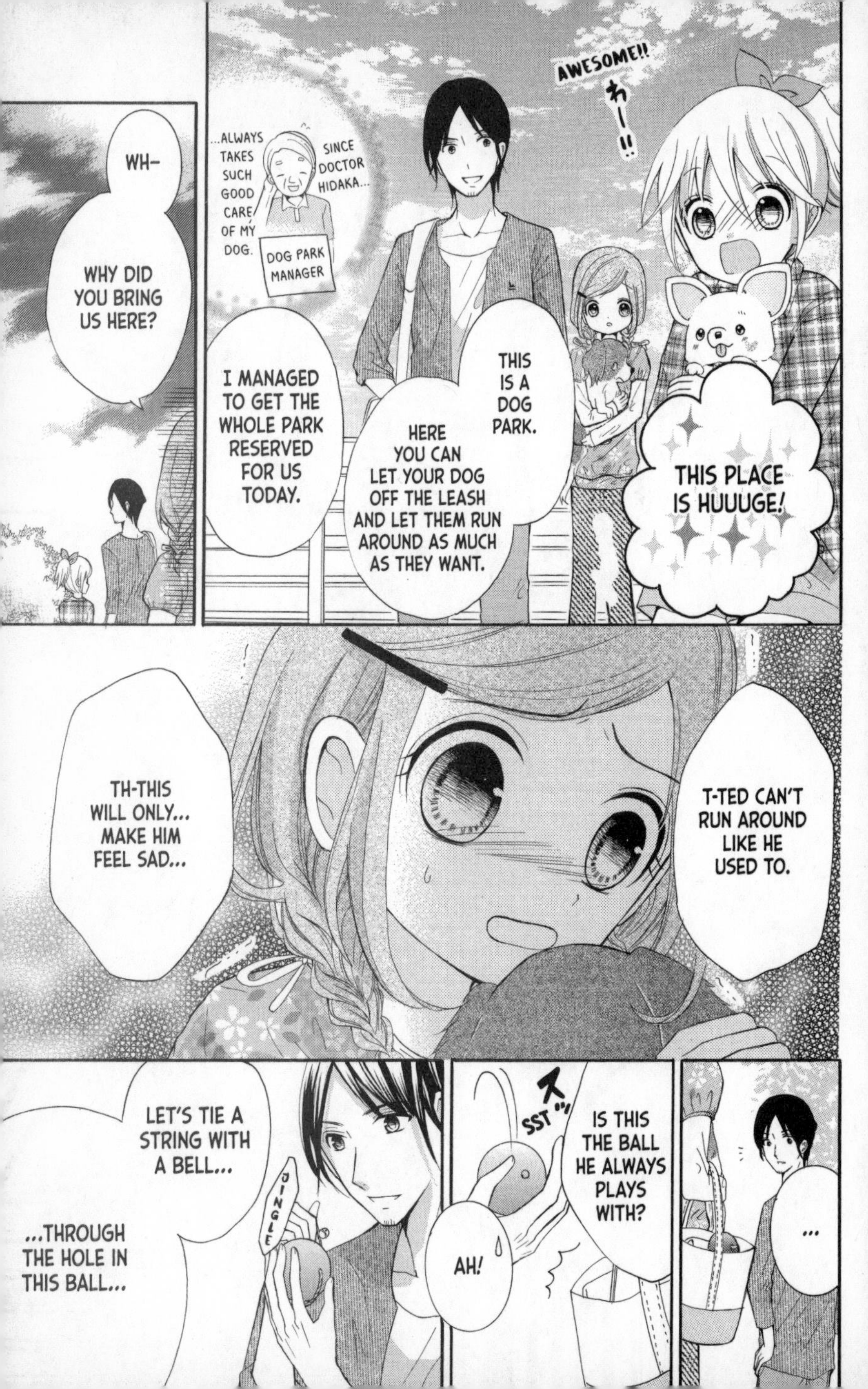
AWESOME!!
わー!!
THIS PLACE IS HUUUGE!
THIS IS A DOG PARK.
HERE YOU CAN LET YOUR DOG OFF THE LEASH AND LET THEM RUN AROUND AS MUCH AS THEY WANT.
I MANAGED TO GET THE WHOLE PARK RESERVED FOR US TODAY.
SINCE DOCTOR HIDAKA...
...ALWAYS TAKES SUCH GOOD CARE OF MY DOG.
DOG PARK MANAGER
WH-
WHY DID YOU BRING US HERE?
T-TED CAN'T RUN AROUND LIKE HE USED TO.
TH-THIS WILL ONLY... MAKE HIM FEEL SAD...
...
IS THIS THE BALL HE ALWAYS PLAYS WITH?
ス
SST ッ
AH!
LET'S TIE A STRING WITH A BELL...
JINGLE
...THROUGH THE HOLE IN THIS BALL...

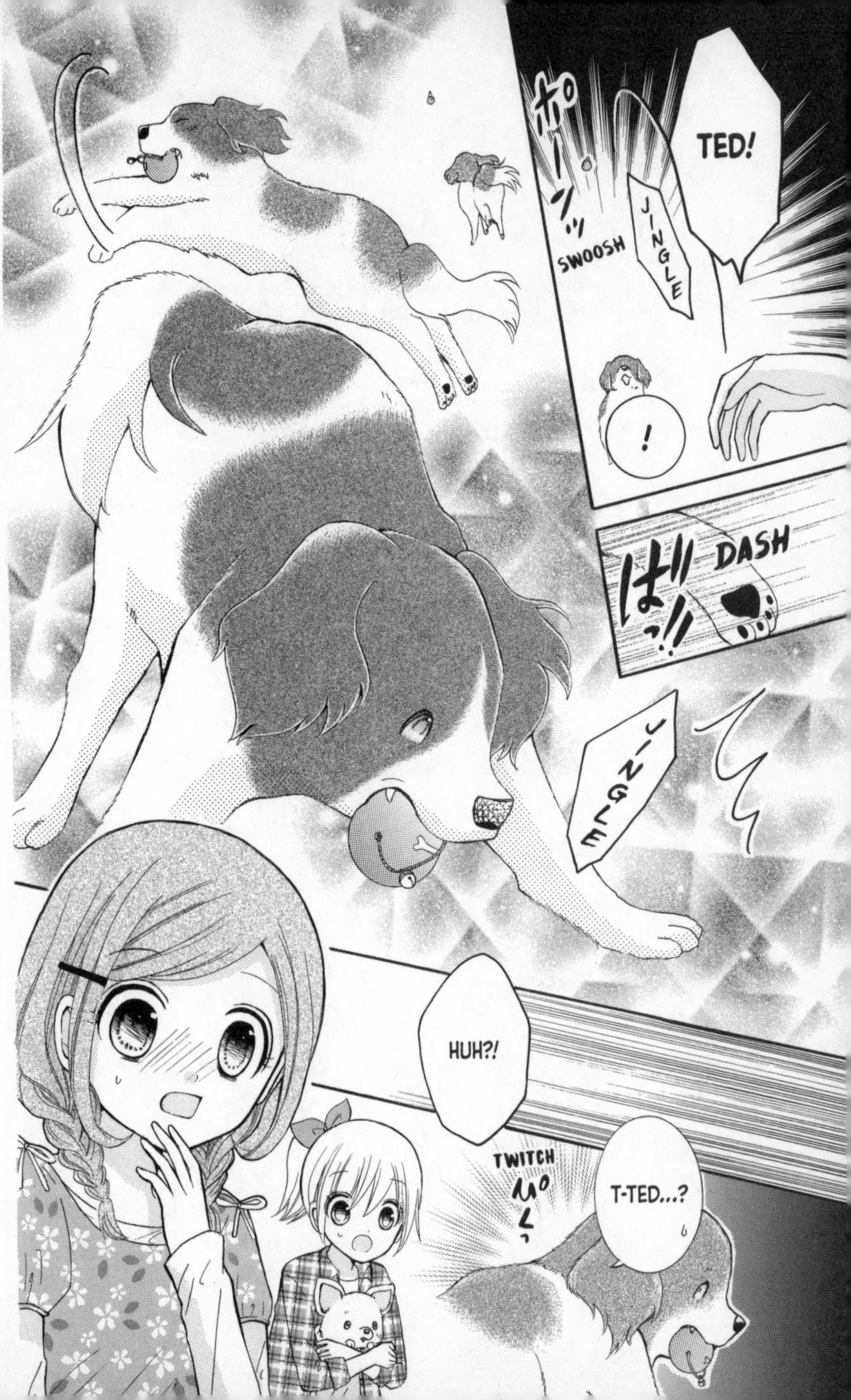
TED!
SWOOSH
JINGLE
!
DASH
JINGLE
HUH?!
TWITCH
T-TED...?

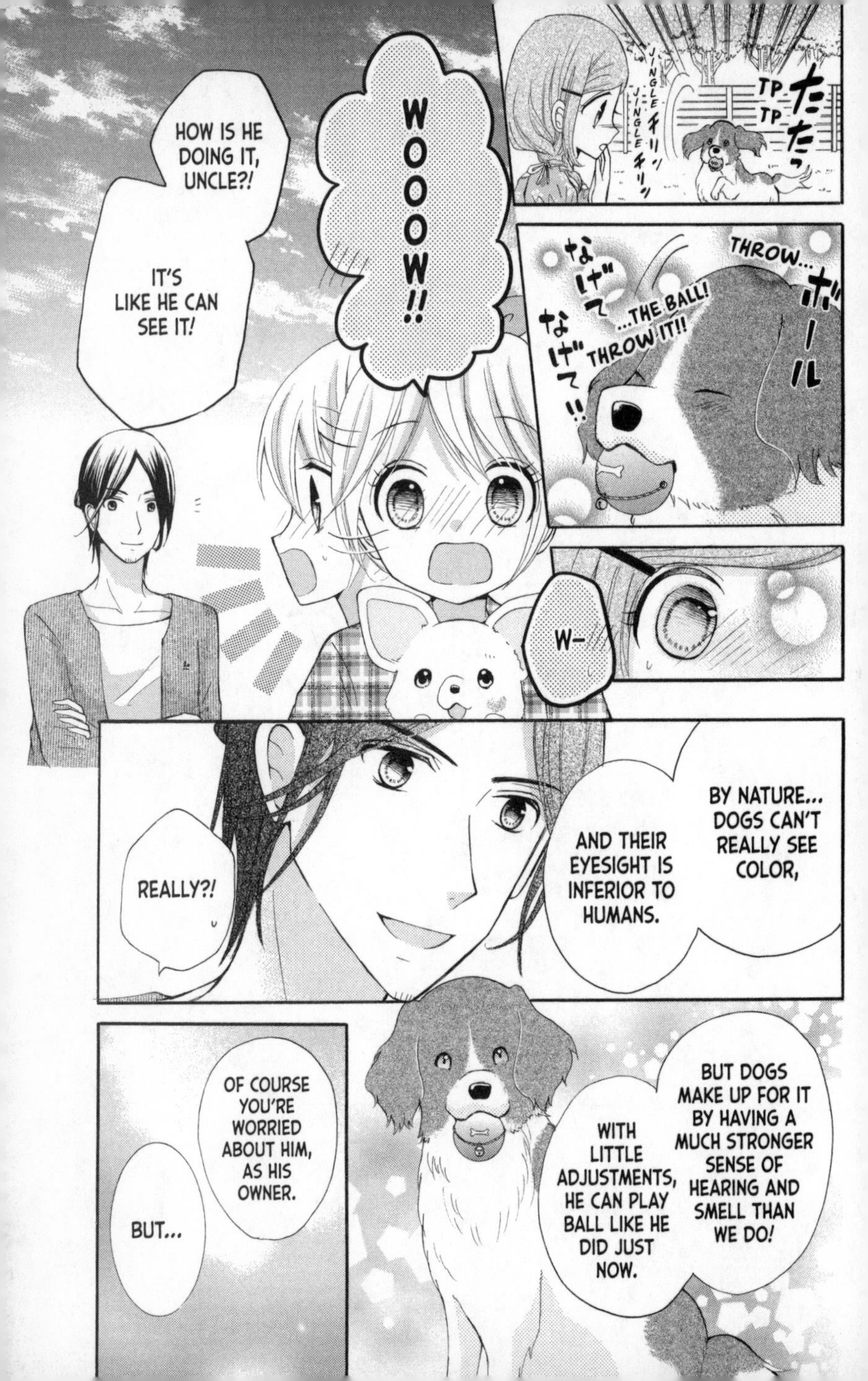
TP TP
たたっ
JINGLE JINGLE
チリッ チリッ
THROW...
ボール
...THE BALL! THROW IT!!
なげて なげて!!
W-
WOOOW!!
HOW IS HE DOING IT, UNCLE?!
IT'S LIKE HE CAN SEE IT!
BY NATURE... DOGS CAN'T REALLY SEE COLOR,
AND THEIR EYESIGHT IS INFERIOR TO HUMANS.
REALLY?!
BUT DOGS MAKE UP FOR IT BY HAVING A MUCH STRONGER SENSE OF HEARING AND SMELL THAN WE DO!
WITH LITTLE ADJUSTMENTS, HE CAN PLAY BALL LIKE HE DID JUST NOW.
OF COURSE YOU'RE WORRIED ABOUT HIM, AS HIS OWNER.
BUT...

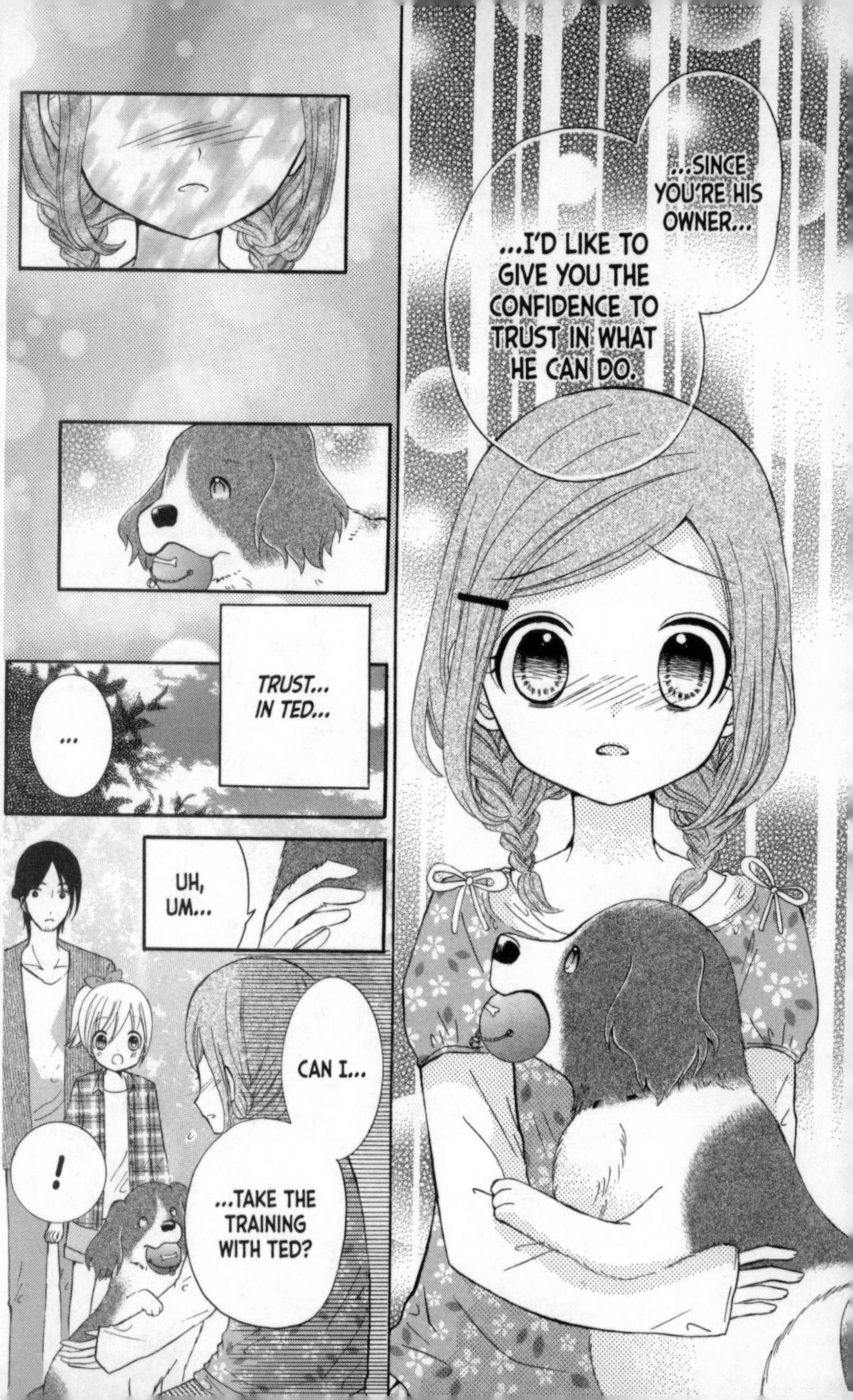
...SINCE YOU'RE HIS OWNER...
...I'D LIKE TO GIVE YOU THE CONFIDENCE TO TRUST IN WHAT HE CAN DO.
TRUST... IN TED...
...
UH, UM...
CAN I...
...TAKE THE TRAINING WITH TED?
!

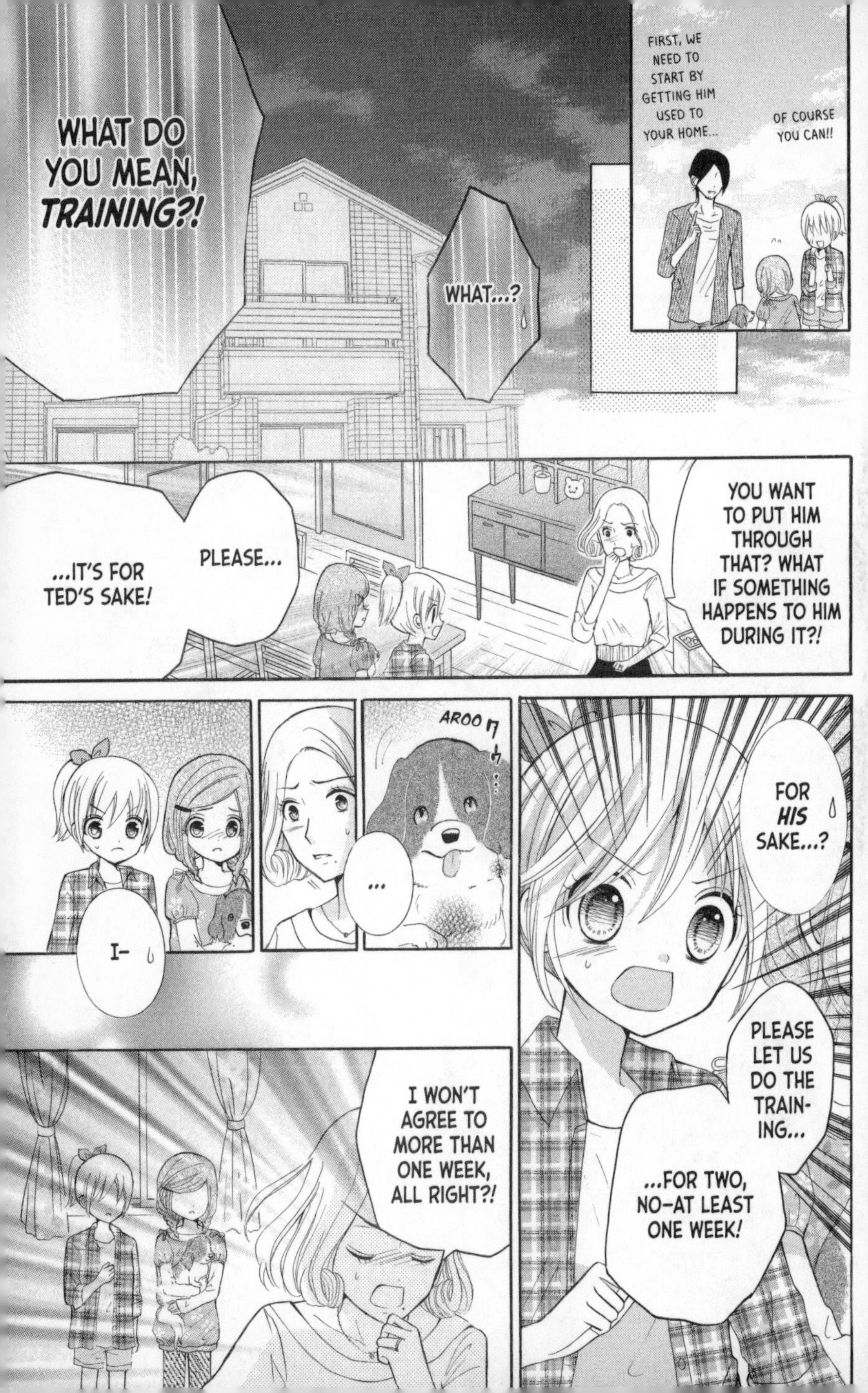
OF COURSE YOU CAN!!
FIRST, WE NEED TO START BY GETTING HIM USED TO YOUR HOME...
WHAT...?
WHAT DO YOU MEAN, TRAINING?!
YOU WANT TO PUT HIM THROUGH THAT? WHAT IF SOMETHING HAPPENS TO HIM DURING IT?!
PLEASE...
...IT'S FOR TED'S SAKE!
FOR HIS SAKE...?
PLEASE LET US DO THE TRAIN-ING...
...FOR TWO, NO—AT LEAST ONE WEEK!
AROO
...
I–
I WON'T AGREE TO MORE THAN ONE WEEK, ALL RIGHT?!

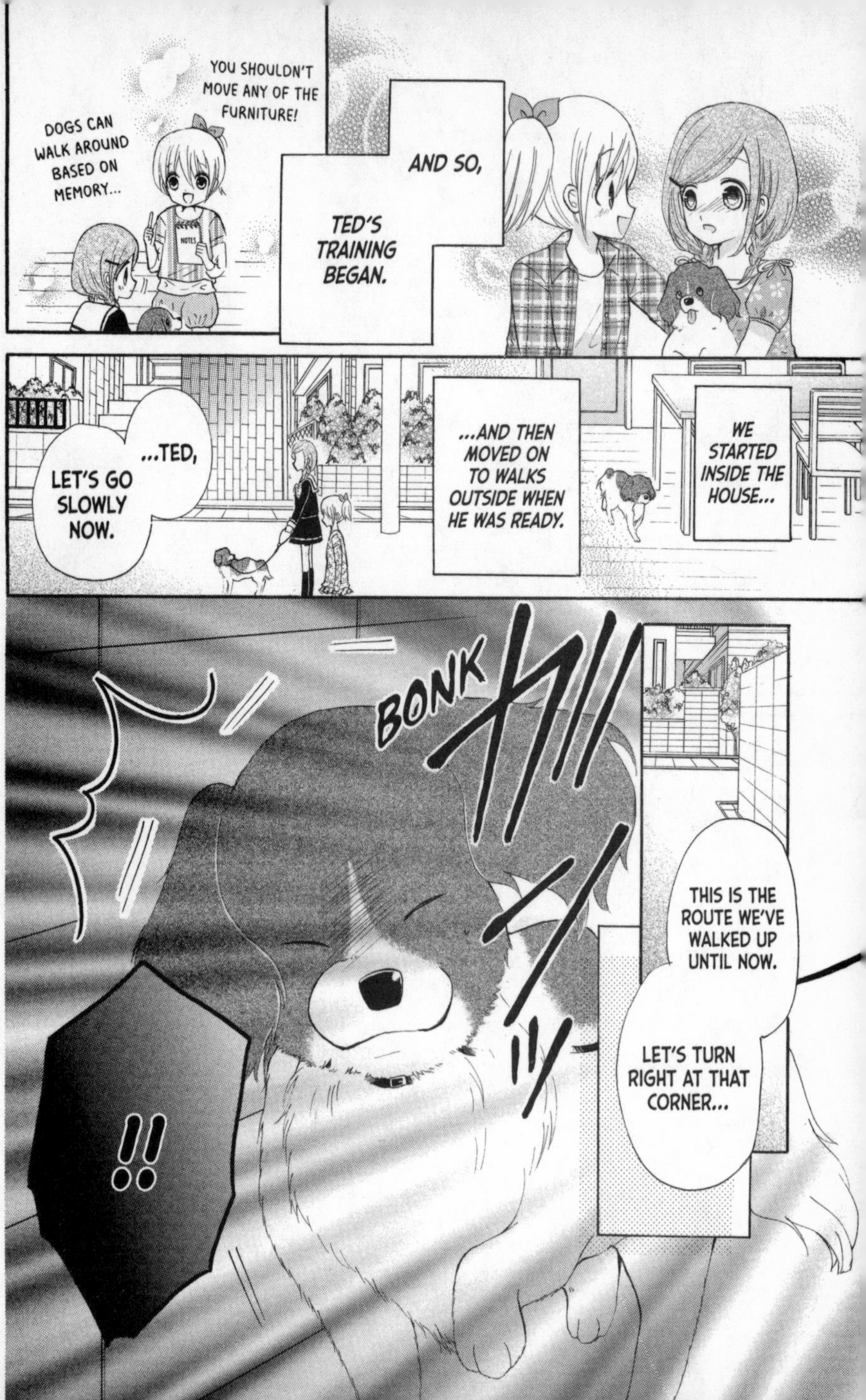
AND SO, TED'S TRAINING BEGAN.
YOU SHOULDN'T MOVE ANY OF THE FURNITURE!
DOGS CAN WALK AROUND BASED ON MEMORY...
NOTES
WE STARTED INSIDE THE HOUSE...
...AND THEN MOVED ON TO WALKS OUTSIDE WHEN HE WAS READY.
...TED, LET'S GO SLOWLY NOW.
THIS IS THE ROUTE WE'VE WALKED UP UNTIL NOW.
LET'S TURN RIGHT AT THAT CORNER...
BONK
!!

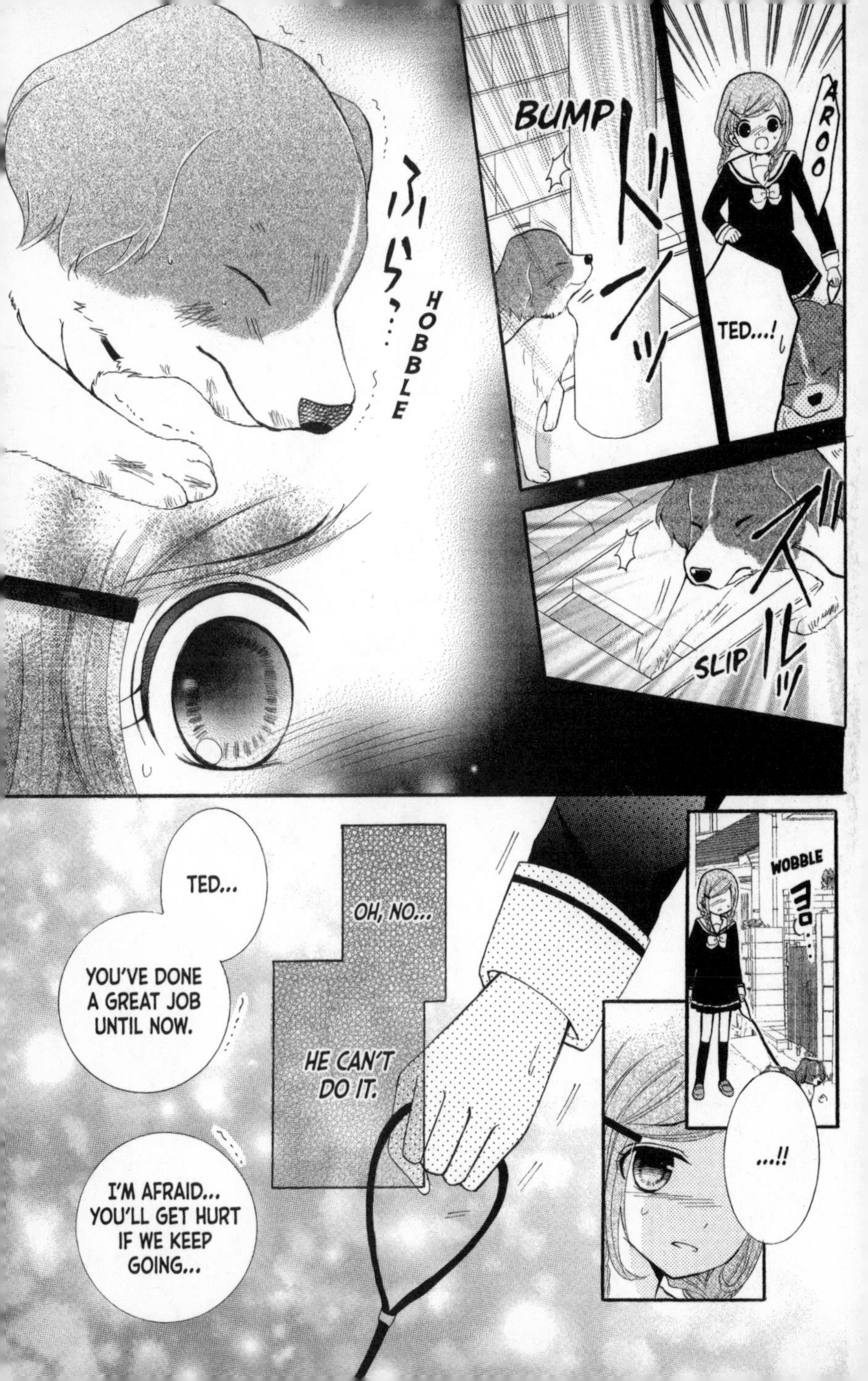
AROO
TED...!
BUMP
SLIP
ふらっ...
HOBBLE
WOBBLE
ヨロ...
...!!
OH, NO...
HE CAN'T DO IT.
TED...
YOU'VE DONE A GREAT JOB UNTIL NOW.
I'M AFRAID... YOU'LL GET HURT IF WE KEEP GOING...

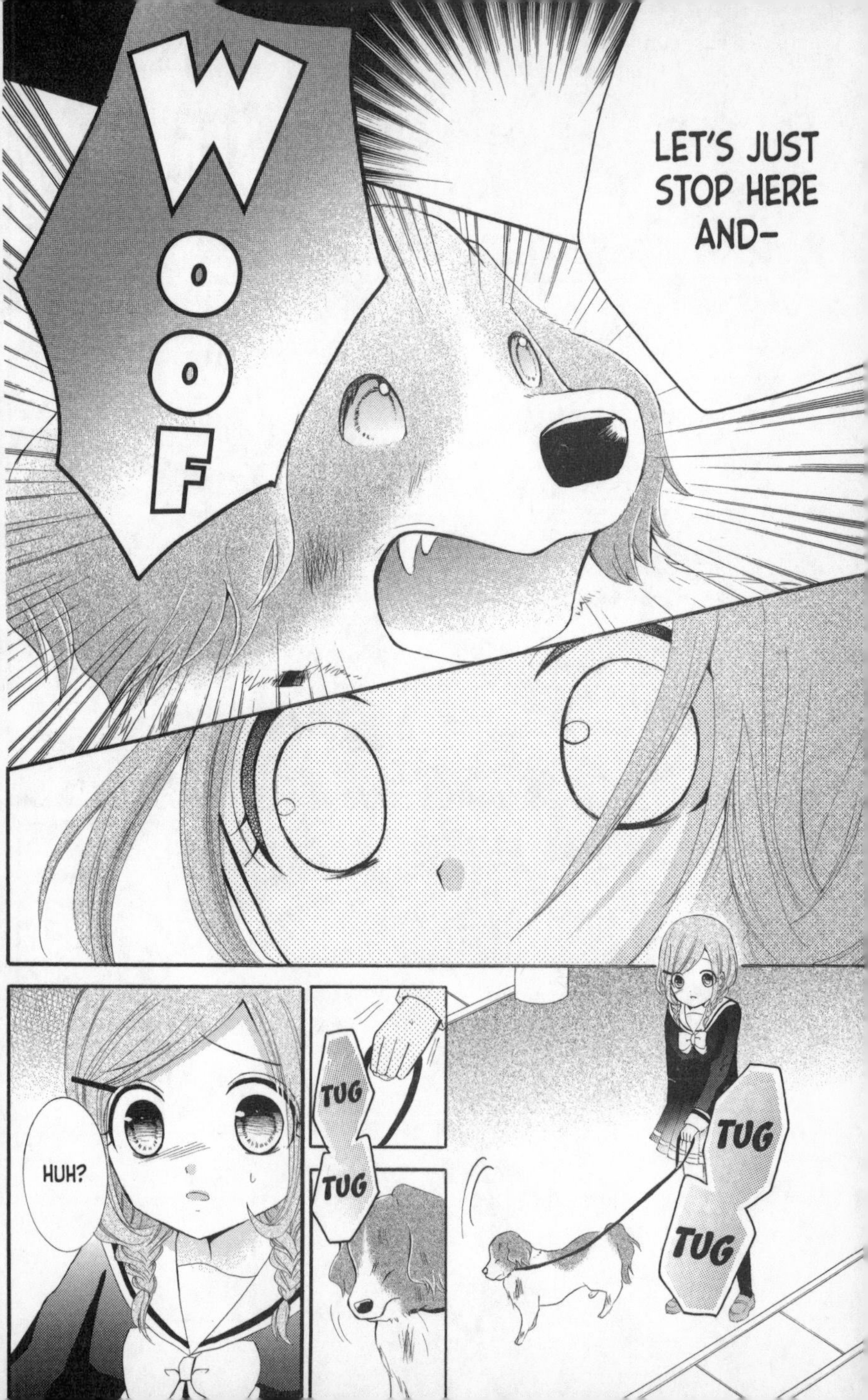
LET'S JUST STOP HERE AND-
WOOF
TUG
TUG
TUG
TUG
HUH?

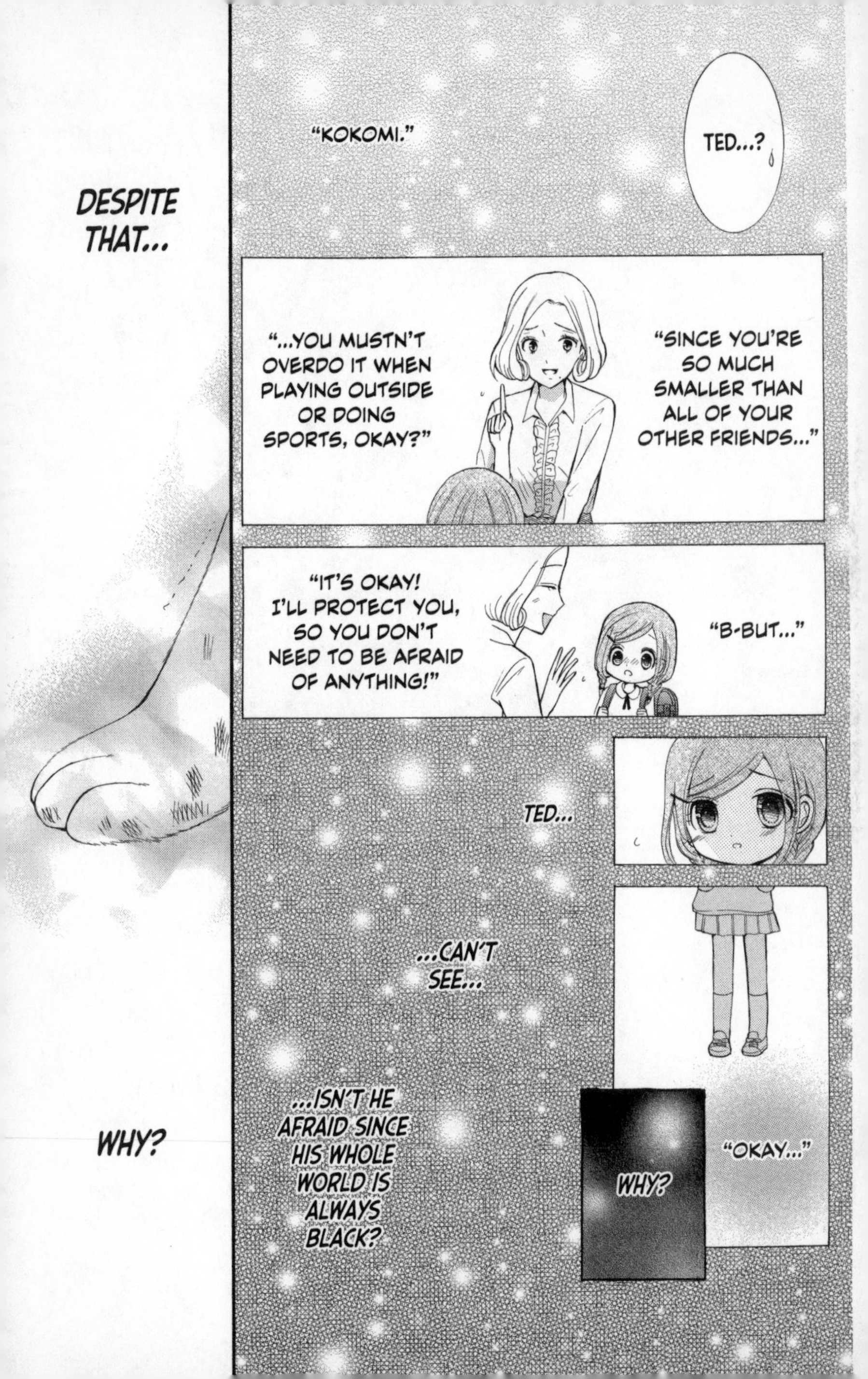
TED...?
"KOKOMI."
"SINCE YOU'RE SO MUCH SMALLER THAN ALL OF YOUR OTHER FRIENDS..."
"...YOU MUSTN'T OVERDO IT WHEN PLAYING OUTSIDE OR DOING SPORTS, OKAY?"
"B-BUT..."
"IT'S OKAY! I'LL PROTECT YOU, SO YOU DON'T NEED TO BE AFRAID OF ANYTHING!"
TED...
...CAN'T SEE...
"OKAY..."
WHY?
...ISN'T HE AFRAID SINCE HIS WHOLE WORLD IS ALWAYS BLACK?
DESPITE THAT...
WHY?

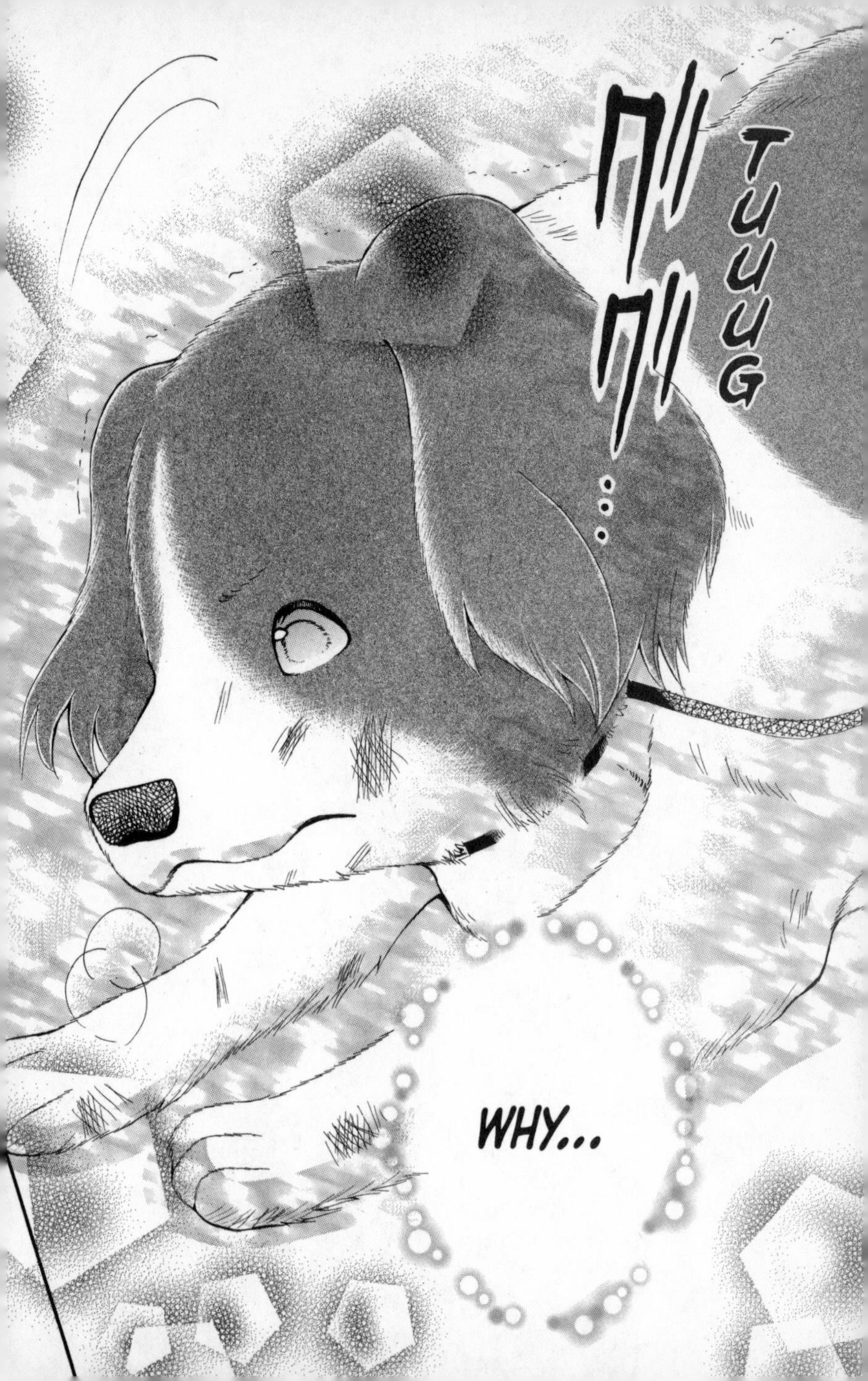
TUUUG
...
WHY...

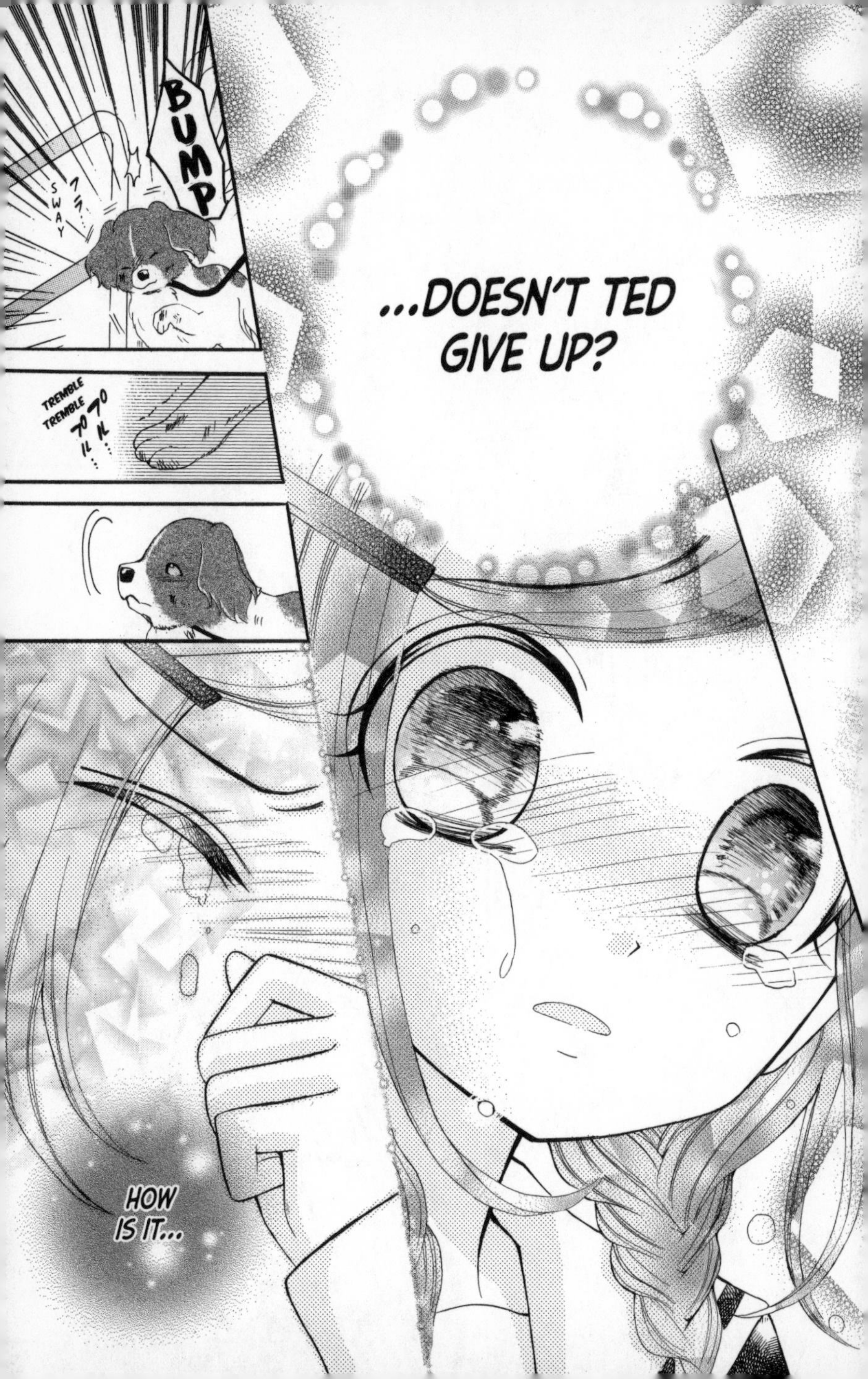

BUMP
SWAY
フラ…
TREMBLE TREMBLE
フルフル…
HOW IS IT...
...DOESN'T TED GIVE UP?

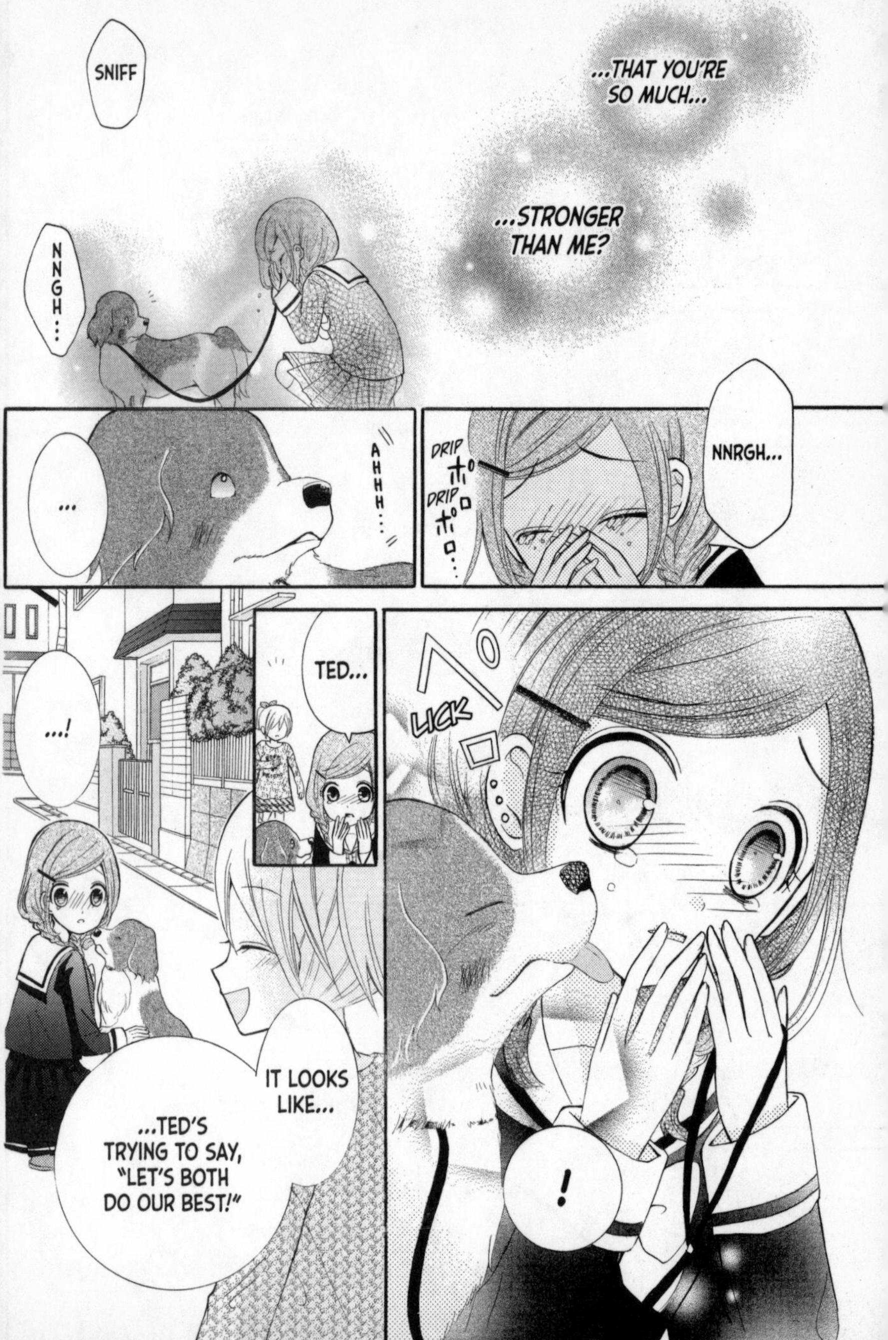
...THAT YOU'RE SO MUCH...
...STRONGER THAN ME?
SNIFF
NNGH...
NNRGH...
DRIP DRIP
AHHH...
...
LICK
!
TED...
...!
IT LOOKS LIKE...
...TED'S TRYING TO SAY, "LET'S BOTH DO OUR BEST!"

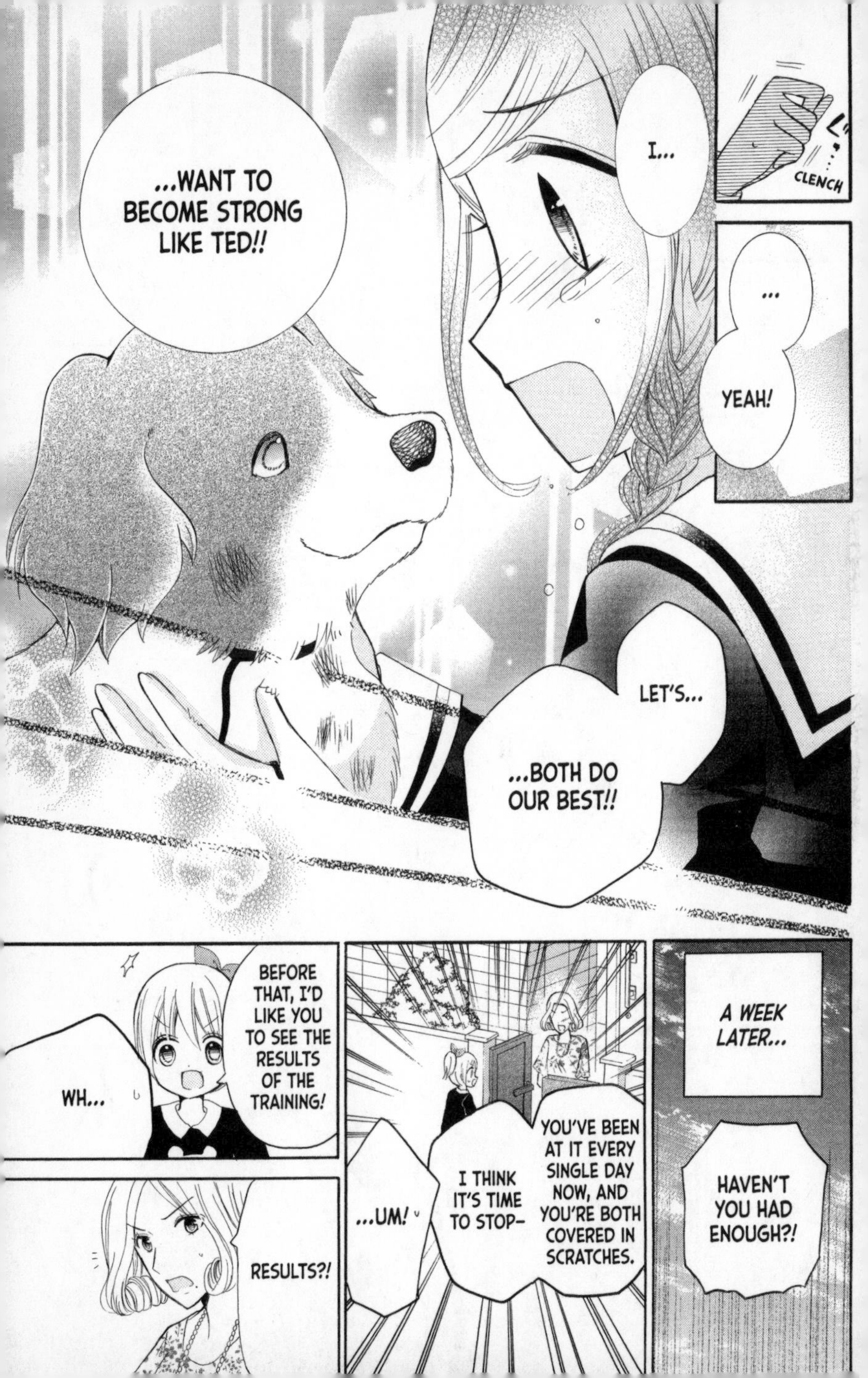
CLENCH
...
YEAH!
I...
...WANT TO BECOME STRONG LIKE TED!!
LET'S...
...BOTH DO OUR BEST!!
A WEEK LATER...
HAVEN'T YOU HAD ENOUGH?!
YOU'VE BEEN AT IT EVERY SINGLE DAY NOW, AND YOU'RE BOTH COVERED IN SCRATCHES.
I THINK IT'S TIME TO STOP–
...UM!
BEFORE THAT, I'D LIKE YOU TO SEE THE RESULTS OF THE TRAINING!
WH...
RESULTS?!

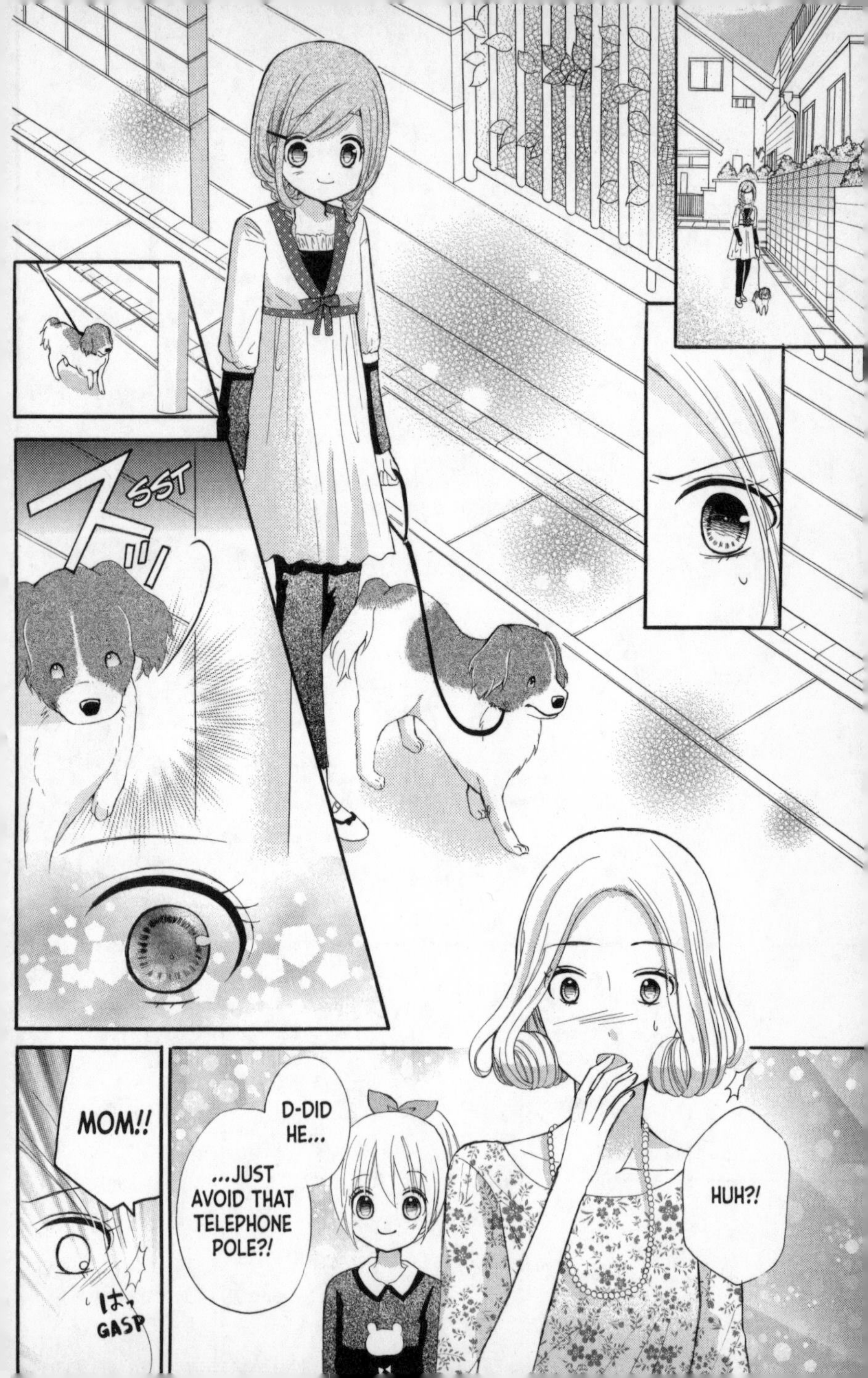
スッ
SST
D-DID HE...
...JUST AVOID THAT TELEPHONE POLE?!
HUH?!
MOM!!
はっ
GASP

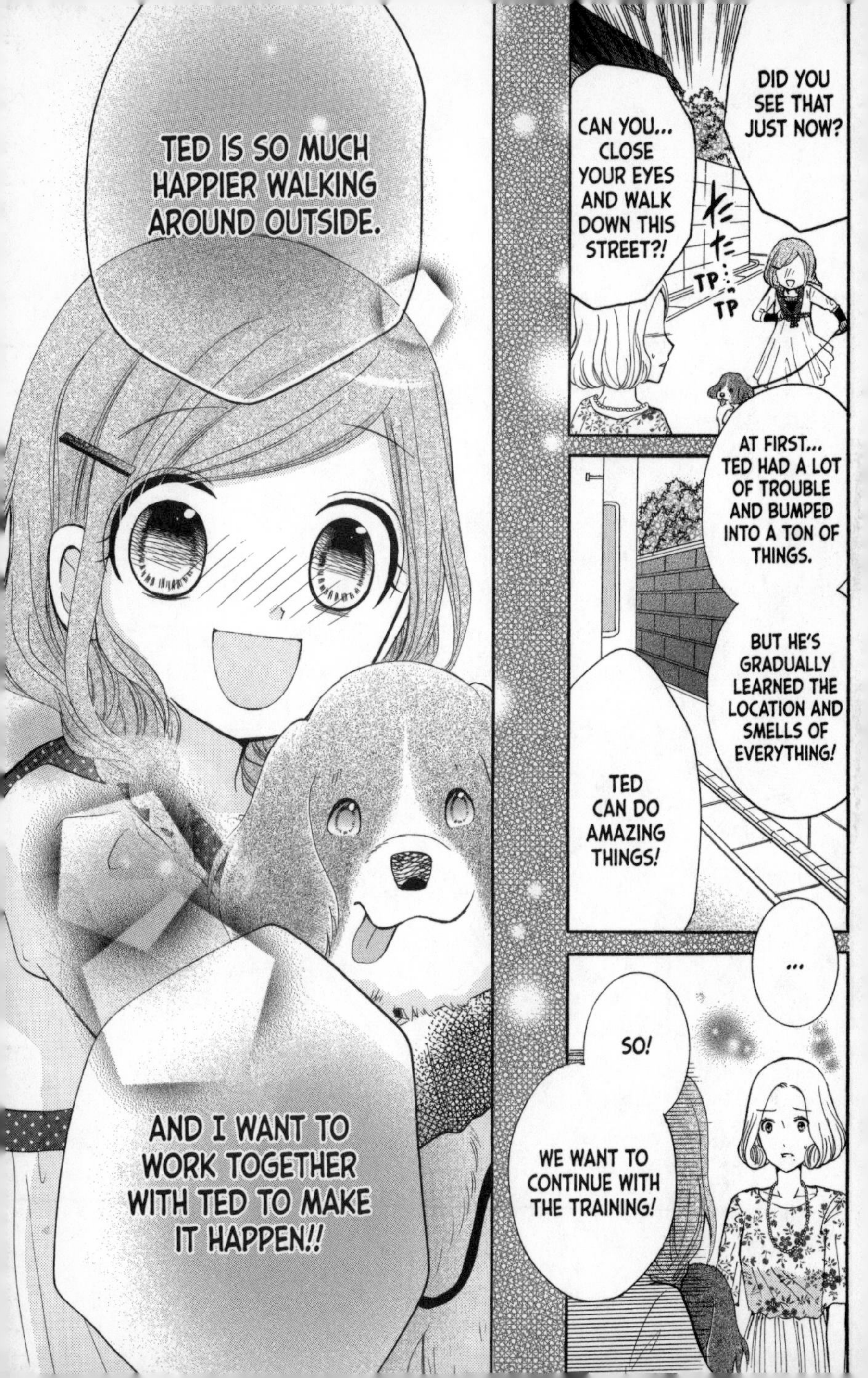
DID YOU SEE THAT JUST NOW?
CAN YOU... CLOSE YOUR EYES AND WALK DOWN THIS STREET?!
TP TP
AT FIRST... TED HAD A LOT OF TROUBLE AND BUMPED INTO A TON OF THINGS.
BUT HE'S GRADUALLY LEARNED THE LOCATION AND SMELLS OF EVERYTHING!
TED CAN DO AMAZING THINGS!
...
SO!
WE WANT TO CONTINUE WITH THE TRAINING!
TED IS SO MUCH HAPPIER WALKING AROUND OUTSIDE.
AND I WANT TO WORK TOGETHER WITH TED TO MAKE IT HAPPEN!!

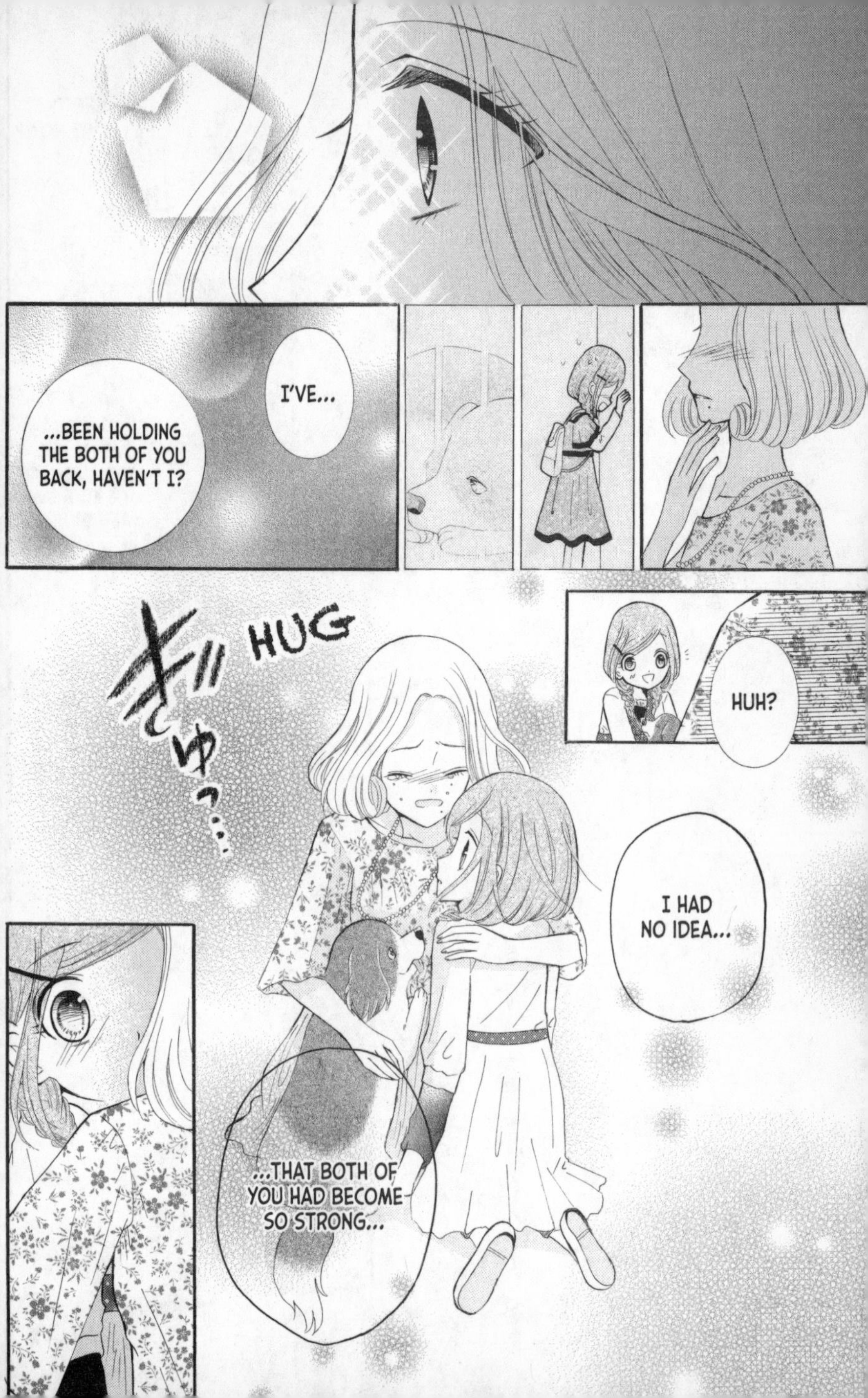
I'VE...
...BEEN HOLDING THE BOTH OF YOU BACK, HAVEN'T I?
HUH?
ぎゅっ…
HUG
I HAD NO IDEA...
...THAT BOTH OF YOU HAD BECOME SO STRONG...

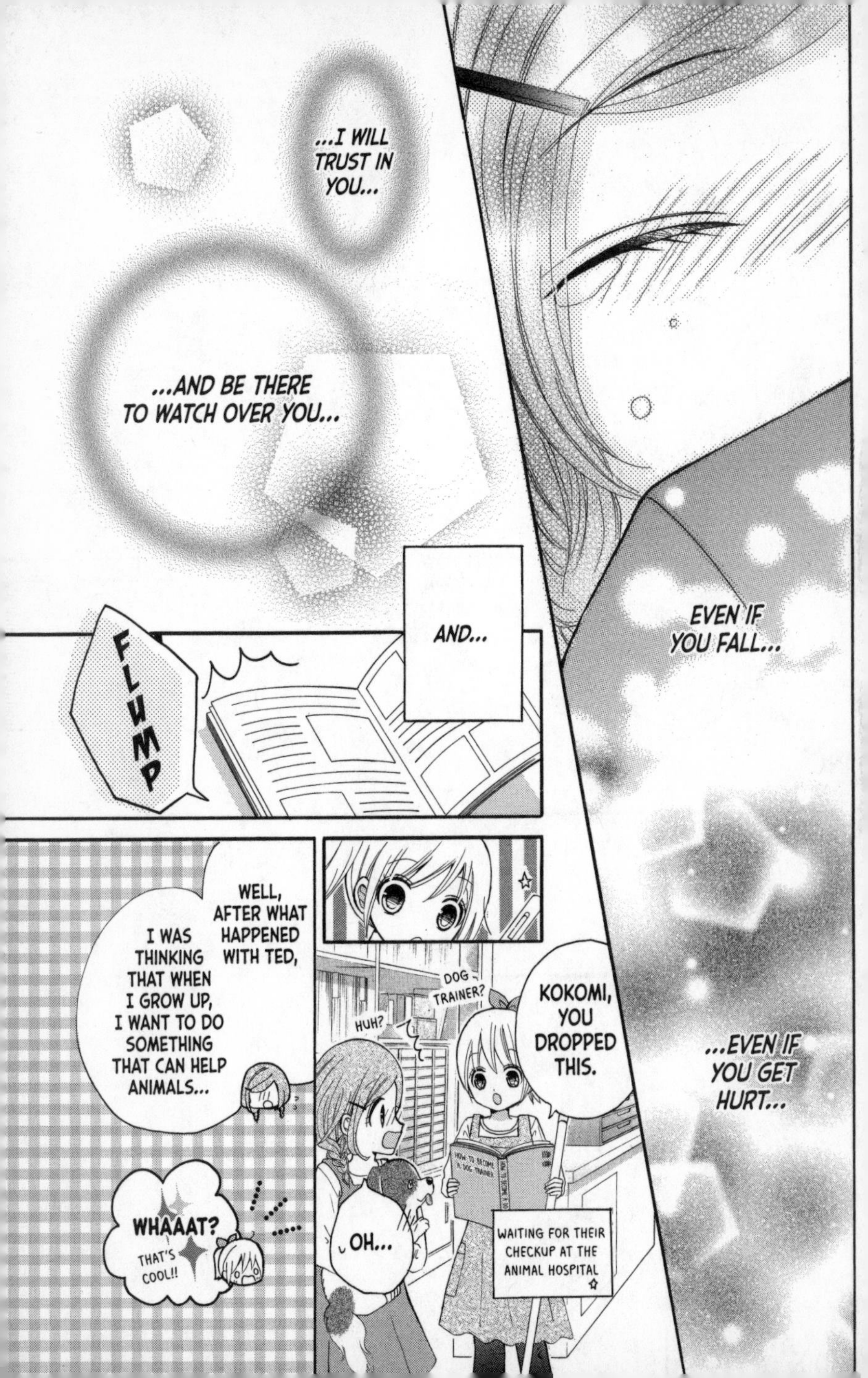

EVEN IF YOU FALL...
...EVEN IF YOU GET HURT...
...I WILL TRUST IN YOU...
...AND BE THERE TO WATCH OVER YOU...
AND...
FLUMP
WAITING FOR THEIR CHECKUP AT THE ANIMAL HOSPITAL
KOKOMI, YOU DROPPED THIS.
HOW TO BECOME A DOG TRAINER
DOG-TRAINER?
HUH?
OH...
WELL, AFTER WHAT HAPPENED WITH TED,
I WAS THINKING THAT WHEN I GROW UP, I WANT TO DO SOMETHING THAT CAN HELP ANIMALS...
WHAAAT?
THAT'S COOL!!

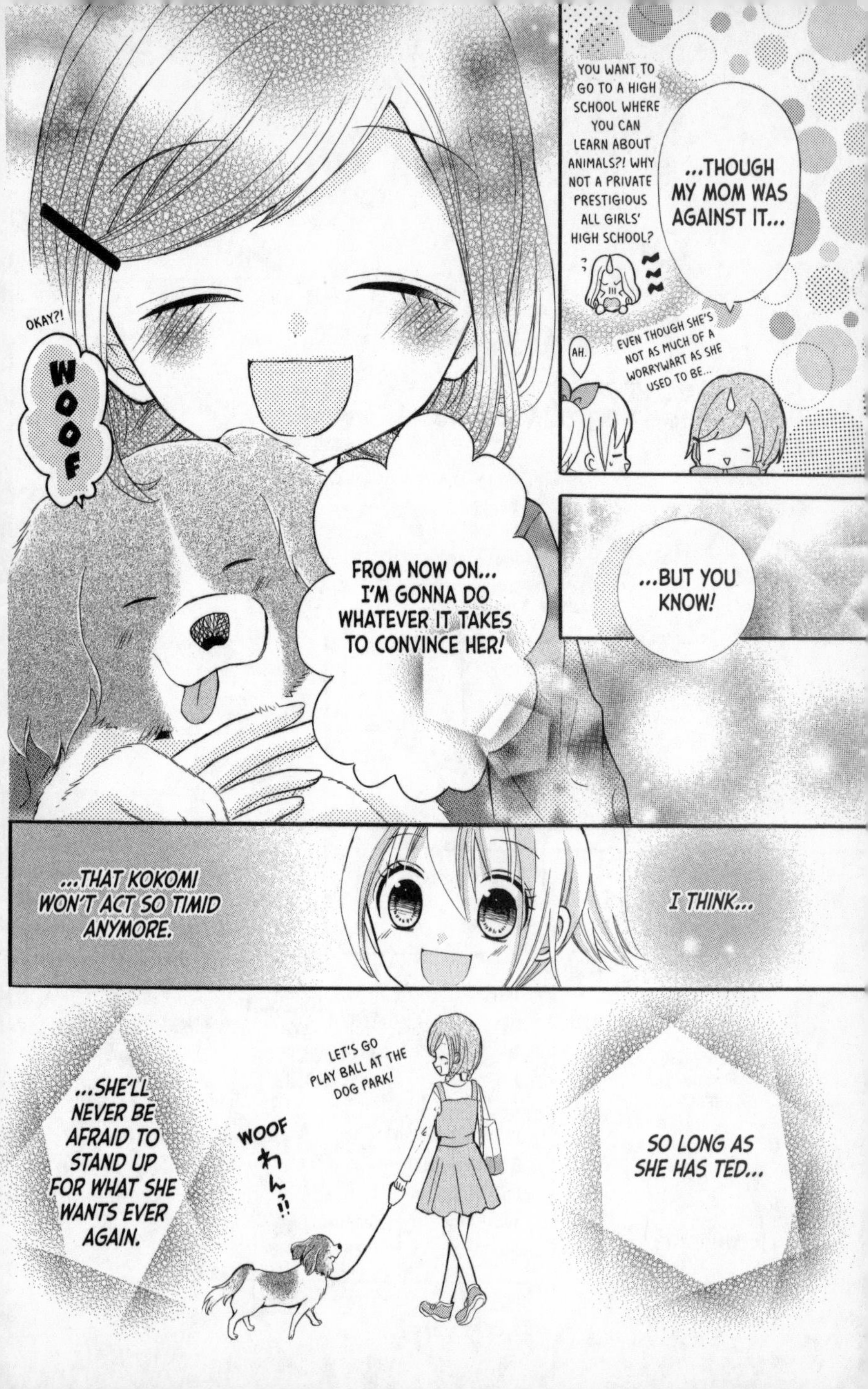
...THOUGH MY MOM WAS AGAINST IT...
YOU WANT TO GO TO A HIGH SCHOOL WHERE YOU CAN LEARN ABOUT ANIMALS?! WHY NOT A PRIVATE PRESTIGIOUS ALL GIRLS' HIGH SCHOOL?
EVEN THOUGH SHE'S NOT AS MUCH OF A WORRYWART AS SHE USED TO BE...
AH.
...BUT YOU KNOW!
FROM NOW ON... I'M GONNA DO WHATEVER IT TAKES TO CONVINCE HER!
WOOF
OKAY?!
I THINK...
...THAT KOKOMI WON'T ACT SO TIMID ANYMORE.
SO LONG AS SHE HAS TED...
LET'S GO PLAY BALL AT THE DOG PARK!
WOOF
わん?!
...SHE'LL NEVER BE AFRAID TO STAND UP FOR WHAT SHE WANTS EVER AGAIN.

BEHIND THE SCENES

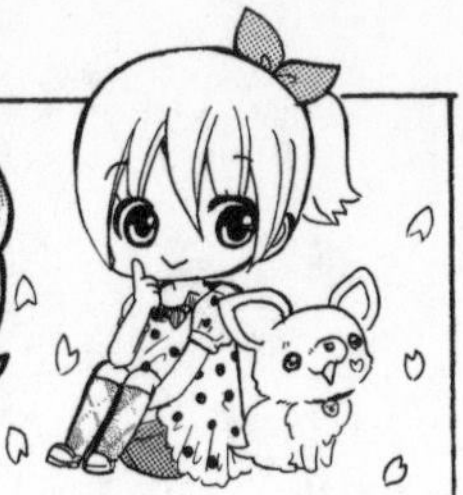

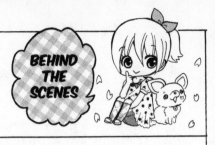

THANK YOU FOR READING UP UNTIL THIS POINT~ ☆

THOSE WHO HAVE FINISHED READING THE STORY, YOU'RE WELCOME TO READ THESE BEHIND-THE-SCENES TIDBITS!

☆☆ ↓↓

"TINY LIVES" TWO-PARTER

<THE MANY KITTENS I MET ONE DAY> & <I WANT TO SAVE THESE TINY LIVES>

THE FIRST **TWO-PARTER** FOR THE SERIES!! NORMALLY EACH CHAPTER HAS A SELF-CONTAINED STORY, SO IT WAS THE FIRST TIME WE COULD END A CHAPTER WITH "TO BE CONTINUED IN THE NEXT CHAPTER...!" WHERE WOULD BE THE BEST PLACE TO PUT THE CLIFFHANGER?! AND HOW SHOULD THE STORY COME TO ITS CONCLUSION?! THIS WAS A TRIAL-AND-ERROR KIND OF CHAPTER FOR ME. AND ON TOP OF THAT, THIS CHAPTER WAS ALSO HARD TO WORK ON SINCE IT PROBABLY HAS THE HEAVIEST THEME OF ALL SO FAR. TO MAKE UP FOR IT, THE GUEST CHARACTER SEIRA WHO APPEARED IN THIS CHAPTER WAS A BRIGHT AND ENERGETIC KIND OF GIRL, SO THAT REALLY HELPED. THANK YOU, SEIRA.

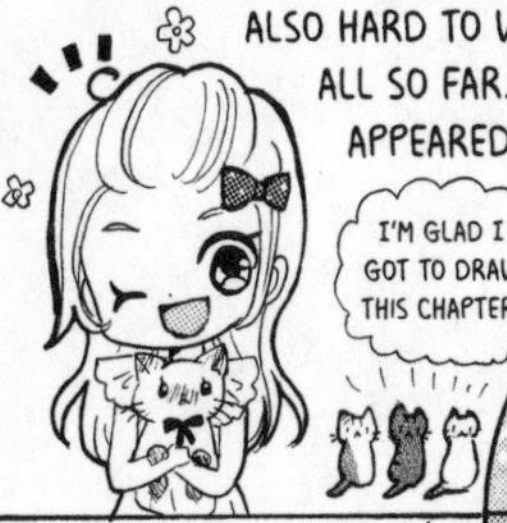
I'M GLAD I GOT TO DRAW THIS CHAPTER!

CHAPTER 15

<HAPPY THE BLUE BIRD OF HAPPINESS>

OUR FIRST BIRD PATIENT. AS I WROTE THIS CHAPTER, I REMEMBERED HOW MY FRIEND'S PET BIRD ACTED WHEN I WAS OVER AT THEIR HOUSE, LIKE HOW IT SAT ON MY HEAD (LOL). SO, HAPPY LANDING ON YUZU'S HEAD WHEN THEY FIRST MET WAS FROM ACTUAL EXPERIENCE.

ALSO, WHEN I WAS DRAWING THIS CHAPTER, IT REALLY HIT ME HOW I SHOULD BECOME AN EARLY BIRD, TOO...

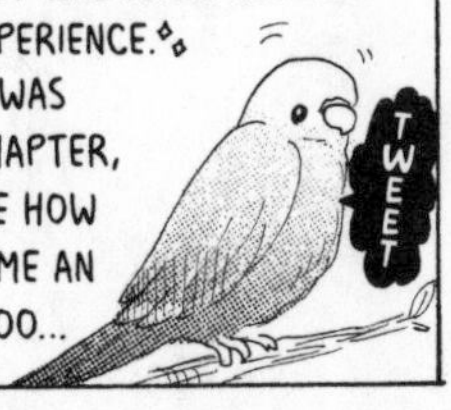
TWEET

CHAPTER 16

<TED THE BALL-LOVING DOG>

THERE ARE LOTS OF THINGS THAT ANIMALS ARE GOOD AT, SO THIS CHAPTER REALLY FOCUSED ON THAT FOR TED. THE MORE I RESEARCHED HOW BLIND ANIMALS COULD USE THEIR SUPERIOR EARS AND NOSES TO WALK, I COULDN'T STOP THINKING HOW AMAZING DOGS AND CATS ARE. I KNOW TED'S MY OWN CHARACTER, BUT I REALLY WANTED TO SEE HIM SUCCEED WITH HIS TRAINING.

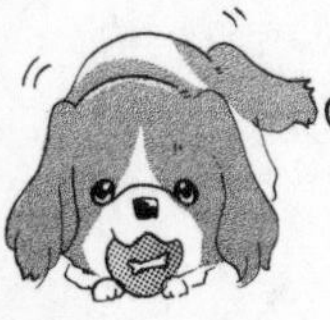

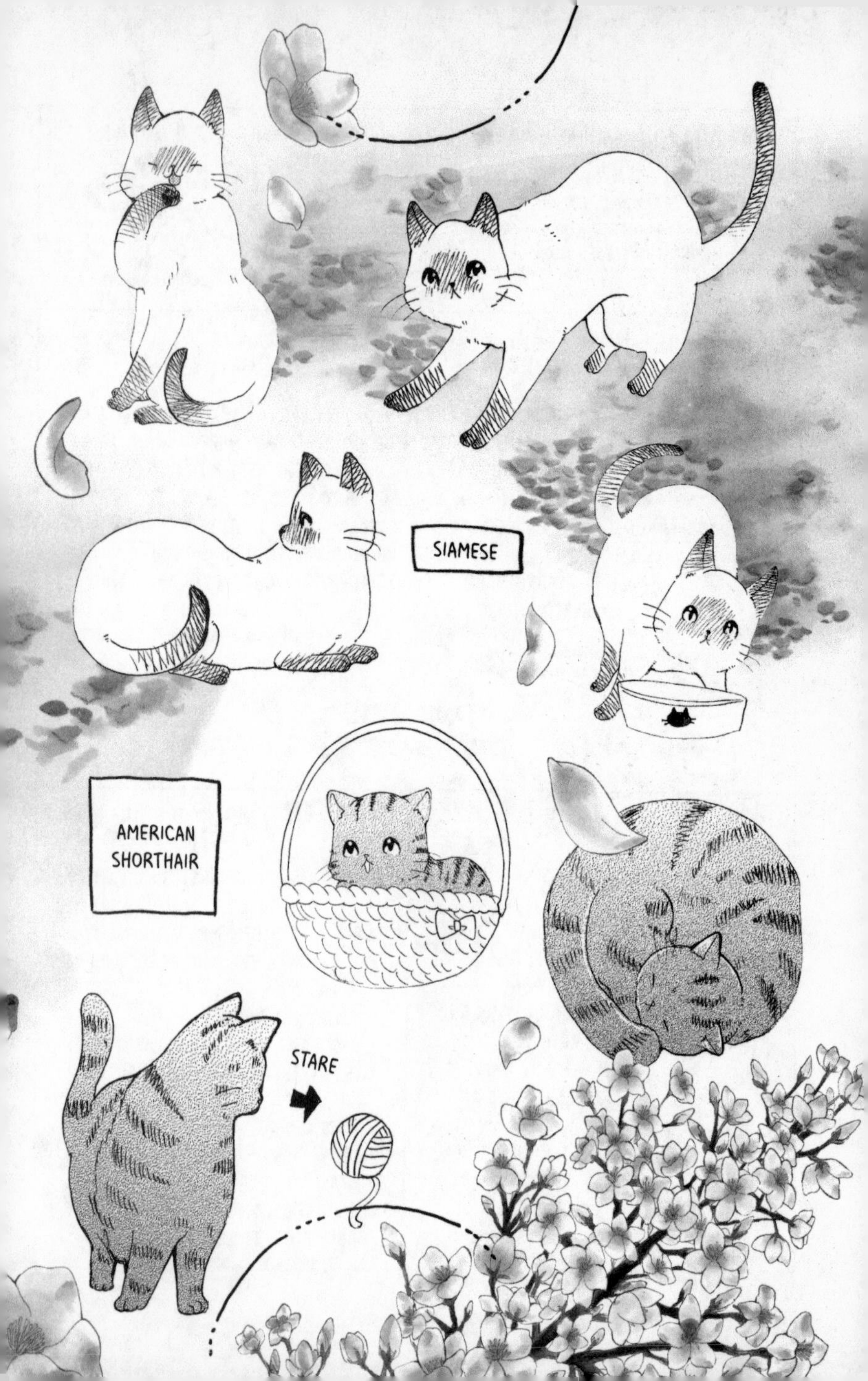
SIAMESE
AMERICAN SHORTHAIR
STARE

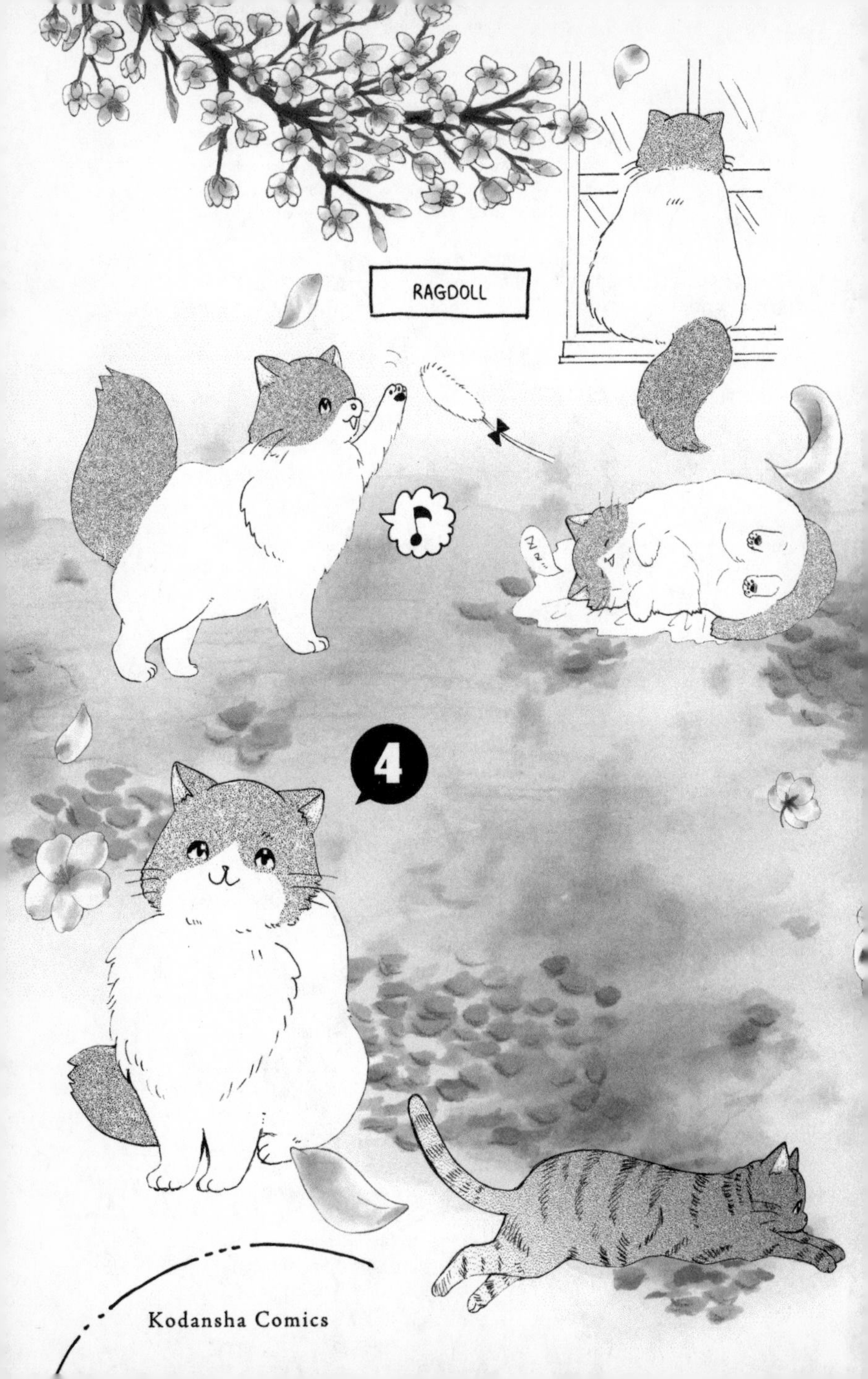
RAGDOLL
4
Kodansha Comics

A Kodansha Comics Trade Paperback Original
Yuzu the Pet Vet 4 copyright © 2018 Mingo Ito © 2018 NIPPON COLUMBIA CO., LTD.
English translation copyright © 2020 Mingo Ito © NIPPON COLUMBIA CO., LTD.

All rights reserved.

Published in the United States by Kodansha Comics, an imprint of Kodansha USA Publishing, LLC, New York.

Publication rights for this English edition arranged through Kodansha Ltd., Tokyo.

First published in Japan in 2018 by Kodansha Ltd., Tokyo as *Yuzu no Doubutsu Karute ~Kochira Wan Nyan Doubutsu Byouin~*, volume 4.

ISBN 978-1-64651-080-1

Original cover design by Tomoko Kobayashi

Printed in the United States of America.

www.kodanshacomics.com

9 8 7 6 5 4 3 2 1
Translation: Julie Goniwich
Lettering: David Yoo
Editing: Haruko Hashimoto
Kodansha Comics edition cover design by Matthew Akuginow

Publisher: Kiichiro Sugawara

Director of publishing services: Ben Applegate
Associate director of operations: Stephen Pakula
Publishing services managing editor: Noelle Webster
Assistant production manager: Emi Lotto, Angela Zurlo
Logo and character art ©Kodansha USA Publishing, LLC